OPHER MARLOWE

Longman Critical Readers

General Editor:

Stan Smith, Research Professor in Literary Studies, Nottingham Trent University

CHRISTOPHER MARLOWE

Edited and Introduced by

RICHARD WILSON

LONGMAN
LONDON AND NEW YORK

Addison Wesley Longman Limited
Edinburgh Gate
Harlow
Essex CM20 2JE
United Kingdom
and Associated Companies throughout the world.

*Published in the United States of America
by Addison Wesley Longman Inc., New York*

First published 1999

ISBN 0–582–23706–8 CSD
ISBN 0–582–23707–6 PPR

Visit Addison Wesley Longman on the world wide web at
http://www.awl-he.com

British Library Cataloguing-in-Publication Data

A catalogue record for this book is available from the British Library

Library of Congress Cataloging-in-Publication Data

A catalog record for this book is available from the Library of Congress, USA

Christopher Marlowe / edited and introduced by Richard Wilson.
      p.   cm. — (Longman critical readers)
   Includes bibliographical references and index.
   ISBN 0–582–23706–8. — ISBN 0–582–23707–6 (pbk.)
   1. Marlowe, Christopher, 1564–1593—Criticism and interpretation.
 I. Wilson, Richard, 1950– .   II. Series.
 PR2673.C46   1999
 822'.3—dc21   98–46865
                                                                CIP

Set by 35 in 9½/11½pt Palatino
Produced by Addison Wesley Longman Singapore (Pte) Ltd.,
Printed in Singapore

Contents

Contents

General Editors' Preface

The outlines of contemporary critical theory are now often taught as a standard feature of a degree in literary studies. The development of particular theories has seen a thorough transformation of literary criticism. For example, Marxist and Foucauldian theories have revolutionised Shakespeare studies, and 'deconstruction' has led to a complete reassessment of Romantic poetry. Feminist criticism has left scarcely any period of literature unaffected by its searching critiques. Teachers of literary studies can no longer fall back on a standardised, received methodology.

Lecturers and teachers are now urgently looking for guidance in a rapidly changing critical environment. They need help in understanding the latest revisions in literary theory, and especially in grasping the practical effects of the new theories in the form of theoretically sensitised new readings. A number of volumes in the series anthologise important essays on particular theories. However, in order to grasp the full implications and possible uses of particular theories it is essential to see them put to work. This series provides substantial volumes of new readings, presented in an accessible form and with a significant amount of editorial guidance.

Each volume includes a substantial introduction which explores the theoretical issues and conflicts embodied in the essays selected and locates areas of disagreement between positions. The pluralism of theories has to be put on the agenda of literary studies. We can no longer pretend that we all tacitly accept the same practices in literary studies. Neither is a *laissez-faire* attitude any longer tenable. Literature departments need to go beyond the mere toleration of theoretical differences: it is not enough merely to agree to differ; they need actually to 'stage' the differences openly. The volumes in this series all attempt to dramatise the differences, not necessarily with a view to resolving them but in order to foreground the choices presented by different theories or to argue for a particular route through the impasses the differences present.

The theory 'revolution' has had real effects. It has loosened the grip of traditional empiricist and romantic assumptions about language and literature. It is not always clear what is being proposed as the new agenda for literary studies, and indeed the very notion of 'literature' is questioned by the post-structuralist strain in theory. However, the uncertainties and obscurities of contemporary theories appear much less worrying when we see what the best critics have been able to do with them in practice. This series aims to disseminate the best of recent criticism and to show that it is possible to re-read the canonical texts of literature in new and challenging ways.

RAMAN SELDEN AND STAN SMITH

The Publishers and fellow Series Editor regret to record that Raman Selden died after a short illness in May 1991 at the age of fifty-three. Ray Selden was a fine scholar and a lovely man. All those he has worked with will remember him with much affection and respect.

Acknowledgements

The publishers are grateful to the following for permission to reproduce copyright material:

The editors, *English Literary Renaissance* for the article 'Malta: *The Jew of Malta*, and the Fictions of Difference: Colonialist Discourse' by Emily C. Bartels in *ENGLISH LITERARY RENAISSANCE* 20:1 (winter 1990) 1–16; the author, Jonathan Goldberg for his article 'Sodomy and Society: The Case of Christopher Marlowe' in *SOUTHWEST REVIEW* 69 (1984); International Thomson Publishing Services and the author, Professor Hilary Gatti for an edited version of the article 'Bruno and Marlowe: *Doctor Faustus*' in *THE RENAISSANCE DRAMA OF KNOWLEDGE: GIORDANO BRUNO IN ENGLAND* by Hilary Gatti (1989) 89–113, and Stephen Greenblatt, for an edited version of the essay 'Marlowe, Marx and Anti-Semitism' in *LEARNING TO CURSE: ESSAYS IN EARLY MODERN CULTURE* by Stephen Greenblatt (1990) 40–56; Johns Hopkins University Press for the essay 'Theatre of the Idols' Marlowe, Rankins and Theatrical Images' by Jonathan Crewe in *THEATRE JOURNAL* 36 (1984), the article '"Here's Nothing Writ": Scribe, Script and Circumspections in Marlowe's Plays' by Marjorie Garber in *THEATRE JOURNAL* 36 (1984) 321–333 & 302–320, and the article 'Visible Bullets: *Tamburlaine the Great* and Ivan the Terrible' by Richard Wilson in *ENGLISH LITERARY HISTORY* 62 (1995) 47–68; Oxford University Press for the article 'The Rites of Violence: Marlowe's *Massacre at Paris*' by Julia Briggs in *REVIEW OF ENGLISH STUDIES* 34 (1983) 257–278; Oxford University Press/ The University of California Press for the essay 'Legitimating Tamburlaine' from *FAULTLINES; CULTURAL MATERIALISM AND THE POLITICS OF DISSIDENT READING* by Alan Sinfield, 237–245. © Alan Sinfield 1992 and © 1992 The Regents of the University of California; University of Pennsylvania Press for the essay 'King Edward's Body' from *MARLOWE, SHAKESPEARE AND THE ECONOMY OF THEATRICAL EXPERIENCE* by Thomas Cartelli (1991) 121–135; Simon & Schuster/Duke University Press for the essay '*Doctor Faustus*: Subversion Through Transgression' by Jonathan Dollimore in *RADICAL TRAGEDY: RELIGION IDEOLOGY AND POWER IN THE DRAMA OF SHAKESPEARE AND HIS CONTEMPORARIES* (Harvester, 1984) 109–119; Simon & Schuster/ St Martin's Press for the essay 'Representing "Women" and Males:

Acknowledgements

Gender Relations in Marlowe' by Simon Shepherd in *MARLOWE AND THE POLITICS OF ELIZABETHAN THEATRE* (Harvester, 1986) 178–207 © Simon Shepherd; Stanford University Press for the edited essay 'Marlowe and the observation of Men' in *SOVEREIGNTY AND INTELLIGENCE: SPYING AND COURT CULTURE IN THE ENGLISH RENAISSANCE*' by John Michael Archer (1993). © 1993 by the Board of Trustees of the Leland Stanford Junior University, and 'Play the Sodomites, or Worse' in *SODOMETRIES: RENAISSANCE TEXTS, MODERN SEXUALITIES* by Jonathan Goldberg (1992). © 1992 by the Board of Trustees of the Leland Stanford Junior University.

In Memoriam Dinos Patrides

Dead shepherd, now I find thy saw of might . . .

1 Introduction

The Ruffian on the Stair

The primal scene of Marlowe criticism was scripted by the dramatist himself, when, at the climax of *The Massacre at Paris*, the 'King's Professor of Logic' is rudely interrupted in his study at the Sorbonne, as 'fearful cries come from the River Seine, / That fright poor Ramus sitting at his book' (*Mass.*, 1.7.1/21).[1] This Peter Ramus is the same literary theorist that Faustus repudiates in his first words, for teaching 'no greater miracle' than that 'to dispute well' is 'logic's chiefest end' (*Faust*, 1.1.8); and Marlowe's bitterness at his own Cambridge education – in which Ramus had been the reigning god – is blatant now, as the Professor's 'bedfellow' screams that 'The Guisians are / Hard at the door and mean to murder us' (*Mass.*, 1.7.8). It was Ramus, Michel Foucault explains, who codified the ancient – and modern – idea that 'Language is not what it is because it has meaning', but because 'words group syllables together',[2] but now reality bursts in to sweep away this superstition of signifiers without sense. The Duke of Guise is the crudest of Marlowe's Machiavellian anti-heroes, yet he sums them all up in his disgust that 'such a simple sound' as the word 'Religion . . . Of so great matter should be made the ground' (*Mass.*, 1.2.68). If it is true, as theorists say, that meaning is a mere system of differences, 'To shuffle or cut' like a pack of cards, 'take this as surest thing', he gloats, 'That, right or wrong, thou deal thyself a king' (*Mass.*, 1.2.66–91). So, when he confronts the scholar in his library, he turns murder into a revenge *viva* on language and power, condemning Ramus not for being a Protestant, but 'a flat dichotomist' – or structuralist – who 'didst never sound anything to the depth', and taught that there is 'nothing but epitomes' and signs. This Regius Professor stands for the entire ivory tower of literary criticism, it seems, with its formalist philosophy that there is nothing outside of texts:

1

To contradict which, I say, Ramus shall die:
How answer you that? Your *nego argumentum*
Cannot serve, sirrah. – Kill him.

(*Mass.*, 1.7.26–38)

'To kill a man because of his views on literature', George Steiner
has said, 'is a sinister tribute to literature – but a tribute, none the
less'.[3] He was thinking of Stalin's KGB, but it was in the same spirit
of poetic justice that Marlowe's contemporaries returned again and
again to the episode he stages here, adapting it to their belief that
books determine even their writers' deaths, like that of Shakespeare's
Cinna, torn to pieces by the Roman mob 'for his bad verses'.[4] In
those versions the death of the author demonstrated the vengeance
of his own words, but in *The Massacre at Paris* there is no such irony.
For when Ramus in desperation disowns those other 'blockish
Sorbonnists' who 'Attribute as much unto their works / As to the
service of the eternal God', it is not words but Guise's brutality
which silences him for good: 'Why suffer you that peasant to
declaim? / Stab him, I say, and send him to his friends in hell'
(51–5). Perhaps Marlowe sensed that Ramus's religion of rhetoric
would soon be dissolved in the Enlightenment system of
representation, when language would become simply a window on
the world; but what is disturbing about this dramatisation of the
murder of the bookman is that it occurs at the hands of a character
whose thuggish cruelty, energy and charisma are so clearly meant
to be irresistible. It is in this sense that the assassination of Ramus
is a paradigm of the problem presented to Marlowe criticism.
The scandal posed by Marlowe for his critics is not Renaissance
hyperbole, baroque bloodletting, or modern homosexuality; the
embarrassment is that in his work the power of speech, violence
and virility is juxtaposed to the impotence of literacy, culture and
criticism itself. Marlowe's aggression savagely defies the world of
art. In fact, this studiously academic writer seems driven by a
detestation of everything that his critical readers represent, so they
find themselves compelled, in play after play, to collude in the
imagination of their own end:

Old men with swords thrust through their aged sides,
Kneeling in mercy to a Greekish lad,
Who with steel pole-axes dash'd out their brains.

(*Dido*, 2.1.197–199)

'He worshipped all the possessors of sheer animal flesh unspoiled
by intellect – young toughs, sailors, soldiers, fishermen':[5] from

Marlowe to Mishima, the quandary posed for academic critics by
the literary cult of homoerotic violence has always been its anti-
intellectualism. For by valorising aggression and destructiveness,
such desire is inevitably 'the killer of civilised egos'.[6] Thus, in
Marlowe the ruffian on the stair or 'Hard at the door' is intent on
obliterating not just his own teacher, but every reader and thinker,
as the murder of Ramus is followed by the butchery of schoolmasters
and all other 'Protestants with books' (*Mass.*, 2.1; 2.3). When
Shakespeare introduces the enemies of academia, they are repulsive
louts, such as Jack Cade; but Marlowe makes them the most hypnotic
and desirable figures on stage. Radical critics who are committed to
toppling the institution of literature are in the disconcerting position,
therefore, of encountering in this canonical writer a cult of the
iconoclast as their own nemesis. They are in the situation, that is
to say, of Marlowe's central character, 'learned Faustus', whose
entrapment by Lucifer, the 'most dearly loved of god', and his
'bewitching fiend', Mephistophilis, is the archetypal case of the
anaemic intellectual infatuated by annihilating physicality, like that
of the boy actor who plays Helen as both 'more lovely' and more
damaging 'than flaming Jupiter'. The legend of Faustus has usually
been interpreted as a myth of the will to knowledge, but Marlowe
also stages it as a fable of the seductiveness of dumb ignorance. As
the beautiful devil himself jeers at the pathetic pedagogue: 'when
thou took'st the book / To view the scriptures, then I turn'd the
leaves / And led thine eye' (*Faust*, 1.3.65; 5.1.112; 2.102). And as the
scholars break into the Doctor's charred study the morning after
they have heard 'such fearful shrieks and cries' inside, they discover
the carnage of the ultimate mugging of helpless brains by heedless
brawn. Like the murder of the greatest of all classical scholars,
Winckelmann, at the hands of a Neapolitan rent boy, a scandalous
police report itemising the 'limbs all torn asunder' must now stand
for an intellectual's entire revolt from reason and pursuit of death:

> The devils whom Faustus served have torn him thus:
> For twixt the hours of twelve and one, methought
> I heard him shriek and call aloud for help,
> At which time the house seemed all on fire
> With dreadful horror of these damned fiends.
>
> (*Faust*, 5.3.8–12)

Faustus's burning library and dismembered body remind
Marlowe's critics of this author's final contempt for their world of
books. If *Doctor Faustus* closes on the scene of such a crime, with an
embarrassed university hastening to 'give his mangled limbs due

burial . . . though Faustus' end be such / As every Christian heart laments', (*Faust*, 5.3.14–16) then that may be because in each of Marlowe's works there is the same descent from the library – with its Bibles, Greek and Latin manuscripts, medieval moralities, and Renaissance maps – to the libido – with its blood, brutality, desire and death. The sado-masochistic ritual staged in *Edward II* by Gaveston for the 'pliant king', in which 'a lovely boy in Dian's shape' is bait to lure an actor dressed as the legendary voyeur Actaeon to his horrific death (1.1.61–70), is a paradigm of the process that, in play after play, turns the safely literary into the savagely literal. Not for nothing was this writer the most literal-minded translator of Ovid and Lucan, respectively poets of the power of sex and the sexuality of power. For as one of the most influential current critics, Stephen Greenblatt frets, Marlowe's 'cruel, aggressive plays' seem to reflect a life also lived on the edge: 'a courting of disaster as reckless as any that he depicted on stage'. Reports of the dramatist's 'extremely dangerous blasphemies and equally dangerous homosexuality', leave Greenblatt confused whether 'this is a man whose recklessness is out of control', or one 'so coolly mocking that he can calculate his own excess', but what is certain is that 'This is play on the brink of an abyss'. According to this reading, it is because we 'have lived after Nietzsche' that we can appreciate this theatre of extremity;[7] but it might be as true to say that the post-modern reaction to a drama that so compulsively stages the dance of desire and death is shaped by coming after Foucault, the philosopher who taught that 'to master life is given only to a cruel, reductive and already infernal knowledge that only wishes it dead'.[8]

The Burning Library

Marlowe's reverence for the satanic beauty that threatens to destroy 'learning's golden gifts' (*Faust*, Pro, 24) places literary theorists who make a religion of the text in a cruelly ironic light. A theatre which foregrounds iconoclastic festivals, like the one when Tamburlaine orders a vast bonfire of 'all the heaps of superstitious books / Found in the temples' (*2 Tam.*, 5.2.173), is uniquely challenging to this 'historically well-determined little pedagogy which teaches the pupil that there is nothing outside the text . . . and that it is therefore unnecessary to search elsewhere'. For what Foucault reviled as 'A pedagogy which gives to the voice of the master limitless sovereignty to restate the text indefinitely',[9] reads its own deconstruction in those material flames whose 'flaring beams' (*Hero*, 2.332) torch the end of every one of Marlowe's works. The comedy of theory's encounter with a drama that despises not only the vanity of literary critics, but literature itself, is played out, for instance, in the case of Marjorie Garber, a self-appointed *belle dame sans merci* of American academia. Her 1976 essay, 'Infinite riches in a little room: closure and enclosure in Marlowe', had taken Marlowe's fascination with the myth of Icarus seriously enough to present all his plays as varieties of labyrinth: not coincidentally, the favourite figure of French theorists, from Bataille to Deleuze, for the inescapable prison house of words. Dedicated to the memory of W.K. Wimsatt, the godfather of (the old) New Criticism, Garber's essay also looked forward to New Historicism when it described Marlowe's theatre as a claustrophobic nightmare, in which characters attempting 'to prison and wall each other up', succeed only in incarcerating themselves, as 'play after play finds closure in enclosure', with the artisan not enclosing, but enclosed. Here Dido's grotto, Edward's dungeon, Barabas's cauldron, Tamburlaine's coffin, and Faustus's hell each enact the entrapment of language itself:

> The list of enclosures is striking and consistent, [and suggests] another kind of enclosure, one equally germane to the nature and possibility of power. I refer to the limit represented by language. . . . Manifestly, however great its power, language is ultimately an enclosure. Once uttered, a phrase . . . conveys the speaker into the power of his hearers, whether on or off stage.[10]

Primed on Barthes and Derrida, Garber's updating of Marlowe revealed the Renaissance dramatist to be a post-structuralist *avant la lettre*, caging his protagonists in mazes of their own making, like the murderous messages 'returned to sender' from Mortimer and the Duchess of Guise, which each rehearse the theory of the Death of the Author three hundred years before its time. What Umberto Eco derided as this 'frenchified affectation of inscribing everything and seeing everything inscribed', (Umberto Eco, *Travels in Hyper-reality*, trans. William Weaver (London: Picador, 1987), p. 245) was taken by Garber to a logical extreme in a 1984 essay which can now be read as the founding document of post-modern Marlowe criticism. ' "Here's nothing writ": scribe, script, and circumscription in Marlowe's plays' (Chapter 2) added to the airless confinement of her earlier essay the asphyxiating sensation that if these Elizabethan characters are literally scripted in *characters*, as mere figures of written speech, then they are liable to be casually snuffed out with an article and wiped from the slate. The influence here was Foucault's notorious pronouncement, at the end of his book, *The Order of Things*, that the figure of 'man' will soon be 'effaced, like a face drawn in sand at the edge of the sea';[11] and Garber's interpretation of Faustus was indeed as the 'last man', his identity a palimpsest of 'Lines, circles, letters, and characters', to be scrawled and cancelled as instantaneously as the tattoo which first scarifies and then vanishes from his arm. Prefaced with an epigraph from *The Jew of Malta* – 'The meaning has a meaning' – this was a reading that confirmed the aptness of reviewing Marlowe's stage – with its archives, inventories, despatches, contracts, maps, and wills – as a theatre of the all-conquering word: an analysis that was gratifying to critics sure there was nothing outside the library of their world. For if Marlowe's characters were themselves finally 'nothing' on this view, being composed, like Arcimboldo portraits, out of the hell of other people's words, then the meaning of their meaning so little was paradoxically that their writing meant so much:

> Faustus, Mortimer . . . and Tamburlaine . . . are ultimately cancelled or slain by their own hands: by their handwriting, by their signatures, by their seals, by writing against the hand of the playwright, against the hand of history, fable, legend, Scripture, and inscription.

To diagnose the deaths of Marlowe's characters (and, by extension, of the author) as suicide by their own signatures or 'hands', might be thought to make as much of a fetish of the scene of writing as those post-modernists who in the 1980s asserted that even fascism was an effect of words. Yet this was the implication of Jonathan Crewe's 'Theatre of the idols: Marlowe, Rankins, and theatrical images' (Chapter 6), which considered *Tamburlaine the Great* as itself constitutive of the anti-theatricality surrounding the writer's demonisation and destruction. Like Garber, Crewe was supported in this interpretation by Derrida's theory that language always deconstructs itself by turning its own metaphors back upon themselves, and his point was similarly to present Marlovian drama as a writing against the self. Playwright and puritan were mirror-images, by this light, since Marlowe's psychopathic monsters were as collusive with the moral campaign against theatre as anti-theatrical literature was a homage to the infectiousness of the stage. So, pulpit and playhouse scripted each other in Marlowe's London, Crewe argues, and just as the firebrand William Rankins relied on theatrical metaphor, so the dramatist played, quite literally, into his enemy's homicidal hands. This was an analysis that marked the zenith of the New Historicist idea, earlier explored in Greenblatt's essay on *The Jew of Malta* (Chapter 9), that identity is constructed and destroyed by discourses to which it is ostensibly opposed. In a much-hyped study of Tudor England, *Renaissance Self-Fashioning* (1980), Greenblatt would popularise this grim picture of civilisation deadlocked in chains of textuality;[12] but the argument was already clear when he defined Barabas's 'egotism, duplicity and murderous cunning' as conditions, not of exclusion, but of *centrality* to the culture he would try to use them to destroy. For like Karl Marx (himself a Jew), Marlowe deploys the caricature of the Jew as a rhetorical mirror of society itself:

> Marlowe and Marx seize upon the Jew as . . . a way of marshalling deep popular hatred and clarifying its object. . . . Both writers focus attention upon activity that is seen as at once alien yet central to the life of the community, to direct against the activity the anti-Semitic feeling of the audience. . . . Twentieth-century history has demonstrated with numbing force how tragically misguided this rhetorical strategy was.

Playing with fire, Marlowe's flirtation with anti-Semitism, like his toying with homophobia, originates, Greenblatt alleges, from a self-destructiveness that is the opposite of Marx's goal of self-emancipation. Read, therefore, by the flames of the Holocaust, Barabas's 'dark playfulness' with the tropes and stereotypes of his own oppression reduces him, as much as Garber's Faustus, to 'a senseless lump of clay, / That will with every water wash to dirt' (*Faustus*, 1.2.270). Programmed to 'vanish from the earth in air, / And leave no memory' that they ever were (221), Marlowe's creations are all, with such hindsight, devoured by their own words. To Greenblatt, himself Jewish, the violence of this rhetoric on which Hitler drew is stored in its 'sleaziest materials': 'that collection of social scraps and offal . . . hard little aphorisms, cynical adages, worldly maxims – all the neatly packaged nastiness of his society', which Barabas turns against himself. To Garber, meanwhile, Faustus's nemesis was decided 'In the library of Corpus Christi' at Cambridge, where his creator absorbed the poison in 'Archbishop Parker's magnificent bequest of books and manuscripts'. But whether as speech or writing, it is language these critics accuse when they identify the evil genius of Marlowe's world. 'All language is Fascist', Barthes stated, not because it prevents, but because it *compels*;[13] and Hilary Gatti seems to agree, when she turns specifically to Marlowe's quarrel with Ramus and the academic discourse of his time (Chapter 15). Dissecting Faustus's first and last soliloquies line by line, Gatti shows how they echo arguments against the university establishment by Giordano Bruno, himself a victim of both Oxford, which expelled him for defending heliocentrism, and the Inquisition, which burned him at the stake. In this analysis, *Doctor Faustus* is a battle between rival books which the heretic is sure to lose: crushed not only by the Anglican platitudes of the Chorus, but by the Catholic dogma of Mephistophilis, the very model of a Grand Inquisitor:

> Words, Bruno had written, must be the servants of meanings, not meanings the servants of words, as the grammarians make them ... [But] it is here that Faustus, to use another Brunian expression, loses the race, unable to pit against the smooth expertise of Mephistophilis's oratory new doctrines and new words. He can only ask question upon question, and cry at the familiar, expected answers: 'O thou art deceived.'

Overwhelmed by the sheer weight of the dominant religious discourse of his day, Faustus 'brings his speech and his life to a close', Gatti observes, with a weary acceptance that 'he has no choice but to die in terms of the inevitable scenario: "Ugly hell gape not; come Lucifer, / I'll burn my books".' Thus, it is the Doctor's own library which fuels the pyre on which he burns in this interpretation; and though she does not mention it, Gatti's account of Faustus's subjection to 'a reigning metaphysic too strong and entrenched to resist' is very close to the theory of Louis Althusser, that ruling ideology reproduces itself by 'interpellating' (or calling) individuals as its subjects through institutions such as colleges and schools. According to Althusser (who was influenced by his own Catholic education) the paradigm of all such 'Ideological State Apparatuses' is the Church, and Gatti's commentary on Faustus's subjugation to its 'intellectual authority and dominion' corresponds exactly to the Althusserian thesis that Christian ideology works by addressing individuals as reflections of 'the Other Subject' who is God: just as men need God, 'the Great Subject needs subjects as his *mirrors* ... even in terrible inversion of His image, i.e. sin'. In Althusser's theory, the individual is thus 'interpellated as a free subject in order that he shall (freely) accept his subjection';[14] and likewise 'the pessimism of Marlowe's final tragic vision', Gatti decides, is that Faustus 'experiences his death in a Christian universe', unable to voice an alternative except in ever 'weaker negative verbs' and 'hypothetical grammatical forms'. Once again, then, in Marlovian drama, the library is literally an Inferno the hero enters without hope. For Gatti, as for Garber and Greenblatt, this Renaissance burning library was an *auto da fe*, and the 'Hell' that is 'discovered' to Faustus is a pyre, like Bruno's stake, composed of pages from his own books:

There are the furies tossing damned souls
On burning forks. Their bodies broil in lead.
There are live quarters broiling on the coals
That can never die. This ever-burning chair
Is for o'er-tortured souls to rest them in . . .
But yet all these are nothing. Thou shalt see
Ten thousand tortures that more horrid be.

(Faust, 5.2.128–37)

'Now, Dido, with these relics burn thyself' exclaims Marlowe's
heroine as she stokes her funeral pyre with Aeneas's writing, 'These
letters, lines, and perjur'd papers, all / Shall burn to cinders in this
precious flame' (*Dido*, 5.1.292–301). Self-immolated on the Latin lines
that lit the Roman world, the act of suttee committed by the African
Queen can stand for the sacrifice of all the victims of literature,
according to the New Historicist interpretation. This oppressive view
of theatre's entanglement with texts is put into historical perspective
by Foucault, however, when he argues that 'literature' is a discourse
that arises precisely during the crisis Marlowe stages, when rhetoric
gives way to reading, and books offer the fraudulent contract that
cheats Faustus: the deceit of a flight 'towards infinity', which is in fact
a fall into the bottomless abyss of words. For it is only in the modern
epoch of the Library, Foucault contends, that texts have enslaved the
reader with the illusion that they exceed the real.[15] Such is the gloss
on Marlowe's bonfire of vanities offered by Graham Hammill, in an
essay that draws a line under New Historicism's terror of literature
by explaining its magic as merely that 'suspension of disbelief' in
signs on which capitalism thrives. So, whereas Greenblatt was
overawed by Marlowe's 'will to play', Hammill identifies it as merely
a function of early modern commodification, when literary language
became the sign of signs in the new system of universal exchange.
Thus, the tragedy of Faustus is the historical one of the subject
of 'global capitalism', duped by the performative promise of his
'necromantic books' into 'eroticised exchange with a succubus' who
is distinctly *not* 'the face that launched a thousand ships', but a 'lovely
boy', with whom the Doctor plays a 'hapless . . . wanton' girl. Faustus
desired to be 'ravished' by books (*Faust*, 1.1.48/109; 5.2.97–115), and
in this interpretation the act of sodomy is indeed the ultimate
'suspension of disbelief' in the 'literariness' that is his doom:

> The play registers Faustus as a subject of literariness – a subject
> whose Imaginary identification is to be a character in a story not
> his own, whose Symbolic identification is to burn his books, and
> whose Being locates him by the representational logic of sodomy.

It is a form of subjectivity that Faustus cannot escape, not because he has overreached the bounds of humanism, but because he is inescapably committed to the literary.[16]

The story with which Faustus identifies, Hammill points out, is the same sado-masochistic one as Gaveston directs for Edward, but which the Doctor stages, when Benvolio dares to play 'Actaeon, and turn to a stag', by casting himself in drag: 'And I'll play Diana, and send him horns presently'. This is a game that involves unleashing 'a kennel of hounds shall hunt him so / As all his footmanship shall scarce prevail / To keep his carcass from their bloody fangs'; yet when the drunken youth is dragged 'through the woods / Amongst the pricking thorns and sharpest briars', Faustus is the first to see that it is how 'he intended to dismember me' (*Faustus*, 4.2.52/98; 3.93). Hammill reads this as a rehearsal, therefore, of the hero's own death, when he too is ripped apart and 'devoured by his favourites', as Actaeon was in the homosexual version of the myth. According to Foucault, the logic of all such sado-masochistic rituals is to purge the lust for blood and death by means of 'a continuous irony';[17] but in this revision it is precisely the ironic 'literariness' of the savage Actaeon game which traps Edward and Faustus in a quest for some ultimate limit experience that climaxes in the horror of their deaths. Where earlier critics had interpreted the Icarus myth as the key to Marlovian drama, therefore, Hammill sees the Actaeon legend as the index to the so-called 'Marlowe effect', which pivots each of the plays on a razor edge between transcendence and its terminus.[18] And when he too dates this 'effect' to the era when literature, with its endless craving to transgress, superseded rhetoric, with its zeal for order, he explains what Foucault meant when he wrote that 'Rhetoric was a means of postponing the burning of libraries'. The conflagration that consumes Faustus's mutilated corpse, at the end of his Actaeon play, is nothing less, on this view, than the fire to which all of Marlowe's language (as the first modern literature) aspires:

A 'Literature' that comes into existence at precisely the moment when a language appears that appropriates all other languages in its lightning flash . . . where death and the wavelike succession of words to infinity enact their roles. From this moment the space of language is not defined by Rhetoric, but by the Library . . . substituting for Rhetoric the simple, continuous, and monotonous line of language left to its own devices, a language fated to be infinite because it can no longer support itself upon speech . . . a language of the Library [where] either all books are already contained within the Word and must be burned, or they are contradictory, and, again, must be burned.[19]

Confessions of a Mask

'See that in the next room I have a fire, / And get me a spit, and let it be red-hot' (*Edward*, 5.5.31–2): the flaming poker with which Lightborn sodomises Edward II is the irresistible phallic signifier, to post-modern criticism, of Marlowe's arsonist lust for absolute symbolic power. Even more than those pyrotechnics of 'fiery meteors . . . Flying dragons, lightning [and] fearful thunderclaps', with which Tamburlaine aspires to repeat the incendiary seductiveness of Helen, and burn the topless towers of Asia (*2 Tam.*, 3.2.1–13), the devilish fire that is 'bravely' inserted into the body of the king, so 'none shall know which way he died' (5.4.25/7), appears to instantiate the suicidal self-destructiveness of this desire. What certain commentators have said of Foucault's own demise from AIDS, that (like Nietzsche's syphilis) 'Foucault's death was the result of thinking Foucault's thoughts', lurks behind the assumption that Marlowe's career similarly conformed to 'A Faustian pact, whose temptation was instilled by the deployment of sexuality: to exchange life in its entirety for the sovereignty of sex . . . sex worth dying for'.[20] That, at least, is one implication of Jonathan Goldberg's 1984 essay, 'Sodomy and society: the case of Christopher Marlowe' (Chapter 3), which takes as its premise Foucault's demolition of the 'repressive hypothesis' and insistence that, far from repressing sexual deviance or desire, these are what modern authority *produces* to be its defining foil. The philosopher overshadows Goldberg's argument most darkly, therefore, in its proposition that Marlowe's identity as dramatist, sexual dissident and spy was constructed by the discourses not of revolt, but of Elizabethan empire itself. On this view, the sodomy which defined the playwright's outlaw status should be seen not as a positive act, but as a rebellion licensed by the nation state. Like the counterfeit coining with which he was also charged, or the histrionics of his heroes, Marlowe's love of boys was thus merely the reverse of the official stamp:

> Like the heroes he created, Marlowe lived and died in the impossible project of the marginalized, negativized existence permitted him. Marlowe and his heroes live lives . . . in the realization that rebellion never manages to find its own space, but always acts in the space that society has created for it. To play there is to be nowhere and to recognize that the solidity of discourse carries with it the very negations in which such play can occur.

Comparing the fates of Marlowe and Oscar Wilde, Goldberg ended this depressing essay doubting 'whether we can ever find an authenticity not capable of being crushed by the society in which we exist'. It was a conclusion which revealed the pessimistic depth to which gloom about 'the solidity of discourse' would plunge the humanities in a period when desire was deconstructed as 'an effect of domination, rather than a source of resistance to it'.[21] The weight of this dismal criticism was that of Foucault's account, in *The History of Sexuality*, of how in all earlier societies 'the sodomite had been a temporary aberration', but with the onset of the modern state 'the homosexual was now a species'. Far from being the natural disposition of an essential self, therefore, homosexuality began to be constructed, according to this argument, as 'a product of the encroachment of power on bodies and their pleasures'.[22] It was an analysis given relevance to Marlowe by Alan Bray's *Homosexuality in Renaissance England* (1982), which confirmed that while acts of sodomy had long been condemned, it was only with the emergence of a homosexual subculture of bars and cruising places in seventeenth-century London that English homosexuality became an object 'to be fixed on and recognised. . . . Its visibility was its bane.' Foucault had warned that 'Visibility is a trap'; and in Bray's history the dramatist was one of the earliest victims of such entrapment, his 'defiant assertion of homosexuality' being an assumption of the role of 'the stock figure of the sodomite in the satirical literature' of his time: an 'abomination' whose 'horrible crimes' even the homosexual James I declared he 'was bound in conscience never to forgive'. Bray concedes that 'Marlowe was a very unusual individual', whose identification with the demonised category of sodomite was years before its time; yet as Goldberg likewise laments, by embracing what his society rejected as his own 'negativized identity', this Elizabethan renegade helped to corral homosexuality within that 'sphere of radically threatening otherness', the ghetto where it has remained, 'menaced and vulnerable', to this day.[23]

In the satire of Marlowe's England, sodomites burned in 'fire and brimstone raining from heaven upon them and their cities'. Typical, according to Bray, was a poem by the humanist Du Bartas that imagined the destruction of Sodom as a fire in a homosexual club: 'Here one perceiving the next chamber burning, / With sudden leap towards the window turning, / Thinks to cry "Fire!"; but instantly the smoke / And flame . . . his voice do choke.' Homosexuality was locked in a fatal clinch with this punitive morality, in the Foucauldian account, from the day when individuals such as Marlowe exchanged the invisibility of the barracks or college for the visibility of the negative stereotypes against which modern heterosexuality is defined.[24] Just how insidiously the dominant ideology persists in constructing Marlowe was Goldberg's theme, therefore, when he returned to the dramatist in his study of 'Renaissance Texts and Modern Sexualities', *Sodometries*, in 1992. Here his target was the influential feminism of a critic such as Lisa Jardine, whose book *Still Harping on Daughters* (initially mistaken for a radical primer on Renaissance drama) perpetuated the violent hierarchy that sent Marlowe to his death. As Goldberg objects, Jardine's thesis – that because 'mincing and lisping' boys played women on Marlowe's stage, his 'perverted sexual tastes' are to blame for the 'misogyny' of these roles – depends on the myth of homosexuality as effeminacy, and it polices heterosexuality as the norm beside which 'sexual deviancy' is (in her words) 'unhealthy' and 'misdirected', a 'distorted obsession' that pollutes 'legitimate sexual relations' with the 'gratuitous sub-erotic', as it literally *travesties* straight relationships in 'dubious sex'. For Jardine, 'perverted sexuality is the inevitable accompaniment of female impersonation', so it is no surprise that with such banal prejudices about 'misplaced passion', 'deliberate decadence', and 'the most extreme of unnatural lusts', such feminists should become embroiled in a bitter feud with gay theorists.[25] What is troubling, Goldberg contends (Chapter 5), is that such an inane homophobia should slip into critiques of Marlowe's staging of sodomy offered even by those who do not treat it as 'symptom of his "pathological" condition'. Thus, even gay criticism has been inflected by this form of feminism:

> For Simon Shepherd sodomy serves only to expose the fundamental sameness of sexual experience. Paradoxically, he reads Marlowe's stance as achieving precisely the same purpose that cross-dressed scenes are taken to serve by critics who read boys and women as identical . . . the power relationship is the same in both cases. Thus when he looks for instances of sodomy in Marlowe, he finds them in effeminized men.

For a critic such as Shepherd, Goldberg objects, Marlowe's sodomy merely reproduces, rather than resists, the gendered structure of heterosexual power, because Shepherd sees male/male relations as reflections of male/female ones, with 'the less empowered male written into the female position'. Thus, by caricaturing homosexual relations as predatory, exploitative, and differential, Shepherd unwittingly repeats the cliché that they are an extreme form of masculine supremacism. 'How easily this view of homosexuality becomes homophobic', as Goldberg warns, was evident throughout Shepherd's book, *Marlowe and the Politics of Elizabethan Theatre*, which was expressly written 'out of rage against queer-bashing', as typified by those critics who denigrated the dramatist for his 'unhealthy interest in unnatural vice', 'attraction to sex and sadism', or 'that taste for cruelty that is so often found in the abnormal'.[26] For one of the oddities of Shepherd's account of ' "Women" and Males' in Marlowe (Chapter 4) was that he actually seemed to share this moralistic disgust with sado-masochism, since he demonised it as the paradigm of 'masculine power', from which, 'as a man committed against patriarchy', he wished to separate the drama. This obliviousness to the ways in which gay men like Foucault would explore the performative potential of sado-masochistic eroticism, and so distinguish gay from straight machismo, betrayed how much Shepherd's tabloid rhetoric remained locked, as Goldberg notes, into the 'modern regime of heterosexuality' it supposedly despised. A way out of this impasse, ventured by Jonathan Dollimore in his critique of *Doctor Faustus* (Chapter 14), was opened up by Foucault's revelation (prompted by his S/M experiments) that 'limit and transgression depend upon each other', so that Faustus's 'masochistic sacrifice' can be read as a blueprint for 'sub-cultural transgression', turning 'the identity conferred upon the deviant', as gays have done, back upon oppression. This would be the subject of Dollimore's later book, *Sexual Dissidence* (1991); but in his 1984 commentary on Marlowe, 'transgressive reinscription' remained only a tantalising projection:

> In *Doctor Faustus* sin is . . . a conscious and deliberate transgression of limit. . . . Out of such conditions is born a mode of transgression identifiably protestant in origin: despairing yet defiant, masochistic yet wilful. Faustus is abject yet his abjectness is inseparable from arrogance, which reproaches the authority which demands it, which is not so much subdued as incited . . .

In the 1980s gay theorists still shared the same gendered concept of power as homophobes and feminists; but what is explosive about Marlowe's theatre of sodomy, Goldberg came to realise, is that it escapes the normative structure of male/female oppression, precisely because it is not a carnival of cross-dressing. Quoting the critic William Empson, therefore, Goldberg counters that Marlowe's difference from all his contemporaries is that, instead of tamely disguising boys as women, he presents 'the unmentionable sin for which the punishment was death as *the proper thing to do*'.[27] So, in *Hero and Leander*, the boy may think Neptune takes him for a woman, when 'the lusty god embraced him, called him love', but the joke is his naivety: 'Thereat smiled Neptune, and then told a tale, / How that a shepherd, sitting in a vale, / Played with a boy' (*Hero*, 2.193). The reference is to Marlowe's famous lyric, *The Passionate Shepherd to his Love*, and like the object of the poem, Leander discovers that 'if these pleasures may thee move' it is because he is definitely *not* a girl. Again, in *Edward II*, the transvestite scene of a 'boy in Dian's shape' is never staged, Goldberg notes, and as 'Neither Gaveston nor Edward wear dresses, the link of boy and woman is disarmed.' Instead (as Faustus shows) it is the man who plays Actaeon, 'By yelping hounds pull'd down', who is the homoerotic focus of the myth (*Edward*, 1.1.61–70). So, where he had formerly seen Marlowe caught in what Foucault termed the 'perpetual spiral of power and pleasure',[28] Goldberg now thinks his dramatisation of sodomy disrupts the subject/object binarism of heterosexual ideology. The prototype of such disruption would be *Dido Queen of Carthage*, which here becomes a problematisation (written to be acted entirely by adolescent boys) of those institutions – the army, school, and playhouse – of which 'the unmentionable sin' is 'the dirty secret truth'. In this reading, therefore, when Aeneas deserts Dido, he denies not only effeminisation of warriors by women, but heterosexuality itself, for empire is shown to be an enterprise built upon the sodomy with which the play begins – with Jupiter 'dandling Ganymede upon his knee' – and which is mimicked by a queue of boys throughout. The effect is, of course, to subvert the discourses that privilege a 'masculine' state over an 'effeminate' stage, so Goldberg's 1992 coda cancels his earlier one, and challenges Marlowe's critics with a far more positive prospect of resistance:

> It has been my assumption that Marlowe's radical rethinking of the possibility of being a sodomite was not widely shared in his time. . . . Marlowe's singularity [lies] in the value he attached to what his culture so vehemently opposed. Hence, it is possible, imperative, to recognise in Marlowe a site of political resistance. To recognise too that this could have literary consequences . . . and even Shakespeare would be implicated.

By emphasising how Marlowe's sodomites defy the transvestite myth imposed by feminists, Goldberg liberates homosexual desire from heterosexual fantasy. As he notices, the dramatist himself gives sodomites their own history: 'Great Achilles lov'd Hephaestion, / The conquering Hercules for Hylas wept, / And for Patroclus the stern Achilles droop'd' (*Edward*, 1.4.394). Marlowe's genealogy of male lovers was part of the long struggle, in this sense, 'to reverse the discursive positioning of homosexuality and heterosexuality: to shift heterosexuality from the position of a universal subject to an object of interrogation, and to shift homosexuality from the position of an object to a position of legitimate subjectivity'.[29] Foucault had anticipated this reversal, when he stressed that 'Discourses are not once and for all subservient to power or raised against it . . . a discourse can be both an instrument of power and a starting point for an opposing strategy'.[30] And that is also the premise of Bruce Smith, in his pathbreaking contribution to what has come to be called queer theory, *Homosexual Desire in Shakespeare's England*, where he discusses Marlowe as the first to 'introduce to us the possibility of a homosexual subjectivity', by 'showing that power works in more than one direction', since 'a sodomite can take revenge on satirists'. Like Goldberg, then, Smith highlights how feminists misread a strategy that, far from traducing same-sex love as imitation marriage, presents the goddess of the family, Juno herself, as an (unsuccessful) imitator of Ganymede. Even the murder by his father of the 'mincing minion', Calyphas, is distanced, on this view, by the fact that his muscle-bound killer, Tamburlaine, is the homoerotic pin-up of the play; while *Edward II* seems designed to 'transpose stereotypes of sodomy into situations in which they do not fit'. As Smith attests, Marlowe's point is not that either king or lover are female impersonators, but that they are *two men*, so that 'The power play between them is nothing so simple as a man exerting dominion over a woman':

> The dynamics of gender between Edward and Gaveston are not, then, what the satirists would have us believe. . . . Edward substitutes a man for a woman, but not because the man is like a woman. Far from it. The misogyny of *Edward II* does not equate homosexuality and effeminacy; it insists on their separation.[31]

For queer theorists, such as Goldberg and Smith, it is the exclusive *maleness* of Marlovian drama that lifts it, like the violence of his heroes, outside the knowledge of Elizabethan morality and modern feminism: 'Friendship that yields to marriage; adolescent desire that cools with age; transvestite disguise that is cast aside; laughter that drowns the voice of "Ganymede" – all of these strategies for having it both ways, for entertaining homoerotic desire but keeping it in place, are rejected.'[32] Just how baffled by this 'normalizing of the attractions of the deviant' heterosexuality remains, is confirmed by Thomas Cartelli, with his unusual effort to extend Reader Response Theory to Elizabethan theatre by reconstructing the reactions of the original audience to Marlowe's staging of sodomy. In 'King Edward's Body' (Chapter 11) Cartelli muses that 'if a lovely girl were substituted' for the boy in Gaveston's masque, 'the scenario would not be considered decadent'; but since 'One cannot respond to such images without associating with the "men" who "delight to see" the boy's private parts', Marlowe 'succeeds in making accomplices of playgoers' in a 'pornographic refinement of eroticism' climaxing in the homicidal 'rape' of the king. So, once again, on this reading, it is the Actaeon legend that frames the voyeurism of Marlowe's stage, and when enacted by Edward's murderer, 'challenges the audience to acknowledge its complicity in his performance'. This meditation resembles controversy over modern novelists such as William Burroughs; and though Cartelli's claim that 'As Lightborn . . . drives a hot poker into Edward's anus . . . the separation between audience and stage is suspended' seems as dubious as his confidence that no 'normal' playgoer would ever delight to see a boy naked (he assumes that *The Passionate Shepherd* is addressed to a girl), the essay reminds us of the feral otherness of Marlowe's writing: its absolute negation of 'the normative heterosexual order' that was being fabricated (even though Cartelli believes it to be transhistorical) just as these plays were first performed.

That it is heterosexuality and its nuclear family which is the new construction in Marlowe's England, as 'a fragile and inadequate alternative to older institutions like patronage, pederasty, and the dynastic household', is the historical starting point of John Archer's sophisticated decoding of the world of Renaissance sodomy and spying in 'Marlowe and the observation of men' (Chapter 12). This extract thus serves as a corrective to those who import anachronistic assumptions about the universality of homophobia into Renaissance literature, for Archer echoes Foucault in affirming that until the category of 'sodomite' was invented, 'homosexual practice . . . was the barely visible mortar' that held society together. The elegance of the essay that follows is that it combines this sexual history with another Foucauldian idea: that there was a shift in the early modern state from spectacle to surveillance, a shift in which Marlowe was implicated as both an object and agent. The link is Freud's theory of paranoia as fear of being the object of an unseen gaze, a form of castration anxiety; and in *Sovereignty and Intelligence*, from which this chapter comes, Archer images the Elizabethan court as in this sense literally *paranoid*, being a world of eroticised males regimented into compulsory heterosexuality under the eyes of an all-seeing, or emasculating, female. For, as *Dido* clearly shows, in the Renaissance 'effeminacy was associated with heterosexuality, not love between men', and Marlowe, the 'playwright, lover of boys, and spy', was thereby caught up in a lethal erotics of exhibitionism and concealment. So, in *Edward II*, it is the royal favourites who figure his vulnerability as the dramatist and secret agent of a regime moving from display to discipline, and from pederasty to paranoia; and the

'English agent' who in *The Massacre at Paris* relays to Elizabeth news of the assassination of the Protestant and homosexual Henri III may even be his self-portrait: an omen of Marlowe's own fate in the new era of surveillance.

The Bonfire of Vanities

Queer theory reminds us that Marlowe's plays were written under imminent threat of death, like that stoked up for sodomites by a homophobic Christianity: 'For while in the stinking mire / Of his foul lust he lies, a lightning flash / Him and his love at once to dust doth dash: / The abhorred bed is burnt, and they as well / Coupled in plague as sin are sent to hell.'[33] Christopher Ricks contextualises this sense of doom in an essay on Marlowe and medicine, *'Doctor Faustus* and Hell on Earth', in which he argues that what makes Faustus's contract meaningful is 'the guarantee that he will live for another twenty-four years in a society haunted by plague'. Ricks's 1985 article compares the impact of bubonic plague to that of AIDS; but it is strictly historicist in insisting that it is 'the pressure of plague' upon a play composed in 1592–93, a period of pestilence and the last year of its author's life, that explains its obsession with passing time: 'The centre of the play is visited by curses of plague; the beginning and the end speak of the visitation of plague itself; which thereby swathes the play. First, the literal plague; last the eternal plague that is Hell.' Ricks deplores the 'cordon sanitaire' which has sealed *Faustus* from 'even the biographical facts' about 'Marlowe's involvement' with the catastrophic history of his time;[34] and he agrees, therefore, with the Cultural Materialist critic Alan Sinfield, who similarly relates the violence of *Tamburlaine* to contemporary reactions to the plague (Chapter 7). Taking seriously its hero's claim to be 'the scourge of God and terror of the earth', Sinfield argues that the tragedy prises apart the rhetoric that legitimates state violence as a natural disaster like disease. So the actual contexts of Tamburlaine's threat 'To scourge the pride of such as Heaven abhors' (2 *Tam.*, 4.1.147–52) were those Elizabethan slums where the poor were sermonised that epidemics were caused not by 'overcrowding, unsatisfactory hygiene, and bad housing,' but as divine punishment for their own lives:

> As with today's AIDS 'plague', the neatest technique of legitimation blames the victim: 'So our inventions beget sin, sin provokes the wrath of God, the wrath of God sends the plague among us', [Bishop] Andrewes explained. Plague actually did

afflict mainly the people who usually lost out and were blamed when things went wrong. . . . [But] Andrewes did not resign everything to God – at the height of the epidemic, he fled his deanery.

Historicist criticism returns us to the chilling fact that what was visualised on Marlowe's stage as a figure of speech was inflicted on his contemporaries for real. This is the theme of Richard Wilson's account of the geopolitics of *Tamburlaine* (Chapter 8), which alludes in its title, 'Visible bullets', to Greenblatt's proposition, in an essay called 'Invisible bullets', that while plague or famine may break our bones, words will surely kill us. By contrast, Wilson restores Marlowe's plague metaphor to historical reality, with a reading that insists on the literal truth of Tamburlaine's threat to 'scourge' his victims with 'the deadly bullet gliding through the side' (*2 Tam.*, 3.4.4). Prompted by an episode at one of the early performances of the tragedy, when 'a player's hand swerved, his calliver being charged with bullets, and killed a child and a woman' in the audience, 'Visible bullets' reconstructs the bloody trail that connects the pogroms of the fictional despot to the genocide perpetrated with English weapons by Queen Elizabeth's ally, Ivan the Terrible: 'the incident reminds us of the materiality of Marlovian culture . . . the covert cycle that links Persepolis to Deptford'. As much detective-work as critique, the essay reveals how these texts legitimate international racketeering to supply arms in exchange for access to the Tsar's new Asian conquests, a conspiracy rigged by Marlowe's backers in the Muscovy Company. The discovery of the playwright's involvement in this gun-running thus suggests a startling solution to his stabbing, based on the fact that the murder-scene was no tavern, but the office where the fraud was fixed. Marlowe died, according to this fresh source material, a pawn in the Great Game of empire that was so lucrative to Bankside spectators who were also *speculators* in global exploitation. This is criticism that deliberately breaks the structuralist taboo of 'The Death of the Author', therefore, to implicate both the dramatist and his drama in the holocaust ignited by imperialism:

So burn the turrets of this cursed town
Flame to the highest region of the air,
And kindle heaps of exhalations,
Death and destruction to the inhabitants!
Over my zenith hang a blazing star . . .
Threatening plague and famine to this land!

(*2 Tam.*, 3.2.1–9)

Christopher Marlowe

Historicising *Tamburlaine* at the crossroads of the first global empires, 'All those commodities transported from Persepolis to Deptford are traded, we grasp, for these "bullets like Jove's thunderbolts, / Enrolled in flames and fiery mists" (*1 Tam.*, 2.3.19), and the poet's pyromania has its genesis in that warehouse where a kinsman "quietly" consigned munitions to the arsonist of Moscow.' The same acuteness to the deadly material realities of Marlowe's will to power informs Emily Bartels's account of *The Jew of Malta* (Chapter 10), which again answers Greenblatt's belief that this tragedy simply rehearses the 'will to endless play' by locating it in the Mediterranean island where it is set, and the actual period dramatised, when Malta became the strategic key to Europe's world-wide domination. Where New Historicist critics had bisected Renaissance literature on structuralist lines, to expose the polarity dividing Self from Other, white from black, or West from East, Bartels here makes a deconstructionist move, by showing how an indeterminate location subverts such binarism, for 'the play represents Malta as a place of difference within itself . . . outside binary opposition. As the object of imperialist conflict, the island emerges as a third term whose meaning is dictated from without.' Thus, though the action takes place after the siege of Malta in 1565, Marlowe visualises the West's worst-case scenario 'by rewriting history and presenting the Turks as victorious'. The result is to relativise fictions of difference, for here the opposing power is Spain: England's Catholic demon. So, the paradox that 'my enemy's enemy is my friend' underpins this plot, as Marlowe constantly introduces third parties, beginning with the placeless Jew, Barabas, and his slave Ithamore, to explode the polarities on which both identities and colonies depend. Thus, *The Jew of Malta* becomes a machine for 'self-colonization', fuelled by what Bartels calls, in her 1993 book on Marlowe and imperialism, *Spectacles of Difference*, the genocidal destructiveness of the 'stranger within':

> For what Marlowe's plays show is that the discourse of domination, whether in the 'dark continent' or on the English throne, was inexorably dependent upon the circumscription of another. . . . And what had to be denied even as it was displayed was the difference within – the horror that in the heart of darkness sat the English themselves. . . . For on Marlowe's stage there is no denial of the difference within – no denial . . . that the darkness of the 'dark continent' as of the worlds beyond is 'ours' rather than 'theirs'.[35]

The Conradian echoes in Bartels's coda confirm how a more literal historicism than New Historicism discovers Marlowe's drama deep in the heart of darkness of his time. And of no text is this 'new literalism' more telling than *The Massacre at Paris*, which has almost unique status for an Elizabethan play of reporting a topical event. In fact, its subject, the St Bartholomew's Day Massacre of Protestants in Paris in 1572, was infamous as the most horrific atrocity of the sixteenth century, a collective crime that gave the age the very word 'massacre' and traumatised contemporaries as much as Auschwitz or Hiroshima in our own. Here, then, in what may be his final script for the stage, Marlowe at last realised the holocaust towards which his work had aimed. Yet, because the text appears incomplete, *The Massacre at Paris* has been dismissed as a chaotic shambles; exactly the same misreading, Julia Briggs points out (Chapter 13), as once blinded commentators to the social logic of the type of bloodbath it enacts. In fact, our understanding of early modern riots (and so, of Marlowe's play) has been transformed by the research of the French *Annales* school of historians; in particular, by *Carnival at Romans*, Emmanuel Le Roy Ladurie's book on an uprising that erupted in the French town at Mardi Gras in 1580. Extended by Natalie Zemon Davis to the entire welter of the French Wars of Religion, Ladurie's 'microhistory' revealed the symbolic repertory and festive rhythms of religious blood-letting, and underlined 'how characteristic was the St Bartholomew's Day scenario. A marriage – one of the great rites of passage – and then wedding masques turned into rites of violence.'[36] Briggs deploys this idea of sacrificial bloodshed, therefore, to show not only how accurately Marlowe's reportage relays the grisly choreography of a people's purge, but how the charisma of its instigator, Guise, might compel even Protestant collusion. The sinister implication of this reading, of course, is that, through such a seductive anti-hero, Marlowe systematically sets out to lure his audience into a willing complicity in the spectacle of its own extermination:

> The Elizabethan audience may have reacted to the violence with excitement, as if they were watching real events, witnessing an execution or participating in a lynching, so that they laughed with the murderers, thus freeing themselves of responsibility and compassion, as the religious rioters seem to have done . . . a reaction that would have forced a Protestant audience to see the massacre from a standpoint identical with that of the Catholic murderers . . .

'Fire Paris, where these treacherous rebels lurk. . . . As Rome, and all the popish prelates there, / Shall curse the time that e're Navarre was king': the final lines of *The Massacre at Paris* become, in Briggs's version, simply a compulsive rekindling of the same conflagration that the Catholic villain had earlier lit. 'Those never-dying flames / Which cannot be extinguish'd but by blood' (1.2.35) illuminate a theatre, according to this reading, that draws its energy from the torchlit parades where the actual revellers of St Bartholomew's Day danced their masque of death, and the order to burn Paris brings a fitting climax to a drama that demands (as Walter Benjamin wrote of Fascist art) a 'self-alienation that experiences aesthetic pleasure from its own destruction'.[37] All through his career Marlowe dreamed of falling towers in burning cities, so he ended his last play, the only one set at the moment of writing, with the promise, we can infer, of such an apocalypse of his own. And if biographers are right, and this dramatist's admiration for the mass-murderer Guise dates from his infiltration, as a 'treacherous rebel' himself, of the Catholic League in France, then the possibility that 'the English agent' who carries the order to 'Fire Paris' is his own self-portrait appears suicidally nihilistic. As Charles Nicholl observes, there comes a point in weighing Marlowe's double-agency when 'The interesting question is not how much his political position influenced his work as a writer, but the opposite question that no one has asked: how much did his position as a writer influence his political work?'[38] It is an axiom of New Historicism that the purpose of playing is not merely to hold a mirror up to nature, but to 'shape the fantasies by which it is shaped, beget that by which it is begotten'.[39] If that is so, then the newest historicism concludes that the ultimate victim of Marlowe's imagined bonfire of vanities was the fantasist and pyromaniac contemporaries saluted as 'our best for plotting', the author himself.

Saint Marlowe

He was murdered in the docks, where he had been enticed, according to police informers, for an assignation that ended in savage violence over payment of a young male prostitute. But rumours persist that he was the target of a political assassination, ambushed by enemies he had betrayed, or outraged with his work. His art provoked church and censors by glamorising the underclass of peasants, students, hustlers, and racketeers who were drawn to the slums by the consumer boom that was transforming the ancient city into a modern capital. He dressed them in the crowns and robes of kings, and then featured them in blasphemous or pornographic versions of classical myths and medieval histories. His preferred settings were the biblical landscapes of the Mediterranean and the Middle East, where Muslims and Jews confronted the Christians with their own barbarity. These he decorated with thugs and angels, and lit with a magic realism. He liked to sign his works with small personal appearances, tempting fate with these masochistic hints that he was the author and agent of so much sensuality and suffering. And in his last unfinished testament he broke all rules of taste by staging one of the most atrocious massacres of recent times as a carnival of sodomy and sadism. So there were many who said he had willed his end in a proxy suicide, to perish at the hands of the underworld he loved, this sexual and religious heretic, who had imaged Christ as a pederast, but had been protected for so long by powerful friends. His name was Pier Paolo Pasolini, and his career and death in 1975 have such uncanny parallels with Marlowe's that it appears as if the same narrative controls the destiny of both the modern film director and the Renaissance dramatist. And when we also compare the fate of Marlowe's own contemporary, the painter Caravaggio, the pattern seems undeniable. This discourse of desire and death is that which modern culture assigns to the artist as sexual outlaw.

'I think that all men in Christianity ought to endeavour that the mouth of so dangerous a member may be stopped': the sexual innuendo in a dossier on Marlowe slipped to the police three days before his murder typifies the orthodox reaction to his words, which prompted calls for censorship as late as the 1960s. His mouth had to be shut to end his contempt of God, wrote his accuser, a spy named Richard Baines, who claimed to be scandalised by Marlowe's ribaldry that 'St John was bedfellow to Christ and used him as the sinners of Sodom'. This tip-off was corroborated by the dramatist Thomas Kyd, who alleged how 'he would report St John to be our Saviour's Alexis', meaning 'that Christ did love him with extraordinary love', and taunt 'That all they that love not tobacco and boys are fools'. When he was murdered in Deptford on 30 May 1593, it was easy, therefore, for the establishment to blame his desires for his death, branding him with the classical writer Lycophron: 'shot to death by a rival, as Marlowe was stabbed by a bawdy serving-man, a rival in his lewd love'. Known only for poems to boys, Lycophron was a prototype of the author killed (like Orpheus) for his homosexuality, and his martyrdom suggested how Marlowe's story belonged to an age-old scenario of deviance and disaster. From the very first comments of the critics, then, his work was subjected to a narrative in which his language, sexuality and death were all judged to have defied the limits imposed by God. That, stabbed through the brain, he 'died swearing' only seemed to confirm the aptness of a critique that equated his penis with his pen and his language with his life.[40] As Simon Shepherd has noted, this construction of 'Marlowe-as-homosexual' has been essential to the marginalised status accorded his works, for 'Marlowe-as-homosexual is always understood as a flawed writer because of the obsession he could not control'.[41] Thus, as early as 1597, Cromwell's schoolmaster, Thomas Beard, was setting the academic tone by rejoicing that 'The Theatre of God's Judgement' had silenced 'this play-maker and poet of scurrility':

> Who by giving too large a swinge to his wit, and suffering his lust to have full reins, fell (not without desert) to that outrage that he denied God and His son. But see what a hook the Lord put in the nostrils of this barking dog: it so fell out that . . . he stabbed his own dagger into his own head. . . . The manner of his death being so terrible that it was not only horrible to all that beheld him, but a manifest sign of God's judgement, in that he compelled his own hand which had written those blasphemies to be the instrument to punish him, and that in his brain, which had devised the same.[42]

It is Foucault's analysis of the 'rules of exclusion' that determine the 'author function' which helps to unravel this configuration, when he proposes that the modern concept of authorship was fabricated at the end of the sixteenth century 'according to the manner in which Christian tradition had authenticated or rejected texts', and that 'modern criticism uses methods similar to those of Christian exegesis when trying to prove the value of a text by its author's saintliness'.[43] So, what made Marlowe crucial, according to this theory, was that he was a figure at the intersection of two of the defining discourses of modernity: when criticism was devising the institution of authorship just as law was normalising sexuality. As the most scandalous Elizabethan writer, Marlowe was present at the birth of both modern authorship and sexual dissidence, and it was this coincidence which it was the work of critics to confront. For long, however, there was no contradiction, since, as Edmund Rudyard sneered in 1614, such a 'poet and filthy play-maker' proved how sodomy was soldered to the stage: 'Hearken, ye brain-sick poets and players, that betwitch idle ears with foolish vanities . . . what fell upon this profane wretch. Mark this, ye players, that live by making fools to laugh at sin.' In early commentaries Marlowe's sodomy was simply seen as evidence of the vice of the theatre, where, to the horror of the Puritan Philip Stubbes, 'every mate sorts with his mate, everyone brings another home, and in their secret conclaves they play the Sodomites or worse'. And for three centuries Ben Jonson's scorn for 'Marlowe's mighty line' as a perversion 'from nature' cued critics to attribute

the 'lust for power in his writings' to what Romantics like Charles
Lamb identified as his 'thirst for unrighteousness', and even the
homosexual campaigner, J.A. Symonds, as 'the day-dreams of his
deep desires'. So, by the time of Freud, a moraliser such as George
Bernard Shaw could conveniently diagnose the dramatist as
psychotic in his infatuation for the ruffian on the stair:

> Marlowe, the moment the exhaustion of the imaginative fit
> deprives him of the power of raving, becomes childish . . . itching
> to frighten people with terrors and cruelties . . . and wallowing in
> blood, violence, muscularity and animal passion, as only literary
> men do when they become depraved by solitary work, sedentary
> cowardice, and starvation of the sympathetic centres.[44]

The 'rules of exclusion' had always demoted Marlowe from the
canon for his sexual heresy, so it was merely a reversal of this
discourse when modernists, led by T.S. Eliot, denied his dissidence in
order to secure his canonicity. Sanitised by Eliot as 'a deliberate and
conscious workman', the blaspheming pederast was normalised by
modernism into Marlowe the 'conservative and objective artist'. With
titles such as *A Study in Renaissance Moral Philosophy* and *Suffering
and Evil in the Plays of Marlowe*, the critics of mid-century erased the
Elizabethan's unAmerican activities to reassure their campuses.[45]
Yet, as Thomas Dabbs points out in his book, *Reforming Marlowe*,
'the subjective Marlowe of the romantic school and the objective
Marlowe' of modernism remained in deadlock even in the 1990s,
with the return of 'Marlowe as an "estranged" subversive' in
Greenblatt's portrait of 'the artist bravely forging human values
in the face of an abysmal universe'.[46] For the critical reader at the
millennium, therefore, the quandary posed by Marlowe is analogous
to that provoked by the philosopher of normalisation himself,
according to David Halperin in his recent 'gay hagiography',
Saint Foucault: whether to 'reduce personal life to the merely *private*,
neglecting the connection between thought and experiences of
sexual and political subjection, or to seek in fantasy life, sexual
preoccupations, and artistic tastes the key to understanding books'.
To a queer theorist like Halperin, this choice between 'the silence of
discretion' and 'chatter of psychologizing' misses the point of 'the
political character' of a life like Foucault's, 'of his struggle against the
modern "technologies of the subject" whose operations he described';
and the same can be said of the writer who, more than any other,
exposed those operations, even as he suffered them, at the moment
they were born. What Halperin maintains of Foucault can be applied
equally to Marlowe, when he insists:

If we learn anything from him, it is not to canonize him as the exponent of some doctrine, but as someone whose understanding of his location enabled him to devise modes of resistance to the conditions which circumscribed him. That ability to reflect critically on the circumstances that constrained his own activity may account for why his life, as much as his work, continues to serve as a compelling model.[47]

Millennial Marlowe will be canonised, according to this celebration, not for pious orthodoxy, but for the perversion, violence, cruelty and excess that formerly disqualified him from sainthood. It is a paradox of such a reversal that the reason why critics are so fascinated by the death of this author, as Thomas Healy admits, is that 'we know so much about it', thanks to the machinery of discipline and punishment that destroyed him. For though Healy objects that 'there is no evidence to confirm the intellectually dangerous character his reputation has made him', that character was precisely the one constructed by the state to justify his silence; just as the poison of his words was the legend invented to negate his person. Like Healy, Richard Dutton has cited 'the normality of the treatment Marlowe received' from the censors as proof of conformism; but these revisionist moves to naturalise the plays by 'discriminating between the man and his writings' seem disingenuous about what Halperin calls 'the cultural imperative to maintain public respectability by pandering to prejudice and upholding normalizing standards'.[48] It is too late now for the system that marginalised Marlowe to manoeuvre to coopt him. The playwright who staged the scandal of a paedophile god, sado-masochistic killer, immigrant Jew, sodomite king, subversive intellectual, and Catholic terrorist, will be canonised not for normalising them, but for dramatising their difference from the normality they outraged. A sainted Marlowe will be the patron, in this sense, of that inversion of normative values to which queer theorists aspire, when they assert that deviance is not something to be rehabilitated, but a position 'to be exploited and explored: a privileged site for the criticism and analysis of culture'.[49] Like his hero, Aeneas, who carried boys through the burning library, this Saint Christopher will be staged and studied for his perversity 'In managing those fierce barbarian minds' (*Dido*, 1.1.92):

With balls of wild-fire in their murdering paws,
Which made the funeral flame that burnt fair Troy.

(*Dido*, 2.1.217)

Notes

1. All quotations from Marlowe are from *Christopher Marlowe: The Complete Plays*, ed. J.B. STEANE (Harmondsworth, Penguin, 1969).

2. MICHEL FOUCAULT, *The Order of Things: An Archaeology of the Human Sciences*, trans. anon. (London, Tavistock, 1970), p. 35.

3. GEORGE STEINER, *Language and Silence* (Harmondsworth, Penguin, 1969), p. 290.

4. WILLIAM SHAKESPEARE, *Julius Caesar*, ed. T.S. DORSCH (London, Methuen, 1955), 3.3.30.

5. YUKIO MISHIMA, *Confessions of a Mask*, trans. MEREDITH WEATHERBY (New York, New Directions, 1958), p. 65.

6. GUY HOCQUENGHEM, *Homosexual Desire*, trans. DANIELLA DANGOOR (Durham, NC, Duke University Press, 1993), p. 150.

7. STEPHEN GREENBLATT, 'Marlowe and the will to absolute play', in RICHARD WILSON and RICHARD DUTTON (eds), *New Historicism and Renaissance Drama* (London, Longman, 1992), p. 82.

8. MICHEL FOUCAULT, 'Un plaisir si simple', *Gai Pied*, 1 (April 1979), p. 10: trans. *Fag Rag*, 29, p. 3. Quoted in JAMES MILLER, *The Passion of Michel Foucault* (London, HarperCollins, 1993), p. 28.

9. MICHEL FOUCAULT, 'Mon Couer, ce papier, ce feu', *Padedia* (September 1971), pp. 583–603, esp. p. 602: trans. GEOFF BENNINGTON, *Oxford Literary Review*, 4 (1979), pp. 9–28.

10. MARJORIE GARBER, ' "Infinite riches in a little room": closure and enclosure in Marlowe', in ALVIN KERNAN (ed.), *Two Renaissance Myth Makers: Christopher Marlowe and Ben Jonson: Selected Papers of the English Institute, 1975–76*, (Baltimore, MD, Johns Hopkins University Press, 1977), pp. 3–21, esp. pp. 11–13.

11. MICHEL FOUCAULT, *The Order of Things*, p. 387.

12. STEPHEN GREENBLATT, *Renaissance Self-Fashioning from More to Shakespeare* (Chicago, Chicago University Press, 1980).

13. ROLAND BARTHES, 'Inaugural lecture, College de France', in SUSAN SONTAG (ed.), *Barthes: Selected Writings* (London, Fontana, 1983), pp. 457–78, esp. p. 461.

14. LOUIS ALTHUSSER, 'Ideology and ideological state apparatuses (notes towards an investigation)', in *Essays in Ideology*, trans. anon. (London, Verso, 1984), pp. 127–70, esp. pp. 167–9.

15. MICHEL FOUCAULT, 'Language to infinity', in *Language, Counter-Memory, Practice: Selected Essays and Interviews*, ed. and trans. DONALD BOUCHARD (Oxford, Basil Blackwell, 1977), pp. 53–67.

16. GRAHAM HAMMILL, 'Faustus's fortunes: commodification, exchange, and the form of literary subjectivity', *English Literary History*, 63 (1996), pp. 309–36, esp. p. 336. Regretfully, this important essay was published too late to be included in the present volume.

17. MICHEL FOUCAULT, 'Sept propos sur le septieme ange', preface to JEAN-PIERRE BRISSET, *La grammaire logique* (Paris, Gallimard, 1970), quoted in JAMES MILLER, *The Passion of Michel Foucault* (HarperCollins, London, 1994), p. 279.

Christopher Marlowe

18. LEAH MARCUS, 'Textual indeterminacy and ideological difference: the case of *Doctor Faustus*', *Renaissance Drama*, 20 (1989), p. 5.

19. FOUCAULT, 'Language to infinity', pp. 66–7.

20. MICHEL FOUCAULT, *The History of Sexuality: Introduction*, trans. ROBERT HURLEY (Harmondsworth, Penguin, 1978), p. 206.

21. JONATHAN DOLLIMORE, *Sexual Dissidence: Augustine to Wilde, Freud to Foucault* (Oxford, Oxford University Press, 1991), p. 44.

22. FOUCAULT, *History of Sexuality*, pp. 43 and 48.

23. ALAN BRAY, *Homosexuality in Renaissance England* (London, Gay Men's Press, 1982), pp. 65 and 92; MICHEL FOUCAULT, *Discipline and Punish: The Birth of the Prison*, trans. ALAN SHERIDAN (Harmondsworth, Penguin, 1977), p. 200.

24. PHILIP STUBBES, *The Anatomy of Abuses*, ed. FREDERICK FURNIVALL (London, New Shakespeare Society, 1882), vol. 2, p. 3; BRAY, *Homosexuality*, pp. 59 and 79.

25. JONATHAN GOLDBERG, *Sodometries: Renaissance Texts, Modern Sexualities* (Stanford, CA, Stanford University Press, 1992), pp. 112–15; LISA JARDINE, *Still Harping on Daughters* (Hemel Hempstead, Harvester Wheatsheaf, 1983), pp. 20–4; LISA JARDINE, ' "Girl talk" (for boys on the left), or marginalising feminist critical praxis', *Oxford Literary Review*, 8 (1986), pp. 213–14.

26. JOHN BAKELESS, *The Tragical History of Christopher Marlowe* (Cambridge, MA, Harvard University Press, 1942) (2 vols), vol. 1, p. 112; J.B. STEANE, *Marlowe – A Critical Study* (Cambridge, Cambridge University Press, 1964), p. 234; PHILIP HENDERSON, *And Morning in His Eyes: A True Portrait of Christopher Marlowe* (London, Boriswood, 1937), p. 290.

27. WILLIAM EMPSON, 'Two proper crimes', *The Nation*, 163 (1946), pp. 444–5.

28. FOUCAULT, *History of Sexuality*, p. 45.

29. DAVID HALPERIN, *Saint Foucault: Towards a Gay Hagiography* (Oxford, Oxford University Press, 1995), p. 57.

30. FOUCAULT, *History of Sexuality*, pp. 100–1.

31. BRUCE SMITH, *Homosexual Desire in Shakespeare's England: A Cultural Poetics* (Chicago, Chicago University Press, 1994), pp. 209–10, 213–15.

32. Ibid., pp. 222–3.

33. Du Bartas, quoted in BRAY, *Homosexuality*, p. 59.

34. CHRISTOPHER RICKS, '*Doctor Faustus* and Hell on Earth', *Essays in Criticism*, 35 (2) (April 1985), pp. 101–20, esp. pp. 104 and 108; permission to reproduce this essay in the present collection was refused by the author.

35. EMILY C. BARTELS, *Spectacles of Strangeness: Imperialism, Alienation, and Marlowe* (Philadelphia, University of Pennsylvania Press, 1993), pp. 173–5.

36. NATALIE ZEMON DAVIS, *Society and Culture in Early Modern France* (Oxford, Polity Press, 1987), p. 173.

37. WALTER BENJAMIN, 'The work of art in the age of mechanical reproduction', in *Illuminations*, trans. HARRY ZOHN (London, Collins, 1973), p. 244.

38. CHARLES NICHOLL, *The Reckoning: The Murder of Christopher Marlowe* (London, Jonathan Cape, 1993), pp. 170–1.

39. LOUIS MONTROSE, '*A Midsummer Night's Dream* and the shaping fantasies of Elizabethan culture', in RICHARD WILSON and RICHARD DUTTON (eds), *New Historicism and Renaissance Drama* (London, Longman, 1992), p. 130.

40. MILLAR MACLURE (ed.), *Marlowe: The Critical Heritage* (London, Routledge, 1979), pp. 35–8 and 46.

41. SIMON SHEPHERD, *Marlowe and the Politics of Elizabethan Theatre* (Brighton, Harvester, 1986), p. xii.

42. MACLURE, *Marlowe*, pp. 41–2.

43. MICHEL FOUCAULT, 'What is an author?', *The Foucault Reader*, ed. PAUL RABINOW (Harmondsworth, Penguin, 1986), p. 110.

44. WILLIAM TYDEMAN and VIVIEN THOMAS, *Christopher Marlowe: State of the Art* (Bristol, Bristol Classical Press, 1989), pp. 2, 7 and 10; MACLURE, *Marlowe*, pp. 198–9.

45. T.S. ELIOT, 'Notes on the blank verse of Christopher Marlowe' (1919), in *Collected Essays* (London, Faber, 1961), p. 45; ROY BATTENHOUSE, *Marlowe's 'Tamburlaine': A Study in Renaissance Moral Philosophy* (Nashville, Tenn.: Vanderbilt University Press, 1941), quoted in THOMAS DABBS, *Reforming Marlowe: The Nineteenth-Century Canonization of a Renaissance Dramatist* (Lewisburg, Bucknell University Press, 1991), p. 137; DOUGLAS COLE, *Suffering and Evil in the Plays of Christopher Marlowe* (Princeton, NJ, Princeton University Press, 1962).

46. DABBS, *Reforming Marlowe*, p. 139.

47. HALPERIN, *Saint Foucault*, pp. 153 and 162.

48. THOMAS HEALY, *Christopher Marlowe* (Plymouth, Northcote House, 1994), p. 13; RICHARD DUTTON, 'Shakespeare and Marlowe: censorship and construction', *Yearbook of English Studies*, 23 (1993), p. 29; HALPERIN, *Saint Foucault*, p. 147.

49. Ibid. (Halperin), pp. 60–1.

2 'Here's Nothing Writ': Scribe, Script, and Circumscription in Marlowe's Plays*

MARJORIE GARBER

In America in the 1980s New Historicism was a critical movement to restore texts to historical contexts, but as products of prior discourses, rather than works of individual authors. Influenced by Jacques Derrida's theory that 'There is nothing outside the text', New Historicists were preoccupied by the ways in which bodies and identities are *prescribed*, and Marjorie Garber's essay implied an elective affinity between this criticism and Marlovian drama, which also demonstrated how human beings are (sometimes literally) *circumscribed* by the effects of texts. As Tamburlaine redrafts the map of the world; Faustus signs the devil's pact; and Mortimer punctuates Edward's death warrant, we see that in these plays the pen is mightier than the sword, and that their dominant metaphor for power is *writing*. But there is a sharp edge to this poststructuralist theme, Garber concludes, because the characters who 'make their mark' in Marlowe's plots are themselves undone by signatures and signs, which are *inscribed* with 'point, period, and punctuation by another hand': that of the terminating writer himself. Marlowe cancels his own creations, according to this reading, in a travesty of Christ, appropriating the symbolism of the eucharist to a new religion of the autonomous author. In an earlier essay, entitled 'Infinite riches in a little room', Garber had described Marlowe's stage as a claustrophobic prison house of words; but by returning to the biography of the playwright, she now suggests that what remains 'outside the text' is history itself – albeit, a history mediated through other books, like those that the author read himself.

The meaning has a meaning

(*The Jew of Malta*, IV. iv. 91)

Although Marlowe has been justifiably praised for the dramatic force of his characters' spoken discourse, another dimension of his drama

---

* Reprinted from *Theatre Journal*, 36 (1984), 301–20.

which raises larger questions of power has received less attention – the trope of writing and unwriting. Patterns of intertextual reference, texts 'deconstructing' or undoing other texts, and authors asserting competing authority recur throughout Marlowe's plays. This drama of the word is played out in *Tamburlaine* with special reference to the Koran and the conqueror's map of the world; in *Faustus*, with reference to the Eucharistic testament and the sorcerer's 'deed of gift' to Lucifer. In *Edward II* a letter serves as the material embodiment of the concept of countertext as counterplot. In all these instances, the act of writing or signing conveys, not just a struggle between contending characters, but a struggle for mastery of stage and text between the playwright and his inscribed characters.

With his 'persuasions more pathetical' than the eloquent god Hermes and his 'working words', Tamburlaine is less often regarded as a writer than as a rhetor or orator.[1] Not only is he magniloquent, he is also enraptured with the very sounds of words – won over by the language of Menander's phrase, 'And ride in triumph through Persepolis', as much or more than by the idea embodied in that phrase (*Part 1*, II. v. 49–50). In some ways he seems both the perfect speaker for, and the perfect auditor of, Marlowe's fabled 'mighty line'. In addition to the resounding periods of his speeches Tamburlaine is adept in the language of signs, although – or perhaps because – his semiotic codes are far from subtle. The sequence of white, red, and black tents to be pitched before Damascus unequivocally herald clemency on the first day, warfare on the second, and death on the third, and when the Median lord Agydas, who has imprudently counseled Zenocrate against accepting Tamburlaine's suit, is presented with a naked dagger, he has no difficulty in deciphering its meaning: 'He needed not with words confirm my fear, / For words are vain where working tools present / The naked action of my threatened end. / It says, Agydas, thou shalt surely die' (*Part 1*, III. ii. 92–95).

Tamburlaine is likewise a master of speech-acts, whose natural syntax is a performative illocutionary utterance, as he asserts to his admiring lieutenant: 'Well said, Theridimas; speak in that mood, / For *will* and *shall* best fitteth Tamburlaine' (*Part 1*, III. iii. 40–41). The Prologue to *Part 1* describes Tamburlaine as 'Threatening the world with high astounding terms, / And scourging kingdoms with his conquering sword' (5–6), and this twinship of sword and word, echoed in the first scene by Mycetes' fearful compliment to Theridimas ('thy words are swords' [74]) will be a constant factor throughout the two *Tamburlaine* plays.

Equally striking, however, is Tamburlaine's participation in transactions of writing and unwriting, revision and correction. Appropriately, the text that he writes and later unwrites is a map, the metonymic sign of the world he seeks to conquer, and, according to his own figure, his pen is the conquering sword.

> Zenocrate, were Egypt Jove's own land,
> Yet would I with my sword make Jove to stoop.
> I will confute those blind geographers
> That make a triple region of the world,
> Excluding regions which I mean to trace,
> And with this pen reduce them to a map,
> Calling the provinces, cities and towns,
> After my name and thine, Zenocrate.
> Here at Damascus shall I make the point
> That shall begin the perpendicular.
>
> *(Part 1,* IV, iv. 78–87)

This speech reads almost like a primer in figurative language. His 'sword' (79) becomes a pen, ostentatiously brandished ('this pen' [83]), and the act of writing is simultaneously one of microcosmic miniaturization ('reduce them to a map' [82]) and of naming, or more properly, renaming. 'Point', in line 86, is both a sword's point and a punctuation mark. The 'map', present here only imaginatively, will become a visible stage property in his death scene at the end of *Part 2*, at a moment when, paradoxically, the unconquered territories are furthest from Tamburlaine's grasp. Here in *Part 1*, however, the map offers a displaced metonymic alternative to the already common Elizabethan metaphor of the world as a stage.

Moreover, behind the sword–pen metaphor stands another which is in a sense its inverse. Tamburlaine's sword is his pen – but Marlowe's pen is Tamburlaine's sword. Just as Tamburlaine's 'working words' and 'high astounding terms', rather than his martial might, are the real instruments of his conquest – conquest of Theridimas, Zenocrate, and the audience – and the territory to be conquered is not Egypt or Damascus but the Elizabethan stage and the imaginative space of drama, so Marlowe's pen is the instrument of writing behind Tamburlaine's redrawing of the map of the world. In the very next scene, Act V, Scene i, occurs the famous Marlovian set piece on the limits of language and the power of poetry:

> What is beauty, saith my sufferings, then?
> If all the pens that ever poets held
> Had fed the feeling of their masters' thoughts,
> And every sweetness that inspired their thoughts,
> Their minds, and muses on admired themes;
> If all the heavenly quintessence they still
> From their immortal flowers of poesy,

Wherein, as in a mirror, we perceive
The highest reaches of a human wit;
If these had made one poem's period,
And all combined in beauty's worthiness,
Yet should there hover in their restless heads
One thought, one grace, one wonder, at the least,
Which into words no virtue can digest.

(*Part 1*, V. i. 160–173)

Here, too, is unconquered and unconquerable territory, rendered inaccessible by the limits of mortality. Again, as in the figure of the map, we have compression or reduction – all heavenly quintessence distilled into 'one poem's period'. 'Period' carries the primary signification of 'unit of poetry', but the diachronic associations of temporality and limit are also present; this period is an end which yet remains stubbornly elusive, inconclusive. Indeed, the presence of beauty is valorized by an absence – the inexpressibility of that 'one thought, one grace, one wonder' which 'no virtue can digest'. 'Digest', like 'still' (i.e., 'distill', 1. 165) and 'reduce' in the previous passage, connotes contraction or compression, again parallel or analogous to the metaphor of the world as a stage, but here (as in Shakespeare's Prologues to *Henry V*) the apparent diminution and inadequacy is at the same time a paradoxical claim for aggrandizement through acts of individual and collective imagination.

The dramatic contiguity of the two 'pen' speeches – pointed as they are by Tamburlaine's deictic 'this pen' as he indicates his sword – marks a contest between Tamburlaine and Marlowe suggestively similar to those that may be discerned in other plays between Marlowe and Faustus, or Marlowe and Mortimer. As always, the arbiter of this competition will be the reader or audience, since it is we, and not Tamburlaine, who hear the dangerous doubleness implicit in his words, the metatheatrical or metapoetic referent. And, like the others, this one is intrinsically an unequal contest. Both the scales and the author's hand are tipped, as becomes clear in a third reference to the 'pen' as the instrument of power and limit, the Prologue to *Tamburlaine, Part 2*. Here, in a characteristically Marlovian placement on the borders or margins of the central text, we find both a quietly incontrovertible assertion of authority such as to throw Tamburlaine's ensuing struggles into an increasingly ironic light, and, at the same time, an apparent syntactical awkwardness or ambiguity, which first permits – and then enforces – an interpretative crisis of referentiality.

The general welcomes Tamburlaine received,
When he arrived last upon our stage,

Hath made our poet pen his Second Part,
Where death cuts off the progress of his pomp,
And murderous fate throws all his triumphs down.
But what became of fair Zenocrate,
And with how many cities' sacrifice
He celebrated her sad funeral,
Himself in presence shall unfold at large.

(Prol., 1–9)

Tamburlaine's reappearance on the stage is explicitly attributed to
the audience's enthusiastic reception of *Part 1* ('general welcomes')
and to the poet, whose 'pen' has now become a powerful causative
and creative verb governing the actions and the fate of the play's
protagonist. Tamburlaine himself appears in this Prologue as a
syntactical object rather than an acting subject, a figure whose
dramatic destiny is to be cut off by death and thrown down by
murderous fates – all themselves agents invented and empowered
by the poet's controlling pen. The possessives in 'his pomp' and
'his triumphs' clearly refer to Tamburlaine, as does the pronominal
promise that 'himself in presence shall unfold' the events to be
portrayed. But it is also quite clear that someone else is present here
– the poet-playwright Marlowe, whose absent presence provides a
peculiarly invulnerable vantage point from which to dispose and
'unfold at large'. The 'his' in 'his Second Part' could denote either
'Tamburlaine' or 'our poet', and this potential for ambiguity offers an
interesting second reading for 'himself in presence' in the Prologue's
final line. The poet survives his poems. In a sense, the Prologue
means to mean Tamburlaine by 'himself' – but the playwright's
presence becomes insistent and all-powerful precisely because of
his absence from the temporal and spatial limits of the stage.

The death foretold in the Prologue comes to Tamburlaine not in
glorious battle – a theatre in which he remains invulnerable to defeat
– but rather directly following his decision to destroy a sacred text,
the 'Alcoran' or Koran of the Mohammedans. Editors and critics have
never been exactly sure how to interpret the burning of the Koran,
an action which might reasonably have been thought gratifying to a
Christian audience, likely to enhance rather than to worsen the hero's
prospects for salvation and survival.[2] Yet Tamburlaine, who has
murdered and plundered his way with impunity across the known
world, slaughtering emperors and virgins indifferently as they
crossed his path in his self-appointed role as the 'scourge of God',
now finds himself 'distempered suddenly' (*Part 2*, V. i. 216) as a
result of his incineration of an Islamic book – or, as Tamburlaine
describes it, 'the writ / Wherein the sum of [Mahomet's] religion

rests' (188–189). We may want to join previous commentators of *Tamburlaine* in questioning the significance of 'Mahomet's' writ.[3] Why should the destruction of *this* book, presumably anathema to believing Christians in the period, put Tamburlaine in mortal jeopardy?

It is difficult to say what Marlowe could have thought or known about the textual nature of the Koran. The first Latin translation dates from 1143, and was published at Basle in 1543 by Theodor Bibliander; the text was afterward rendered into Italian, German, and Dutch, though it was not translated into English until the middle of the seventeenth century by Alexander Ross. There is a copy of the Koran in the library of Marlowe's College at Cambridge, Corpus Christi, but it was acquired after the playwright's death, during the time of the Commonwealth.[4] Nevertheless, the Koran was considered an appropriate and valuable library resource in the period and copies were accessible in England during Marlowe's life.

In Arabic 'Koran' or 'Qu'ran' means 'The Recital', and the Koran's origins are traditionally described in a story not unlike Bede's account of the singing of Caedmon's 'Hymn'. One night, it is said, Mohammed, having retired to a cave to meditate, was awakened by the Angel Gabriel, who commanded him to 'Recite!' 'What shall I recite?' Mohammed asked. Three times the order was given and the same reply received, until the Angel told him, 'Recite in the name of your Lord, who created, created man from clots of blood! Recite! your Lord is the Most Bountiful One, who by the pen taught man what he did not know.'[5] The contents of the Koran, like those of the Jewish Torah, are interpreted by believers in terms of the symbolism of the book: the universe is a book, the letters of the book are the elements of the cosmos. As one recent Islamic commentator writes, 'God speaks and His speech is crystallized in the form of a Book. . . . God-as-Being is The Book *par excellence*, and . . . on the level of Being, the pole of Substance is the first reflection of this Book; the Word, which is its dynamic complement, then becomes the Pen, the vertical axis of creation. In contra-distinction man too has an aspect of Word represented by his name: God created man in naming him.'[6]

As we can see from this account, the radical symbolism of the Koran thus offers an odd congruence to that of Marlowe's play: pen, speech, word, book, and name are all modes of creativity that seek to embody timelessness through actions in time; the choice of a dominant metaphor of *writing*, a term which circumscribes such alternate verbal activities as speech and naming, underscores the degree to which textuality is seen as an essential paradigm for all other kinds of relation. The dynamic tension between Word or Pen and Book is analogous to that between a narrative, plot, or sequence of dramatic events and the novel, play, or history that contains it.

Acts of writing and reading are intrinsically acts of communion, not figural equivalents of the activity of 'crystallization', but the ground of that activity – not ideas about the thing, but the thing itself.

Suppose, then, we were to alter the terms of our question about *Tamburlaine* and the Koran slightly and ask not 'which *book*' (Christian or Moslem) but 'which *text*' is privileged by the dramatic action. Instead of concerning ourselves, as have earlier critics, primarily with the theological or doctrinal differences between the Islamic sacred scriptures and the Christian Bible, we might consider for a moment the text (or, in Tamburlaine's phase, 'the writ') which supplies the ground of belief for the play's protagonist, and the containing or competing text (or 'writ') which ironically circumscribes him without his knowledge, and represents the Marlovian inscription or signature, the power of the poet's pen. In place of the binary opposition Koran/ Bible, then, we will discover the triad Koran/map/play. The Koran is 'Mahomet's' narrative, and the narrative or plot as followed by the captive Turkish kings. 'I will', vows Tamburlaine, 'with the flames that beat against the clouds, / Incense the heavens, and make the stars to melt, / As if they were the tears of Mahomet, / For hot consumption of his country's pride; / And till by vision or by speech I hear / Immortal Jove say, "Cease, my Tamburlaine" / I will persist, a terror to the world' (*Part 2*, IV. ii. 197–203). The 'flame of fire' that consumes the Koran is part of this same incendiary, obliterating rhetoric. In its stead, Tamburlaine designs his own text of conquest, a text which is to be without margins or boundaries, without limits: the map of the world.

As we have already noted, the map in *Part 1* is present only as a verbal referent, an imaginary idea drawn by Tamburlaine's sword as pen, and inscribed with provinces, cities, and towns bearing his name and that of Zenocrate. At the close of *Part 2*, when it is produced as a stage property for the scrutiny of the dying hero, the map is in effect again 'reduced', to use his word; the world-as-a-stage now contains a world-as-a-map, the alternative models for macrocosm as microcosm now nested inside one another in the manner of a Chinese box or a Russian doll. In a sense, the audience has been waiting, dramatically speaking, for this presentation of the map to Tamburlaine, since he has repeatedly assured us of his determination to conquer the world, of which the map has been established as a potent sign, to be written in and by his own hand. But when 'a map' is finally brought to him, at his command, it comes as an ironic emblem of what he cannot have: 'Give me a map; then let me see how much / Is left for me to conquer all the world, / That these, my boys, may finish all my wants / [*One brings a map*]' (V. iii. 124–126). This map, too, is an absent presence – a pictorial representation that graphically reifies the absence of total conquest.

Tamburlaine's long but instructive reading of this map (V. iii. 127–161) charts an important shift in the speaker's mood and tone. It begins as a narrative account of the *Tamburlaine* plays, marking geography by dramatic incident with the imprisonment of Bajazeth and his Empress. The confident omnipresence of the first person pronoun and the performative verb ('I began to march towards Persia' [128]; 'I took The Turk' [129–30]; 'Thence marched I into Egypt and Arabia' [131]) is quickly replaced by acknowledgments of incompletion and inability: 'I meant to cut a channel' (135); 'To Asia, where I stay against my will' (143). The point to which he has come, and from which he cannot depart except by death, is described as 'from Scythia, where I first began, / Backward and forwards near five thousand leagues' (144–145). What Tamburlaine here describes as a simple act of measurement (in either direction the distance is 5,000 leagues) in fact delineates a movement he himself can no longer physically emulate, since now he 'stay[s] against [his] will', himself taken prisoner by impending death. The reading of the map here becomes disjunctive and dislocating, ironically mocking the hero with what he has not done and cannot do, and that mockery becomes more pronounced when he turns in line 146 from the conquered to the unconquered world.

Shakespeare may well have been remembering or half-remembering Tamburlaine's imagined 'golden mines, / Inestimable drugs and precious stones' and 'rocks of pearl that shine' (152–153, 157) inaccessible to the mortal conqueror in his account of Clarence's dream in *Richard III*, another undiscovered country whose sight is a sign of impending death: 'Wedges of gold, great anchors, heaps of pearl, / Inestimable stones, unvalued jewels, / All scatt'red in the bottom of the sea' (*Richard III*, I. iv. 26–28). Almost surely Shakespeare had Tamburlaine in mind when he makes Hotspur – that most Marlovian (and Tamburlainian) of figures – declare *his* intention to rewrite the map of England for his territorial advantage by rechanneling the river Trent (*1 Henry IV*, III. i. 100–102).

But Tamburlaine's reading of the map does not rewrite it. Indeed, Tamburlaine reveals, unwittingly, that he has lost that special power over speech and speech-acts he once confidently claimed as his. Throughout *Parts 1* and *2* we see and hear him justify that boast, continually speaking in the imperative mood: 'I *will* confute those blind geographers' (*Part 1*, IV, iv. 80); 'They *shall* be burnt' (*Part 2*, V. i. 174); 'And till I die thou *shalt* not be interred' (*Part 2*, II. iv. 132). But in the final map reading scene – Tamburlaine's death scene – his *wills* and *shalls* have been rendered empty of performative power, translated from the imperative mood into a simple future tense devoid of the ability to command: 'And *shall* I die, and this unconquered?' (V. iii. 151); 'And *shall* I die, and this unconquered?' (159). In asking to see the map which will show him 'how much / Is left for me to conquer all the world' (125) Tamburlaine resigns his power to rewrite the map, the world, and the play. The regions that remain unconquered, unmarked by his name or Zenocrate's, mock him again with their elusive anonymity.

'Resign' (from Latin *resignare*, to un-sign, unseal or cancel) is Tamburlaine's own word choice. He will 'resign' his 'place and proper title' (176–177) to his son, 'that these, my boys, will finish all my want' (126). His former 'working words' have now been reduced to mere illusory illocutions – for as Marlowe's original audience would have known (and as any attentive spectator will deduce from the previous events of the play) Tamburlaine's sons could not fulfill their father's grand design for conquest. Thus warning his son and chosen successor against the fate of Phaethon, whose attempt to emulate his father's godlike power plummeted him to an all-too-human death, Tamburlaine pronounces his own epitaph, resigning himself as he does so to another author's performative language: 'Tamburlaine, the scourge of God, *must* die' (249). For Tamburlaine's true successor, as well as his predecessor, the signatory before whom he 'must' resign, is the playwright who holds the powerful pen, and whose absent presence has transformed the protagonist's speech-acts into iterable acts of dramatic writing. Here, a Marlovian hero sets out to rewrite history, and finds that he can indeed inscribe 'his story' better than can his onstage rivals, only to discover himself at the last revised, re-signed and rewritten by the unseen rival he cannot overreach, the author who makes prologues and epilogues, who alone can 'begin the perpendicular' (*Part 1*, IV. iv. 87) and 'finish all [his] wants' (*Part 2*, V. iii. 126).

This paradoxical re-signing also presents itself as a puzzling dilemma in *Doctor Faustus*. 'What means this show? Speak, Mephistophilis', demands Faustus in his peremptory – and slightly querulous – fashion. 'Nothing', replies the equable and witty Mephistophilis, a born deconstructer. 'Nothing, Faustus, but to delight thy mind, / And let thee see what magic can perform' (*Doctor Faustus*, II. i. 82–84). Yet Mephistophilis, of course, does not mean 'nothing' – or means it only in a deliberately ironic and doubling sense. For the magic show he produces to delight and distract Faustus's mind comes at a crucial point in the dramatic action – the point when Faustus has just attempted to sign away his soul. When Faustus stabs his arm and begins to write in blood his 'deed of gift of body and of soul' to Lucifer, he exclaims, 'My blood congeals, and I can write no more' (II. i. 61), and Mephistophilis, drily acknowledging the legendary thermal properties of hell, announces he will 'fetch

thee fire to dissolve it straight'. Faustus's problematic effort at
inscribing and subscribing is one of the key signatures of the play.
Faustus must write in order that he be damned.

But even in his failure to write, Faustus is caught up in a ceremony
of signing that puts him into conflict and competition with, as well as
mimetic parody and imitation of, not one but two other authors, or
authorities – the author of the play, and the Author of the Universe,
who is also the Author of the Scriptures. For it is the unwilled
appearance of an inscription on Faustus's arm, advising him to flee,
that sets Mephistophilis on to his diversionary tactics, and produces
the magic demonstration – a representation which is, in turn,
described as 'nothing'. At this pivotal moment, the play becomes
a plot of simultaneous writing and unwriting – the more Faustus
would write, the more 'here's nothing writ'.

Marlowe's *Doctor Faustus* begins, not with an act of writing, but
with a scene of *reading*. 'Settle thy studies, Faustus, and begin', says
the protagonist to himself (I. i. 1), invoking, as he does so often, his
own magic name – throughout the play he will address himself in
this curious and characteristic vocative third person. He reviews the
possible primary texts of study – Aristotle's *Analytics*, written in
Greek, Galen's medical treatises, in Latin, Justinian's *Institutes* on
Roman law, and 'Jerome's Bible' – the Vulgate – all the classic works
of the humanistic heritage – and he rejects them all in favor of magic.
What does he mean by magic?

> Lines, circles, letters, and characters;
> Ay, these are those that Faustus most desires.
> Oh, what a world of profit and delight,
> Of power, of honor, and omnipotence,
> Is promised to the studious artisan!
>
> (I. i. 52–56)

Lines, circles, letters and characters – these are indeed the signs
and signifiers of magical arts. But more specifically and locally in
Marlowe's play they are the elements of *language*, of writing. 'Oh,
what a world of profit and delight.' We do not need the reminder
of Horace here to see Faustus as a man enraptured by the idea
of making, of poesis, of poetry – of becoming author of himself.

'O Faustus, lay that damned book aside, / And gaze not on it'
(71–72) urges the Good Angel. 'Read, read the Scriptures' (74). But
Lucifer and Mephistophilis are always at hand to offer him other
texts. Throughout the play, Faustus's reading is bound up with
questions of textual authority. Even when, at the close of the play,
he pledges in a famous gesture to 'burn my books!' (V. i. 331), he is

corrected, overruled, and overwritten by the Chorus in the Epilogue: 'Burned is Apollo's laurel bough / That sometime grew within this learned man' (Ep., 2–3). Although Faustus himself vows to become 'conjuror-laureate', in his own dangerous phrase, in the opening moments of the play he is counseled by his fellow conjurors, Valdes and Cornelius, to first learn 'the words of art' by means of which he will soon become 'perfecter' than they at conjuring (I. iv. 34; i. 159). Advised by Valdes to carry with him not only 'Bacon's and Albanus' works', traditional medieval texts of magic, but also 'the Hebrew Psalter and New Testament' (155–56), he withdraws with his colleagues to dinner, where 'after meat / They'll canvass every quiddity' (164–165).

When we next see Faustus he is a practicing conjuror, and also explicitly a writer, an inscriber as well as a circumscriber, accompanied by Lucifer and four attendant devils. 'Faustus, begin thine incantations', he counsels himself, echoing and transmuting his first line in the play, 'and try if devils will obey thy hest':

> Within this circle is Jehovah's name,
> Forward and backward anagrammatized;
> Th'abbreviated names of holy saints,
> Figures of every adjunct to the heavens,
> And characters of signs and erring stars,
> By which the spirits are enforced to rise:
>
> (I. iii. 8–13)

Writing the name of Jehovah is a manifestly taboo or forbidden act. Faustus's blasphemous enterprise is, however, doomed to self-subversion. For to anagrammatize the name of Jehovah – to rearrange its letters so as to form a new word – is merely to replicate the original pious replacement of the tetragrammaton, YWVH – a term the Jews considered too holy for utterance, and therefore pointed with vowels from the Hebrew word 'Adonai', or 'Lord', as a direction to the reader to substitute a permissible euphemism for the ineffable name. Jerome actually incorporates this substitution when he speaks of 'Jehovah' in his vulgate translation of Exodus 6:3, and he is followed in this practice by Wyclif and other English translators.

Moreover, the sacred tetragrammaton itself signified God's power by virtue of its ambiguities. The most widely accepted etymological explanation of YWVH associates the word with the Hebrew *hayah*, 'to be', construing the term as it might be written or pronounced in full as either *Yahveh*, 'He who causes to be', or *Yahuah*, 'He who indeed will (show himself to) be', employing the third person singular masculine of the imperfect tense of the verb 'to be' in its oldest form. As the complexity of tense and syntax in the English rendering indicates, the name of God was itself a multivalent sign, declaring by its linguistic and grammatical form that God transcended the ordinary limits of time and individual history.[7] Faustus attempts to undo the existence and power of the Author of the Scriptures by placing His name in time, by writing the Name forward and backward inside a circle, and thereby asserting his own role as a new author and a new authority. In doing so, however, he performs an inadvertently pious transcription of a name which had always been ineffably multiple and indeterminate.

At the same time, Faustus's attempt to invert the name of God is doomed by the very nature of the written language itself. For to a reader and speaker of English (or, indeed, of German, the language of Faustus's Wittenberg) Hebrew writing *is* backward, its characters inscribed from right to left upon the page Correctly understood, correctly read, backward is forward and forward is backward – as it will be, indeed, throughout *Doctor Faustus*. The Bad Angel repeatedly urges Faustus to 'Go forward in that famous art' of magic (I. i. 75; II. i. 15), while the Good Angel and the Old Man implore him to repent and go back to God. Likewise the Chorus points darkly in the Epilogue to Faustus as an unhappy example of those 'forward wits' who suffer a 'hellish fall' because they are enticed 'To practice more than heavenly power permits' (Ep., 7–8).

The idea that language can be made to go forward and backward at will, continually writing and unwriting itself, is one that we will hear Faustus frequently express in one form or another. When, for example, Mephistophilis suggests that because of his sacrilegious pranks the Pope will have him excommunicated with bell, book, and candle, Faustus answers merrily, 'Bell, book and candle – candle, book, and bell, – / Forward and backward, to curse Faustus to hell!' (III. ii. 97–98), and at the beginning of Act II as he waits in his study to see if Lucifer will accept the terms of his bargain, we hear him caution himself, 'Now go not backward; Faustus, be resolute' (II. i. 6).

If Faustus is able to 'be resolute' to 'go not backward', it is by vowing to invert, or 'unwrite', the ritual and the sign at the heart of Christ's contract. He continues his self-address:

The God thou serv'st is thine own appetite,
Wherein is fixed the love of Belzebub:
To him I'll build an altar and a church,
And offer lukewarm blood of new-born babes.

(II. i. 11–14)

This mockery of the Mass is only one of several hinted at in the play. Another will come when Faustus, made invisible, snatches the 'meat' and 'wine' from the Pope, who should himself be dispensing the Eucharist. The friars with bell, book, and candle intone 'Cursed be he that stole his Holiness' meat from the table!' and 'Cursed be he that took away his Holiness' wine!' (III. ii. 103, 113), and this rather comic malediction is immediately followed by a scene in which Robin and Dick enter with a cup they have stolen from the vintner. The pregnant Duchess of Anholt requests that Faustus procure her 'no better meat than a dish of ripe grapes' (IV. v. 18).[8] Indeed, when Faustus first takes up conjuring, he does so over 'meat' shared with his disciples, Valdes and Cornelius, an event to which his servant Wagner's 'wine, if it could speak', could testify (I. ii. 7). That off-stage meal is not self-evidently a Last Supper, or a parody of one. But when we look at all these Eucharistic gestures in the light of the central writing scene with which we began, each apparently trivial incident suggests and contributes to a prevailing pattern. For the writing of Faustus's 'deed of gift of body and of soul' is the making of a testament – a last testament and a new testament. Written in blood, substituting blood for ink, it superscribes – or rather, attempts to superscribe – Christ's own testament of body and blood.

In law a testament is a will, a formal declaration, usually in writing, of a person's wishes as to the disposal of his property after his death. Faustus writes not one but two such testaments in the course of the play. One, explicitly described as 'Faustus' latest will' (V. i. 154) and 'my will' (156), bequeaths his real property, his 'wealth, / His house, his goods, and store of golden plate, / Besides two thousand ducats ready coined' to his servant Wagner (V. i. 2–4). The other, the 'deed of gift' (II. i. 59, 89), is likewise in law 'an instrument of writing', and has, as we have seen, been written and signed previously; it pledges 'body and soul, flesh, blood, or goods' (110–111) to Lucifer and his agent Mephistophilis. Prefaced by study and reading, then, the dramatic life of Faustus is demarcated within the play by these two acts of writing, which are in several senses equally acts of playwriting.

A third sense of 'testament', of course, is that described in the Scriptures: a covenant between God and man. This is the primary meaning of the word in the passage from St Mark – the source for the rite of the Holy Eucharist – where Jesus says to his disciples, giving them bread, 'Take, eat, this is my body', and giving them wine, 'This is the blood of the new testament, which is shed for many'. The new testament of Christ renews and fulfills the old testament of Moses and the prophets, and the Epistle to the Hebrews combines the two latent meanings of testament as 'covenant' and 'will', explaining that Christ 'is the mediator of the new testament, that by means of death, for the redemption of the transgressions that were under the first testament, they which are called might receive the promise of eternal inheritance. For where a testament is, there must also of necessity be the death of the testator. For a testament is of force after men are dead; other wise it is of no strength at all while the testator liveth. Whereupon neither the first testament was dedicated without blood' (Hebrews 9:15–18).

By Marlowe's time a 'testament' was clearly a book or text as well as a 'deed', a speech-act committed to writing. As we have seen, Valdes refers to the 'New Testament' as a 'work' that can be carried into a secret place as an instrument of magic, together with the works of Bacon and Albanus, and in the *Faerie Queene* Red Crosse gives Prince Arthur 'a booke, wherein his Saveours testament / Was writ' (I. ix. 19). But in the play, the insistent, or at least repeated, act of making a will reifies the implicit analogy (and disjunction) between Christ's written testament and Faustus's willful deed, a conjunction of word and practice which is itself replicated by the act of writing – and performing – the play. Both words, *'will'* and *'deed'*, incarnate the speech-acts they embody, transforming by the very act of executing them a spoken pledge into an inscribed written artifact. 'What might the staying of my blood portent?' asks Faustus when his blood congeals. 'Is it unwilling I should write this bill? / Why streams it not, that I may write afresh? / Faustus gives to thee his soul' (II. i. 63–66).

'See, see, where Christ's blood streams in the firmament!' he will later cry, when hell is discovered and the clock strikes eleven. 'One drop would save my soul, half a drop' (V. i. 286–287). 'Why streams it not?' 'See . . . where Christ's blood streams.' Faustus's timely writer's block is yet another sign he will not heed, or read, and so he *signs*. As the Old Man will point out, now only the sacrament of Christ can correct or erase this error in writing: 'thy Savior sweet / Whose blood alone must wash away thy guilt' (V. i. 63).

It is frequently observed that in *Doctor Faustus* Marlowe demonstrates his indebtedness to the morality tradition, in the retention and subversion of such figures as the Good and Bad Angels, the Seven Deadly Sins, and the repentant Old Man.[9] Yet his play also owes – and pays – a debt to the other native dramatic heritage of the English Renaissance stage, the miracle or cycle play, performed on the Feast of Corpus Christi, that celebrates the Eucharistic miracle of transubstantiation. And the doctrine of transubstantiation is itself, manifestly, the quintessential metaphor. According to that doctrine, the bread and wine of the Eucharist *are* the body and blood of Christ, though their exterior semblance remains the same as before, just as Christ on earth *is* the Word made Flesh. As we shall see all these metaphors of transformation participate in the writing and unwriting – the re-signing – of Marlowe's text.[10]

When Marlowe went up to Cambridge in 1580–81, it was as a member of 'the Ancient and Religious Foundation of Corpus Christi and the Blessed Virgin Mary', so named after the medieval Guilds which had united for the founding. Marlowe entered Corpus Christi College as a Canterbury scholar under a provision made by the celebrated Archbishop Matthew Parker, Master of Corpus from 1544 to 1553. In the library of Corpus, endowed with Parker's magnificent bequest of books and manuscripts, Marlowe read plots and exotic place names which he would incorporate into *Tamburlaine* and *Edward II*; there, too, he might have found and transposed the haunting, disembodied final line of *Doctor Faustus*, 'Terminat hora diem; terminat Author opus' – a phrase that occurs in precisely that form in a manuscript from the Archbishop's collection.[11]

But Corpus Christi College itself, its eponymous sacrament, and its Name-Day Festival in celebration of that sacrament, offered a potential source and text of a somewhat different kind, and one equally relevant to Marlowe's work. In the 1550s, the College found itself besieged by the complex and troublesome question of the nature of the Eucharistic sacrament, the doctrine of transubstantiation and the Real Presence of Christ's body and blood. For a College founded and named in honor of the Guild of the Precious Body of Jesus Christ such an issue was inevitably a sensitive one. In his official revision of Cranmer's Forty-Two Articles, Archbishop Parker struck a precarious balance between claims for a real, corporeal presence and the reformer's reduction of the sacrament to a purely figurative sign: 'The Body of Christ is given, taken, and eaten in the Supper, only after an heavenly and spiritual manner. And the mean whereby the Body of Christ is received and eaten in the Supper is Faith.' H.C. Porter wryly observes, 'that was a hit – a palpable hit – at the Real Absence.'[12]

When we consider such theoretical and doctrinal issues as the Real Presence (or Absence) and the dogma of transubstantiation in terms of the semiotics of theatre,[13] we can see the remarkable, though risky, opportunity offered to the dramatist – especially a young and daring dramatist like Marlowe, who had almost surely, by the terms of his scholarship, studied for holy orders, and who could not in any case have avoided the ferment or the controversy, whatever his own ultimate religious choice. If the Corpus Christi Day procession was the most picturesque event in medieval Cambridge's civic drama, the Mass was English Christendom's purest moment of theatre. In fact, the Protestant liturgical reformers' attempt to turn the Mass into a communion was directly analogous to the Tudor and Elizabethan dramatists' efforts to transform the nature of the theatrical experience. The Protestant reformers set out to alter the central ceremony of Christian worship in England from a sacrifice offered to God by a priest on behalf of the people to one which suggested, in both words and actions, a feast in which the worshippers entered into communion with Christ by receiving the elements of the Eucharist.[14] The worshippers became, in effect, a participating audience, whose belief insured the efficacy of the performance.

In a manifest way, the theatrical medium offered a special opportunity for articulating – or disarticulating – semiotic problems of presence and absence, since by the convention of dramatic transactions a character may be at once 'absent' and 'present' from the stage, like the ghost of Old Hamlet in Gertrude's closet, or Banquo at the banquet in *Macbeth*.[15] For Marlowe, the 'invisible' presence of Faustus at the Pope's feast in Act III, scene ii provides a telling, and, at the same time, safely comic, commentary on presence and absence in the Mass. The feast as staged in *Faustus* is doubly an anti-Mass, both because the Pope approaches the meat and wine in an epicurean rather than a sacramental manner, and because he is physically prevented from partaking of the 'troublesome banquet' (80) by Faustus's prankish intervention. Neither locally nor spiritually, then, is a 'real presence' distributed or consumed. Faustus himself becomes a visible absent presence who effects a series of locally present absences.

The visual element of tour-de-force and practical joke in this scene would very likely have been intensified by the onstage appearance of the cowled friars, for the canonical office for Corpus Christi was written, at the request of Pope Urban IV, by the most illustrious of Dominican Friars, Saint Thomas Aquinas. The text of *Faustus* is not explicit about the order to which the Pope's attendant friars belong, but the Dominicans, or Black Friars, were the traditional Preaching Friars. Moreover, Marlowe's company would already have possessed a set of black friars' robes, since the friars in *The Jew of Malta* are described as 'friars of Saint Jaques' (III. iii. 33), so-called after the Dominican church of St Jacques in Paris. That the Pope's bumbling friars would belong to the same order as the learned and eminent Friar who set the office for Corpus Christi Day and defined the Eucharistic sacrament is an incidental, but perhaps not accidental, irony whose effect would be more directly felt by a sixteenth century audience than by a modern one.

For any audience interested in semiotics and the magical properties of signs, however, it is instructive to consider Saint Thomas's compositions for Corpus Christi Day as a kind of subtext for *Doctor*

Faustus. The festival's magnificent hymns explicitly acknowledge an analogy between the transforming power of language (the word and the Word) and the transubstantiation of bread and wine into flesh and blood. The hymn *Pange, lingua, gloriosi* declares, '*Verbum caro, panem verum / Verbo carnem efficit / Fitque sanguis Christi merum*' ('By his word, the Word-made-Flesh changes true bread into flesh / And makes wine into the blood of Christ'). The conspicuous wordplay on word (*Verbum, verum, Verbo*) and flesh (*caro, carnem*) offers a poetic equivalent to the transubstantiation of the two species, bread and wine, into their divine counterparts. Here, then, is yet another version of sacred writing, Eucharistic magic words at work, the opposite of Faustus's 'anagrammatized' and inverted Black Mass on Jehovah's name.

Perhaps even more suggestive are lines from another of Saint Thomas's Corpus Christi hymns, '*Panis angelicus fit panis hominum; / Dat panis caelicus figuris terminum*' ('Thus Angels' bread is made the bread of man; / the heavenly bread puts an end to types and figures').[16] In this case the concept of ending (*terminum*) familiar throughout *Faustus* is expressed as a paradoxical form of beginning – the end of the Old Testament in the realization of the New, the end to types and figures itself figured forth in the Incarnation of Christ. 'This Sacrament, the embodied fulfillment of all the ancient types and figures, 'Saint Thomas calls it.[17] And this is just what Faustus, for all his vainglory, is not; he *is* a figure, a representation, a terminable fiction, a dramatic creation who perversely tries to turn blood into ink as an act of willful self-inscription – the antithesis of a creating Word who selflessly transforms wine into blood as an act of grace.[18]

The play's instrumental triad of blood/wine/ink is thus divisible into two binarisms, blood/wine and blood/ink, where one is associated with Christ and seems clearly holy, the other associated with Faustus's devilish bargain, and therefore unholy. Yet this division will not stay divided. *Someone* intervenes, inscribing Faustus's arm with a warning, yet another sign:

> But what is this inscription on mine arm?
> *Homo, fuge!* whither should I fly?
> If unto God, he'll throw me down to hell.
> My senses are deceived; here's nothing writ:
> Oh yes, I see it plain; even here is writ,
> *Homo, fuge!* Yet shall not Faustus fly.

> (II. i. 73–78)

Moreover, the determinedly blasphemous '*Consummatum est*, this bill is ended', (II. i. 73), pronounced as he signs his name to the deed of gift, once again indicates the incommensurability of the devilish and the divine, now through Faustus's radical misunderstanding of time and sequence. Christ on the cross could put a period, a point, an end, to the sentence that was God on earth, the Word made Flesh, just as His sacrifice, emblematized in the sacrament of the Eucharist, 'put an end to types'. But, as Faustus will later discover, 'no end is limited to damned souls' (V. i. 312). The continually iterated word 'limit', which for Faustus means both scope and bound, is both his temptation and his downfall. He strives to limit others and in himself to exceed all limits, to write his life backward and forward as he chooses. And, like the hapless victims of fairy tale wish-fulfillment trials, he gets, ironically, just what he bargains for, the letter of the law, and has to suffer the excessive consequences. His is a *life sentence*, both compound and complex, as well as a sentence of death.

Stanislavski suggested to the actors in his theatre that they think of their characters in terms of verbs rather than nouns, since 'every objective must carry in itself the germ of action'. Thus the actor should express himself in some form of the sentence 'I wish to do [X]'.[19] Michael Goldman has justly observed that 'what ravishes the Marlovian actor can never be contained within what a method actor would call an "objective" ', since 'the ravished man's desire swells beyond any specific goal'.[20] For Faustus, however, this act of striving is both more boundary breaking and more doomed, because the verb after which he strives, that which he wishes to *do*, is God's verb, the verb intrinsic and implicit in Jehovah's name, the verb 'to be', 'to pre-exist', which has neither beginning nor end. 'Stand still, you ever moving spheres of heaven, / That time may cease, and midnight never come. / . . . / The stars move still, time runs, the clock will strike, / The devil will come, and Faustus must be damned'. (V. i. 277–285).

Faustus's 'will' becomes, at the last, both a noun and a verb. His deed of gift is not a divine metaphor like Christ's Eucharist, but instead a fallen, time-bound, and limited dramatic metonymy, based upon an accidental or contingent connection with magic and magical power, rather than an essential similarity. His power is transumptive rather than authoritative; his will and deed are not the plot of the play, but a counterplot countenanced by another author. Thus, though he claims that 'a sound magician is a demi-god' (I. i. 63), his own powers are derived from his perverse testament, and rather than integration and transubstantiation he incurs dispersal and displacement at the play's end.

The comic scenes in Act IV have shown the audience a Faustus with a false head and leg, both of which are removed without personal injury, and with apparently magical effect. But this dismemberment is repeated in a different spirit in the final scene, when an appalled and awestruck scholar discovers the necromancer's scattered remains. 'Oh, help us heaven!' he cries, 'See, here are Faustus' limbs / All torn asunder by the hand of death', and a few moments later, 'We'll give his mangled limbs due burial' (V. i. 337–338, 348). Here once again we find a curious intertextual relation between *Doctor Faustus* and the liturgical office for Corpus Christi Day. In the Fifth Breviary Lesson Saint Thomas writes of the miracle of the Eucharist, 'Nothing more marvellous, for there it comes to pass that the substance of bread and wine is changed into the body and blood of Christ. He is there, perfect God and perfect man, under the show of a morsel of bread and a sup of wine. He is eaten by his faithful, *but not mangled*. Nay, when this Sacrament is broken, in each piece he remains entire.'[21] The Latin phrase is *sed minime laceratur*, and *laceratur* is usually rendered as 'mangled' in English translation. The ceremony of Faustus's dispersal – which is the play – offers, then, one more disjunction, rather than conjunction, with the Eucharistic rite. 'The appearance of bread and wine remain, but the Thing is not bread or wine', continues the lesson. Yet it is precisely Faustus's tragedy that he is reduced to the 'accidents' of his appearance, the ironic stage buffoonery of the clown, less than the sum of his parts.

Early in the play, Wagner anticipates this radical dismemberment when he threatens a Clown with punishment unless the Clown agrees to bind himself as his servant: 'I'll turn all the lice about thee into familiars, and make them tear thee in pieces' (I. iv. 22–23). Even at this point the trope of fragmentation is firmly tied to the blasphemous de-centering of the Eucharist; the Clown equably replies, 'you may save yourself a labor, for they are as familiar with me as if they had paid for their meat and drink.' An audience inclined to dismiss this exchange as merely low and not very forceful banter might find itself disconcerted to hear Mephistophilis echo it, much later, in a characteristic inversion of forward-backward language: 'Revolt [i.e., turn back to Satan from God] or I'll in piecemeal tear thy flesh' (V. i. 85). Rather than being integrated into the metaphor of the body and blood of Christ, Faustus is excluded and de-centered, displaced. To the triad of blood/wine/ink we can here perhaps add a second, equally concerned with the metatheatrical materials of Marlowe's art: flesh/bread/and props or stage properties: a wooden leg, a false head. Faustus is incarnated as a dramatic character, not an autonomous author, and, as Marlowe's written supplement to his play, *terminat Author opus*, declares, the author, not the self-inscribed character, ends the work. Marlowe signs his own writ, which must be executed. 'The clock will strike, / The devil will come, and Faustus must be damned.'[22]

Because of the way it employs the Eucharistic sacrament and the riddle of the creating Word, *Doctor Faustus* provides the most obvious and explicit examples of the trope of writing and unwriting in Marlowe's plays. As we have seen, however, a similar pattern of texts echoing and subverting other texts can be found in the two parts of *Tamburlaine*, where the Koran and the map of the world occupy the textual positions of the Eucharist and Faustus's fatal 'deed of gift'. In *Edward II* as well we find a crucial written object which again expands the issue of dramatic authority to a struggle for mastery between the playwright and his written characters. Indeed in *Edward II* the term 'character' takes on a suggestive second meaning, since the play's final peripety turns on Mortimer's 'unpointed' letter *author*izing the murder of the king. It is often remarked that the manner of Edward's death is ironically just, a punishment that fits the crime. But Mortimer, the king's competitor, will die with equal dramatic justice. His own 'hand' will lead him to the executioner's block – to what might in his case almost be called the 'writer's block'.

Like *Doctor Faustus*, *Edward II* begins with a crucial scene of reading. Gaveston appears onstage reading aloud from Edward's letter which announces the old king's death, Edward's accession to the throne, and Gaveston's own dramatic opportunity. He may now leave France, and enter England – and the play. This is the first of several written documents that serve as potential scripts for action: 'the form of Gaveston's exile' already signed with the names of earls, to which Edward is forced to 'subscribe' his own name ('Instead of ink I'll write it with my tears' [I. iv. 86]); heraldic 'devices' that greet Gaveston's arrival with transparent derision, and are described by Edward as 'private libeling' of his friend (II. ii. 34); a note of execution; and a spate of letters; a letter from Gaveston to Lady Margaret, his intended wife; a letter from the Frenchman Levune, concerning Mortimer; a letter from Mortimer to Leicester and Berkeley, commanding the removal of the king to Berkeley Castle; a letter from Edward, resigning the crown.

These letters and documents set the audience's expectations, and provide a literary and dramatic context for the climactic 'unpointed' letter sent by Mortimer in the fifth act. As was the case with the textual properties in *Tamburlaine* and *Faustus*, the unpointed letter is pivotal precisely because it is indeterminate. As Hebrew is written and read from right to left, and therefore 'backward' to an English sensibility, so Latin, because it is an inflected language, can be written and read so as to mean two apparently opposite things. Mortimer gloatingly tells us that

... he that is the cause of Edward's death,
Is sure to pay for it when his son is of age;
And therefore will I do it cunningly,
This letter, written by a friend of ours,
Contains his death, yet bids them save his life.

[*reads*]

'*Edwardum occidere nolite timere bonum est*:
Fear not to kill the King, 'tis good he die.'
But read it thus, and that's another sense:
'*Edwardum occidere nolite timere bonum est*:
Kill not the King, 'tis good to fear the worst.'
Unpointed as it is, thus shall it go,
That, being dead, if it chance to be found,
Matrevis and the rest may bear the blame,
And we be quit that caused it to be done.

(V. iv. 3–16)

He will indeed 'be quit', but in an ironic way. For here is a performative utterance with a vengeance. This 'unpointed' letter is in fact very pointed, precisely because it is unpointed, or unpunctuated. It is both limited and limitless, open and closed. Gurney, receiving it, says he 'know[s] not how to conster it' (V. v. 15), but Matrevis is sure at once of the meaning and the design: 'Gurney, it was left unpointed for the nonce' – that is, on purpose, '*Edwardum occidere nolite timere*, / That's his meaning' (16–18).

At the end of the play, inevitably, the letter reappears to accuse Mortimer and condemn him to death. As he had foretold, the son who bears the name of his father, Edward III, confronts him with his deed:

Mortimer.	Who is the man dare say I murdered him?
K. Edw. III.	Traitor, in me my loving father speaks,
	And plainly saith, 'twas thou that murdredst him.
Mortimer.	But hath your grace no other proof than this?
K. Edw. III.	Yes, if this be the hand of Mortimer.

[*Showing letter*]

. . . .

Mortimer.	'Tis my hand; what gather you by this?
K. Edw. III.	That thither thou didst send a murderer.

(V. vi. 40–48)

Like Matrevis, Edward III has no difficulty in pointing or punctuating the unpointed letter, nor in pointing an accusatory finger at its author. ''Tis my hand.' Earlier Mortimer had said that the letter was 'written by a friend of ours', an apparent inconsistency often noted by editors (V. iv. 6).[23] But it is perfectly possible for the hand to be his, and the writing another's. Conceivably, he has copied or rewritten a strategem devised by another offstage author; certainly he is both copying and reading, as well as being entrapped by, the play's overreaching author, Christopher Marlowe. Significantly, he now begins to speak about a different kind of 'point': 'There is a point, to which when men aspire, / They tumble headlong down: that point I touched' (60–61). The point, the period, the limit, the punctuation mark is inscribed by another hand. *Terminat Author opus.*

'I seal, I cancel, I do what I will' Mortimer had exulted after sending the fateful letter to its destination (V. iv. 51) – and here again we find writing and unwriting at once; 'here's nothing writ'. For to cancel is to obliterate writing by drawing lines across it, to deface, to cross out, and thus to render deeds and documents invalid. Perhaps significantly, both Faustus and Mortimer are dismembered at the ends of their plays – 'Faustus' limbs / All torn asunder by the hand of death', Mortimer beheaded, his head presented to the young king and offered up by him to the hearse or coffin of his murdered father. Yet both characters, like Tamburlaine in his way, are ultimately cancelled or slain by their own hands: by their handwriting, by their signatures, by their seals, by writing against the hand of the playwright, against the hand of history, fable, legend, Scripture, inscription. 'Nothing, Faustus'. 'Here's nothing – writ.'

Notes

1. *Tamburlaine, Part 1*, I. ii. 211; II. iv. 25. All citations from Marlowe's plays are to RUSSELL A. FRASER and NORMAN RABKIN (eds), *Drama of the English Renaissance*, Vol. I, *The Tudor Period* (New York, Macmillan, 1976).

2. See SAMUEL C. CHEW, *The Crescent and the Rose: Islam and England during the Renaissance* (New York, Oxford University Press, 1937), pp. 434ff. Stephen Greenblatt comments on the burning of the Koran: 'The effect is not to celebrate the transcendent power of Mohammed but to challenge the habit of mind that looks to heaven for rewards and punishments, that imagines human evil as "the scourge of God."' *Renaissance Self-Fashioning: from More to Shakespeare* (Chicago, University of Chicago Press, 1980), p. 202.

3. Both Harry Levin and Irving Ribner address the question of why the burning of the Koran should lead to Tamburlaine's illness and death, placing that particular book, and other 'supersticious bookes' pertaining to the Islamic faith, in the context of Marlowe's own acknowledged or presumed beliefs about Christianity, mortality, and heroism. Neither, however, explores the textual implications of the Koran in its own right. (H. LEVIN, *The Overreacher: A Study of Christopher Marlowe* [Cambridge, MA, Harvard University Press, 1952], p. 51; I. RIBNER, *The Complete Plays of Christopher Marlowe* [Indianapolis, Odyssey Press, 1963], p. xxviii.).

4. See H.P. Stokes, *Corpus Christi* in *Cambridge College Histories* (London, F.E. Robinson, 1898), p. 196.

5. N.J. Dawood (ed. and trans.), *The Koran* (Harmondsworth, Penguin Books, 1956; rev. edn, 1974), p. 9.

6. Frithjof Schuon, *Understanding Islam*, trans. D.M. Matheson (Baltimore, MD, Penguin Books, 1972), pp. 51–2.

7. W. Gunther Plaut and Bernard J. Bamberger, *The Torah: A Modern Commentary* (New York, Union of Hebrew Congregations, 1981), pp. 425–6.

8. The sacramental interchangeability of the two species, bread and wine (or in *Faustus*'s terms 'meat' and 'grapes'), had been firmly asserted by the Council of Trent: 'It is most true that there is as much contained under either species as under both, for Christ exists whole and entire under the species of bread, and under every part of the species, whole too and entire under the species of wine and under its parts.' (*Council of Trent*, Sess. 13, cap. 3. Cited in Matthew Britt (ed.), *The Hymns of the Breviary and Missal* (New York, Benzinger Brothers, 1948), pp. 167–8.)

9. For example, David M. Bevington, *From Mankind to Marlowe: Growth of Structure in the Popular Drama of Tudor England* (Cambridge, MA, Harvard University Press, 1962); Nicholas Brooke, 'The moral tragedy of *Doctor Faustus*', *Cambridge Journal*, 5 (1952), pp. 662–87; David Kaula, 'Time and the timeless in *Everyman* and *Doctor Faustus*', *College English* 22 (1960), pp. 9–14.

10. See C.L. Barber, ' "The form of Faustus' fortunes good or bad" ', *Tulane Drama Review* 8 (1964), pp. 92–119. Barber suggests that 'We can . . . connect the restriction of the impulse for physical embodiment in the Protestant worship with a compensatory fascination in the drama with magical possibilities and the incarnation of meaning in physical gesture and ceremony' (p. 97), and argues persuasively that the imagery of orality and devouring, eating and being eaten in *Faustus* is linked to the protagonist's own 'blasphemous need, in psychoanalytic terms' (p. 107).

11. Parker MS, 281, fol.78*v*. Cited in John Bakeless, *The Tragicall History of Christopher Marlowe* (Cambridge, MA, Harvard University Press, 1942), I, 293.

12. H.C. Porter, *Reformation and Reaction in Tudor Cambridge* (Cambridge, Cambridge University Press, 1958), p. 67.

13. Barber suggests the connection between sacramental doctrine and a major shift in semantic perspective when he speaks of the 'semantic tensions' involved in viewing the Eucharist as a 'bare sign': 'the whole great controversy centered on fundamental issues about the nature of signs and acts, through which the age pursued its new sense of reality', 'Faustus' fortune', p. 97.

14. T.M. Parker, *The English Reformation to 1558*, 2nd edn (London, Oxford University Press, 1966), pp. 99–100.

15. See Thomas Cartelli, 'Banquo's Ghost: The Shared Vision', *Theatre Journal* 35 (3) (1983), pp. 389–405.

16. '*Sacris solemniis juncta sint gaudia*'. Texts and commentaries on the Corpus Christi hymns can be found in Britt, *Hymns*, pp. 166–93. I am indebted to Michael J. O'Loughlin for this suggestion.

17. Thomas Aquinas, 'Sixth lesson for Corpus Christi Day', in *Selected Writings*, ed. M.C. D'Arcy (London, Dent, 1939, rev. edn. 1964), p. 40.

18. A passage in the *Summa Theologica* comments with provocative pertinence on the whole question of metaphor and metonymy as it relates to the Eucharistic

sacrament, *'Hic est calix sanguinis mei* is a figurative expression, which can be understood either by metonymy or by metaphor. Metonymy signifies the container for the contained, and the sense, which is then, *This is my blood contained in the chalice*, is justifiable, for Christ's blood is sacramentally consecrated as drink for the faithful, an idea better conveyed by the term *cup* than *blood*. By metaphor Christ's Passion is signified, as when he himself said, *Father, if it be possible, let this chalice pass from me*. This sense of the consecration formula is then, *This is the chalice of my Passion'* (*Summa Theologica*, 3a, lxxviii, 3.1). Quoted in THOMAS AQUINAS, *Theological Texts*, ed. and trans. THOMAS GILBY (London, Oxford University Press, 1955), pp. 370–1.

19. CONSTANTIN STANISLAVSKI, *An Actor Prepares*, trans. ELIZABETH REYNOLDS HAPGOOD (New York, Theatre Arts Books, 1936), p. 116.

20. 'Marlowe and the Histrionics of Ravishment', in ALVIN KERNAN (ed.), *Two Renaissance Mythmakers: Christopher Marlowe and Ben Jonson* (Baltimore, MD, Johns Hopkins University Press, 1977), p. 22.

21. THOMAS AQUINAS, *Theological Texts*, p. 366.

22. For another perspective on the dismemberment of Faustus, see EDWARD A. SNOW, *'Doctor Faustus* and the Ends of Desire', in ALVIN KERNAN (ed.), *Mythmakers*, p. 94ff.

23. For example, FRASER and RABKIN (eds), *Drama of the English Renaissance*, I, 335, fn 5.

3   Sodomy and Society: The Case of Christopher Marlowe*

JONATHAN GOLDBERG

If modernist critics tended to read Marlowe's writing through his biography, post-modernist critics interpret the life through the plays. Jonathan Goldberg's essay is an instance of this provisional 'return of the author', with its proposition that Marlowe's identity as dramatist, sexual dissident and spy was constructed by the discourses of Elizabethan power, as a foil or shadow to its orthodoxy. On this view, the sodomy that epitomised Marlowe's transgressive status should be seen not as a positive act, but as a merely symbolic rebellion, licensed by authority to be its negative Other. Like the counterfeit coining with which he was also charged, or the histrionics of his heroes, the author's homosexuality was thus merely the reverse of the official stamp. This is an interpretation which applies a familiar New Historicist argument – that Renaissance theatre functioned, like Carnival, as a safety-valve, 'where countervoices were acted out' – to forward the pessimistic prospectus that opposition can never be spontaneous, but is always instigated and curtailed by power; a theory itself deriving from Michel Foucault's attack on the 'repressive hypothesis' and insistence that authority *produces* resistance as its defining ground. Much of the fatalism of American academia in the 1980s is distilled into this account of Marlowe as the double-agent of his own oppression, whose relevance to contemporary gay and oppositional cultures is as a precocious warning that 'rebellion never manages to find its own space', but always occurs in the space society allows. Though the essay is open-ended, Goldberg seems to repeat New Historicism's dismal post-1968 theme, that 'There is subversion, no end of subversion, only not for us'.

Within a few days of his mysterious death, a document appeared labeling Marlowe as an atheist and a homosexual. Signed by Richard

* Reprinted from *Southwest Review*, 69 (1984), 371–8.

Baines, the note lists some nineteen charges said to represent Marlowe's opinions 'Concerning his Damnable Judgment of Religion, and scorn of gods word'.[1] . . . At first glance, the list can appear rather random in its organization, a series of opinions on the truth of the gospels occasionally intermixed with more overtly political utterances and, towards the end, pausing for one moment to insert a bit of sexual bravura: 'That all they that love not Tobacco & Boies were fooles.' I would like to suggest, however, that this document, arranged to fit the preconceptions of the authorities to whom Baines was reporting, reveals the constitution of homosexuality within the social text. Although the document is usually referred to as the Baines libel, it speaks a discursive truth.

To place this document within the social discourses that give it its voice, I rely on Alan Bray's brilliant book, *Homosexuality in Renaissance England*.[2] Bray argues that there were no discrete terms for homosexual behavior in the period; *sodomy* always was embedded in other discourses, those delineating anti-social behavior – sedition, demonism, atheism. In *sodomy* English society saw its shadow: the word expressed sheer negation, an absence capable of taking root in anyone, and necessarily to be rooted out. In homosexuality so construed and so entangled with religious, political, and cosmic subversion, the most fundamental malaises of Elizabethan society were given expression. These are the contexts voiced in the Baines libel. There was, Bray argues, no recognition of homosexuality *per se*, no terms to identify a homosexual except within a seditious behavior that knew no limits. For homosexual acts were not localized in Elizabethan society; homosexual persons were not identified. Rather, sodomy was disseminated throughout society, invisible so long as homosexual acts failed to connect with the much more visible signs of social disruption represented by unorthodox religious or social positions.

What was Marlowe's place in Elizabethan society? What made him a likely object of Baines's accusations? These are the questions raised by the conjunction of the libel and the argument Bray makes about the social invisibility of the sodomite. They are not easy questions to answer. The facts of Marlowe's life, and, particularly, of his death, do not easily reveal themselves. Here is what the standard biographies report.

On 18 May 1593, the Privy Council issued a warrant for Marlowe's arrest; two days later he presented himself and agreed to remain in London until he was called again. Some two weeks later, on 30 May 1593, Marlowe spent the entire day in the house of one Eleanor Bull in the company of three male companions. They talked, dined, strolled in the garden; after dinner, a dispute arose, and, in the course of the argument, Marlowe received a wound in the eye from which he died instantly. On 1 June, he was buried. On 2 June, a copy of Baines's allegations against Marlowe was made and sent to the queen.

This narrative is full of questions. We do not know why the Privy Council ordered Marlowe's arrest – it may as easily have been to secure his testimony against someone as to charge him with criminal activity. We certainly do not know that allegations of treason, blasphemy, atheism, or sodomy were involved. Nor do we know whether the fact that Marlowe had not been recalled before the Privy Council by 30 May means that the case, whatever it was, had been dropped, or whether it was still pending. We do not know if the Baines document was related to the case, nor if it bears some connection to Marlowe's death. Its date of composition cannot be determined. We do not even know whether Eleanor Bull's establishment was a public tavern or a private house.

We do know, however, that the three men with whom Marlowe spent his last day had all served in various capacities as government spies, and that Marlowe's murderer, Ingram Friser, was released after a month's imprisonment. Records show Friser transacting business on the day of his release for Sir Thomas Walsingham, a close relative of Sir Francis Walsingham, Queen Elizabeth's Secretary of State and head of her secret service. Marlowe spent eight hours in the company of these men because he shared their social connections; he, too, had been patronized by Sir Thomas; he, too, had been employed as a government spy. One of these men had acted as a double agent, securing the crucial evidence for the conviction of Mary Queen of Scots. Marlowe, however, had a place with such accomplished double agents, men whose business it was to voice what society regarded as inexorably opposed to it. He is reported to have traveled in France, and there to have presented himself as a Catholic sympathizer. As a government agent, Marlowe was given an identity that was, at one and the same time, a counter-identity. What Elizabethan society called Other, it also employed in its service. The Baines libel records this voice – the voice, that is, of Marlowe's rebellion against his society which is also the rebellion which his society employed him to voice. The Baines libel, in short, speaks from the position of a socially sanctioned *double agency*, and speaks in the recognition that such a position permits. What adds full impact and eeriness to this is the strong likelihood that this identity constituted as an Otherness was in fact Marlowe's *real* identity. There is, of course, no way to say simply what a real identity is in such a construction. But what I would suggest is that it locates a place for a homosexual identity in Elizabethan society.

The Baines document will clarify what I mean.

The first four allegations are directed against religion, undermining the priority of Christian belief by insisting on the radical historicity of religion and its political uses. Moses is called a juggler, the wandering in the wilderness a way of founding 'everlasting superstition . . . in the hartes of the people', Adam a latecomer in human history. In short, 'the first beginning of Religion was only to keep men in awe', the fourth allegation reads. Machiavelli might be speaking. Yet, in placing these opinions in Marlowe's mouth, Marlowe is allowed to bring to its ultimate destination an impulse which also stands as a cornerstone of normative Renaissance culture and political conservatism, the humanist's desire for authentic history which had led to such accomplishments as labeling the Donation of Constantine a forgery or to the production of an authoritative biblical text. Humanistic philology, in performing such activities, had not been operating in a pure or apolitical fashion; the scholarly work served emerging states and reforming churches; political sinecures were the scholar's reward. In the libellous accusation, an arm of the state is turned back against it; the state's use of religion is affirmed as a scandal. The alleged opinions, in brief, recognize the subversive potential in an apparatus of state power.

The next set of allegations also concerns religion, but the emphasis now lies on the Bible as fiction. Christ is read as a bastard, his mother as a whore, and his father as a carpenter; and thus his crucifixion as evidence that 'the Jewes . . . best knew him and whence he Came'. Marlowe is said to have regarded Catholicism as a 'good Religion', thanks to its elaborate ceremonies; 'all Protestantes are Hypocriticall asses'. The logic of these accusations is thus revealed. Reading the Bible literally, as a good Protestant, the Marlowe of Baines's text realizes that only Catholic mystification can save the text from its gross palpability. Marlowe turns Protestant hermeneutics on its head, and Catholicism emerges as a 'good Religion' merely because it embraces the fictions of ceremony rather than indulging in the Protestant hypocrisy which pretends to a literalism that it will not see through. Once again we could describe the voice assigned to Marlowe here as the articulation of a founding cultural antithesis. The perception that society itself is a matrix of fictions, and that one of its strongest fictional components involves the denial of its fictionality, describes, too, the double agency that generates Marlowe's identity. These allegations, in fact, seize hold of such possibilities when Marlowe is reported to have said 'That if he were to write a new Religion, he would undertake both a more Excellent and Admirable methode', adding 'that all the new testament is filthily written'.

It is at this point that the allegation of sodomy is made, coming after charges that Christ knew the whorish woman of Samaria dishonestly and was 'bedfellow' of John the Evangelist, 'that he used him as the sinners of Sodoma'. The sexual irregularity of Christ's behavior represents a full literalization of the incarnation; it also authorizes Marlowe's praise of the love of boys and tobacco. Baines's Marlowe coopts the Bible through a misreading rooted in the demystifying historicity of earlier claims. Once again, the radical reading arises from a possibility offered to Protestant readers. Once again, then, mainstream habits of thought and central tenets of Elizabethan culture produce their own subversion.

Soon after Marlowe's death, his fellow playwright and sometime roommate, Thomas Kyd, was charged with atheism; in response, he insisted that Marlowe, not he, held irregular opinions. In one of two letters written in his own defense, Kyd produced a list, briefer than Baines's, of Marlowe's beliefs. This time, Marlowe is said to have called St Paul a juggler; Kyd claims that Marlowe told him that to write in imitation of St Paul could only lead to bad poetry. What is striking in Kyd's allegations is that it opens with the charge of Christ's sodomy: 'He would report St John to be our savior Christes *Alexis* . . . that is that Christ did love him with an extraordinary love.' The allusion, of course, is to Virgil's second eclogue, Corydon's lament about the unforthcoming Alexis. The overt homosexuality of the Virgilian text coupled with the demystification of the Bible once again arises from a central habit of Renaissance thought, the conjunction of classicism and Christianity.

Perhaps what needs further glossing is the coupling of the love of boys with tobacco. Tobacco has a particular historical valency that ought not to be overlooked; colonizing activities were directed to its importation, and support of tobacco could be taken as a sign of patriotism. Early in the Baines allegation, the juggling of Moses had been compared invidiously to the talents of 'one Heriots being Sir W Raleighs man'; Raleigh and Heriot, in fact, were often suspected of atheistical beliefs; but Raleigh was also the queen's instrument in exploring the virgin territories of the new world, and Heriot, serving as a government spokesman, had written an account of Virginia praising the importation of tobacco. Once more, sodomy has been placed in a context in which official government positions and their accompanying malaise both speak.

Indeed, the Baines document moves from sodomy to its most explicit political allegations, questioning St Paul's (and by extension, Luther's and the Elizabethan state's) prescriptions about obedience to magistrates, and including the bizarre claim in which Baines's Marlowe says he has as much right to mint coins as the queen –

asserting, too, that he had learned the art from 'one poole', a fellow prisoner in Newgate. Marlowe *had* spent time in Newgate, charged as an accomplice to a murder, and one Poole was in fact the double agent who had deceived Mary Queen of Scots, and with whom Marlowe spent his final day. The bizarre declaration has other connections as well, for it translates into the public realm the earlier assertions about Marlowe's power as a writer of fictions; these coins are the counterfeit representations upon which political economy rests, and which Marlowe claims to have seen through and to be able to better. Such claims hold the key, too, to the final pair of allegations with which the Baines document ends. 'That the Angell Gabriell was Baud to the holy ghost, because he brought the salutation to Mary' and 'that on[e] Ric Cholmley hath Confessed that he was perswaded to Marloe's Reasons to become an Atheist.' Seemingly unrelated, the final charges point to the insidious powers of persuasion upon which authority – and authoring – rest.

This final point leads, of course, to the aspect of Marlowe that I might have been expected to have started with, his identity as an author. Although that is never explicitly charged against him in Baines's note, the spectre of the theater lurks behind his text. It is there, for instance, in the word *juggler*, which includes in its range of associations con man, cheap entertainer, magician, trickster, storyteller, conjurer, actor, and dramatist, as Stephen Greenblatt has noted.[3] The conjunction of boys and tobacco also summons up the theater, with its boy actors and profligate audience, the object of puritanical horror and government legislation. Even false coins might call up a phrase from Sir Philip Sidney's *Defence* which defines poetry as 'a representing, counterfeiting, or figuring forth'.[4] The demystifications in the document, in short, authorize its voice, lending it the authority writers and monarchs shared, not necessarily very comfortably. For the document, we might say, *legitimizes* Marlowe, but much as the theater was legitimated, at once placed and policed, censored and yet situated in the 'liberties', on the border of the city, allowed a certain sphere of freedom to represent what might not be said within the city's confines, to give the illusion of autonomous and full discourse.[5] The theater was at once marginalized and supported by the government; when James I came to the throne of England, he took the theaters under his patronage. Elizabeth had said, in 1586, that 'princes are set on stages in the sight and view of all the world', and James repeated her remark in his treatise on kingship, the *Basilikon Doron*.[6] In it, he also listed crimes that were treasonous and warranted death. Among them was sodomy. James, of course, was notorious for his overtly homosexual behavior. Yet, his treatise does not simply dissimulate; rather, it shows that sodomy was so fully politicized that no king could possibly apply the term to himself. Marlowe's theatrical milieu, as hospitable to homosexuality as any institution in the period can be said to have been (boy actors were regularly suspected of being what they counterfeited) is the place, in short, where the counter-voices of the culture were acted out.

The theater was permitted to rehearse the dark side of Elizabethan culture; it was a recreative spot where sedition could wear the face of play, where authors could make assertions as potent as monarchs'. In the theater, kings were the puppets of writers; greatness was mimed; atheists, rebels, magicians, and sodomites could be publicly displayed. And nowhere, of course, more strikingly than in Marlowe's heroes, the sodomitical Edward II, for instance, the Jew of Malta, Faustus and Tamburlaine. Marlowe's identity in his culture comes from his rehearsal of these counter-positions, and the words of Richard Baines, government spy, report how Marlowe, a fellow spy, acquired a counter-identity at once countenanced and denounced by his society. Like the heroes he created, Marlowe lived and died in the impossible project – as author, government spy, and sodomite – of the marginalized, negativized existence permitted him. Marlowe and his heroes, Stephen Greenblatt says, live lives in the recognition of the void, in the realization (I mean that both ways) that rebellion never manages to find its own space, but always acts in the space that society has created for it. To play there is to be nowhere and to recognize that the solidity of social discourse carries with it, as its support and as its own undermining, the very negations in which such play can occur. When Marlowe's audience assembled to see *The Jew of Malta*, they were greeted by a prologue spoken by Machiavelli, telling them, 'I count religion but a childish toy / And hold there is no sin but ignorance'.[7] Baines's note ascribes to Marlowe the rhetoric of his inventions. Marlowe is charged with *being* what he and his society allowed existence only as *negations* and *fictions*. Marlowe was not just playing.

That negativized identity has repercussions that stretch into our own time, however great the historical differences between the place of homosexuality in Renaissance society and ours. In the years between Marlowe and us, homosexuality has fastened upon what society has rejected as the place in which an antithetical discourse and a claim for social placement could be made. At the turn of this century, as the example of Oscar Wilde suggests, it was, in part, in *theatricality* that such claims were made. And it was also in theatricality that, at first, Wilde was saved. It was because he was charged with *posing* as a 'somdomite' (not with being one) that he filed his libel suit; when he ultimately was convicted, he maintained that it was for writing a beautiful letter, a prose poem like one of Shakespeare's sonnets to his young man. The authenticity of inauthenticity was the ground upon which Wilde met his society. The history of homosexuality in the past 100 years has been of its emergence in the sphere of otherness to which it has been confined, its foundation in a discursive sphere in which it attempts to lay claims to a radically threatening otherness. Yet, it is always menaced and vulnerable, and whether we can ever find an authenticity that is not capable of being absorbed by, and crushed by, the society in which we exist, is the question raised, it seems to me, by the case of Christopher Marlowe.

Notes

1. A facsimile and transcription appear on pp. 308–9 of A.D. WRAIGHT, *In Search of Christopher Marlowe* (New York, Vanguard Press, 1965). An up-to-date summary of information about Baines can be found in C.B. KURIYAMA, 'Marlowe's nemesis: the identity of Richard Baines', in KENNETH FRIEDENREICH, ROMA GILL, and CONSTANCE B. KURIYAMA (eds), '*A Poet and a Filthy Play-maker': New Essays on Christopher Marlowe* (New York, AMS Press, 1988), pp. 343–60.

2. ALAN BRAY, *Homosexuality in Renaissance England* (London, Gay Men's Press, 1982). Bray's book remains the best treatment of its subject; however, there are some problematic aspects to its theory and practice that have become clearer to me since I wrote this essay. It was pp. 83–90 of EVE KOSOFSKY SEDGWICK's *Between Men: English Literature and Male Homosocial Desire* (New York, Columbia University Press, 1985) that first alerted me to areas of his work that needed scrutiny, and I have continued this critique, while continuing to rely on Bray's work, in 'Colin to Hobbinol: Spenser's Familiar Letters', *South Atlantic Quarterly* 88 (1989), 107–26, esp. pp. 111–14.

3. See 'Invisible bullets: Renaissance authority and its subversion', *Glyph* 8 (1981), 40–61, esp. pp. 42ff., which consider the Baines and Kyd allegations. (The essay appears in a final form in STEPHEN GREENBLATT, *Shakespearean Negotiations* [Berkeley and Los Angeles, University of California Press, 1988]). This is perhaps the appropriate place to note my indebtedness throughout this essay to Greenblatt's work, not least to his treatment of Marlowe in *Renaissance Self-Fashioning* (Chicago, University of Chicago Press, 1980).

4. *A Defence of Poetry*, ed. J.A. VAN DORSTEN (Oxford, Oxford University Press, 1966), p. 25.

5. Cf. STEVEN MULLANEY, *The Place of the Stage* (Chicago, University of Chicago Press, 1988), pp. 1–59.

6. For further discussion, see my *James I and the Politics of Literature* (Baltimore, MD, Johns Hopkins University Press, 1983; Stanford, CA, Stanford University Press, 1989), pp. 113–16.

7. *The Complete Plays of Christopher Marlowe*, ed. IRVING RIBNER (Indianapolis and New York, Odyssey Press, 1963), p. 179.

4 Representing 'Women' and Males: Gender Relations in Marlowe*

SIMON SHEPHERD

While American New Historicists were exploring the textuality of history, in Britain so-called Cultural Materialist critics continued to emphasise the historicity of texts, and Simon Shepherd's 1986 book on Marlowe was an important statement of their conviction that Renaissance drama radically questioned the beliefs and values that went to shape the modern world. Written 'out of rage against queer-bashing', Shepherd's polemical chapter on gender relations therefore examines the ways in which Marlowe ironises the normative assumptions that underpin masculine power. This involves an alertness to performance of the plays on stage, since Shepherd proposes that Marlowe's use of costumes, props and space works to problematise the male gaze through which women are objectified. An unspoken influence here is the Lacanian journal *Cahiers du Cinema*, which pioneered analysis of the politics of vision, and the result is to affirm that Faustus's fetishising of Helen, or Tamburlaine's worship of Zenocrate, is as much designed to highlight sexism as is Aeneas's overt exploitation of Dido. That these female parts were originally played by boys further subverts our expectations about representations of gender, Shepherd maintains, for what Marlowe stages with his strutting musclemen is the exclusion of women from the locker-room of male desire. Masculinity is exposed as a rhetorical construct in these dramas, most pointedly in Edward's sodomy, where the eroticising of *adult* males disrupts the subject/object binarism on which a privileged spectatorship depends. In contrast to the pessimism of American New Historicists (Chapter 3), therefore, Shepherd reads this 'Marlowe-who-isn't-Shakespeare' as an incitement to gay and feminist critics to collaborate in an education programme that is militantly 'socialist and anti-patriarchal'.

---

* Extracted from *Marlowe and the Politics of Elizabethan Theatre* (Hemel Hempstead, Harvester Wheatsheaf, 1986), 178–207.

The politics of Elizabethan theatre must encompass its representation of gender relations as well as kingship or class. For some time feminist critics have argued the need to explore the works of Shakespeare and his contemporaries, but Elizabethan theatre presents a problem in that there are fewer 'women' in plots and they are represented in conventional ways. Marlowe in particular is difficult because of the sodomy: commentaries on Marlowe imply that nothing needs to be said because his view of sex is all too clearly obsessive, nor indeed ought anything to be said because such things are best left unspoken. Therefore, almost out of sheer bloody-mindedness and rage against queer-bashing, I want to speak of Marlowe's treatment of gender and of sodomy.

Implicit in my remarks on Elizabethan theatre was a concept of sexual political analysis that studies what happens to women characters in stories. At its worst it is concerned with what is represented rather than how it is represented, and tends to assume that texts work realistically. But where the artworks are male-authored and performed entirely by men, it seems necessary to ask how the female is identified, what devices signal womanhood. Even the most thoughtful male portrayal of a woman character can assume that certain modes of discourse or appearance are 'female'; the male writer always selects his 'woman's' language according to his own assumptions, looks at her with a male gaze. But what is male need not be masculine: it may be possible to find male texts that question the ways men in patriarchy look at women, or indeed texts that call attention to their own strategies for representing women in patriarchy; males can question the operation of masculine power. When the role of the male representer of 'woman' is not examined, when 'she' is studied as a character in her own right, that which is male is assumed to be beyond comment, normal, natural – an assumption central to masculine power. To question this assumption, and what it supports, it is necessary to comment on that which is male, to see how maleness is defined, to make men in texts into case studies of the representation of maleness. My own position as a man committed against patriarchy leads me to think that maleness is the problem, and I think a reading can be made of Marlowe which sees his texts as problematising the male and masculinity (much of which has been hidden by the 'explanation' of sodomy). So my study here moves from the handling of women characters to the questioning of masculinity.

There are few women characters in Marlowe's plays, the major ones being Dido, Zenocrate and Abigail. Dido is not much written about because the whole play is seen as minor; Abigail, on the other hand, is seen to have real emotions which show up the iniquity of her father; Zenocrate is not a character but a device that helps to characterise the male hero. This sort of criticism not only compels its readers to interpret everything from the viewpoint of a central male, but it replaces specific stage pictures with an abstracted model of female–male contrast. So pervasive is this view as applied to *1 Tamburlaine* that I'll need to centre my analysis on that text.

Zenocrate first enters as part of the loot of an ambush: the written text insists that Tamburlaine's men carry treasure, and his syntax balances woman and loot: 'The jewels and the treasure we have ta'en / Shall be reserv'd, and you in better state . . .' (I. ii. 2–3). The text insists that, although silent, she has to remain on stage for the whole scene since she is given the last line. The staging thus marks the woman not so much as passive and silent (which would fit with the recommendations of the dominant religious and social ideology) as captured and silenced; treated as treasure in a world where men fight and negotiate. The movement of the scene climaxes in the establishment of male community, the welcoming of Theridamas the foe into the gang, watched by the woman. This portrayal of the 'woman's place' may, of course, be paralleled in the notorious blurring of girl and gold in the speech of Barabas the Jew after she steals his treasure for him. She is replaced by money in that she is physically separated from him, being 'above', and Barabas hugs the money-bags that she throws down. The scene encourages interrogation of the ideological values which are seemingly so emotively, so 'naturally', expressed. The relations of possession assumed by such metaphors are revealed when Barabas celebrates the satisfaction of his desires without thinking of how they have been satisfied. The split staging of the scene simultaneously points up how it is the active agency of Abigail that enables Barabas's satisfaction but how it is only the inanimate money bags which cross the distance between them. To this fetishising of objects within gender relations we must return.

Another point of comparison between the Zenocrate and Abigail scenes here, and a second point about the presentation of 'woman's place', is that men control stage space. The capture of Zenocrate scene turns into the persuading of Theridamas, which she watches. The scene in which Abigail steals the gold begins with Barabas alone bemoaning his lot; Abigail's appearance above provides a new interest, fostered by her lines: 'here, behold, unseen, where I have found / The gold' (II. i. 22–3). She addresses the audience and is engaged in activity; he is addressing Barabas and is sitting down: the split staging potentially invites comparison of he and she. As the gold crosses the stage space between them his mood changes and he becomes more energetic, and she is faded out of the scene. But

I have to say, of both scenes, that they only *potentially* invite gender comparison, since the narrative interest in each case centres on the male project – how each central male will deal with the new crisis. So the texts could be said to work in a sexist way, marginalising the woman (except that Marlowe does not forget Zenocrate). It is possible, however, to show Marlowe's staging trying to foreground the male gaze, to show specifically the male control of stage space. This is the reading I would make of the Agydas scene in *1 Tamburlaine*, Act III, scene ii. Agydas is a courtier captured with Zenocrate and he tries to urge her to resist and hate Tamburlaine; she, however, now speaks of her admiration for him:

> As looks the sun through Nilus' flowing stream,
> Or when the morning holds him in her arms,
> So looks my lordly love, fair Tamburlaine;

> > (III. ii. 47–9)

She then weeps because she considers herself unworthy of him. Unknown to her, Tamburlaine and his men are watching the conversation. Their appearance has the effect of estranging the intimacy in that the audience hears Zenocrate's words in a context different from that in which she intentionally speaks them. Her deliberately ornate picture of how Tamburlaine looks is seen not to fit with the Tamburlaine who is in fact looking at her, from whom an audience may well expect some violent response against Agydas. The personal expressivity of the woman is made into extravagant redundance when the audience watches it in awareness of the watching male. Zenocrate's emotion is not insincere, in fact the internalising of the unequal power relations is pathetic, but it is devalued on a stage overseen by the male gaze.

The other person who is looked at is Agydas, and the distancing of his words produces another sort of knowledge. For Agydas is trying to persuade Zenocrate that Tamburlaine is not the man for her since he is barbarous and fiercely martial. In addressing her, Agydas is constructing a picture of her, referring to her 'heavenly face' and her 'dainty ears' which will be offended by talk of war and blood. Although at first it may seem 'natural' to address the virginal heroine thus, the construction of the scene places Agydas's words as attempted manipulation; watched over Tamburlaine's shoulder, what Agydas is seen to be doing is plotting, and the characteristics ascribed to the woman do not so much arise from what she is as from how she may be used in a world of male politics. Such an awareness prepares an audience for the next scene in which Bajazeth and Tamburlaine match one another's brags, in a series comparing their names, their religion, their captains' brags, then their wives: Bajazeth's wife Zabina is praised as a mother, Zenocrate for her beauty. Tamburlaine's speech describing her is very beautiful but it falls into place as part of male competition: it is not so much that Zenocrate is beautiful as that Tamburlaine's project requires her to be seen as beautiful; masculine power maintains itself by insisting on the difference of those who are not masculine (Marks and de Courtivron, 1981, p. 219).

As the play goes on Zenocrate is steadily more silenced. In the two jubilant Act IV scenes she breaks the mood by asking for pity for her father. In the first, Tamburlaine claims he has 'sworn' and can't break his word, and in the second she is not allowed the space to plead for her father. The sorrow and pity may be seen as traditional characteristics which mark femaleness, but the writing of these scenes makes them awkward disruptions. More importantly, they are ineffectual, for Tamburlaine constructs a certain image of Zenocrate to which he dedicates his conquests but this image is not the real woman. Thus in the famous address to her during the siege of Damascus he describes her weeping:

> With hair dishevelled wip'st thy watery cheeks,
> And, like to Flora in her morning's pride,
> Shaking her silver tresses in the air
>
> (V. ii. 76–8)

But the poetry suppresses the fact that it is in his power to remove the cause of her weeping, for the poetry, initially, arises precisely to describe her weeping – it is a condition for *his* poetry that *she* weeps. She is also absent, the description of her replacing her physical presence, much as previously his image of her coexisted with his denial of her feelings. This moment in the playtext shows, I think, how the ideology of what woman should be, the preferred beauty, passivity, goodness, originates in the man.

What the text does not do is explain why the ideology takes the shape it has. Tamburlaine's first formal address to Zenocrate associates her with his ambitions of conquest:

> Thy person is more worth to Tamburlaine
> Than the possession of the Persian crown,
> Which gracious stars have promis'd at my birth.
>
> (I. ii. 90–2)

Here the feeling for Zenocrate, especially the fetishising of her chastity, fits into place in the imperial project. Tamburlaine tells

Theridamas that Jove has sent him this Soldan's daughter, which
argues that he is destined for fame; she is a partner who may
fittingly be contrasted with Bajazeth's wife; finally, the fact that her
chastity has been guarded allows her father to yield to Tamburlaine
and consolidate the empire – his treatment of Zenocrate works to his
profit.

It might be argued that it is only natural to treat Zenocrate as
chaste since, as a character, she has no desires; that the text is not
showing sexist ideology, but is sexist. But here again I would argue
that Marlowe makes the male way of looking and of addressing seem
strange, if not contradictory, rather than natural. For example, when
Tamburlaine addresses Zenocrate as 'lovelier than the love of Jove, /
Brighter than is the silver Rhodope' (I. ii. 87–8), the speech sees her
in positions of power, being attended on by Tartars and drawn on
a sled by milk-white harts, but she has to listen as a captive: the
visual/verbal contrast shows that the poetry refuses to recognise the
real and present power relations. This first example connects up with
all the others I have looked at in that poetry is used ideologically to
tell Zenocrate what she is and to conceal the conditions under which
it addresses her. The stage here is doing what written poetry cannot
do, in that it shows the person addressed and the conditions under
which s/he is addressed. The context suggests that the poetry is not
'natural' expression but a means of reinforcing an unequal gender
power relationship.

In *The Jew of Malta* the text makes a joke of love poetry precisely by
dislocating it from context. The slave Ithamore promises the whore
Bellamira: 'I'll be thy Jason, thou my golden fleece; / Where painted
carpets o'er the meads are hurl'd' (IV. ii. 96–7); the classical fantasy is
sustained for ten lines of couplets, but as soon as Pilia-Borza enters
Ithamore asks if he has the gold from Barabas. The two men discuss
the Jew's reaction and Ithamore prepares another blackmail note with
which Pilia-Borza leaves, remarking (ambiguously) 'You'd make a
rich poet, sir' (l. 130). The two 'lovers' then return to their love-talk.
Two different sorts of text are made by Ithamore, blackmail notes
and love poetry, the first discussed with a man, the second with a
woman. And all the time Ithamore is being tricked by the other two,
so a poetry in which he is the Jason and she the fleece misrecognises
the power relations. So too the emotional expressivity is seen, by the
structuring, to be an illusion – Ithamore makes poetry for Bellamira
as he makes blackmail notes. Marlowe may deconstruct this further
by parodying his own lyric 'Come live with me and be my love', as it
were declaring his own authorship behind Ithamore: and at the same
time asking questions about the status of his own love lyric and its
unspoken context.

The placing of the language of gender relations within financial concerns, and the questioning of sincere expressivity, are appropriate to the world of *The Jew of Malta*. I used the example to try to broaden my point, from 1 *Tamburlaine*, that the language of male poetry, so natural to Elizabethan culture perhaps, is foregrounded and estranged in Marlowe's plays, which then allow exploration of its values. From here another point can be made, that instead of enjoying the description of the person addressed the focus concentrates on the speaker, so that the operation of male desire is studied. An example, from 1 *Tamburlaine*, is Arabia's dying speech to Zenocrate. As her former betrothed, he makes a claim upon her and enters wounded to die in her arms; before dying he wishes that his 'deadly pangs' 'Would lend an hour's licence to my tongue, / To make discourse of some sweet accidents' (V. ii. 359–60). The style of the speech, with its antithetical phrasing, its alliteration, its conceit of sweet pain, shows Arabia already to be making his discourse, and that discourse is visually shown to be an imposition on Zenocrate. She and her maid have sat among corpses in silence, with the noise of battle off-stage; Arabia appears and places his bleeding body in her arms, bringing the blood close to her, yet his speech ignores her distress. He says 'Lie down, Arabia, . . . let Zenocrate's fair eyes behold' (ll. 343–4), making himself performer and she the audience. The man creates a picture, the conditions of its creation are violent; the woman speaks of herself as 'the cursed *object*'.

This double effect of male looking recurs. In 2 *Tamburlaine*, Zenocrate is arranged into a patriarchal tableau: 'now she sits in pomp and majesty, / When these, my sons, . . . Placed by her side, look on their mother's face' – their look creates her pomp; and written into Tamburlaine's look is the destruction, for the sons are 'more precious *in mine eyes* / Than all the wealthy kingdoms I subdued' (I. iv. 17–20; my italics). At the end of the great scene of her death, after all the fantastic visions of battering the shining palace of the sun and shivering the starry firmament, he gives orders that the town where she has died will be burnt – and that order is real. A scene later he enters to a dead march with her hearse and the image of the town burning; he makes a memorial to her and then suddenly gives his sons a lesson in warfare. The woman is literally now an object in a male world, and the process of memorialising her creates destruction. So too, notoriously, in *Doctor Faustus* the hero's poetry to the Helen apparition envisages mass destruction – 'for love of thee / Instead of Troy shall Wittenberg be sack'd' (xviii. 106–7) – male competition and rape. In 2 *Tamburlaine* an audience sees a town burning but here it is only imagined in poetry, so it is less noticeable (for years male scholars found this a highpoint of poetry); but part of the strategy of *Faustus* is to trap its audience with the pleasurable. The context for Helen's second appearance, however, establishes how the man uses the picture of the woman: Helen's 'sweet embraces may extinguish clear / Those thoughts that do dissuade me from my vow' (ll. 94–5). In Faustus's gaze Helen changes status from the magic show put on for the curious scholars, after which Faustus says nothing, to the object of desire which promises an end to the doubts arising in the real world; the image remains an image but becomes desired: 'Helen', despite the poetry, is still not Helen but a spirit. I don't know how much the presence of a boy actor would contribute to 'Helen's' impermanence here, but I think in *1 Tamburlaine* Marlowe uses acting conditions to point up the fetishising within the narrative of Zenocrate. It is thought that *Tamburlaine* would have been performed with four boys in the cast (Bevington, 1962), which means that the Zenocrate actor would have doubled as one of the virgins who plead with Tamburlaine. Thus in the single identity of the actor an audience sees the 'woman' (as a virgin of Damascus) denied and destroyed while it also sees the same 'woman' (as Zenocrate) praised and adored. The doubling seems to add to the structure of male picture-making of women and male violence that is insisted on as a characteristic of male looking at women.

Zenocrate is captured, wooed and exposed to slaughter: through it all she remains chaste. The fetishising of her chastity is not simply seen as an element of male psychology, but is given material specificity in the play in that her father can agree to her marrying Tamburlaine. Through most of the text she places her father in opposition to Tamburlaine. She was seized on the way to her father and at the end of the play he enters to her as her lover's captive, but the absent father of the text is not, on account of her, in opposition: while she is silent in the last minutes of the play, they agree on an alliance: her role is to satisfy them both. It is the patriarchal arrangement of property marriage rather than the father–lover opposition of romance that structures the final scene. More importantly, the chastity fetish can be seen to be historically specific. The propaganda of Elizabeth's rule presented her as the chaste virginal monarch. She was compared to the classical goddesses Pallas Athene and Astraea, the last being associated both with justice and with empire.

[...]

1 Tamburlaine explores the Elizabethan ideology of chaste rule by showing what the imagery suppresses. For although the Soldan (like some male critics) can accept that Tamburlaine's treatment of Zenocrate is a mark of his essential honour, the corpses still lie at his feet. Tamburlaine invites an audience to look at Zenocrate's face 'shadowing in her brows / Triumphs and trophies for my victories' (V ii 448–9) but what the stage also shows are the corpses which Zenocrate pities. She may be 'shadowing' in two senses: looking distressed from her experiences or theatrically presenting ('shadow' was a word used of actor or acted); Tamburlaine selects only one of these meanings. The end scenes of crowning and promised marriage of the chaste woman do not conceal the bloodiness of the adventures earlier, despite Tamburlaine's speeches. The absolutist rhetoric of personal virtue is inhumane. [. . .] Situated historically, this element of 1 *Tamburlaine* deconstructs an imagery which both legitimated Elizabeth's personal rule and structured Elizabethan thinking about sexual relations.

Gendered Language

One contemporary theory in feminism suggests that the differences between masculine and feminine are structured by the acquisition of language. While this may be debated in our society (Lovell, 1983), in the Renaissance women were excluded generally from the education offered by academic institutions (Ong, 1982), which meant an exclusion from Latin and from rhetoric. Men learn to work with language, women merely speak. [. . .] This notion of the gendering of language may be illustrated, I think, in *Edward II* where Isabella's early speech of grief contrasts with the stripped-down language of the other characters. It seems overblown: 'Like frantic Juno will I fill the earth / With ghastly murmur of my sighs and cries' (I. iv. 179–80). Isabella cannot 'fill' the earth because it is already filled with a different sort of speech, and her language is both private and non-functional. Although she can talk articulately, when all the men re-enter she is silent. The silence is shown by her talking in dumb-show to Mortimer, a political intervention that cannot be heard. During the play Mortimer specifically curtails her emotional utterances: 'Cease to lament, and tell us where's the king?' (II. iv. 31), 'Nay, madam, if you be a warrior, / You must not grow so passionate in speeches' (IV. iv. 15–16). Isabella learns to be a proper warrior for as her relationship with Mortimer develops so her speech uses stylistic devices that make it sound more 'rational', less passionate. Through her language she becomes masculinised, less emotional.

Isabella is more sympathetic when she is emotional than when she is rational. Although this can be taken to be part of the play's attack on the discourse of masculinity, the association of emotion and its language with woman is nevertheless derived from dominant ideology. As we have seen, the woman was supposedly more inclined to be governed by passion or hysteria. My argument is that Marlowe's texts encourage exploration both of the portrayal of that emotion and of its value. In Renaissance plays women characters often move from distress to passion, if not to hysteria and madness. The emotional trajectory is, however, re-plotted in Zenocrate who, at the precise moment that emotional collapse might be expected – the discovery of the corpses, which Marlowe holds back for a while – instead delivers a most formally patterned oration. With the repeated line 'Behold the Turk and his great emperess' she presents the corpses, noting at the end of her speech that she had been insufficiently emotional: 'pardon me that was not moved with ruth / To see them live so long in misery' (V. ii. 305–6). Far from collapsing into 'female' hysteria, Zenocrate takes on the role of Presenter, a role that was traditionally the male narrative voice of truth against the mimesis of emotion. From addressing herself as the grieving woman Zenocrate turns, in one of the play's breaches of 'realistic' continuity, to present to the audience. In a similar way the text of *Dido* changes its source at the farewell of Dido and Aeneas. Virgil's account has her break down with emotion, verbally defeated, and the poetry then describes Aeneas's emotion. In the play it is Dido who has the fullness of speech, the male is silent and he leaves silently; she only cries after he has gone. As speaker she is the central emotional focus.

One of the implications of female passion is that a woman's inner emotions will always be revealed. When Zenocrate does not collapse, the moment of expected transparency becomes opaque, the privileged insight is not offered. This complication of the viewing relationship is clearer with Isabella in *Edward II*, for her language of private grievance feels almost embarrassingly overwritten in the context of the rest of the play; there is nearly impropriety in its attempted fullness, which unsettles theatrical pleasure. The emotion hence is made difficult to respond to, stylistically opaque rather than transparently expressive. (It is possible that there are similar problems of 'tone' with Abigail.)

Woman's emotionalism was commonly seen as a bad thing, that which debilitated her from governing. Yet Zenocrate's distress at slaughter is preferable to Tamburlaine's tableaux; nevertheless Isabella loses sympathy as she becomes less emotional. The problems of value are highlighted in *Dido, Queen of Carthage*, for Dido was supposedly a woman whose desires tried to obstruct the project of empire by delaying Aeneas on his way from Troy to Italy. The relevance of this story to an English audience derives from the myth of London as the new Troy, so Dido takes her place as yet another type of the passionate woman, the antithesis to virginal rule. In the

play Venus compels Dido to love Aeneas so that she will provide
him with the materials necessary to refurbish his expedition. In the
centre of the play Venus argues with Juno about her hostility to
Aeneas and they discuss the possibility of marrying him to Dido,
though it looks unlikely in view of his imperial plans. The scene
is placed to locate the 'love' within the project of empire. The end
of the play focuses on the loser Dido, alone with the relics of her
relationship with Aeneas which she burns before immolating herself.
The image of the abandoned woman is intensified by giving the last
speech of the play to Dido's sister Anna, who throughout the play
has desired Iarbas, who in turn desired Dido. The imagery of the
flames and self-destruction is a traditional moral labelling of desire,
but nevertheless it is the passion not the empire-builder which
occupies the dramatic focus.

My analysis of *Dido* will need to be fuller to show properly how
it contributes to the revaluing of passion; it will include further
discussion of the markers of feminine and masculine difference.
I have kept this play separate because its performance conditions
were different, being a play for boy actors. Neither fully-grown man
nor woman, the boy takes both sex roles. With voices and bodies
sounding and looking alike, other means have to be used to signify
gender, and *Dido* uses props. In a pattern of scenes the relationship
is articulated through fetishised objects. In Act III Dido and Aeneas
swear love and fidelity, which Dido celebrates by dressing Aeneas
in her jewels: 'These golden bracelets, and this wedding-ring, /
Wherewith my husband woo'd me yet a maid' (III. iv. 61–2). She
takes the 'male' part of wooer, the powerful woman dressing a man
as she wants to see him, choosing to transfer her tokens of allegiance
from one man to another. But the sexual articulation of the gesture is
given different meaning by the narrative context, that the gods have
landed Aeneas here so that Dido's wealth can be used to mend his
fleet. The jewels as they move express two different commitments.
They also mark perpetual separation, for two people cannot wear
the same jewel at one time: Dido's power is delimited by Aeneas's.

In Act IV Dido tries to prevent Aeneas's departure by giving him
coronation jewels, but he rejects the crown and sceptre that he holds:
'A burgonet of steel and not a crown, / A sword and not a sceptre
fits Aeneas' (IV. iv. 42–3). Nevertheless she convinces him to stay
and he exits wearing the jewels, which in one sense do fit him in that
they are riches. By contrast the scene ends with Dido talking to the
tackling, oars and sails that she has ordered removed from the ships
to prevent departure. The pomp of Aeneas's exit to play the role
of Dido's husband is matched by her private speech addressed to
inanimate objects. For Aeneas she creates a public role and finery,

for herself she ties knots in rope. The mythological fantasy for
Aeneas is balanced by a rejection of myth: she tells the oars:

> The water which our poets term a nymph,
> Why did it suffer thee to touch her breast
> And shrunk not back, knowing my love was there?
> The water is an element, no nymph.

(ll. 144–7)

The props only function in the man's world, the jewels creating a role
for Aeneas to play, the tackling useless off the ship. The narrative of
the scene apparently tells of Dido's power, but the contrasts of
public/private, meaningful/useless objects, poetry/failed poetry
build a distinction between 'masculine' and 'feminine'.

In her final scene Dido lays out more objects: the sword Aeneas
swore love by, the garment she first dressed him in, the 'letters, lines,
and perjur'd papers' (V. i. 300). The woman is again surrounded by
redundant objects – a tableau to be used again with Zenocrate and
the corpses, and Olympia and the funeral pyre. This time the objects
have been made redundant for her by the man: she is visually
defined as static recipient, no longer handling jewels but treacherous
texts. When she was first divinely caused to love Aeneas the love
was shaped by her position of wealth and power as a ruler:

> His glistering eyes shall be my looking-glass, . . .
> His looks shall be my only library;
> And thou, Aeneas, Dido's treasury

(III. i. 85, 89–90)

Like the property, he will reflect and confirm her power. From this
unequal relationship the play moves to another version of it as
Aeneas takes the wealth and continues on his journey. The departure
of her 'looking-glass' makes Dido lose her grip on reality, to have
'thoughts of lunacy'. Her sister urges: 'remember who you are' (V. i.
263), but what constitutes 'Dido' is now a problem. She burns herself
alongside his relics. She learnt to define herself by the male world
and becomes its leavings. It takes away her power and produces her
lunacy. Thus her 'passionate' end is an indictment of masculine
action. Gender is articulated through objects that have private and
public meanings; personal feeling expressed through objects is not
separable from control and competition. The definition of gender is
shaped by the project of empire. The play invites sympathy with the
redundant woman and her fantasies, lunacy and false texts. When
she asks for an avenger to rise up and plough Aeneas's countries

with the sword, Dido repeats an English hostility to Italy; but so too the passionate woman urges destruction of the lands of the descendants of Troy, which has another meaning in Tudor myth (where London is new Troy).

As a representation of woman the picture of Dido is that of defeat and powerlessness. The relics of Aeneas suggest what has made that picture, but the stage image does not challenge the pathos of the woman victim. The force of the play may perhaps depend on its conditions of production and its intertextuality. As a boys' play it was probably performed in some richly decorated hall: the wealthy furnishings and dress of the audience are themselves ironised by a narrative in which property treacherously constructs and exploits human relations. By ending the play with Dido's death, the passionate woman is given major emphasis – not only against Aeneas who is already a contradictory figure, but against the usual emphasising of properly chaste women in boys' plays.

[...]

Marlowe's texts, then, could be said to explore the construction of gender difference in representation and to problematise it. Expectations about 'feminine' speech and emotionalism are questioned, assumed values rejected. At moments the privileged male gaze, which oversees the differentiation of gender, has its power and pleasure unsettled.

Manliness and Sodomy

Assumed values of sex roles derived from the ideology of manliness, which Elizabethan plays persistently affirm. [...] The ideology of manliness, or masculinity, inscribes the individual within interpersonal competition and denigrates emotion without action.

In the light of this formulation, *Edward II* could be interpreted to show, unsympathetically, such masculinity. The barons frequently draw swords, scenes of quarrelling rapidly become physically violent; Spenser advises Edward to 'refer your vengeance to the sword' (III. ii. 126). The sword supplies many phallic puns on the Renaissance stage and its frequent usage in *Edward II* marks both the masculinity and the violence of interpersonal communication: 'henceforth parley with our naked swords'; 'We never beg, but use such prayers as these' – *seizing sword* (I. i. 126; II. ii. 153). Other chivalric weaponry is also foregrounded, with much talk of advancing standards to the battlefield and Elder Spenser directed to carry his 'truncheon' when he brings troops to express his 'love' for the king. Love in the play is structured by competition, Mortimer advising Isabella not to lament the loss of Edward's love but 'Cry quittance, madam, then, and love not him' (I. iv. 197).

The association between masculinity and violence is regarded by most commentators not as a critique but as a personal kink of Marlowe's deriving from his homosexuality, a viewpoint which, based on wonky ideas about homosexuality, suppresses Marlowe as sexual political thinker beneath Marlowe the compulsive. Thus the attack on masculinity is seen only as a symptom of a sick condition. There is no space to engage with the ideological ramifications of such commentary. More important, perhaps, is to look at the 'homosexual' scenes.

First, however, the word 'homosexual' has to be erased, since Elizabethan culture had no conception of 'homosexuality' as a positive form of sexuality in its own right (the word itself is a nineteenth-century invention). When the Elizabethans spoke of sodomy or buggery they tended to speak of debauchery (more broad than homosexual activity) and the words were loaded with overtones of disorder and unnaturalness; yet homosexual acts took place, and despite the fuss prosecution was rare. Marlowe's texts can be seen to make definitions of their own and maybe even to question the values in sodomy: not so much 'compulsion' as interrogation.

The most normative representations are the sodomite behaviours of Henry III and (possibly) Mycetes. Both are bad kings: Henry III's obsession with his 'minions' leads him to ignore public responsibility and the Guise bid for power. He only wants to 'delight himself', and the choice of male minions marks the disorder. Mycetes is an incapable king who uses counsellors to speak and fight for him. He refers to Meander whom 'I may term a Damon for thy love' (1 *Tamburlaine*, I. i. 50); he invites Theridamas to bring back corpses: 'Go frowning forth; but come thou smiling home, / As did Sir Paris with the Grecian dame' (ll. 65–6). Mycetes illustrates the problem about identifying homosexuality: there is no talk of minions, but there is a self-indulgent incapability marked by inappropriate sexual references (in male company). Both kings are more given to personal (sexual) appetite than public order, a reverse of what constitutes manliness.

Sodomy here may be made sense of as political labelling. More notorious is the opening to *Dido* – 'minor and quickly forgotten', gulps one editor; unnecessary and therefore obsessional, think others. (Why is it that homosexuals are obsessional and heterosexuals are not? – are their sexual lives so boring?) 'Jupiter dandling Ganymede upon his knee' is discovered: Jupiter offers Ganymede love and protection from his wife Juno, and gives him some of her wedding jewels; Ganymede promises embraces in return for a jewel for his ear and a brooch for his hat. The giving of jewels between 'lovers' will be echoed later in the play, as will the gestures, for example when Dido sits Cupid on her lap (thinking him Ascanius) and he asks: 'What will you give me? Now I'll have this fan' (III. i. 32). And again, when the Nurse carries 'Ascanius' (as he asks her to) and talks of her desire for 'love' although she is old. Comparison of the three similar scenes (older figures carrying boys) sees the Nurse mocked for her sexual desire and Dido commencing on a tragic infatuation: only Jupiter is successful. The Nurse and Dido are both tricked by Cupid disguised as Ascanius (who could be performed by the Ganymede actor), and they and Anna are abandoned by mortal men. This treatment of women's emotion is initiated by Jupiter's threats against Juno, just as a 'love' expressed through jewel giving is likewise going to mark sexual relations.

The gods could be expected to provide a frame of commentary which highlights the moral mistakes of mortals, even while it influences action. The authority of this frame is immediately undercut in *Dido* by the sodomy, so that there is no rational overview beyond the chaos of passions. More importantly, the assumption that rationality is male and passion female is challenged, and male desire is foregrounded at the start of a play about a woman who classically exemplifies destructive desire. That male desire is associated with power over others, particularly humiliation of women, and commercialised 'love'. Thus the first scene relates to, but radically shifts evaluation of, Dido's collapse from 'female' passion. Instead of ideological affirmation that women by *nature* have fatally ungovernable desires, these desires are seen to be produced, shaped and exploited by a power structure dominated by men. Jupiter takes from others to give to Ganymede, Aeneas just takes; Dido gives all. Jupiter can choose the sex object he prefers, Aeneas can leave; Dido, Anna, the Nurse either cannot choose their sexual objects or cannot fulfil their desires.

Dido questions how power facilitates desire: it refuses the mystification of male innocence in a world dominated by men. It also refuses the sexual tease, the cross-gender scenes, which boys' plays are capable of, for the dramatic thrill of the same-sex seduction aids in the policing of desire: the near-sodomy is produced by disorder in the plot and will be avoided when all comes right or 'truth' is revealed. *Dido* begins with the fact of Jupiter's sodomy and shows it to be truer to male sexual contact – with women – than moralist writings allowed.

Marlowe's 'compulsion' could still be argued to be present at a different level of the representation, since the play makes male sex

objects, in particular Aeneas: the text has the boy actor lovingly
dressed on stage. At the same time the scenic construction works
powerfully to draw Aeneas alongside Ganymede and Cupid, all alike
as sex objects who get what they want. The failures are the 'female'
sex objects. The text homosexualises male success, the empire-builder
is also sex object; this staging contradicts an ideology that sees the
man as the lover and the author of love discourse directed at another,
for he in turn may be desired; it unsettles a belief that men represent
a *quality*, whereas women can be reduced to their physicality. These
possibilities question representation of male power in that there may
be something beyond the controlling male look. I suspect this
uncertainty about the way male figures are being looked at
contributes to the anxiety about Marlowe's 'obsession'.

The sexualising of the male becomes more unsettling in texts for
adult actors, since the gender divisions may be more clearly marked
with boys only as women. The best example of this is the temptation
of Theridamas in *1 Tamburlaine*. The scene looks like simple bribery,
with the loot laid out and Tamburlaine's talk of money and power.
Yet Techelles notes that Theridamas's 'deep affections make him
passionate' (I. ii. 164), writing passion into the scene's expectations;
and Tamburlaine notes the majesty of his looks. Theridamas feels
enticed by 'strong enchantments' and admits he is 'Won with thy
words and conquered with thy looks' (l. 228). Rhetorical words are
designed to 'win', but the 'looks' raise a problem. Tamburlaine may
still be wearing rich armour but he says 'Jove sometime masked in
a shepherd's weed' (l. 199) as if to explain himself. Zenocrate had
earlier been impressed with his appearance. The 'looks' may not be
just a promise of wealth; and indeed wealth is marginalised by the
terms of the final allegiance gesture:

Thus shall my heart be still combined with thine,
Until our bodies turn to elements,
And both our souls aspire celestial thrones.

(ll. 235–7)

The men holding hands suggests fealty-swearing, a common scene
(see Fleischer, 1974), yet the language also implies betrothal
(Greenblatt also notes this is a 'passionate' love scene (in Kernan,
1977, p. 56)).

The looks of Tamburlaine twice work on apparent enemies;
during the scene he dresses himself (at least once). While he puts
on captured armour he talks to Zenocrate, transforming himself
while he talks. This has the effect of drawing attention to the speaker
rather than the spoken to, visually centring him: he is both powerful

speaking presence and object to be looked at, yet what he wears is illegal, is dressing up, non-authoritative. Tamburlaine as much as Aeneas, I would suggest, is fetishistically dressed. When this happens the text locks the viewer into a contradiction between (narcissistic) identification with Tamburlaine (the star actor, the successful leader unlike Mycetes) and specular pleasure in Tamburlaine as erotic object to be looked at (see the terms used by Flitterman, 1981, p. 247). This difficulty experienced in theatrical viewing foregrounds a problem about maleness. The scene is not just a tactical tempting of an enemy, but is structured so that what happens to Zenocrate balances Theridamas (see Hattaway, 1982, p. 58). Zenocrate is represented as the silenced woman on the margin of a formed male–male relationship. Zenocrate with the treasure has object status, Theridamas promises social power. The male group forms around Theridamas; the women, prisoners, money are piled up elsewhere. Again masculinity is associated with wealth and power, a power consolidated by male mutual appreciation to the exclusion of women.

It could be argued that Marlowe explores a contradiction within thinking about sodomy, for sodomy between clowns and commoners passes without note. In rulers sodomy matters because it apparently marks an improper excess of desire, as in Mycetes or Henry III. Dominant ideology suggests that the male ruler's sexual interest in other men is a deviation from true rule; but Tamburlaine's interest in Theridamas is a consolidation of his power. Within patriarchy men maintain an exclusive power, so the real object of their desire is in fact male achievement: this is misrepresented, or deflected, by attacks on sodomy, which aim to affirm masculine power by seeing the proper man as rational against disordering female desire. But in the Marlowe plays the relationships of Jupiter and Ganymede or Tamburlaine and Theridamas are seen to be based on economic and military gain – the relationships are shaped by the interests of masculine social power. It is the economics of gender power rather than an ascribed nature of gender which shapes social relations.

Edward II centres the issue of sodomy. The choice of emphasis is largely Marlowe's. The unnamed homoeroticism of Tamburlaine is named in *Edward*, but at the same time the play challenges its value. Edward's language is gendered female when it talks of mythology and role-play, Lancaster and others describe it as 'passions'. The prison-cell agonising about kingship is said to be a waste of time, embarrassing in front of the silent messengers; the attempt to move Lightborn is redundant. Against this Edward can speak the language of the sword. He is inconsistently masculine. Thus when Elder Mortimer lists the 'mightiest kings' who 'have had their minions' – 'Great Alexander', 'conquering Hercules', 'stern Achilles' – the adjectives are important as a contrast with Edward (I. iv. 393–6). The two Mortimers are used to discuss the terms on which manliness accepts sodomy. Elder Mortimer argues Edward should 'freely enjoy' Gaveston because he 'promiseth as much as we can wish' (ll. 401–2) – the terms of 'personal' freedom are measured, the ideology of the 'free' individual questioned. Younger Mortimer cannot forgive Gaveston's base birth nor the spending of national wealth, but is unoffended by the 'wanton humour'. The allowed sodomy conforms to the established structures of wealth and class . . . plus ça change.

The 'humour' is seen as a passing phase, a 'toy', the dismissable personal disorder. But Edward replaces Gaveston with Spenser and he desires more fiercely the more he is opposed. Moralistic history notes only the fatal effects of personal desire in a 'wilful' or 'humorous' monarch, but it does not ask what produces the 'humour' nor what shapes it. Marlowe's text explores the connections of personal and social, and the shaping of disorder by 'order' (rather than vice versa). 'Love' is structured within reward and patronage in the play: Gaveston and Isabella both feel themselves *robbed* of Edward. It is spoken by discourses of 'public' diplomacy and 'private' emotion, leading to the contradiction of barons whose 'loving' is ironised early on and overtly violent later. Competitive discrimination is, contradictorily, inscribed into the expression of 'love': 'I love him more' says Isabella 'Than he can Gaveston' (I. iv. 304–5); Edward will love Isabella *if* she loves Gaveston. Thus Edward's defiance: 'They love me not that hate my Gaveston' (II. ii. 37) – his identification with his lover is established and strengthened by opposition.

Interpersonal relations are constructed as competition by masculinity, and Edward's 'humour' is itself thus shaped and strengthened by denial. Not so much a 'toy', the desire is more permanent than its object. The personal disorder of moral biography is here shown to be shaped by the accepted order; the sodomy is not so much an individual case-study of an anomaly but part of a debased form of human relations. The privileged viewpoint of the spectator of moral biography is unsettled, since for most of the play it is difficult to find either an overview or identification point, as the language has no emotional plenitude with its brutal plainness, its devalued 'love', its embarrassing expressiveness. It is a very male play though not an enjoyably male-centred one. Masculinity is not privileged over sodomy: there is little pleasurable or reassuring differentiation between order and disorder, personal and social.

One of the play's most expressive images comes, crucially, at the end. The figure of Edward III is used to close the play, and consequently, I think, is less inspected. His attachment to his father is only explicable as 'natural' feeling, where little else in the play has this status. Yet memory of his father causes him to weep (for the last 70 lines) for which he demands space:

Forbid me not to weep; he was my father,
And had you lov'd him half so well as I,
You could not bear his death thus patiently

(V. vi. 34–6)

The measuring of love repeats an idea; but the tearful memory of a father contrasts with Edward II's memory of his own father, which hardens him. The manliness of Edward III here is a problem: the emotionally expressive, embarrassing tears are not manly; the orders to punish the murderers, while he weeps, are. Edward claims 'in me my loving father speaks' (l. 41), yet 'loving' is a perfunctory word now. The tears, on the other hand, are not shown to be a trick.

The final tableau has Edward putting on mourning robes and offering Mortimer's head to the hearse of his father, asking that his tears 'Be witness of my grief and innocency' (l. 102). The image feels full, but the last word is a problem: how is Edward innocent? He and the country are free of the oppressive protector and the incapable father, and he combines the toughness of the one with the emotionalism of the other. It could be a picture of the proper ruler. At the same time, it is a completely male picture, it suppresses the figure of Isabella with her very different earlier status, it is emotional and brutal. Edward has given the order for death and he is shown to construct the scene, so in this sense he is not innocent. On the one hand the tableau is satisfyingly balanced, but on the other it questions whether any manly male is innocent, whether the blend of emotion and brutality is ever avoidable.

I have let the discussion of sodomy return to manliness in following the narrative of *Edward II*. What that discussion has avoided is any question of the naturalness of being manly, an evasion facilitated by thinking in terms of sodomitic disorder versus manly order. Yet the doubts about constructed manliness at *Edward's* end are given force by the earlier project of *2 Tamburlaine*, with which I shall finish. For the follow-up to the conquest play concerns consolidation, the wooing is followed by training sons. Tamburlaine warns that his sons will not inherit 'unless thou bear / A mind courageous and invincible' (*2 Tamburlaine*, I. iv. 72–3), and he sets about building this. The historical specificity of this idea is late Elizabethan concern over royal succession and factional squabble over candidates for rule. Most succession plays press the urgency of the problem by showing a sick father, but Marlowe's text shows how personal rule reproduces itself through an unquestioned ideology of leadership.

The play, however, does question by setting up debate: Zenocrate suggests that Tamburlaine's description of brutality 'Dismays their minds before they come to prove / The wounding troubles angry war affords', but her son Celebinus says 'these are speeches fit for us' (ll. 86–8). The woman speaks of 'proving', experiencing; the young man of 'fitness', observation of rules. Talking of proving, Zenocrate is like Abigail who learns from 'experience', even like Dido who is emotionally distressed by Aeneas's brutal description of the destruction of Troy. This is not 'female' emotion against 'male' reason, but experience – one form of knowledge – against inherited rules – another. So the grimness in Tamburlaine's final lesson in manliness, the killing of the cowardly Calyphas, comes in the emphasis on rule. To those who plead for Calyphas he says: 'Know ye not yet the argument of arms?' and goes on to speak of himself as a conqueror: 'I must apply myself to fit those terms' (IV. i. 98, 153). Manliness is an argument, a rhetorical construction, to be learnt. The 'terms' precede the person and shape him. Constructed according to rules, the manly man still practises real violence. In the centre of the play, father and sons construct a memorial to their dead mother, fixing her in art and writing. Then they break off and Tamburlaine talks at great length about military matters, ending by cutting his arm to teach them fit courage. While he speaks and while he privileges the image of himself, a destroyed town burns and Zenocrate's hearse is on stage. The manliness is experienced by the audience as a tiresome speech and a flash piece of theatre, suppressing mention of the contradictions in the deaths it mourns and makes.

In these ways the order that is manliness is alienated. Its claim to express the inner person in social action is shown as a repression of experience and a construction of an inner person, not so much expressed as trained. In particular, manliness invents pictures of women and denies them feelings. These sorts of ideas seem to me altogether more complex than homosexual 'compulsion' would describe.

References

BEVINGTON, D.M. *From 'Mankind' to Marlowe* (Cambridge, MA, Harvard University Press, 1962).

FLEISCHER, M.H. *The Iconography of the English History Play* (Salzburg, Salzburg Studies, 1974).

FLITTERMAN, S. 'Woman, Desire and the Look: Feminism and the Enunciative Apparatus in Cinema', in J. CAUGHIE (ed.), *Theories of Authorship* (London, Routledge and Kegan Paul, 1981).

HATTAWAY, M. *Elizabethan Popular Theatre* (London, Routledge and Kegan Paul, 1982).

KERNAN, A. (ed.) *Two Renaissance Mythmakers* (Baltimore, MD, Johns Hopkins University Press, 1977).

LOVELL, T. 'Writing Like a Woman – a Question of Politics', in F. BAKER et al. (eds), *The Politics of Theory* (Colchester, Essex University Press, 1983).

MARKS, E. and DE COURTIVRON, I. *New French Feminisms* (Brighton, Harvester, 1981).

ONG, W.J. *Orality and Literacy* (London, Methuen, 1982).

5 'Play the Sodomites, or Worse': *Dido Queen of Carthage**

JONATHAN GOLDBERG

A decade after interpreting Marlowe's sexual dissidence as mere shadow-play (Chapter 3), Jonathan Goldberg returned to the question of sodomy with a new sense of its radical potential to deconstruct categories of gender and power. His chapter on *Dido Queen of Carthage* forms part of a study of male homosexuality in Anglo-American culture, and was expressly written in reaction to Simon Shepherd's cooption of Marlowe to contemporary gay and lesbian politics (Chapter 4). Ironically, however, Goldberg now asserts that Shepherd underestimates Marlowe's transgressive potential, because his view of homosexuality simply replicates heterosexual power relations, with effeminised lovers, such as Edward, Mycetes, or Henri III, dominated by macho men. By contrast, Goldberg interprets Marlowe's earliest play (written to be performed entirely by boys) as a dramatisation of institutions – school, army, and theatre – themselves constructed upon sodomy, the 'unmentionable sin' that unravels every power system, including the imperialism of which it is the 'dirty secret truth'. When Aeneas deserts Dido, therefore, he rejects not only the effeminisation of men by women, but heterosexuality itself. The empire of Cecil Rhodes and Baden Powell is an enterprise that will depend, we infer, on the sodomy with which Marlowe opens his play, when Jupiter 'dandles Ganymede upon his knee', and which is then simulated with a catalogue of different boys throughout. In the words of William Empson, Marlowe's drama thus 'insists that the illicit is the proper thing to do', and the effect is to demolish the heterosexism that separates a 'masculine' state from the 'effeminate' stage. Goldberg's interpretation illustrates Marlowe's explosive relevance to modern debate: in this case, specifically the controversy over gays and the military in Britain and America.

---

* Extracted from *Sodometries: Renaissance Texts, Modern Sexualities* (Stanford, CA, Stanford University Press, 1992), 125–43.

> Like frantic Juno will I fill the earth
> With ghastly murmur of my sighs and cries,
> For never doted Jove on Ganymede
> As much as he on cursèd Gaveston.
>
> (*Edward II*, 1.4.178–81)

Isabella's reference to Jove and Ganymede recalls the opening scene of Marlowe's *Dido Queen of Carthage*, where the curtains of the discovery space are drawn to reveal *'Jupiter dandling Ganymede upon his knee'* (1.1.sd). With the exception of Simon Shepherd, Marlowe's critics have attempted to ignore that scene, treating it as an embarrassment, a joke, or a symptom of his 'pathological' condition.[1] As Shepherd argues, however, that opening has everything to do with the play that follows: '*Dido* begins with the fact of Jupiter's sodomy and shows it to be truer to male sexual contact – with women – than moralist writings allowed.'[2] In Shepherd's account, the predatory nature of the sodomitical relationship between Jupiter and Ganymede discloses a power relationship constitutive of masculinity and male desire, not its aberration, and not to be distanced from masculinity in its more usual form, as when, for example, Aeneas abandons Dido. Shepherd thus points to an overturning in the sexual sphere congruent with Greenblatt's arguments about race, religion, economy, and knowledge in *The Jew of Malta* or *Doctor Faustus*. Sodomy, Shepherd contends, founds masculinity; rather than its negation, it is its truth. This argument could be put beside William Empson's crystalline remark that Marlowe insists on the *properness* of behaviors and beliefs stigmatized as fundamentally antisocial, for Shepherd also calls into question moralistic judgments and the stability of the ontological categories upon which they are supposed to rest. Valuably, Shepherd marshals sodomy against homophobic discourses, not least of all that to be found in much of the criticism of Marlowe.

Insofar as Shepherd sees sodomy as a deconstitutive locus, his argument parallels one about the work that sodomy, that confused category, can do. Shepherd also notes that *Dido* 'refuses the sexual tease, the cross-gender scenes, which boys' plays are capable of' (p. 201), that cross-dressing is not how Marlowe represents male/male desire. For Shepherd, however, this refusal to disguise sodomy under some more acceptable form of sexual relation serves to expose the fundamental sameness of sexual experience. Paradoxically, Shepherd reads Marlowe's stance as achieving precisely the same purpose that cross-dressed scenes are taken to serve by critics who read boys and women as identical to each other. For Shepherd, the power relationship is the same one in both cases. Thus when he looks for instances of sodomy in Marlowe, he finds them in effeminized men, 'bad kings' (p. 199) like Henry III or Mycetes in *Tamburlaine*, or, more generally, in any man who displays 'female' emotion, or any man put into the 'feminine' position of being the object of the sexual gaze of another man. While such scenes deconstruct ontological differences between male and female, in Shepherd's reading of them, they nonetheless preserve the gendered structure of power relations. Hence, Shepherd can argue that sodomy is the truth of heterosexuality because he understands male/male relations as versions of the power differential in male/female ones, and because he writes the less empowered male into the female position.

How easily this view of homosexuality can become homophobic (rather than serving as a weapon against the homophobia and misogyny that conflate the position of women with the sodomite) is evident in a recent essay by David Lee Miller on 'Hero and Leander'.[3] Like Shepherd, Miller has a commitment to revealing the male oppression of women. For him this happens not only in Leander's treatment of Hero, but also in the narrator's investment in Leander. Miller shares Shepherd's supposition that for a man to look with desire at another places the one gazed upon in a female position. This view is not entirely supported by the poem; Leander may think Neptune has mistaken him for a woman when he attempts to embrace him, but he has not: the sea god thinks he is seizing Ganymede. (The difference between Leander and Neptune here parallels that between Gaveston and Edward II.) In Miller's view, Leander is represented as both masculine (with Hero) and feminine (with the narrator), the site of what then gets termed the 'bisexuality' of the privileged masculine view of the poem (p. 763). In other words, Miller takes the homosexual gaze of 'Hero and Leander' to be the normative locus of male domination. Marlowe's poem becomes a piece of evidence for the timeless structure that psychoanalysis reveals; so doing, and fully within the grip of that discourse, Miller scapegoats homosexuality as the source of gender oppression (of the oppression of women; Miller never considers the discrimination against gay men rife in our culture, or against sodomites in Marlowe's). Shepherd, on the other hand, takes the same structure (of the gaze, of gender oppression) to be the site of a protofeminist intervention that Marlowe is performing. Rather than condemning Marlowe as a perpetrator, he sees him, from the vantage point of (his) sodomy, seeing through the structures of oppression.

In commendably seeking to forge an alliance between feminist and antihomophobic work, Shepherd's argument nonetheless runs the danger of supplying ammunition for Miller's argument. For Shepherd also thinks that the traffic in women is a ruse for male desire for other men; embracing sodomy as the nasty secret of all male sexuality, whatever its object, Shepherd sees Edward as feminized: 'Edward's language is gendered female when he talks of mythology and role-play'; he is 'inconsistently masculine' (p. 204). *Edward II*, he says, 'centres the issue of sodomy' (p. 204); 'the sodomy' of Edward and his lovers, Shepherd argues, 'is not so much an individual case-study of an anomaly but part of a debased form of human relations. . . . Masculinity is not privileged over sodomy: there is little pleasurable or reassuring differentiation between order and disorder, personal and social' (p. 205). Masculinity, as Shepherd sees it, involves male competition and oppression; the peers, in his view, condemn Edward but condone male/male relations so long as power differentials are maintained. True enough: but, for Shepherd, for Edward to be a sodomite, he must be both male and female, and the sodomy the peers condemn in him is his effeminization.

This is, undoubtedly, a route of homophobia. But it is therefore important not to collapse all sexuality, as Shepherd does in marking Edward as 'inconsistently masculine', into the same sexuality. Certainly, Shepherd is right to view sodomy as the 'center' of the play, and one that decenters it; a center without a center, a void, sodomy ruins difference. But it also allows for difference – sexual difference, gender difference – and allows for ways of conceiving sexual relations and gender construction that cannot be reduced to the normative structure of male/female relations under the modern regimes of heterosexuality.

The complexity in defining sexuality and gender in Marlowe lies in the ungroundedness – the undecidability – of these differences. By this, I don't mean to deny power differentials or to suppose some utopian state of egalitarianism can be found in Marlowe. Rather, I would recall Empson's fundamental insight: Marlowe affirms *as proper* what his society sees as warranting death: his unflinching representation of the death of Edward is one sign of this, a making manifest of sodomy as the ungrounded truth of the play. So doing, Marlowe glimpses the destruction of the social as constituted; what he is affirming is not something that can be taken into the social order, not its secret other, not its dark truth. This is what makes it difficult to use categorical terms which are themselves always under pressure, to treat male and female, masculinity and femininity, hetero- and homosexuality as ontologically pregiven rather than as in the process of a deconstitutive construction that also must be thought through in its historic specificity, for sodomy is not homosexuality *tout court*, nor are male/female relations of alliance the same as heterosexuality.

Further consideration of *Dido Queen of Carthage* will clarify these arguments. The play begins in a way that would seem to support Shepherd, since the relationship between Jupiter and Ganymede is explicitly positioned against women, against Juno: 'Come, gentle Ganymede, and play with me. / I love thee well, say Juno what she will' (1.1.1–2). Jupiter titillates Ganymede with sadistic promises to rack his queen. By the end of their scene together, he also performs an action that is repeated throughout the play, giving gifts to the boy, a feather from the wings of the sleeping Mercury who lies at his feet, and, even more spectacularly, the 'linkèd gems / My Juno ware upon her marriage day' (ll. 42–3). This is, explicitly, 'theft' (l. 45), and the point seems equally explicit. To legitimize the illicit relationship opposed by Juno, Jupiter marries his 'sweet wag' (l. 23), or, more accurately, appropriates a sign of marriage for their relationship. A moment later, Venus arrives, complaining that in toying with Ganymede, Jupiter has forgotten the plight of her son, pursued by avenging Juno. Venus accuses Jupiter of 'playing with that female wanton boy' (l. 51), Ganymede, when he should be attending to her 'sweet boy' (l. 74), Aeneas.

The movement of this opening scene, brief as it is, is extraordinarily slippery. It begins in a misogyny that structures the relationship between Jupiter and Ganymede as an opposition to Juno – an opposition to women, but, more particularly, to his wife, to marriage and the goddess who represents that social institution. It slides into a misogyny based on the appropriation of the relationship between Jupiter and his wife. Venus castigates this simulated marriage, and in her scorn for the 'female . . . boy', she redirects Jupiter to *her* boy, to a proper male/male relationship rather than the improper one. Venus is a moralist at this moment, and she is also the voice of antitheatricality, attacking the cross-dressed boy who has been turned into a woman, or has been given the attributes of a woman. Antitheatricalists, following Tertullian, regularly term the theater a court of Venus; here, in a typically Marlovian twist, Venus has their voice. Indeed, as she calls Jupiter to attend to the claims of empire, she echoes the final pages of Stephen Gosson's *School of Abuse*, which argue that rather than wasting their time in the theater, young men should be training in arms and entering military careers.

There is, in the opening lines of the play, a route from sodomy to masculinity, but it is not the direct one in which male/female relations are seamlessly superimposed on male/male ones. The route from one male/male relation (Jupiter and Ganymede's) to another (Jupiter and Aeneas's) is structured by Venus's antitheatrical response to the relationship between Jupiter and Ganymede, and it passes through and is mobilized by the misogyny that is attached to male/male relationships in which one male plays the part of a woman. Perverse moralist, Venus is not staking out a claim for marriage, for she opposes Juno, but she is insisting on male/male relations (the promotion of Aeneas's career) that follow from maintaining gender propriety in the sexual sphere. Thus, the movement in this brief scene suggests both the similarity of male/male and male/female relations and their difference. If Ganymede can be dressed in female attire, it is because of the differences in age and power between the god and his boy; these provide the transfer point so that their relationship parodies Jove's marriage to Juno. But this is also a transformation of the relationship as originally conceived, where Jupiter's relationship to Ganymede represents an antithesis to his marriage to Juno, not its simulation.

The play that follows never recovers that oppositional moment; rather, its structuring effect leads to the representation of male/female relations caught up within simulation. Dido repeatedly invests her relationship to Aeneas with all the signs of her former marriage. If this theatricalization initially stays within the proprieties of gender – in their first meeting, she clothes him in the garb of Sichaeus (2.1.80) – later, when she actually renames him Sichaeus, she simultaneously gives him the jewels and the wedding ring that Sichaeus had given her (3.4.58–63). This cross-gendering culminates when she crowns Aeneas in her place, and retiring within, sends him into the streets of Carthage to be king in her place (4.4.35–92). These are scenes of a displaced cross-dressing, versions of the scene between Jupiter and Ganymede excoriated by Venus. Played out between a man and a woman they effectively challenge what either gender can be under the heterosexual regime of a Venus. If they look like the cross-dressed relation of Jupiter and Ganymede, it would appear that the parody is already installed in 'natural' relations.

As in the *Aeneid*, Aeneas enters the walls of Carthage by passing through a picture gallery; the image of heroic masculinity that he represents is reenacted throughout the play – in his refusal of the relation with Dido and, with that, a defense against women and against effeminization. The simulation of marriage is disallowed, not in order to defend the proprieties of marriage (Venus opposes Juno), but to expose marriage as a deforming institution, for men *and* for women. When Venus lures Jupiter to aid her son, Jupiter warmly responds in his vision of 'bright Ascanius, beauty's better work' (1.1.96), as if the refusal of marriage could lead back to his original idyll with Ganymede. Similarly, when Aeneas looks at the image of Priam on the walls of Carthage, and believes it is really Priam that he sees, his son knows better: 'Sweet father, leave to weep. This is not he, / For were he Priam he would smile at me' (2.1.35–36). Ascanius casts the true relationship with Priam as a version of the relation of Ganymede and Jupiter. Jupiter dreams of a futurity modeled like Ascanius's recognition on an irrecoverable past. Such futurity is thought of in a pedophiliac vein, Ascanius as a replacement for, or a version of, Ganymede, an attempt in history to recapture the moment upon which the curtains opened as the play began, a moment as immediately lost, the primal moment that unravels as the opening scene proceeds:

> What is't, sweet wag, I should deny thy youth,
> Whose face reflects such pleasure to mine eyes,
> As I, exhaled with thy fire-darting beams,
> Have oft driven back the horses of the night,
> Whenas they would have haled thee from my sight.
>
> (1.1.23–27)

So Jupiter describes the initial idyll, that refusal of temporality that also marks Ganymede's original mythic status: a mortal who achieves eternal youth without ever having to die. The very violation of the conditions of human being here is the deontological ground of an impossibility unthinkable within the licit, not even thinkable as the miming (il)licit of cross-dressing.

These opening lines glance at a desire that echoes throughout the play in the substitution of Cupid for Ascanius; over and again, Dido plays with the boy as Jupiter had with Ganymede. That attempted replay of Jupiter's part is as impossible for her as it is for him to recapture the lost idyll, and for similar reasons: just as Venus voices a redirection of male/male desire through the route of its abuse as the abuse of women, so Dido, as a woman limited by the possibilities of marriage or its simulation, is incapable of taking on Jupiter's role. Her attempt at simulation is her undoing. The original relationship between Jupiter and Ganymede, like the sodomy in *Edward II*, initiates simulations – it is the groundless ground upon which simulation thrives; thereby it opens difference.

This is clearest when Dido crowns Aeneas and gives him her throne; acting like Jupiter, she constitutes him *as* Jupiter: 'Now looks Aeneas like immortal Jove', she says, 'O where is Ganymede to hold his cup / And Mercury to fly for what he calls?' (4.4.45–47). Dido's self-abandonment implicitly includes an acknowledgment of just what makes her abandonment inevitable, the difference between her relationship with Aeneas and Jupiter's hold on him as the vehicle of his desire. Aeneas attempts in this scene, as elsewhere in the play, to refuse what Dido offers; 'O keep them still' (l. 44), she insists, referring to crown and sceptre, and by extension, everything with which she has invested him. The nature of Aeneas's resistance is registered a scene earlier, in his first attempt to abandon Dido. To Achates' call that

> This is no life for men-at-arms to live,
> Where dalliance doth consume a soldier's strength,
> And wanton motions of alluring eyes
> Effeminate our minds, inured to war

(4.3.33–36)

– lines that recall both Gosson's charge that theater effeminates the mind as well as his call to arms – Aeneas responds, 'I may not dure this female drudgery' (l. 55). Effeminization, not his reconstitution as Jupiter, lies at the hands of Dido. In the hands of Jupiter, Aeneas abandons his desire for Dido. The heroism he embraces is not allowed to recover a sodomy untarnished by the ways in which it is deformed by the pursuit of his proper career. Made to serve Jupiter's sodomitical vision, he comes closest to avowing it as his own when Ascanius is restored to him – and he is reprimanded by Mercury for doing so: 'Spendst thou thy time about this little boy, / And givest not ear unto the charge I bring?' (5.1.51–52). Aeneas is not allowed any desire except to heed the imperial call; he is positioned at the crossroads of the conflicting desires of Dido (to undo marriage, to be Jupiter) and of Jupiter (to undo marriage, to be Jupiter without Juno and attached to Ganymede or his historical avatars). As the site where these impossible desires cross, Aeneas embodies a hollowed-out heroic masculinity.

In the highly charged final scene between Dido and Aeneas, Marlowe allows Virgil's Latin text into his own, has Aeneas say, *'Italiam non sponte sequor'* (5.1.140, 'I do not pursue Italy of my own volition'. Aeneas speaks Latin in response to Dido's Latin, and at the end of the play, concluding her suicide speech, Dido speaks Virgil's lines again, to foretell unremitting war between Carthage and Rome. 'Live, false Aeneas! Truest Dido dies!' she continues, ending in Virgil's Latin: *'Sic, sic juvat ire sub umbras'* (5.1.312–13), 'Thus, thus, I am pleased to go beneath the shades.' Dido's truth is that she has been spoken by the Virgilian text. Marlowe, having rewritten that text so that it begins with the scene between Jupiter and Ganymede, and ends with a series of imitative suicides that follow Dido's, claims, citing Virgil, that his text coincides with his source. In his rewriting, Juno's ire is caused by her husband's relation with Ganymede (see 3.2.40), and Dido's by Aeneas's role in furthering Jupiter's pedophiliac empire. If, as Shepherd argues, sodomy structures heterosexuality, it does so insofar as Dido's desire – as woman's desire – simulates it.

This simulation is oppositional even as it is imitative. Like Isabella, Dido plays the sodomite, cloaking adultery in the (cross-dressed) trappings of marriage. Her illicit desire cannot be made licit, and not least because relations between men and women are seen as and represented as leading to the effeminization of men. But her relationship cannot be the sodomitical one of male/male relations either, for her gender under the presumptive sexual regimes of Juno and of Venus bars her from that.

Aeneas's abandonment of Dido, and his desire for her, are written into Marlowe's delegitimation of heterosexual relations as a deforming of masculinity, of men's relations with women and with other men. Aeneas's misogyny, which is also an antitheatricality, and an opposition to cross-dressed relationships (he speaks not only with Gosson's voice, but also with his mother's), serves a desire that is also not Aeneas's own, not a function of his volition, but of the cultural impossibility of desire as constructed within the protoheterosexism of empire-building. This does not justify Aeneas's abandonment of Dido – despicable from any angle – but it does register his impossible position, for he also has been abandoned by women, and first of all by Venus, who nonetheless propels his career. (One need not read this as merely a misogynist instance supposedly showing what women do to men but also as displaying what the institutional possibilities for women – marriage, adultery, motherhood – do to both women and men.) At the end of the play Aeneas is able to leave Carthage thanks to Iarbas, the man who hopes to marry Dido once his rival is out of the way, and Iarbas's suicide is one of those that Marlowe adds to the plot. A rivalry between men for a woman translates into an alliance of heterosexuality and misogyny. The sodomitical order is also a misogynistic one, but it, not heterosexuality, lends Dido's voice its power – and its pathos. She, unlike Aeneas, but like Jupiter, is a site of volition. A true Marlovian hero, her situation is even more untenable than that of Edward II. She is the locus of a double negation, structured by heterosexual and homosexual misogyny, and the implacable hate that she voices, to her own undoing, is the oppositional ground on which she stands, one that depends upon the identity and difference of these doubled and divided desires. What she wants even Jupiter barely can have (he loses it almost as soon as he starts talking; it is an irrecoverable past). In this play, there can be no marriages, not even the one simulated by Jupiter and Ganymede. (Jupiter's gift-giving only provokes Ganymede to ask for more.) Aeneas, too, is doubly divided and undone; the false life which is his truth comes from occupying a position between Jupiter and Dido, between sodomitical desire and a heterosexuality that simulates it and opposes it, as cross-dressing does too, and that is destructured by misogyny. Neither desire is his own, and the pursuit of fame and glory, a soldier's life in the service of empire, rests upon the doubled negations that lead him to say of himself, what I do is not of my volition.

'The definition of gender is shaped by the project of empire', Shepherd astutely writes (p. 195). Aeneas, the empire builder, is sent on his way by a misogyny that is doubly structured, by sodomy and by heterosexual relations (between men and women and as they restructure male/male relations and mark the impossibility of sodomy), a structure of identity and difference that produces man and woman as opposing categories, neither of them self-identical nor identical to each other. There is no place in this structure for the 'female . . . boy'. The play rehearses antitheatrical arguments and endorses them as the grounds for its scandalously improper proper, sodomy that is not assimilable to heterosexuality or to heterosexist homophobia. Aeneas is not effeminized and, despite himself, he resists Dido's simulations. His pursuit of empire serves Jove's and Venus's designs, but it is not propelled by his own sodomitical desires. If sodomy is the secret of Aeneas's heterosexist misogyny, as Shepherd contends, it is a secret precisely because its articulation could only repeat Venus's response to the initial scene of the play, the homophobia that sees sodomy as a travesty and as a transvestite version of heterosexuality. In this play, written to be performed by boys, and arising out of an educational system whose summit was the kind of familiar translation of Latin that Marlowe reveals in the play (a pedagogy that is also pedophiliac in its structure),[4] Marlowe aligns a number of all-male institutions – the school, the acting companies, the military – that constitutionally depend on not recognizing their propinquity to the unmentionable sin. That sin is more than mentioned in the play; it opens it and structures what follows. But if sodomy is the truth in the play, the truth of empire, it can be recognized within the licit only as the illicit, as the dirty secret. Here again, what Empson says of *Edward II* is true, that Marlowe sees the illicit as the proper thing to do, even gives it its own authorizing voice in Virgil's Latin text. That improper proper, in quite different ways, structures the relationship of Dido and Aeneas as the site where false and true meet and divide, the restructured difference between heterosexuality and homosexuality.

The play's project is radically conceived, not least in its deformations of the institutional and textual sites upon which it rests. As in *Edward II*, more than overturning is involved as the play drives towards a truth that undermines categorical oppositions even as it regrounds them in a volition that can never be made legitimate. The situation here is like the one that Jonathan Crewe argues for in an analysis of the relationship between *Tamburlaine* and antitheatricality. 'The issue of Tamburlaine's cultural egregiousness', Crewe writes, just those qualities that the antitheatricalists fasten on, and akin to the monstrosity of desire revealed in *Edward II* or *Dido Queen of Carthage*, 'is continuously renegotiated within the play, and in being so, seemingly brings within the realm of the negotiable most of the constitutive categories of Elizabethan cultural and political order' (p. 327).

Dido Queen of Carthage takes on a number of those categories, most crucially the question of the construction of gender in its relationship to theater and to the imperial project. Effectively, it rewrites Gosson's *School of Abuse*, even as it appears to echo it. Posing itself against cross-dressing, it aligns the career of the empire builder with the heterosexist misogyny that founds masculinity on the resistance to effeminization – the effect of woman on man – and against this it offers the scandal of sodomy as the possibility of a difference unthinkable within the discourse of the licit. The play offers a reading of the conjunction of a cultural and a political order, theater and empire, that structures Gosson's tract, and destructures its premises: that theater effeminates the mind; that military exploits are properly masculine.

[...]

It has been my assumption throughout this chapter that Marlowe's radical rethinking of the possibility of being a sodomite was not widely shared in his time, that the deconstructive energies he bequeaths are not assimilable to the subsequent discourses of sexual difference. But by this I do not mean to suggest Marlowe's singularity save in the value he attached to what his culture so vehemently opposed. Hence, it is possible, imperative, to recognize in Marlowe a site of political resistance. To recognize too that this could have literary consequences. A rereading of Elizabethan drama through what Marlowe makes available might be undertaken, and even Shakespeare would be implicated.

[...]

The route to such rethinking is not through cross-dressing as it has been understood; the way to understand these relations lies in the discourse of sodomy, and Marlowe provides leverage upon such relations. One might see, then, that what cross-dressing in Shakespeare defends itself against is not only effeminization but something even more threatening, something that can resist assimilation to the logic of heterosexual simulation.

Notes

1. To the critics cited in SIMON SHEPHERD, *Marlowe and the Politics of Elizabethan Theatre* (New York, St Martin's Press, 1986) might be added JACKSON COPE, 'Marlowe's *Dido* and the Titillating Children', *English Literary Review*, 4 (1974), pp. 315–25. Cope sees that the opening scene responds to antitheatrical arguments about boys and to the fact that boys were impressed, giving further grounds for suppositions of abuse, but he nonetheless regards the opening scene as farce.

2. SHEPHERD, *Marlowe and the Politics of Elizabethan Theatre*, p. 201. Further citations appear parenthetically in the text.

3. 'The Death of the Modern: Gender and Desire in Marlowe's "Hero and Leander"', *SAQ*, 88 (1989), pp. 757–87.

4. For the special pertinence of Ganymede to humanism, see LEONARD BARKAN, *Transuming Passion* (Stanford, CA, Stanford University Press, 1991), pp. 48–59, 67–74.

6 The Theatre of the Idols: Marlowe, Rankins, and Theatrical Images*

JONATHAN CREWE

Marlowe's rebel status had been constructed by Victorian critics to accord with a sentimental idea of the Elizabethan playhouse as a site of riot and delinquence, in resistance to the Puritan authorities. A key insight of New Historicism, however, born of the American entertainments industry, is that culture is never simply set over against power, but is (as Stephen Greenblatt writes) 'one of power's essential modes'. That art and power reinforce each other is the theme of Jonathan Crewe's reading of *Tamburlaine the Great*, which views Marlowe's megalomaniac protagonist as an embodiment not of repulsive abnormality, but of society's unacknowledged desires. So, by making such monstrosities, Marlowe was presenting Londoners with idols of themselves, yet thereby incorporating into theatre the very fear and loathing that fuelled Puritan phobia about the playhouse. Just as the enemies of playing, such as William Rankins, betrayed their guilty fascination with drama through their theatrical metaphors, Marlowe therefore projected on to the stage his critics' own worst case. Later dramatists would refine this aversion therapy into a warning of the dangers of performance, but the dynamism of Marlowe's monsters is such that they destroy any safe division between reality and fiction – or civility and barbarism. Crewe's essay reflects a post-modern fixation with the monstrous, but its main stimulus is once more Michel Foucault, who argued that power works not by repression, but by the desires it incites. Sidestepping the old question of whether Marlowe's stage is thereby one of subversion or containment, Crewe interprets the box-office success of *Tamburlaine* as exemplary of Foucault's maxim: power comes not from above, but from below.

No less than that of Shakespeare and Jonson, Marlowe's drama was written in the wake of the antitheatrical campaign initiated in 1579 by Stephen Gosson and pursued by succeeding pamphleteers.[1] With

* Reprinted from *Theatre Journal*, 36 (1984), 321–33.

Tamburlaine, Part 1, then, Marlowe began his career in a cultural and political milieu preconditioned by antitheatricalism. While it might be suggested that Marlowe's drama, like that of his major successors, constitutes a *response* to this antitheatricalism – a simultaneous exploration and defense of the theatrical medium[2] – it is also possible to see both dramatists and antitheatricalists as participants by 1587 in a cultural dialogue about theatre in which questions of chronological priority (of 'attack' and 'response') are not of paramount importance. This will be my assumption in considering the implicit dialogue between Marlowe and the antitheatrical pamphleteer William Rankins, both of whom come on the scene in 1587. My thesis necessarily takes the form of the truism that this dialogue proves inconclusive, yet in propounding that truism I shall examine some of the terms and conditions under which the dialogue proceeds as well as the conceptions of theatre and of the dramatic protagonist around which it revolves.

For both Marlowe and Rankins, the thing at issue is simple but fundamental: what is to be inferred from the nature and above all the magnitude of theatrical images?[3] What does the proliferation and also the scale of such images imply about the culture in which they are produced? For this to have become the thing at issue the authors, of course, had to agree at least tacitly upon the ground of their differences, and substantial agreement of this kind may be perceived between Marlowe (the Marlowe of *Tamburlaine* and *The Jew of Malta* anyway) and Rankins, whose pamphlet entitled *A Mirrour of Monsters* appeared, coincidentally with *Tamburlaine,* Part 1, in 1587.[4] Something like a common cultural anthropology or at least a shared phenomenology necessarily grounds any possible 'debate' about theatre between Marlowe and Rankins.

To say this is not to minimize the degree of political and ideological polarization, even in 1587, around the theatre. But this polarization has traditionally been overemphasized and oversimplified. There was a time when it was said that the Elizabethan antitheatrical campaign was simply a manifestation of Puritan philistinism and sectarian bigotry and was effectively resisted by talented authors. This view was informed by the erroneous belief that Elizabethan pamphleteers and playwrights lived in worlds apart, each speaking a language alien to the other; it was informed by the further belief that Elizabethan antitheatricalism is just one manifestation of an eternal philistinism eternally to be repelled. The antitheatrical attitude – or maybe 'prejudice' – would accordingly have been regarded as an attitude wholly external or alien to the Elizabethan theatre itself.

Now it seems almost self-evident that this reading of the Elizabethan conflict about theatre is a projection into the sixteenth century of the assumptions of nineteenth-century secular aestheticism, a projection that obliterates the facts about Elizabethan plays and cultural history. The defense of drama in the sixteenth century does not confront antitheatricality as an alien phenomenon, but rather acknowledges it as a culturally endemic form of dread to be overcome within the dramatic process. This sixteenth-century defense of drama – conducted more powerfully and systematically in the dramatic literature itself than in expository treatises – is thus always two-faced: the plays that reflect upon and defend theatre against an ostensible antitheatrical 'prejudice' must also embody and virtually become defenses against – or attempted transformations of – the suspect or occult powers of theatre. To the existence of such powers dramatists remain no less committed than do their antitheatrical opponents. Moreover, insofar as the antitheatrical 'prejudice' is culturally constitutive rather than sectarian,[5] and is therefore inescapable, playwrights cannot but stage their own endlessly vexed or divided relation to the subject of that prejudice, namely the theatre itself. And the culturally imputed guilt of theatrical performance, at once denied and betrayed by the very defensiveness of Elizabethan drama, imparts to theatrical defenses the quality of an interminable rationalization.

It is possible to summarize the situation in this way partly because we have become accustomed to recognizing complexities of this order in our reading of Elizabethan dramatic texts. Yet a similar order of complexity, less well-recognized, may be found in antitheatrical texts. While Rankins can draw on powerful sources of authority in his antitheatrical argument, his pamphlet betrays a knowledge of its own belatedness in relation to the *fait accompli* of an overtly theatricalized cultural and political order. The staging and purposes of his argument accordingly become more complicated than they might otherwise be, and Rankins betrays a powerful susceptibility to the phenomena he reviles.[6] Indeed, for him no less than for Marlowe, theatre has virtually come to embody the general problematic of the culture as well as of individual destinies within it, and this implicit concession on Rankins's part gives up more ground than his antitheatrical argument can recover.[7]

Specifically, then, how do Marlowe and Rankins construe the theatrical image? In the case of Rankins, the answer looks easy: *all* theatrical phenomena are 'monstrous', meaning evil, alien, and profoundly threatening to a desired sense of order. This shocked response may reveal something of the sheer novelty and magnitude of staged spectacle in the Elizabethan public theatre, but we may not want to attach too much significance to the charge, at least until the seriousness of its grounding becomes apparent. The charge of 'monstrousness' can be made with varying degrees of intensity or literalness in an Elizabethan context,[8] and there is also a sense in which the monstrous is codified and domesticated in the Elizabethan understanding. The predictable nature and occurrence of the 'monstrous' – to which such authorities as Pliny and St Augustine accustomed Elizabethans[9] – imply the possibility of its continuous regulation by a cultural system of containment and exclusion. Indeed the very threat of the 'monstrous' – of the unassimilably alien or other – functions continuously in the Elizabethan period to define the stable properties of the culture as well as to justify certain political arrangements, whether institutionalized or merely desired. (To speak, for example, of the 'monstrous' regiment of women is to rule out rather than negotiate that possibility.)

Despite what seems to be a continuing anxiety about the 'monstrous', then – can its forms ever fully be stabilized or codified? – an acute dread is not necessarily to be inferred at all times. Yet in Rankins's pamphlet it is as if the threat of the monstrous has suddenly become acute, the phenomenon itself threatening to rupture its containment within the culture and simultaneously to invade from without. Insofar as 'monstrousness' becomes identified with the theatre, that theatre threatens to break out of its containment within the commonwealth and actually to encompass it. Moreover, while monstrousness might seem to belong properly to the biological sphere, it soon becomes evident in Rankins's pamphlet that it exists also in the ideological and social sphere – indeed, it is this derivative or analogical 'monstrousness' rather than the primary biological phenomenon that concerns Rankins.

In Rankins's mind, monstrousness comes to be identified not only with moral transgression and even with demonic possession (anxieties that fuel much Jacobean antitheatricalism, to say nothing of *Dr Faustus*) but also with insupportable transgressions of class and cultural boundaries. To Rankins, the result of such transgressions is the appearance in both the social and the theatrical spheres of new and alien *personae*, ones threatening constitutive cultural definitions of the human. Refusing to acknowledge that *a priori* lawful images and definitions of the human subject (of 'man') might be negotiable within Christian culture and/or within the Elizabethan political world, Rankins perceives only a 'monstrous' threat to those assumed definitions. His perception of such a threat, whether he might have taken it to be manifested in the careers of such Marlovian protagonists as Tamburlaine and Barabas or to be portended by the successful careers of 'upstart' theatrical authors and performers, would only have been reinforced by the startling arrival of Marlowe on the theatrical scene.

This perception of the monstrous is not, however, confined to Rankins's pamphlet or to antitheatricalists, but is also embodied, as the Marlowe concordance shows, in *Tamburlaine* Parts 1 and 2 and *The Jew of Malta* – the two Marlowe plays in which, almost exclusively, that charge is made. To various characters in these plays, both protagonists look monstrous in ways that Rankins would have understood. Predictably, however, the force of the accusation is vitiated by its being generally heard from the plays' losers – the Soldan in *Tamburlaine* or Calymath in *The Jew of Malta*. Even so the charge has been repeated in modern criticism, where the insupportable scandalousness of Marlovian protagonists continues to be registered. Where does Marlowe stand *vis-à-vis* Rankins (or *vis-à-vis* modern critics) on the question of the monstrous?

Even if it could be assumed that he implicitly identifies himself with his protagonists and with everything they represent, thus laughing to scorn the weakly censorious notion that they *are* monstrous, the very poetics of Elizabethan drama would inhibit his capacity to idealize these 'appalling' figures. The conception of the dramatic protagonist, whether tragic or comic, as a negative exemplum is too powerfully entrenched in the sixteenth century for any simple reversal to be probable either at the level of poetic theory or even at that of audience response.[10] (However inclined the audience might be to succumb to the violence and theatrical magnetism of those protagonists, not only Tamburlaine and Barabas but also the audience get 'punished' by the deaths of those protagonists.) For Marlowe to elicit full identification with his 'monsters' would require him to overthrow virtually omnipotent cultural presuppositions of the sixteenth century as well as to purge the attendant anxieties. It is scarcely conceivable that even Marlowe could have fully imagined or desired that full-scale 'liberation'. Indeed, it might seem that the threat of revolutionary change is more anxiously perceived by Rankins than successfully embodied in either the life or works of Marlowe; it might also seem that Marlowe's staged acknowledgment and 'defeat' of threats perceived by Rankins successfully exorcises them rather than fails in an attempt to forestall them. (In which case Marlowe might be taken to defend more effectively against the threat of the 'monstrous' than does Rankins.) However, since pursuit of this line of interpretation can only result in endless question-begging about the 'real' intentions and/or necessary outcome of both authors' work, I shall limit myself to considering the difference that emerges in the constructions that they respectively place upon the 'monstrous'.

Whereas Rankins definitively *classifies* as monstrous all theatrical images and phenomena, Marlowe of course does not; correspondingly,

Rankins seeks simply to preclude the monstrous, whereas Marlowe at least renegotiates its relationship to assumed norms. Although Marlowe seemingly recognizes the destructive potentiality of the monstrous, he also recognizes the possibility that it is not just present *in* the culture but may be constitutive *of* it. The presumed norm may represent the culture's self-alienation or false consciousness, while the monstrous may represent either the 'lost' constitutive powers of the culture itself or else the fundamental truth that dominant cultural fictions belie. In other words, the monstrous rather than the normal may inescapably reveal itself as central to the culture.

A claim of this kind is implicit in Stephen Greenblatt's discussion of Barabas in 'Marlowe, Marx and Anti-Semitism',[11] in which Barabas as alien is taken to embody the inadmissible *truth* not only of the Christian community that reviles him but of the highly energized Renaissance world at large. In *Tamburlaine*, the outlandish Scythian shepherd invades a 'familiar' monarchical order that is either effete (Mycetes) or merely opportunistic (Cosroe). This conventional opposition in the realm of kingship and political order, one that is reproduced in Shakespeare in the opposition between Richard and Bolingbroke, does not in *Tamburlaine* exhaust the political possibilities but rather represents two sides of a bad coin. Not only does Tamburlaine enter and transcend the field of these alternatives, but in doing so he can seem (or claim) to recover culturally constitutive powers – even a 'lost' cultural destiny – the existence of which normally goes unrecognized. The pagan neoclassicism of Tamburlaine's 'Scythian' world, culturally alien only by virtue of a bad paradox under which it may seem archaic, effete, or merely learned, becomes at once the vehicle and the tenor, so to speak, of cultural recovery. Both the 'lawlessness' and the power of those ostensible fictions – superseded, it might seem, only by Christian truth – could facilitate the recovery of an alienated cultural identity.

However that may be, one manifest feature of *Tamburlaine* is the protagonist's movement from an outside to an inside position – from the role of outlaw to that of lawgiver, however 'tyrannical'. Tamburlaine's potential *normativeness* is embodied in the structure of the play and also perceived, even if not consistently so, by those around him. Cosroe asks: 'What stature wields he, and what personage?', to which Menaphon replies:

> Of stature tall, and straightly fashioned,
> Like his desire, lift upwards and divine,
> So large of limbs, his joints so strongly knit,
> Such breadth of shoulders as might mainly bear

Old *Atlas* burthen, twixt his manly pitch,
A pearl more worth, then all the world is plast:
Wherein by curious soverainty of Art,
Are fixt his piercing instruments of sight:
Whose fiery circles beare encompassed,
A heaven of heavenly bodies in their Spheres:
That guides his steps and actions to the throne,
Where honor sits invested royally;
Pale of complexion: wrought in him with passion,
Thirsting with sovereignty and love of arms.

(II. i. 460–474)[12]

The Tamburlaine pictured here (however self-interestedly) by
Menaphon acquires an astounding yet paradoxically ideal or
definitive magnitude. Menaphon's points of reference – Hercules/
Atlas, the geocentric cosmos, ideal monarchy – are all obviously
lawful and even culturally authoritative. In making Tamburlaine
definitively embody this set of images, Menaphon already 'centers'
him, at the same time perhaps unwittingly effecting a cultural
displacement of the hebraic by the hellenic principle (a displacement
that will be repeated in the opposite direction in *The Jew of Malta*).
Menaphon's simultaneous hyperbolic magnification and cultural
'normalization' of Tamburlaine may seem to be facilitated by the
blank verse medium itself, in which a principle of interminable
cumulativeness – hence of inflation without end – coexists with a
metrical rule that bids to become (as in fact it does) the norm for
English dramatic verse. The medium itself, then, may seem to side
with Menaphon's attempt and even to surpass that attempt, enabling
Tamburlaine to continue where Menaphon leaves off. Although
Menaphon's picture will be completed – framed – by his own
attempted closure, the lack of any internal mechanism of arrest
(e.g., the rhyming couplet) means that the boundaries of Menaphon's
representation, which is also an attempted containment of
Tamburlaine, can be violated. In suggesting, moreover, that
Tamburlaine's 'likeness' is not established with reference to any
external paradigm, but only with reference to his *own* desire,
Menaphon's representation embodies a principle of change and
expansion that will rupture it.

This is precisely what occurs when Tamburlaine, paradoxically
redefining the norm, situates himself in an ostensibly lawless or
'imperfect' cosmos in which he is 'alwaies mooving as the restles
Spheares' (II. vi. 876). Then again, refuting Cosroe's attempt to
legitimize his own rule (despite his being a usurper), Tamburlaine
justifies further rebellion by reminding Cosroe that 'the thirst of

raigne and sweetnes of a crowne, / ... causde the eldest sonne of heavenly *Ops*, / To thrust his doting father from his chaire' (II. ii. 863–865). Usurpation and parricide thus get enunciated as the universal rule instead of remaining, perhaps, the secret truth that fictions of legitimacy belie. In short, the issue of Tamburlaine's cultural egregiousness or definitiveness is continuously negotiated within the play, and in being so, seemingly brings within the realm of the negotiable most of the constitutive categories of Elizabethan cultural and political order.

In the context of Rankins's *Mirrour*, it does not really matter how substantial a critique of the protagonist Marlowe may embody in *Tamburlaine* Parts 1 and 2 – how, for example, Tamburlaine may fail to live up to the limitless promise of the blank verse medium, or to make it peculiarly his own – nor does it really matter whether the effect of Marlowe's play would 'really' – given the particular audience – have been to unleash or to exorcise the demonic protagonist. The point is that Tamburlaine at least becomes thinkable, as he does in Menaphon's speech, as the embodiment of the culture's true image(s). A Tamburlaine 'uplifted' by unrepressed desire, by imaginative opportunism rather than preconception, and by his (and his maker's) seemingly guiltless embrace of self-magnifying artifice can appear, at least to some spectators, to be no monster but rather the figure in which the human form divine again manifests itself after a degrading interregnum. This possibility is as evident in Menaphon's speech as is Tamburlaine's participation in an authentic (i.e., erotic rather than chastely alienated or emasculated) relation to the gods: 'About [his shoulders] hangs a knot of Amber haire / ... On which the breath of heaven delights to play' (II. i. 477–479). In almost every sense, Marlowe makes the 'Scythian' – i.e., the conventionally barbarous in Elizabethan terms – not merely oppose but paradoxically represent cultural norms, thus reestablishing a 'lost' or eclipsed scale of perfection. Even if Tamburlaine, like Barabbas, may ultimately seem to embody the madness rather than the higher reason of the culture, that madness can reveal its own constitutive rather than contingent status.

To say all this is to imply that Marlowe, unlike Rankins, establishes a genuine problematic of the theatrical image. His desire or capacity to do so is obviously subject to the most complex determinations, including the influence of sixteenth-century 'prodigious history'. From the mid-sixteenth century onward, a popular genre of apocalyptic historiography – of history conceived under the aspect of the prodigious – became widely disseminated in Europe, entering England at about the time Marlowe and Rankins were writing.[13] Not only would Tamburlaine's career comfortably fit the category of 'prodigious history', lending credence to his own claim to function as the scourge of God, but the dissemination of such histories might lend credence to the notion of a world suddenly turned strange and threatening, yet also newly open to violent assertions of the will and imagination.

On the 'side' of Rankins, however, such a history would presumably have been insufficient to change the authoritative dispensation under which theatrical 'monstrousness' is at once foreseen and prohibited; indeed, that very history might have been taken, as it was by many Puritan preachers, to be a threatening reassertion of divine providence. Whatever the case may be, Rankins grounds his argument in St Paul's canonical pronouncement (reinforced by authoritative voices including that of St Augustine in *The City of God*) against forms of idolatry. In the light of these pronouncements, theatre can be construed as nothing more nor less than the scene of a pagan cult:

> When they [the pagan gentiles] counted them selves wyse, they became fooles: and turned the glorie of the immortall God, unto an image, made not only after the similtude of mortal man, but also of birdes, and foure footed beastes, and of crepyng beastes. Wherefore God gave them up to uncleaneness, through the lustes of their owne heartes, to defyle their owne bodies among themselves. Whiche chaunged his trueth for a lye, and worshipped and served the creature, more then the creator, which is to be praysed forever.[14]

While other antitheatrical writers (and Marlowe as playwright) pick up on the themes of homosexuality and sophisticated 'vice' also treated by Paul in this letter, Rankins confines himself largely to the 'monstrous' deformation and idolatrous transformation of the Christian man to which the theatre supposedly lends itself. For Rankins, the departure from a culturally inscribed Christian image and scale of perfection not only represents a gross moral lapse but also *portends* cultural apostasy. The players are accused, among other things, of '[taking] upon them the persons of Heathen men, imagining themselves (to vaineglory in the wrath of God) to be the men whose persons they present, wherein, by calling on *Mahomet*, by swearing by the Temples of Idolatry, dedicate to Idols, by calling upon *Iupiter, Mars, Venus*, & other such petty Gods, they doo most wickedly robbe God of his honour, and blaspheme the vertue of his heavenly power' (F. 22).

While Rankins denies any power of real transformation to the imaginative metamorphoses enacted by the players, he also reveals a paradoxical anxiety about the players' tendency to forget themselves and become what they act, in doing so possibly communicating their self-delusion to their audiences. The pamphlet's subtitle refers to 'the *infectious* sight of Playes', and it seems that, in spite of its assumed powerlessness to alter the facts, the theatre may nevertheless institutionalize the possibility of profoundly threatening cultural and individual metamorphoses as well as of unprecedented boundary-crossings. The cultural apostasy Rankins fears may be possible, in his terms, only as a lapse into common delusion, but the threatened universality of that lapse carries it beyond the realm of absurdity and into that of horror.[15]

If the authoritative source and some of the cultural determinants of Rankins's argument are fully apparent, and if they seem to authorize a decisive antitheatricalism, they do not however render his own situation uncomplicated or perhaps even make it differ in the last resort from Marlowe's. Rankins embodies the Pauline argument I have quoted in a rather clumsy allegorical fiction that goes as follows. An unidentified narrator decides in his youth to travel abroad to compare the mores of his own country with those of others. This innocent abroad soon finds himself in an 'alien' kingdom called 'Terralbon', an apparent utopia blessed with sound allies, natural abundance, and a flourishing commonwealth ruled over by 'a most vertuous and godlie princesse ... whome God hath annointed, whome Angels doo guide' (F. 1). But this commonwealth is not without 'caterpillers', who, as the narrator tells us, 'some terme ... Comedians, othersome Players, manie Pleasers, but I Monsters' (F. 2). The narrator terms them so because 'under colour of humanitie, they present nothing but prodigious vanitie'. The theatre that has mysteriously come into being in 'Terralbon', and which threatens the integrity of the entire kingdom, constitutes a setting in which 'men doo then transforme that glorious image of Christ, into the brutish shape of a rude beast, when the temple of our bodies whiche should be consecrate unto him, is made a stage of stinking stuffe, a den for theeves, and an habitation for insatiate monsters' (F. 2).

While not too much coherence can be claimed for Rankins's 'translation' of St Paul, he nevertheless seems to undertake a demystification of theatre. Using the analogy between macro- and microcosm, Rankins equates the identity of the players (as distinct from the images they project) with the physical theatre, and perceives them to replicate in their very physical being the unsavory stink and petty criminality of the theatrical milieu. The distinction between playhouse and player and subsequently that between player and audience is abolished, leaving theatre (which also is characterized as a labyrinth) to stand in simple, traditional opposition to the temple.

This feat of reduction does not, however, liberate Rankins from the world of images. Indeed, the specular trope of his own *Mirrour* tends to multiply rather than limit the 'monstrousness' he contemplates, and ultimately to confine his protagonist *within* a theatre of monstrous images – a specular labyrinth. The encompassing both of the culture and of the self by 'monstrousness' thus becomes perspicuous, and the antitheatrical argument tends to succumb hysterically to the revelation of its own impossibility.

Throughout his not unintelligent critique, in fact, Rankins seems to be just spinning his wheels. For example, his antitheatricalism characteristically seizes upon the players and the playhouse rather than specific plays or dramatic genres, and indeed it is as if theatrical fictions are either transparent or non-existent. Moreover, no particular form of drama – or, as Puttenham might say, of dramatic poem – can alter the nature of theatre or mitigate the harmfulness of its constitutive powers and mechanisms. In Rankins's view, the theatre remains the scene of scandalous play, not of drama. The characteristic form taken by that play, as we discover elsewhere in his pamphlet, is masking or masquerading. The particular masque witnessed in the imaginary theatre by Rankins's fictional protagonist celebrates the marriage of Pride and Lust, both taken to be forms of monstrous vanity and to be accompanied by other lesser vanities including Idleness, Flattery and Ingratitude.[16] What is to be inferred from this spectacle is that theatre is incapable of representing (or allegorizing) anything but itself; its own character is manifest in every one of its features and performances, and it possesses no capacity to stage or even to imagine a world other or better than its own. While Rankins does not explicitly develop the point, and indeed it would be difficult to claim that he is making precisely *that* point, the non-representation or self-representation of theatre constitutes a possible restriction widely perceived by Elizabethan dramatists, for whom the counter-possibility of representation or 'otherness' rests, always insecurely, on the power of poetic fictions and on the capacity of the stage to constitute a world apart. Rankins, however, has a point; the question is, what follows?

For Rankins, nothing can save theatre from itself, and any saving powers or distinctions must be established between the theatre and a world outside. The effect of his work as a fiction is thus to project a condition both prior to and different from that of the theatre. He posits a kingdom (Terralbon), a ruler (the blessed princess), an image (that of Christ) and a condition of the self (youthful innocence) both prior to and uncontaminated by theatricalization. From this imagined vantage-point, an attack on theatre becomes feasible, as does the containment or elimination of theatre within a world definitively constituted otherwise. Yet the cultural fact – even the personal fact – with which Rankins must contend is the theatricalization to which all these idealized images either have or shortly will succumb. (If we think that at least the image of Christ is invulnerable to such contamination, we need only think of Nashe's 'monstrous' theatricalization of Christ in *Christ's Tears over Jerusalem* [1593], an effort undertaken in conscious and explicit emulation of Marlowe's *Tamburlaine*.)

It might be claimed that Rankins employs the utopian device to gain critical purchase on the phenomenon of theatricality; it might even be said that the pamphlet upholds its 'mirror' function in presenting the queen with an image of herself and her kingdom as they might be rather than as they are, thus at once implicitly criticizing the status quo and offering a better alternative. But at the fictional level the narrator who makes his way into that theatre never finds his way out of it again. He ends up speaking as a figure trapped in a hell from which he can only cry for deliverance, thus in some measure anticipating and sharing the fate of the Marlovian protagonist. The utopian outside, moreover, reappears transformed on the inside. The very images that are purportedly those of carnal 'luxury' evoke the self-display not just of players but of the queen – of the queen *as* player. The *courtly* masque thus becomes the very form in which theatrical 'monstrousness' definitively manifests itself:

> [Luxuria] rising from hir bed of Securitie, hanged with Curtins of Carelesnes, with valances of Vanitie, she dressed hir head with such costly Calles, Earings, Jewels, Periwigs & Pearls, as if for varietie of attire, she had a store house of trumperie. Nor was there any thing left undone, but that which should be doone. Amongst the rest to make hir seeme more amiable to hir best beloved shee painted hir faire face with spots of shadowed modestie.
>
> (F. 4)

Not only are the blessed princess and her courtiers figures within rather than outside the theatre, but their masquerade must transform the commoners into a theatrical audience and the kingdom itself into a pagan theatre[17] – the scene of a truly popular cult – in which a mysterious conjunction has occurred between extreme forms of narcissistic display and widespread devotion. (Luxuria, says Rankins's protagonist, 'striveth to rule in the hearts of most men' [F. 4].) Monstrous, indeed, yet what is to be done?

Despite its possible utility in the context of factional politics, Rankins's strategy of denial seems more quixotic, frustrated or paradoxically *ineffectual* as a means of defense than Marlowe's overt acceptance. The mounting hysteria of the Puritan attack on theatre (culminating in Prynne's *Histriomastix*) as well as the eventual failure of the Puritan antitheatrical policy may imply no more than inept politics. Yet they may also suggest a fatal refusal to acknowledge what is culturally constitutive at a level beyond the reach of political cures. Although Rankins fictionally projects a non-theatrical self conceived in the image of Christ as the basis of his radical antitheatricalism, the very terms of his fiction betray him, revealing his argument to have been overtaken by the accomplished fact, or at least by its own premises. Even the Pride that he stigmatizes as 'monstrous' does not appear in his allegorical masque under its common medieval name of Superbia, with its connotations of inward swelling or tumidity, but rather under the name of Fastus (spelled 'Faustus' on more than one occasion!), a condition of external deportment involving both lofty disdain and a certain 'fastidious' withdrawal. The shift suggests that the very inwardness of the moral or 'carnal' condition of pride has given way to a corresponding external condition belonging to the theatre, where 'Fastus' personified exists only in a relation between player and the beholder. The very substance of the self, capable of being infected by evil but also of being restored, tends to dissolve within the theatrical world of magnified appearances, allowing no purchase to the argument Rankins tries to articulate.

My argument does not lead now to a dramatic conclusion, since it is thematically bound only to the proposition that Marlowe and Rankins represent a phase in possibly interminable cultural dialogue, one taking place within the context of the theatricalization that it is also 'about'. Perhaps I can conclude only by anticipating the next phase in this dialogue. The theatre of monstrous idols to which Rankins and Marlowe devote their concern remains both a problem and a preoccupation for their successors. Attempts to recharacterize the theatre – or the theatrical protagonist – are widely implicit in the work of Shakespeare among others, but are also undertaken in the Jacobean drama of such authors as Jonson, Chapman, and Ford (the latter two notably in *Bussy D'Ambois* and *Perkin Warbeck*), who attempt to substitute for the overblown, vain, and vainly adored colossus such figures as that of the stoic 'full' man or even of the historically attested and hence finite 'character'. Among other things, however, this project entails a restoration of the interiority – or real substance – that we have perceived dissolving in the theatre of monstrous idols. The pursuit of that end or of comparable ones comes to depend on an ever more intense antitheatricality within the theatre, an antitheatricality that gives to Jacobean drama its violently self-divided and perhaps self-consuming character.

Notes

1. STEPHEN GOSSON, *The Schoole of Abuse* and *Short Apologie of the Schoole of Abuse* (1579), *Playes Confuted in Fine Actions* (1582); HENRY DENHAM, *A Second and Third Blast of Retrait from Playes and Theatres* (1580); PHILLIP STUBBES, *Anatomie of Abuses* (1583).

2. Insofar as the antitheatrical campaign can be regarded as a cause, its unwanted effect is to empower the very institution it attacks. What we call major Elizabethan drama emerges in the wake of that campaign, and it may be suggested that drama discovers itself (i.e., at once finds and displays itself) in responding to antitheatricalism. Something like this constitutive negation is required to make sense both of the intense reflexiveness of major Elizabethan drama and of a qualitative transformation that no evolutionary account can begin to explain.

3. 'Enormities', implying both excessive magnitude and moral transgression, is one of Rankins's terms. It presumably also becomes a term in the Puritan antitheatrical lexicon inasmuch as Jonson responds to it in *Bartholomew Fair*, where he plays on it in a complex and self-referential way. While farcically defusing some of the dread attendant upon theatrical 'enormity' as well as 'idolatry', Jonson does not fully exorcise the demon, which reappears in the guise of a fleshy superabundance.

4. WILLIAM RANKINS, *A Mirrour of Monsters* (1587); repr. edn ARTHUR FREEMAN (New York, Garland Publishing, 1973).

5. A concept of 'prejudice' that at once founds and baffles Western rationality (reasonableness) seems to be called for in JONAS BARISH's *The Antitheatrical Prejudice* (Berkeley and Los Angeles, University of California Press, 1979), though the question of such a literally fundamental 'prejudice' is not explicitly raised. In this chapter I move somewhat fluidly between the categories of the 'cultural' and the 'political', but in doing so I assume in general that a constitutive *cultural* prejudice manifests itself in particular forms and with particular consequences in the Elizabethan *political* world. While there is always a risk that one of the two terms being employed will really be empty, an overdetermined conception of Elizabethan theatricalism and antitheatricalism is indispensable.

6. In this respect Rankins resembles Phillip Stubbes, who, as C.L. Barber points out in *Shakespeare's Festive Comedy* (Princeton, NJ, Princeton University Press, 1959), pp. 21–2, is an unmatched 'anthropological' observer and sensitive recorder of the pagan festivities he excoriates. In addition to acknowledging that the theatre, whether because of its power to 'inchant by charmes' or because of the observer's 'darkesome disposition' (F. 4), exerts a fatal spell Rankins also communicates the theatrical splendor and sensuous appeal of masking: 'Hir handmaid . . . readie to attend the pleasure of hir Ladie cloathed hir in a coate of Sattin of subtiltie, when shee seemed vnto hir selfe a second *Narcissus*. . . . This King . . . thought it best in compleat Armour richlie wroughte in martial maner to marche to the Chappel. . . . Next Curiositie crowned him with Mirtle, made in a Garland stuck full of Roses, and waxed his wings with Oyle of *Narde*, and *Spike* of the sweetest sauours' (Ff. 5–6).

7. Rankins commends sabbatarian legislation and other unspecified if draconian measures against theatrical 'abuses', yet the situation Rankins represents already seems to call for the final Puritan solution of closing the theatres.

8. Presumably the term can never become as completely drained in Elizabethan usage as it characteristically is in modern usage, yet it need not function as

much more than a scandalized expletive, uttered cynically on occasion in Elizabethan contexts. (Notably, for example, by the Christian governor of Malta while preaching to Barabbas on the sin of covetousness.) The word does, however, retain its connection in Elizabethan usage with its root-meanings of portentousness, revelatory spectacle, and outlandishness ('monster' = 'show'), as it does with the notion of 'unnatural' evil. The charge may, therefore, be pressed with the utmost conviction. In applying the term to theatre, Rankins activates not only its morally pejorative connotations but also its reference to spectacular display.

9.   It may seem as if Rankins's moral 'monstrousness' is here being illegitimately conflated with the literal or biological monstrosity of Pliny's codified monstrous beasts and races, or Augustine's exemplary Siamese twins (*City of God*, Bk. XV, Ch. 8). Yet the moral and biological sense remain interlocked at the time Rankins writes in England, and indeed the connection had been strongly reaffirmed in apocalyptic diatribes such as STEPHEN BATEMAN's *The Doome Warning all Men to Judgement* (1581), in which the entire course of human history is reinterpreted under the aspect of the 'prodigious'. A principled separation of biological and moral monstrousness only begins to be effected – notably in France by Ambroise Paré – at about the time Marlowe and Rankins are writing.

10. The commentaries of Sidney and Puttenham on this subject are too well known to need detailed citation.

11. STEPHEN GREENBLATT, 'Marlowe, Marx, and Anti-Semitism', *Critical Inquiry* 5 (Winter 1978), pp. 291–307. (See also Chapter 9 in this volume.)

12. *The Works of Christopher Marlowe*, ed. C.F. TUCKER BROOKE (Oxford, Clarendon Press, 1969).

13. French *histories prodigieueses* are translated into English by Stephen Batemen in 1581, but also by other English authors. The widespread European currency as well as the popular sensationalism of this 'genre' is well discussed by RUDOLF SCHENDA, *Die französische Prodigienliteratur in der zweiten Hälfte des 16. Jahrhunderts* (Munich, Max Huebler Verlag, 1961). Unlike Rankins, Bateman 'reads' prodigies not as manifestations of demonic power in the world but – in more authentically Augustinian fashion – as manifestations of a divine providence threatening doom to a sinful world.

14. This passage from the Geneva Bible is cited by CLARKE HULSE in *Elizabethan Metamorphic Verse* (Princeton, NJ, Princeton University Press, 1982), p. 101. Hulse notes that the particular form of 'antitheatricality' implicit in this letter arises from Paul's confrontation with the practices of a sophisticated hellenistic paganism. In the next paragraph, Paul deals with the 'unnatural' practices of homosexuality and gender-reversal, thus authorizing another version of Elizabethan antitheatricalism and setting the stage for Marlowe's erotic poems as well as for *Edward II*. It is not, however, along this particular axis of hebraism and hellenism that Rankins and Marlowe situate themselves in 1587; the issue remains that of an 'idolatrous' gigantism and adoration of false images. The force and primacy of Pauline antitheatricalism may be inferred, *inter alia*, from Shakespeare's need to confront it in *The Comedy of Errors*, in which the supposition of diabolical juggling and trickery – stigmatized by Paul in his letter to the Ephesians – induces in Antipholus S. an intense but misplaced anxiety. Shakespeare then proceeds to 'defend' theatre as a clarifying agent and as a benign anti-melancholic remedy.

15. CARLO GINZBURG in *The Cheese and the Worms* (Baltimore, MD, Johns Hopkins University Press, 1980), has shown the remarkable extent to which

sophisticated (humanistic) forms of paganism or heterodoxy can be perceived as a political threat in the sixteenth century insofar as they link up with and reinforce residual forms of popular paganism, the ideology of an unregenerate peasantry. As Ginzburg suggests, the reconquest of a peasantry somewhat liberated in the sixteenth century from feudal constraints is accomplished in the peasant wars in Germany and in the Jesuit occupation of the Italian countryside. A similar reconquest is at least partly the object of the Puritan assault on the theatres and popular entertainments in England. For Rankins, but not for him alone, the threatening prospect of a popular conjunction, facilitated by theatrical 'abuses', also arises between the revived paganism of the classical world and a 'new' Muslim paganism figured by the Koran. This anxiety would be intensified by the cross-cultural flow of information and texts (including the Koran) in the sixteenth century, a flow to which, again, Ginzburg testifies.

16. Rankins's conjunction of Pride and Lust, although traditional, would be somewhat misplaced in relation to Marlowe's work. The 'pride' of Tamburlaine is inseparable from a marked asceticism, a sublimation of desire, that is dramatized for example in his relations with Zenocrate. Simple 'lust', at all events, becomes separated from rather than attached to Pride. Even in Rankins's pamphlet, sexuality *per se* tends to be associated with the *comic* behavior of theatrical spectators engaged in amorous intrigues, while Luxuria (lust personified) resolves itself into narcissistic display and self-absorption, in doing so perhaps anticipating the shift in the meaning of 'luxury' from lustfulness to opulence.

17. It is no doubt 'background' of this kind – as well as of the kind to which I refer in note 15 – that informs Milton's *Eikonoklastes* among other documents of the Puritan revolution. Rankins explicitly acknowledges (and also rather unsuccessfully tries to explain away) the fact that the theatre enjoys royal protection; 'But some . . . may object . . . that I . . . alledge more than I dare avouch, to speak against them that are priveleged by a Prince, nay more sworn, servants to the annointed' (F. 2). Both the theatricality of court life and the access to the court of 'upstart' players and playwrights could only confirm the worst Puritan suspicions.

7 Legitimating Tamburlaine*

ALAN SINFIELD

While American New Historicists suspended Marlowe's plays in an interminable oscillation between power and rebellion, British Cultural Materialists interpreted their contradictions as symptoms of the revolutionary conflicts of their day. To Alan Sinfield, therefore, the indeterminacy of *Tamburlaine the Great*, which traps its audience between applause and contempt for its rampaging hero, is an opportunity to prise apart the flaws that fissure the United Kingdom. The *faultline* in Marlowe's tragedy, according to this theory, is the gap between the warlord's claim to divine sanction as 'the scourge and wrath of god', and the brute arbitrariness on which his empire is actually based. This is an ideological contradiction exposed in the excess violence of his language, as when he threatens the peasants who oppose his power with the plague: a trope Sinfield likens to the demonisation by Christians of the victims of AIDS. Such extremist rhetoric allows us to glimpse the hypocrisy of the official legitimation of violence, since Marlowe's tyrant is a prototype of every judge or general who claims for state terrorism moral superiority over the violence it fights. Thus, in the age of the IRA, Marlowe can be seen to give a twist to Louis Althusser's axiom that ideology supersedes repression, for *Tamburlaine* shows that it is the iron fist that underlies the velvet glove. Such a critique is unconcerned by the historical author's actual intentions, for what matters is the potential of a classic text to disrupt the politics of today. Polemical, sloganising, and journalistic, Sinfield's take on Marlowe is part of his onslaught on the institution of English Literature, and could be described itself as an instance of the rhetorical aggression that papers over the cracks in campus radicalism.

In *Tamburlaine* martial endeavor and legitimate succession depend on the production of gender difference and the subordination of the

---

* Extracted from *Faultlines: Cultural Materialism and the Politics of Dissident Reading* (Oxford, Oxford University Press, 1992), 237–45.

111

female and the feminine. Throughout, the men collude in using as a marker of their competing virilities violence against the women they claim as 'theirs'. At the start Mycetes' unfitness to rule is linked with unmanliness; Tamburlaine, meanwhile, is forcing Zenocrate. Like Henry V, he contrives to appear the irresistible wooer without sacrificing his martial stance: 'Techelles, women must be flattered: / But this is she with whom I am in love' (1.2.107–8). In *Henry V*, banishment of the feminine and the female has to be repeated through the play; Tamburlaine, at the height of his achievement, seems to reclaim the feminine. He finds himself moved by Zenocrate's sympathy for her father, the Soldan, and attributes this in lofty 'poetic' terms to her heavenly beauty. Such rapture is problematic:

> But how unseemly is it for my sex,
> My discipline of arms and chivalry,
> My nature, and the terror of my name,
> To harbour thoughts effeminate and faint!

However, it is all right, for beauty contributes to warrior culture:

> Save only that in beauty's just applause,
> With whose instinct the soul of man is touch'd,
> And every warrior that is rapt with love
> Of fame, of valour, and of victory,
> Must needs have beauty beat on his conceits.
>
> (1:5.1.174–82)

Actually, this appropriation occurs immediately after Tamburlaine has killed the innocent Virgins of Damascus and *during* the slaughter of the rest of the people of Damascus, so he is scarcely succumbing to thoughts effeminate and faint. In fact, the only beneficiary of Tamburlaine's change of heart is the Soldan. The latter declares himself 'pleas'd with this my overthrow' (5.1.480) – the fate of his people does not weigh with him – and the play ends with him sponsoring the marriage of Tamburlaine and Zenocrate. Tamburlaine's sudden sympathy for Zenocrate's father was not disinterested, then: it is the Soldan alone who can regularize this union. Negotiation with the female and the conquered is necessary to secure a legitimate line.

   Yet Zenocrate's grief at the continual indiscriminate killing is vividly expressed, and in part 2 the effeminate returns to trouble Tamburlaine in the person of their son Calyphas, whom he murders. He orders that Turkish concubines

      bury this effeminate brat;
For not a common soldier shall defile
His manly fingers with so faint a boy.

(2:4.1.160–62)

Afterwards, Tamburlaine adds, he wants the concubines brought to his tent. The story ends with his death; what does he die of? – where is the pain that prevents him standing? I would show him clutching his groin.

Tamburlaine's claim that his campaigns are divinely ordained is specially provocative because he takes it as license not just to be violent, cruel, and oppressive, as many magnates were, but to rise against established authorities. He does not adduce legal pretexts, but only military conquest. This indifference to orthodoxy renders his enterprise fraught with religious disturbance. Cosroe demands:

What means this devilish shepherd to aspire
With such a giantly presumption,
To cast up hills against the face of heaven,
And dare the force of angry Jupiter?

(1:2.6.1–4)

But Tamburlaine says he is inspired by Jupiter's overthrow of his father: 'What better precedent than mighty Jove?' he asks (1:2.7.17). The questions seem to invite audience speculation.

Many critics have felt that the plays work to ratify at least some of Tamburlaine's presumption at least some of the time. Roma Gill says in her edition that for most of part 1, Tamburlaine is 'superhuman in his relentless ambition, and this sets him beyond considerations of ordinary morality'.[1] Members of an Elizabethan audience would not necessarily have rejected this, despite the homilies and other exhortations to respect established authority. They might have been excited by Tamburlaine's indifference to the ideology of hierarchy and deference, and even by his disregard for ethical injunctions (which somehow always seem designed more for ordinary people than for rulers).

That some such response was conceivable is suggested by Machiavelli, who tells how Giovampagolo Baglioni of Perugia had in 1505 the opportunity to seize his enemy, Pope Julius II, together with all his cardinals, but shrank from such a bold deed. However, Machiavelli says, thoroughly 'evil deeds have a certain grandeur and are open-handed in their way': Giovampagolo might have defied the whole church on earth, and thus 'would have done a thing the greatness of which would have obliterated any infamy and any danger that might arise from it'.[2] On this assumption, people might

113

have been impressed by the panache with which Tamburlaine carries off his impertinent intrusions upon established power. His 'giantly presumption' (Cosroe's phrase just quoted) suggests a Senecan model: the Herculean, godlike hero. Seneca's Hercules is sexually voracious and given to random violence, but he is a demigod and destined for heaven. Such classical precedent might authorize Tamburlaine's amoral aspiration. His foreignness complicates the question, for it seems that early modern English people did not easily identify with Spaniards, Italians, Turks, and Moors. However, Marlowe, here as elsewhere, throws into confusion such identifications, inhibiting any simple perception of the outsider. Tamburlaine, a Scythian shepherd, is not a notorious threat as the Turks were, is twice said to favor Christians, and behaves more honorably than the Christians of Hungary.

If members of an Elizabethan audience viewed Tamburlaine's audacity as somehow exhilarating, the political implications would be uncertain. It may be that respect for conventional pieties and authorities would be undermined. However, it is also feasible that Tamburlaine would be regarded principally as a more adventurous kind of magnate, in which case his bold stance might add credibility to the conspicuous violence and display customarily exercised by the nobility, and hence encourage deference. Simon Shepherd suggests that audiences might have associated Tamburlaine with contemporary hopes for a heroic 'new man' who would defeat Spaniards, Turks, and the rest; such audiences would then have found themselves caught between the success and the cruelty of Tamburlaine, who turns out to be all too like the order he overthrows.[3] Probably there is no deciding between the exciting and the presumptuous readings of Tamburlaine's career (though this is the kind of issue upon which criticism has liked to exercise itself). Both responses may well have occurred; we should be investigating the way the text is set up to license such divergent possibilities.

From a Christian humanist point of view, the best move is to present Tamburlaine as vicious and disruptive of a divinely inspired order, but as ultimately involved in ratifying and restoring that order. In this vein, Elizabethans would see Tamburlaine as a divine agent ('scourge of God') but as acting nevertheless on his own responsibility. By such an argument, God is exculpated yet remains somehow in control; the play seems to show the punishment of sinful passion within a providentially governed universe; and 'order' wins out all round. However, that position is not coherent and was not orthodox. Protestant doctrine could not allow that Tamburlaine might be acting on his own initiative: it held that God does not merely permit violent and arbitrary magnates, he produces them to serve his purposes. 'Vile monster, born of some infernal hag, / And sent from hell to tyrannize on earth', the governor of Babylon calls Tamburlaine (2:5.1.110–11), and in the protestant scheme of things the Scythian shepherd might well be that. But he would still be an instrument of Divine Providence, being employed by the Lord himself to execute the judgments which he has resolved to inflict.

Once again, we do not have to assume that orthodoxy was necessarily persuasive in stage performances of this text. Critics are surely right to say that the *Tamburlaine* plays systematically tease an audience with the prospect of ethical and political closure, thereby calling into question the patterns to which they allude.[4] An evident aspect of this, which has been well noticed, is the disorderly concatenation of classical, Christian, and Islamic religious terminology. Within and alongside that disturbance, Tamburlaine's god is strikingly like that of the protestants:

There is a God, full of revenging wrath,
From whom the thunder and the lightning breaks,
Whose scourge I am, and him will I obey.

(2:5.1.181–83)

This is the god of Bishop Joseph Hall, for instance when the Philistines are destroyed: 'Every man was either dead, or sick: those that were left living, through their extremity of pain envied the dead; and the cry of their whole cities went up to heaven. It is happy that God hath such store of plagues and thunderbolts for the wicked: if he had not a fire of judgment, wherewith the iron hearts of men might be made flexible, he would want obedience and the world peace.'[5] This god was adduced continually to legitimize the violence of the ruling elite. Lancelot Andrewes explained, justifying Essex's attack on Ireland in 1599: 'God stirreth up the spirit of princes abroad to take peace from the earth, thereby to chasten men by paring the growth of their wealth with his "hired razor"; by wasting their strong men, the hand of the enemies eating them up; by making widows and fatherless children, by other like consequents of war.'[6] (I illustrate from Andrewes because he is often presented as a Christian humanist – T.S. Eliot selected him for special approval.) Thus regarded, Tamburlaine and his consequents of war are not so excessive. Or, again, Cornwall putting out Gloucester's eyes and Regan killing his servant are not outrages of a kind that challenges any theodicy or any theory of obedience to rulers, but the kind of thing God arranged for rulers to do in order to pare the growth of our wealth. To a protestant, Gloucester's blinding may have served him right – Edgar, after all, says as much to Edmund:

115

The Gods are just, and of our pleasant vices
Make instruments to plague us.
The dark and vicious place where thee he got
Cost him his eyes.[7]

Notice the plague there: it was a common analogue for the
activities of God and great magnates (plagues upon the Egyptian
people accompanied the dispute between God and Pharaoh in which
the latter's heart was hardened; and I have just quoted Hall rejoicing
at God's 'store of plagues' when the Philistines were defeated). This
was because all three (plague, God, and magnates) worked through
violent intrusions upon the lower orders and, concomitantly, all three
both challenged and required the Reformation doctrine of providence.
By stretching the idea of divine goodness, they provoked the typical
Reformation response. Preaching during the epidemic of 1603,
Andrewes felt obliged to insist that plague derives from God's care
for people: 'the plague is a thing causal, not casual; comes not merely
by chance but hath somewhat, some cause that procureth it. Sure if a
sparrow "fall not to the ground" . . .' – the trope is familiar. As with
today's AIDS 'plague', the neatest technique of control and legitimation
blames the victim: 'So our inventions beget sin, sin provokes the wrath
of God, the wrath of God sends the plague among us', Andrewes
explained.[8] Plague actually did afflict mainly the people who usually
lost out and who usually were blamed when things went wrong. By
the early seventeenth century, Paul Slack has shown, 'plague was
concentrated in clearly distinguishable areas of each town, in the
fringe parishes which were chiefly, though not wholly, inhabited by
the labouring poor'. 'It is exceptional', F.P. Wilson observes, 'to find
a victim of mark and memory in a London plague.'[9] This was because
the poor suffered overcrowding, unsatisfactory hygiene, bad housing,
and rapid turnover of population, and because the better-off left town
(Andrewes did not resign everything to God – at the height of the
epidemic, he fled his deanery). The correlation between poverty and
plague was commonplace by 1603, to the point where the disease was
apprehended as an aspect of the general threat posed by the 'poorer
sort' – and with some reason, for serious outbreaks were accompanied
by a collapse of social discipline, with drunkenness, looting, and
sexual license. Some commentators actually welcomed plague as a
way of reducing the numbers of masterless men and cleansing the
body politic.[10] Such intricate incorporation of plague into themes of
divine and princely rule indicates once more an anxiously aggressive
ideology of social control.

Tamburlaine says God wants him to 'plague such peasants as resist
in me / The power of heaven's eternal majesty'. As elsewhere in the

plays, and this is my point, his rhetoric of divine legitimation is
basically like that of other rulers:

> Villains, these terrors and these tyrannies
> (If tyrannies war's justice ye repute)
> I execute, enjoin'd me from above,
> To scourge the pride of such as Heaven abhors;
> Nor am I made arch-monarch of the world,
> Crown'd and invested by the hand of Jove,
> For deeds of bounty or nobility;
> But, since I exercise a greater name,
> The scourge of God and terror of the world,
> I must apply myself to fit those terms,
> In war, in blood, in death, in cruelty,
> And plague such peasants as resist in me
> The power of heaven's eternal majesty.
>
> (2:4.1.144–56)

These are the usual arguments, but with a provocative slant.
Tamburlaine is explaining a specially nasty action (killing his
'effeminate' son); he allows the word *tyranny* before repudiating it;
explicitly disavows 'deeds of bounty'; admits to 'cruelty'; and
acknowledges, virtually, that it is 'peasants' who bear the brunt. Most
notably, he implies that his divine mission obliges him to be more
vicious than he otherwise might: 'I must apply myself to fit those
terms'. It is 'heaven's eternal majesty' that makes him thus.

[. . .]

Tamburlaine's rhetorical performance tends to foreground such
dissident thoughts, for it throws into relief the claim of all magnates
to divine legitimation. 'Jove himself will stretch his hand from
heaven / To ward the blow, and shield me safe from harm', he says.
Theridamus is impressed: 'Not Hermes, prolocutor to the gods, /
Could use persuasions more pathetical' (1:1.2.180–81, 210–11).
Tamburlaine's rhetoric works. But when others – established
monarchs – use the same rhetoric it fails. Tamburlaine does not,
as the Soldan threatens, rue the day he 'wrought such ignominious
wrong / Unto the hallow'd person of a prince' (1:4.3.39–40); the
Hungarian Christians are not vindicated in their belief that God
wants them to be the scourge of pagans (2:2.1.51–63); Callapine is not
succoured by Mahomet, whom the king of Amasia sees 'Marching
about the air with armed men, / To join with you against this
Tamburlaine' (2:5.2.34–35). The effect of these rival claims is to prise
apart the language of legitimacy and its users. Anyone can allege

divine endorsement – Tamburlaine's way of putting it suggests as much: 'I . . . *am term'd* the scourge and wrath of god' and will *'write myself* great lord of Africa' (1:3.3.44, 245; my emphases). But whether the language sticks will depend on the balance of forces on the ground (Tamburlaine wins because his followers are more committed). In some circumstances plausible deployment of the rhetoric of divine legitimation may tip the balance, but it is still only rhetoric. That is why Tamburlaine gives Mycetes back his crown (1:2.4): what counts is who wins the battle.

Althusser's distinction between ideological and repressive state apparatuses may encourage the thought that the repressive agencies are resorted to when ideology has failed to produce acquiescent subjects. However, the two are linked from the start, for a key ideological maneuver is the legitimation of state violence. The contradictions inscribed in ideology produce very many confused or dissident subjects, and control of them depends upon convincing enough of the rest that such control is desirable and proper. Soldiers have to believe that they are different from terrorists, prison officers that they are different from kidnappers, judges that they are different from muggers; and most of us have to be persuaded to agree. Tamburlaine's assertions that his harsh regime is divinely required, and the mobility of such rhetoric of legitimation, expose the claims made generally by and on behalf of rulers.

The unstable relationship between ideology and military success in *Tamburlaine* lays bare the difficulty of maintaining the distinction between tyranny and lawful rule. Political theory and theodicy – necessarily both – are shot through with alarm that the distinction might be found inadequate, and have generated innumerable anxious attempts to stabilize it. No one in the governing elite was prepared to tolerate lower-class interference, but sometimes it was allowed that tyrannicide might be performed by lesser magistrates. Generally, such theories were endorsed by out-groups – by Protestants in Catholic countries (the Dutch and Huguenots), and Catholics in protestant countries; it is a nice instance of the material basis of ideas. The distinction between tyranny and lawful rule occurred also, inevitably, in arguments about the reasonableness of the Protestant deity: 'To adjudge to destruction whom he will', says the objector to Calvin in Lawne's *Abridgement*, 'is more agreeable to the lust of a tyrant, than to the lawful sentence of a judge'.[11] For Tamburlaine, '(If tyrannies war's justice ye repute)' is a parenthetical question whose validity he denies; he asserts that as God's agent he may kill whom he chooses. Lawne's orthodox response – 'It is a point of bold wickedness even so much as to inquire the causes of God's will' – only restates the problem. Tamburlaine allows an audience to see this, and that the ultimate analogue for him is not the ruler but the god to whom all of them appeal – the monster who is said to legitimate it all.

Notes

1. ROMA GILL (ed.), *The Plays of Christopher Marlowe* (London: Benn, 1965), p. xiii.

2. NICCOLÒ MACHIAVELLI, *The Discourses*, ed. BERNARD CRICK (Harmondsworth, Penguin Books, 1970), p. 178.

3. SIMON SHEPHERD, *Marlowe and the Politics of Elizabethan Theatre* (Hemel Hempstead, Harvester Wheatsheaf, 1986), pp. 142–53.

4. See STEPHEN GREENBLATT, *Renaissance Self-Fashioning: From More to Shakespeare* (Chicago, Chicago University Press), pp. 194, 202–3; ALAN SINFIELD, *Literature in Protestant England* (London: Croom Helm, 1982), pp. 82–83; SHEPHERD, *Marlowe*, pp. 18–22, 149–52.

5. JOSEPH HALL, *Works*, ed. JOSIAH PRATT (London, 1808), 1:274.

6. LANCELOT ANDREWES, *Works* (Oxford, Clarendon Press, 1841), 1:331. The hired razor is from Isa. 7:20.

7. WILLIAM SHAKESPEARE, *King Lear*, ed. KENNETH MUIR (London, Methuen, 1963), 5.3.170–73.

8. ANDREWES, *Works*, 5:224, 234; so also EDMUND GRINDAL, *Remains* (Cambridge, Cambridge University Press, 1843), pp. 113–14.

9. PAUL SLACK, *The Impact of Plague in Tudor and Stuart England* (London, Routledge, 1985), p. 143 and chs. 5–7; F.P. WILSON, *The Plague in Shakespeare's London* (Oxford, Oxford University Press, 1963), p. 172. On the behavior of Andrewes in the plague of 1603, see SLACK, *Impact of Plague*, p. 234.

10. WILSON, *Plague in Shakespeare's London*, pp. 72, 153–54; SLACK, *Impact of Plague*, pp. 239–40, 305–9.

11. WILLIAM LAWNE, *An Abridgement of the Institution of Christian Religion*, trans. CHRISTOPHER FETHERSTONE (Edinburgh, 1587), p. 222.

8   Visible Bullets: *Tamburlaine the Great* and Ivan the Terrible*

RICHARD WILSON

In a 1991 essay entitled 'Invisible Bullets', Stephen Greenblatt had defined culture as a power transparent as the plague carried by colonists to America, and critics were thereafter obsessed by the ways in which Renaissance theatre had 'infected' the New World. But twelve years on, Richard Wilson's essay announced by its title a recall to a more strictly materialist criticism, for which art is shaped by actuality and Elizabethan drama looks as much backwards to the East as forwards to America. So, his view of *Tamburlaine the Great* is a literal *reorientation* of the play towards the Asia where it is set and the London where it was first performed. The implication is that the material determinants for such a text are recoverable from the archives, and Wilson locates these in a connection with the Muscovy Company, led by Marlowe's patrons. In 1587, when *Tamburlaine* was acted, the Company was running a gigantic fraud, the essay reveals, to supply arms in exchange for access to the Tsar's conquests. Seen in this context, Marlowe's Russian epic appears as a prospectus for London's first joint-stock enterprise, which, thanks to the publicity of his 'mighty line', became, in 1599, the East India Company. This is a Conradian tale that situates Marlowe not on the margins, but in the Elizabethan heart of darkness, where his monstrous hero would inspire the speculators who profited from the crimes of Ivan the Terrible. Part of a recent concern with trade and empire, Wilson's essay confirms the 'return of the author', whose death is here a literal consequence of his imagination. For Marlowe was murdered, according to this investigation, not in a tavern, but in the offices of the arms dealers who fired – and then extinguished – his pyromania. If Marlowe's theatre was, as New Historicists claim, a game, then it was 'the Great Game', we infer, played for world domination and in deadly earnest.

---

* Reprinted from *English Literary History*, 62 (1995), 47–6.

On 18 March 1584 Tsar Ivan IV, Emperor and Great Duke of
Vladimir, Moscow and of all Russia, King of Astrakhan, King of
Kazan, and King of Siberia, was carried on a throne into his treasury,
where (in the account of the English emissary Sir Jerome Horsey)
he called for his jewels: the lodestone of the prophet Muhammed,
'without which the seas nor the bounds that circle the earth cannot
be known'; the unicorn's horn encrusted with rubies and emeralds
he had bought for 'seventy thousand marks sterling' from the Welsh
wizard, David Gower; the 'richest diamond of the orient', which
guaranteed chastity; a sapphire that 'cleared the sight, took away
bloodshot, and strengthened muscles'; and an onyx that changed
color in the hand of vice. Armed with these charms, he summoned
the 'Lapland witches' who had foretold his death, to tell them that
'The day was come; he was as heart whole as ever', and that at
sunset they would therefore be burned. Then he 'made merry with
pleasant songs as he useth to [and] called his favourite to bring his
chess board'. The opponent he chose was his rival, Boris Godunov;
but the tsar set out his pieces confidently until he came to the king,
which rolled onto the floor; whereupon 'the Emperor faints and falls
backward. Great outcry and stir; one sends for his physicians,
another for his ghostly father. In the meantime he was strangled
and stark dead.'[1] Thus passed the tsar known as the Terrible: 'This
Heliogabalus', as Horsey reported him, who was 'a right Scythian;
well favoured, high forehead, shrill voice; full of ready wisdom,
cruel, bloody, merciless', and whose Kremlin tomb, 'guarded day
and night, remains a fearful spectacle to such as pass by or hear his
name spoken, who are contented to cross and bless themselves from
his resurrection'. But if there was jubilation in Moscow when the
chancellor sarcastically announced that 'the English Emperor was
dead', there was consternation in London, where the Muscovy
Company had built its fortune on Ivan's despotic word.[2]

The Muscovy Company was England's first joint-stock enterprise,
floated in 1553 with 240 £25 shares, which members sub-divided as
the market value rose during Ivan's reign to £100 by 1557 and £450
in 1572: an exponential growth of 1,800 percent.[3] The Company's
success was thus the reverse of that to which the dying tsar had
physically clung: the triumph of capital as an invisible power
penetrating distant lands. For as Fernand Braudel explains, merchant
companies were engines of a new global economy, pumping
investment from an ever larger public through cycles of expanding
trade. 'At the top of the world of commerce, the real big business'
of the Renaissance was a fourfold operation (import-and-export
and purchase-and-sale) by these international monopolists; and the
Muscovy Company completed a classic circuit when they sold the

English navy Russian cable bought with arms shipped to the tsar.[4]
Distance, volume, and demand made this semi-clandestine trade so
lucrative that by the mid 1580s the Company was declaring goods
worth £25,000 a year (£75,000 at market rates); but the stimulus for
fresh capital on which its directors constantly called was the potential
for new markets at each end of the line: in the Asian territories
conquered by Ivan where, as Horsey wrote, 'great traffic is
maintained with all nations for the commodities which each country
yields'; and in the American colonies founded on the defeat of
Spain.[5] From Virginia to Persia, the Muscovy Company straddled the
shipping and caravan lanes of world trade; but the hub of its activity
was its warehouse in Deptford, where up to £10,000-worth of
cordage was stowed. That 'the fleet which defeated the Armada
was rigged with Russian tackle and cable', was due to the bills and
invoices that meshed in this store, where the Company's London
agent was charged with executing some of the most secret orders of
the state.[6] And this is significant, because from 1576 to 1599 the agent
was Anthony Marlowe, long identified as a Crayford relative of
Christopher Marlowe, and a cause, we may infer, of the dramatist's
fatal connection with the Deptford docks.[7]

'For the silk of the Medes to come by Muscovy into England is a
strange hearing', exclaimed the English ambassador in Paris, when
he learned of the new passage to Asia. It was such multilateralism,
Braudel suggests, that destroyed the fair and elevated the warehouse
into the key instrument of exchange; and Muscovy Company records
reveal its Deptford depot as the nexus of communication between
London and the tsar's domains.[8] With its accumulation of intelligence
and stock, this was one room where 'infinite riches' were truly
circumscribed in the Jew's audit that 'thus trawls our fortune in by
land and sea, / And thus are we on every side enrich'd'.[9] According
to his predecessor, Anthony Marlowe had 'charge of all the business
of the company', including purchase of goods re-exported to Russia,
and was paid a bonus of £200 a year for 'executing the doings thereof
quietly'.[10] In 1587, when the dramatist arrived in London, such
discretion was at a premium, because the stores were at the center
of a gigantic fraud devised by the Company governor, George Barne,
a Woolwich broker, with his brother-in-law, the spymaster, Francis
Walsingham. Their scam was made possible when Ivan's successor
Theodor revoked the Company's monopoly and Horsey rigged a
secret deal between Godunov and his 'good friends' in London.
Since a turnover of a mere £13,500 was declared for 1587, we can
guess that this 'very cunning scheme' cost the shareholders about half
their dividend; and historians surmise that because they employed
Company ships, Barne and Walsingham must have colluded with

Anthony, who was supposed 'to prevent private trade by numbering every truss of cloth and hogshead of brimstone'.[11] The agent was, in fact, himself related to both men; and their conspiracy was presumably sealed with the complicity of the local official responsible for receipt of goods into the royal household: the bailiff of the Clerk of the Greencloth, the very Richard Bull in whose offices on Deptford Strand, long mistaken for a tavern, Christopher Marlowe would eventually pay his own mysterious reckoning.[12]

Ivan's death precipitated a crisis in the Muscovy Company that had loomed since 1580, when the Turks cut the route from Russia to Persia. By 1586 its books were nominally in the red; so at the annual court shareholders moved to censure its board for 'disposing of trade to the discontent of the inferior brethren, by liberality of Mr Horsey towards some of the chief dealers'. The upshot, however, was that 'the whole court with one assent by erecting of hands' voted to write off seventy-five percent of the debt, refloat the Company with a new share issue, and, as Barne assured Lord Burghley (a major promoter), vest control in just ten directors, to avoid future 'inconvenience of forward men's opinions'.[13] By crushing this shareholders' revolt, the City of London was already displaying its genius for insider dealing; and the affair reveals the restrictive practices Anthony Marlowe might have mobilized on behalf of kin. For the Muscovy Company was in reality a cartel of Kent families, linking many of the factors in Russia, such as Walsingham's step-son, Alexander Carlyle, with naval commanders like Hawkins, who married Anthony Marlowe's cousin. Anthony Marlowe's ties with Bull typified this dynastic network: Richard Bull's father had worked as Deptford Master Shipwright for his grandfather and uncle, William and Benjamin Gonson, successive Navy Treasurers; while Bull's employer at the Greencloth, Christopher Browne of Sayes Court, married another of Marlowe's Gonson cousins.[14] Peter Clark comments that though Kent led foreign enterprise, with gentry 'busy sending home carpets and news from India', this was always managed 'for the consolidation of its oligarchy', and the Justices of the Peace who invested in Russia or America shared the moral horizons of the Faversham pirate, Jack Ward, who plundered the Caribbean and Mediterranean for Queen or Sultan 'with exemplary impartiality'.[15] Certainly, the reflotation of the Russia Company as what critics termed a 'monopoly in a monopoly' suggests that if the poet was privy to its accounts, he would have had a sound initiation into the double entries and strange fellows of venture capitalism.[16]

'Give me a map, and let me see how much / Is left for me to conquer all the world, / That these boys may finish all my wants': it is a commonplace that, as Stephen Greenblatt says, Tamburlaine personifies 'the acquisitive energy of merchants and adventurers, promoters alike of trading and theatrical companies', and that the 'historical matrix' of Marlowe's drama was Elizabethan commerce, since 'it is his countrymen that he depicts'.[17] Ivan's deathbed endgame and the career of the Muscovy agent (who did indeed sponsor a playhouse in Finsbury) point to a yet more specific context for what critics have described as the compulsion to repetition of 'the great Tartarian thief' (*T1*, 3.3.171), in the relaunch of Asian trade by Marlowe's patrons: 'Upon a new and clear ground', as they claimed, 'we having nothing to do with the former reckoning.'[18] Stock in the Russia Company, as it was now called, was subscribed in April 1587: *Part Two* of *Tamburlaine* was acted by November; so it cannot be chance that Marlowe's epic of 'the rogue of Volga' (*T2*, 4.1.4) should project what Burghley described as 'the great end of dealing with the Muscovite: discovery of a passage into Asia'.[19] For far from the aimlessness Greenblatt attributes to him, the hero's campaign 'to march toward Persia, / Along Armenia and the Caspian Sea' (*T2*, 5.3.126–27), accords exactly with Company goals; while even his plan to circumnavigate 'along the oriental sea about the Indian continent . . . from Persepolis to Mexico, / And thence unto the Straits of Jubalter [and] the British shore' (*T1*, 3.3.253–59), simply retraces the Company's 1583 voyage to the Moluccas via South America.[20] If Marlowe's atlas was Ortelius's, Tamburlaine's map was actually the one surveyed for the cartographer in 1562 by the Company factor Antony Jenkinson and dedicated to its governor, Sir Henry Sidney of Penshurst.[21] And if his plan to 'sail to India . . . Along the Ethiopian sea' (*T2*, 5.3.135–37) seems deluded for one 'paltry Scythian' (*T1*, 1.1.54), its rationale lies in the Company's own charter to monopolize the entire orient beyond the northeast passage.[22]

Critics long ago decided that in *Tamburlaine* Marlowe 'was playing a great game of chess, with kings . . . for pieces, and for chess-board the *Theatrum Orbis Terrarum*', but they have been slow to historicize this *kriegspiel* in relation to the war-game waged by Elizabethan finance.[23] Yet, as John Hale writes in his survey of *The Civilization of Europe in the Renaissance*, Ortelius's atlas charted 'one of the great sages of sixteenth-century expansion . . . when Muscovy exerted control southwards along the Don and Volga to the Asian trade routes'. Thus, at the very moment when new cartography supplied them with a key to self-orientation, Russian imperialism posed to the traders who made it possible to annihilate 'populations which had courage but no firearms', the ethical problem of the frontier between civility and barbarism. Their doubt about whether Moscow stood in Europe or Asia signified the liminality of a terrain where nomenclature was ceaselessly revised (as it is by Tamburlaine), and 'the preparedness of maps to offer contexts for political developments broke down'.[24] For as Philip II's ambassador reported in 1582, it was London merchants who hoped to gain most from the Russian dream of bathing in the warm waters of the Indian Ocean, since 'they calculated that by these means they might monopolize the drug and spice trades', and by 'bringing goods from Persia to the Volga' circumvent 'the territories of your Majesty and other Christian Princes'.[25] So, if Tamburlaine's *blitzkrieg* was projected from Ortelius's pages, one image would have illustrated the glittering commercial horizons of Elizabethan Londoners. There, bestriding the golden road to Samarkand (where the cartographer notes that 'great Tamber had his seat'), is a figure who seems by size and situation to dominate Asia. Like Tamburlaine, he is represented as a Tartar nomad, with tent and turban; but, as Hale infers, Ortelius thereby merely marks the deep conceptual ambivalence of sixteenth-century Russia.[26] For this Asiatic potentate is, in fact, the first Western portrait of 'John, Great King, Emperor of Russia, and Duke of Moscow', who would soon be infamous as Ivan.

Greenblatt observes that while incessant movement in *Tamburlaine* does indeed 'reduce the universe to the coordinates of a man', such dramaturgy makes 'all spaces curiously alike . . . contriving to efface differences, as if to insist upon the essential meaninglessness of space. . . . Space is transformed into an abstraction.' For Greenblatt, this 'secularization of space' is the register of 'wants never finished and transcendental homelessness'; but Emily Bartels has recently keyed Marlowe's projective space more concretely to Elizabethan travel writing, and countered that 'the lack of differentiation between its worlds' should be viewed not as the sign of existential angst, but of a drive to 'break down the barriers of difference', to 'show that the worlds out there are not so different from Europe. The point is not that space is meaningless, but that the differences assigned to it are empty, overdetermined, or arbitrary.'[27] Bartels argues that when *Tamburlaine* is contextualized within the emerging discourses of ethnography and orientalism, its hero's contradictory mixture of the civilized and savage can be seen as admonitory for England's confrontation with Asia, 'where choosing sides became as difficult as defining them', states were 'accorded both positive and negative attributes', and their subjects were 'emulated *and* feared, not because civility would at any moment devolve into barbarism, but because that civility was coupled to barbarism'. 'East of England', by this reading, Marlowe's game of empire deliberately deprived its players of moral bearings, and filled the Asian landscape with conflicting voices of nobility and savagery, to prove 'one man's hero another man's barbarian'.[28] To Bartels, such moral neutrality 'undermines the

agency of everyone involved'; but this conclusion ignores the extent
to which, as Thomas Cartelli remarks, 'Marlowe's discourse of
mastery was apt to stir the emotions and fulfil the fantasies' of
playgoers by projecting the very dreams to which they aspired.[29] It
underestimates, that is to say, the material investment of Londoners
in the Eastern ventures of their own exotic agents:

> Merchants of the Indian mines,
> That trade in metal of the purest mould;
> The wealthy Moor, that in the eastern rocks
> Without control can pick his riches up,
> And in his house heap pearl like pebble-stones,
> Receive them free, and sell them by the weight.
>
> (*JM*, 1.1.19–24)

'Backwards and forwards near five thousand leagues' (*T2*, 5.3.144),
Tamburlaine's transit into Persia and Turkey recapitulates the
expeditions that regularly earned Muscovy Company shareholders
dividends of 400 percent in the terrible years of Ivan. If Marlowe's
hero is driven, as Greenblatt proposes, by a 'will to absolute play',
his game is for real, since it is the Great one played from the
sixteenth century between the European powers, with its prize of
control of the passes into India.[30] For though Greenblatt thinks that
Tamburlaine pursues a mirage, the prospect he offers his army is
precisely that from which London importers would generate their
wealth: 'Men from the farthest equinoctial line, / [Who] swarmed in
troops into the Eastern India: / Lading their ships with gold and
precious stones' (*T1* 1.1.119–21). In her book on *Cultural Aesthetics*,
Patricia Fumerton describes seventeenth-century East India trade as
a 'perpetual motion machine of deferred expenditure and delayed
profit', whereby Spanish silver would be shipped from England to
India to buy sugar and silk; which would be transported to the
East Indies to exchange with spice; which would be carried back
to England and sold for silver; which would then be reexported in
a circle to the East.[31] The East India Company that perfected this
multilateral system was founded in 1599 by the tycoons of the Russia
Company, including Barne; so if Tamburlaine's loot of 'jewels and
treasure' and 'golden wedges' is constantly 'reserved' for investment
in 'East India and the late-discover'd Isles' (*T1*, 1.2.2, 139, 166), this
chimes with expectation in the City of attaining the jewel in the
imperial crown: the 'diamonds, sapphires, rubies / And fairest pearl
of wealthy India' (*T2*, 3.2.120–21). His portfolio of ships and camels
laden with gold, coral, slaves, carpets, cotton, silk, cassia, and myrrh,
is shrewd enough; for when his joint-stock company divides 'the

gold, silver, and pearl they got in equal shares' (*T2*, 3.5.89–90), the dividend is an earnest of the interests that would drive the Raj.

In the context of the political economy of the great merchant empires, Marlowe's passage to India reads like a prospectus for the recapitalization of a Company that promised to open the golden road to Samarkand and make London the new Antwerp through which jewels, spices, silks, drugs, and metals would flow to Europe.[32] The Prologue predicts that simply to 'hear the Scythian Tamburlaine / Threatening the world with high astounding terms' will make the public 'applaud his fortunes' (*T1*, Prologue 4–8); and the arithmetic of this investment, from 'five hundred foot' and 'odds too great' at the outset (*T1*, 1.2.121–22), to the 'millions of soldiers' he brings 'from Scythia to the oriental plage / Of India' (*T2*, 1.1.28, 67–69), does seem pitched to tell Sidneys in Kent their prospects. Hakluyt's *Voyages* were doctored by Walsingham in 1589, we know, to promote investment in Russia; and it is for calculating shorter odds on cards than on his father's 'shares' that the skeptical Calyphas is disowned.[33] As Tamburlaine instructs the reckless son, Amyras, 'It is not chance' that wins this game, but 'greater numbers' (*T2*, 4.1.47–81), 'Tempt not fortune' is therefore the prudent motto of this Tartar (*T2*, 4.1.84), whose bookkeeping seems primed to Lombard Street. For if the scenario is in fact the blockade of the 1580s, when Turkish 'galleys and pilling brigandines' did 'yearly sail to the Venetian gulf' and 'cut the straits' to deny the 'argosies' of 'fair Europe the wealth and riches of the world' (*T1*, 3.3.248–50; *T2*, 1.1.39–41, 1.3.33), Tamburlaine's hyperbole works, Marjorie Garber notes, to minimize obstacles through the creative accountancy of writing.[34] Like the Company agent's, his pen is his sword as he deletes lines and multiplies figures with supreme indifference to actuality. Historians who view trading companies as states-within-states, which merged private profit into public priorities through the legerdemain of operators such as Walsingham, would find confirmation of their thesis, therefore, in the sleight-of-hand by which this projector maximizes markets, punctures frontiers, and redrafts the geopolitics of continents:[35]

> I will confute those blind geographers
> That make a triple region of the world,
> Excluding regions which I mean to trace,
> And with this pen reduce them to a map,
> Calling the provinces, cities and towns
> After my name and thine, Zenocrate.

> (*T1*, 4.4.73–78)

Edward Said argues that Marlowe's 'oriental stage' helped fabricate the stereotype of Islam as Christendom's other; but what this

Christopher Marlowe

Scythian's breach of the continental blockade demonstrates is a refusal of binarism, a deconstruction of 'the confines and the bounds' of Europe (T2, 1.6.80) that is dramatically enacted by third terms and intermediaries: the Persian defectors, Theridamas and Cosroe; Catholic Europe; India; Africa; America; even the 'land which never was described' east of 'th'Antartic pole' – Australia (T2, 5.3.154).[36] Tamburlaine's subversion of polarity, his urge to 'leap from his hemisphere' (T2, 1.3.51), shift 'the perpendicular' (T1, 4.4.80), 'fix the meridian line' anew (T1, 4.2.38), or 'travel to th'antartic pole, / Conquering the people underneath our feet' (T1, 5.1.133), belongs, that is to say, precisely to the era of the trading companies, when, as Jean-Christophe Agnew relates, long-distance transactions generated just such triangular relations as Marlowe stages.[37] And if Tamburlaine's 'mighty line' expresses by its very attenuation the compound suspended pay-off of those bills of exchange that connected the speculator in Canterbury with the cinnamon-grower in Java, his characterization as a liminary neither Christian nor Muslim, Asian nor European, destines him to dominate a world dependent on mediation of the arbitrageur and agent. For this 'Scythian slave' (T1, 3.3.68) is the placeless New Man or *Conquistador* of the Renaissance; but he is also that most transgressive of all executants of commercial expansion, one of those 'vile outrageous men / That live by rapine and by lawless spoil' (T1, 2.2.23–24), 'A monster . . . famous for nothing but theft' (T1, 4.3.8, 66), or pirate. Braudel reminds us that piracy is the term used by the waning power to stigmatize its rival; and when the Soldan calls Tamburlaine 'a base usurping vagabond' (T1, 4.3.21), Marlowe's eastern world is a mirror that transcends mere orientalism. What we see reflected, of course, are English privateers such as Hawkins: the founders of the so-called Honourable Company.

With 'pillage and murder is usual trades' and 'a troop of thieves and vagabonds' (T1, 4.1.6, 66), the 'sturdy Scythian thief, / That robs your merchants of Persepolis / Treading by land unto the Western Isles' (T1, 1.1.35–38), embodies the ambiguity of the freebooter for a culture in which raiding and trading were modes of the same enterprise.[38] An antique 'curtle-axe' in his belt, Tamburlaine begins as a Robin Hood, who vows, like Shakespeare's bandits, never to prosper 'by lawless rapine from a silly maid' (T1, 1.2.9–10, 43); but his privateering promotes him into a blockade-runner for England's eastern enterprise: 'The only fear and terror of the cruel pirates of Argier, / That damned train, the scum of Africa' (T1, 3.3.55–56). From pillaging London merchants to policing Barbary corsairs, the whole history of buccaneering is thus figured when 'this thief of Scythia' becomes a 'proud King of Persia' (T2, 3.1.14–15). Doubtless this is

Marlowe's version of what the pirate said to Alexander when he objected, 'Because I do with a little ship, I am called a thief: thou doing it with a great navy, art called an emperor.'[39] But the gulf between pirate and emperor, we are constantly reminded, is technology. For if Marlowe's map is up-to-the minute, so too is his analysis (confirmed by authorities such as Geoffrey Parker) that a prerequisite of modern hegemony was armament.[40] Nothing remains, in any case, of Timur the Lame in this juggernaut who bombards and mines, editors notice, according to *The Practice of Fortification* by Paul Ives, a Kent aide to Walsingham (T2, 3.2.62–90).[41] With 'great artillery / And store of ordnance' (T2, 3.2.79–80), 'sulphur balls of fire' (T2, 3.2.41), 'volleys of shot' (T2, 5.1.99), 'light artillery, / Minions, falc'nets, shakers' (T2, 3.3.5–7), and even 'engines never exercised' (T2, 4.1.190), Tamburlaine's pyrotechnics are a state-of-the-art display of early modern European ballistic supremacy. For though the tsar can muster one hundred and fifty thousand Tartars (so Horsey relayed), it is his 'warlike engines and munition' that suddenly 'exceed the force of mortal men' (T1, 4.1.20–29), and he is 'termed the Scourge and Wrath of God' (T1, 3.3.44) precisely because he has been equipped to actualize the Marlovian holocaust, and burn the topless towers of Asia:[42]

> So, burn the turrets of this cursed town,
> Flame to the highest region of the air:
> And kindle heaps of exhalations,
> That being fiery meteors, may presage,
> Death and destruction to th'inhabitants.
> Over my zenith hang a blazing star,
> That may endure till heaven be dissolved,
> Fed with the fresh supply of earthly dregs,
> Threatening a death and famine to this land.
> Flying dragons, lightning, fearful thunderclaps,
> Singe these fair plains, and make them seem as black
> As is the island where the Furies mask.
> Compassed with Lethe, Styx, and Phlegethon.
>
> (T2, 3.2.1–13)

Editors have struggled to locate sources for Tamburlaine's weapons of mass destruction in Byzantine chronicles of the Mongolian Khan, but overlook obvious analogues for 'the flames the cursed Scythian sets on all the towns . . . bordering on the [Black] sea' (T2, 3.2.51–55), in the arsenal of Ivan.[43] Yet if Marlowe was under the patronage of Walsingham, Horsey's despatches would have provided gruesome illustration of both the lethal efficiency of modern armaments and the seriousness of Tamburlaine's threat to 'raise cavalieros higher than the clouds, / And with the cannon break the frame of heaven' (*T2*, 2.4.103–4). In 1569 Sigismund of Poland had warned the English government that 'the Muscovite, made more perfect in warlike affairs with engines of war and ships, will make assault on Christendom, to slay and bind all that withstand him'; and Horsey confirmed how in 1577 'the emperor and his cruel and hellish Tartars set forward with cannon and artillery, munitions, and ten thousand to draw his ordnance over rivers', to 'batter' Reval with 'twenty thousand cannon shot', leaving 'streets lying full of carcasses of aged men, women, and infants'.[44] Observers attributed Ivan's savagery to the death of the tsarina Anastasia (who was then sanctified, like Zenocrate); and Tamburlaine's mania to 'consume with fire' the 'cursed town [that] bereft me of my love' (*T2*, 2.4.137–38), has its precedent in the razing of Novgorod in 1570, when the tsar pitched his pavilion to spectate as 'thirty thousand Tartars . . . ravished, ransacked, and murdered . . . burned all merchandizes and warehouses . . . and set all on fire with wax, together with the blood of seven hundred thousand men, women and children', in an atrocity of which Horsey wrote, 'No history maketh mention of so horrible a massacre'.[45] When Marlowe's warlord pledges, therefore, to 'fill all the air with fiery meteors', so 'it shall be said, I made it red myself' (*T1*, 4.2.51–52), audiences at the Rose would have had no doubt of the real perpetrator of such conflagrations, even though he had smuggled his demand for explosives to Elizabeth in a vodka bottle.[46]

'Hang him up in chains upon the city walls, / And let my soldiers shoot the slave to death' (*T2*, 5.1.108–9): it was during the performance of the 'firing squad' of the governor of Babylon in November 1587 that a 'player's hand swerved, his calliver being charged with bullets, missed the fellow he aimed at, and killed a child and a woman great with child, and hurt another man very sore in the head'.[47] Calyphas had warned how 'bullets fly at random where they list' (*T2*, 4.1.52); and like the 'accidental' slaying of Olympia (*T2*, 4.2.80), the incident reminds us of the materiality of Marlovian culture, with its 'deadly bullet gliding through the side' (*T2*, 3.4.4). It is by his homicidal staging of the victim 'having as many bullets in his flesh, / As there be breaches in the wall' (*T2*, 5.1.158–59), that Marlowe discloses the covert cycle that links the joint-stock company with the tsar's bloodthirsty mafia, the *oprichnina*. All those commodities transported from Persepolis to Deptford are traded, we grasp, for these 'bullets like Jove's thunderbolts, / Enrolled in flames and fiery mists' (*T1*, 2.3.19–20); and the poet's pyromania has its genesis in that warehouse where a kinsman 'quietly' consigned munitions to the arsonist of Moscow. Elizabeth always denied rumors of arms for Russia 'on her royal word'; but Marlowe's incendiary imagination gives away the game.[48] For if Tamburlaine's 'volleys of shot, bullets dipped in poison [and] roaring cannons' are a scourge, that is because they work, as he boasts, like a *pharmakon*, 'as baneful / As Thessalian drugs or mithridate' (*T1*, 5.2.69–70, 159), or fire with fire. Set a thief to catch one, was the Queen's reasoning, at any rate, in secretly agreeing to 'let the Tsar have out of England all kinds of artillery and things necessary for war'.[49] Thereafter, 'Christian merchants that with Russian stems / Plow up huge furrows in the Caspian Sea', were happy to vail to Ivan, as the text records, in return for passage 'on the fifty-headed Volga's waves' (*T1*, 1.2.103, 194–96); and the Kremlin Nero was satisfied with his cargo of invisible 'lead, copper, powder, saltpeter, and brimstone'.[50]

'He is advised by no council, but governeth altogether like a tyrant', wrote Francis Bacon of Ivan the Terrible in 1582; and behind this remark it is possible to detect the equivocalness towards absolutism that made Tamburlaine the barnstormer of Bankside.[51] For though Philip Sidney scorned the 'slave-born Muscovite' who 'calls it praise to suffer tyranny', what impressed investors like his own father was that this ogre 'whose name was synonymous with cruelty' should have waged his wars 'for the right of free trade'.[52] Thus, in spite of atrocities, reported Samuel Purchas, 'his memory is savoury to the Russians, who either of their servile disposition, or for his long and prosperous reign, hold him in no less reputation than a saint'.[53] It was the paradox that Marlowe made the crux of his play, and one that stockbrokers could appreciate, since, out of a race of 'false truce-breakers, subtle foxes, and ravenous wolves, barbarous, yet cunning and unfaithful', the impaler had proved to be the one Russian whose word was his bond.[54] Whether licensing Christian traders or slaughtering the virgins of Damascus, Tamburlaine likewise resolved never to break a promise 'if I have sworn' (*T1*, 4.3.125), since 'that which mine honour swears shall be performed' (*T1*, 5.2.44); and his purge of silk roads and shipping lanes had shown how money knows neither morality nor margins. Marlowe's distant mirror had revealed to Kentish shareholders, indeed, not their polar other, but their mutual interest in a world apart. It had even imaged a Suez canal, cut 'whereas the Terrene and the Red Sea meet . . . That men might quickly sail to India' (*T2*, 5.3.132–35); and if this was literally far-fetched, it was no more so than the project that would preoccupy the Company in 1613, to secure 'the Persian trade by way of the Caspian Sea and Volga, to Archangel and England', by annexing Russia to the Crown.[55] 'Some of the nobility of Muscovy having offered to put themselves under King James', the Privy Council minuted, 'he is full of a scheme to send an army there, and rule that country by a viceroy, and is sanguine of success':

In this project there is no injustice nor any breach or straining of treaties concluded with any other prince or state. Contrariwise, there is in it much glory to His Majesty, much charity towards those oppressed people with whom we have had long commerce, much policy in regard of the increase of our shipping and trade, which must needs augment both our strength and wealth, and much happiness promised thereby to His Majesty and this whole Kingdom.[56]

'The God of heaven and earth would not that all things should be found in one region, to the end that one should have need of another', proclaimed the letter from Edward VI flourished by the first Muscovy merchants when they left Deptford in 1553; so 'All kings in all places under the universal heaven' should give 'aid and help' to such as 'carry good and profitable things as are found in their countries to remote regions . . . and bring from the same things they find commodious for their own'.[57] It was under this gospel of free trade that Marlowe could promote his terrible tsar as an instrument of Hermes, the god of universal commerce (*T1*, 1.2.210): 'He that sits on high and never sleeps, / Nor in one place is circumscriptible' (*T2*, 2.2.50). For as Greenblatt observes, by constituting 'desire of gold' as 'the wind that bloweth all the world' (*JM*, 3.5.3–4), Marlowe's work familiarizes what Christian culture finds terrifying, installing outsiders (such as the Jewish broker) at the epicentre of power.[58] Here, then, in the universalist ideology of the chartered company, and what Immanuel Wallerstein calls its 'interstate system . . . to encompass as many links in the commodity chain as possible', lies the market logic that explains why, in Simon Shepherd's reading, *Tamburlaine* 'traps the audience between the success and cruelty of the hero'.[59] To Shepherd, such an irony produces only 'a sense of powerlessness' in spectators; but this is to undervalue the monetary interest of London's over-horizons *speculators* in breaching any arms embargo.[60] For if Tamburlaine's God, 'Full of revenging wrath' (*T2*, 5.1.181), is 'strikingly Protestant', as Alan Sinfield finds, this is because he is as much a deity of contract law as Faustus's.[61] It is when Tamburlaine burns his universal 'writ' that 'the Scourge of God must die' (*T2*, 5.1.188; 5.2.248); but while he observes those 'solemn oaths, / Signed with our hands' which Catholics break (*T2*, 1.2.66–67), the alien thrives. Marlowe, who was born just as the doctrine of consideration emerged in English law to legitimate exchange, made contract the basis of his plots; and however great or small the sums in that final reckoning in the customs house at Deptford, it would determine his own hour of 'crisis' (*T2*, 5.3.91), when he met with the assassin who had arrived by ferry that very morning hot from the Bourse at Amsterdam.[62]

The day after being pardoned for the murder of Christopher Marlowe, his killers were busy selling 'a number of guns and great iron pieces' on behalf of the Walsinghams.[63] Whatever the deceased's part in the contraband from which his backers profited, the fortunes he predicted in his play had not materialized under Ivan's heirs, and the Company was engaged in disposing of army surplus and settling accounts with the Clerk of the Greencloth at Sayes Court.[64] So, if *Tamburlaine* does dramatize despatches Horsey sent the Company during the Reign of Terror, their contents would confirm the mutuality of all who make a killing out of war.[65] It might have been news of how the barbarous Scythian struck his heir dead for commiserating with his victims that suggested Tamburlaine's (otherwise unsourced) murder of his pacifist son Calyphas; as it may have been the tsar's tragi-comic marriage-proposals to Elizabeth that inspired his devotion to the moon as Cynthia. It is possible that Marlowe was himself drawn by stories of Ivan's homosexuality; but, as his ambivalence hints, this monster who was the prototypical outsider inside Europe – Uncle Joe, or The Russian with whom the West can do Business – was always threatening to become overfamiliar.[66] Shakespeare's joke about the arrival of the 'frozen Muscovite' in the West (*Love's Labour's Lost*, 5.2.265) was very nearly realized in 1580, when Ivan 'prepared many boats and brought his treasure to be embarked, to pass down the river and so into England upon a sudden, leaving the tsarevich to pacify his troubled land'.[67] Though Tamburlaine is heroized by merchants of the Western Isles as the one Russian whose word is good, it is doubtful whether Elizabeth would have honored her own secret promise to grant her 'cousin' asylum. Marlowe, however, recognized the identity trade imposed on both shareholder and savage; and so it was apt that when in 1698 a tsar did visit London to study shipbuilding, it was at Sayes Court in Deptford that Peter the Great encamped. The havoc he wrought there, 'As if a regiment of cossacks in iron shoes had drilled' through John Evelyn's house and precious hedge, might have been intended as a salute to Marlowe's epic of the Scythian who tramples every barrier, with snow on his boots.[68]

Notes

This essay was first given to the conference on Christopher Marlowe and English Renaissance Culture at the University of Kent at Canterbury in July 1993.

1. JEROME HORSEY, *Travels* [BL. Harleian MS. 1813], in *Rude and Barbarous Kingdom: Russia in the Accounts of Sixteenth-Century English Voyagers*, ed. LLOYD EASON BERRY and ROBERT OWEN CRUMMEY (Madison, University of Wisconsin Press, 1968), pp. 304–6.

2. HORSEY, *Travels*, p. 313.

3. THOMAS STUART WILLAN, *The Early History of the Russia Company, 1553–1603* (Manchester, Manchester University Press, 1956), pp. 41–3.

4. WILLAN, *Early History*, pp. 63–6, 91–2; WILLIAM ROBERT SCOTT, *The Constitution and Finance of English, Scottish and Irish Joint-Stock Companies to 1720*, 2 vols (Cambridge, Cambridge University Press, 1912), Vol. 1, pp. 17–22. For arms shipments from England to Ivan, and the opposition from other European governments, see esp. JOSEPH T. FUHRMANN, *The Origins of Capitalism in Russia: Industry and Progress in the Sixteenth and Seventeenth Centuries* (Chicago, Quadrangle Books, 1972), pp. 42–7. For Company profits, see DAVID B. QUINN and A.N. RYAN, *England's Sea Empire* (London, Allen and Unwin, 1983), p. 147.

5. FERNAND BRAUDEL, *Civilization and Capitalism, 15th-18th Century: The Wheels of Commerce*, trans. SIAN REYNOLDS (London, Collins, 1982), pp. 140–2, 403–8; HORSEY, *Travels*, p. 311.

6. WILLAN, *Early History*, pp. 185, 254–5; MILDRED WRETTS-SMITH, 'The English in Russia during the second half of the sixteenth century', *Transactions of the Royal Historical Society*, 4th ser., Vol. 3, p. 95.

7. For Anthony Marlowe, see JOHN BAKELESS, *The Tragicall History of Christopher Marlowe* (Cambridge, MA, Harvard University Press, 1942), pp. 89, 141–2; *Harleian Society Publications* 25 (1887); *Calendar of State Papers, Foreign, 1584–85*, pp. 132–3; *Calendar of State Papers, Domestic, 1591–94*, pp. 396–7, 408; WILLAN, *Early History*, pp. 27–8, 254, 259, 287; EDWARD HASTED, *The History of Kent* (Canterbury, Simmons of Kirkby, 1797), Vol. 2, p. 280. Anthony's uncle, Walter Marlowe, was a charter member of the Muscovy Company, whose son, also named Walter, married the daughter of its governor, George Barne, brother-in-law of Sir Francis Walsingham. See, T.S. WILLAN, *The Muscovy Merchants of 1555* (Manchester, Manchester University Press, 1953), p. 111. Thomas Barne had been sponsored as a haberdasher by one John Marlowe as early as 1535, and the possibility of family ties has been strengthened with the discovery that the dramatist's family originated not in Canterbury, but came from Faversham, which had strong commercial links with London. Christopher Marlowe's father John arrived in Canterbury only about 1556, aged twenty; see WILLIAM URRY, *Christopher Marlowe and Canterbury* (London, Faber, 1988), pp. 12–13, 149–50.

8. WILLAN, *Early History*, p. 58; BRAUDEL, *Civilization and Capitalism*, pp. 94–7.

9. CHRISTOPHER MARLOWE, *The Jew of Malta*, ed. NIGEL W. BAWCUTT (Manchester, Manchester University Press, 1978), 1.1.105; hereafter cited parenthetically in the text and abbreviated *JM*.

10. WILLAN, *Early History*, p. 28.

11. WILLAN, *Early History*, pp. 27, 202–5. The embezzlement perpetrated by Barne, Walsingham and Horsey apparently occurred with the collusion of the Moscow agent, Anthony Marsh, while the Company was officially represented in negotiations with Tsar Theodor by the ineffectual Sir Jerome Bowes. For this murky but immensely lucrative double-dealing, see pp. 165–72, 196–201; and BERRY and CRUMMEY, *Rude and Barbarous Kingdom*, pp. 319–21.

12. For Richard Bull and the office of the Greencloth, see W. URRY, *Marlowe*, pp. 84–5. Bull died in 1590; but his widow Eleanor was herself connected with the Cecils, so may have retained some of his perquisites. In any event, the idea that Marlowe died in a tavern 'is now utterly dissipated [and] what can be concluded is that the supposed ale-wife or bawdy-house keeper of

Deptford came of an ancient armorial family with members close about the Queen' (p. 86).

13. WILLAN, *Early History*, pp. 23, 208–16.

14. For Richard Bull the elder, Master Shipwright at Deptford from 1550 to 1572, see *The Autobiography of Phineas Pett*, ed. W.G. PERRIN (London, Navy Record Society, 1918), pp. xxi–xxiii; *Acts of the Privy Council* 1 (1544), p. 233; 2 (1548), p. 186; 5 (1555), p. 189. This Bull was possibly the son of Thomas, Mayor of Plymouth and erstwhile adversary of the Hawkins family: see JAMES ALEXANDER WILLIAMSON, *Hawkins of Plymouth* (London, Black, 1969), p. 21. For the Gonsons, see Williamson, pp. 242–6, 314–15. Anthony Marlowe's mother was sister to Benjamin Gonson senior, Navy Treasurer from 1549 to 1577, when he was succeeded by his son-in-law, John Hawkins. Christopher Browne married the daughter of Benjamin Gonson junior, Clerk of Ships from 1589.

15. PETER CLARK, *English Provincial Society from the Reformation to the Revolution: Religion, Politics and Society in Kent, 1500–1640* (Brighton, Harvester Press, 1977), pp. 207–9, 302. In 1608 twenty-six of ninety-six Kent Justices were investors in one or more trading company; and of the pioneers of the Russia trade, Richard Chancellor and Henry Sidney were Kent gentry, Barne, Carlyle and Thomas Randolphe were Walsingham's relatives, and Giles Fletcher, George Turbeville, and Horsey were under his patronage (Horsey's *Travels* were dedicated to him); see BERRY and CRUMMEY, *Rude and Barbarous Kingdom*, pp. 3, 61, 88, 253, 262, 320–1. For Jack Ward, the subject of a 1612 play by Robert Osborne, *A Christian Turn'd Turk*, see the *Dictionary of National Biography* and CHRISTOPHER LLOYD, *English Corsairs on the Barbary Coast* (London, Collins, 1981), pp. 48–53.

16. *Journal of the House of Commons* 1:220 (debate on monopolies, May 1604): 'The Muscovy Company has fifteen directors, who manage the whole trade . . . and consign it into the hands of . . . one Agent, and give such account as they please. This is a strong and shameful monopoly; a monopoly in a monopoly; both at home and abroad a whole company has become by this means as one man, who alone hath the uttering of all the commodities of so great a country.'

17. MARLOWE, *Tamburlaine the Great*, ed. G.S. CUNNINGHAM (London, Methuen, 1981); hereafter cited parenthetically in the text and abbreviated *T1* for Part 1, and *T2* for Part 2. STEPHEN GREENBLATT, 'Marlowe and the Will to Absolute Play', in *New Historicism and Renaissance Drama*, ed. RICHARD WILSON and RICHARD DUTTON (London, Longman, 1992), p. 58.

18. For Anthony Marlowe's sponsorship of a playhouse, see WALTER WILSON GREG, *Henslowe Papers* (London, A.M. Bullen, 1907), p. 51, GREENBLATT, 'Marlowe and the Will to Absolute Play', p. 64; WILLAN, *Early History*, pp. 211–12.

19. *Calendar of State Papers, Domestic* 23 (March 1589), p. 287.

20. KENNETH R. ANDREWS, *Elizabethan Privateering: English Privateering During the Spanish War, 1585–1603* (Cambridge, Cambridge University Press, 1964), pp. 203–4; *Calendar of State Papers, Colonial, East Indies, 1513–1616*, pp. 73–4.

21. WILLAN, *Early History*, p. 282.

22. THOMAS STUART WILLAN, 'Trade between England and Russia in the Second Half of the Sixteenth Century', *English Historical Review*, 63 (1948), pp. 308–9; 'Some Aspects of English Trade with the Levant in the Sixteenth Century', *English Historical Review*, 70 (1955), pp. 399–400. Tamburlaine's naval

ambitions may also reflect the fact that in 1585 a Russian fleet of twenty ships was constructed by shipbuilders from Deptford, and by 1587 there were preparations to build twenty more. See FUHRMANN, *Origins of Capitalism in Russia*, pp. 16–7.

23. ETHEL SEATON, 'Marlowe's Map', *Essays and Studies*, 10 (1924), p. 35.

24. JOHN HALE, *The Civilization of Europe in the Renaissance* (London, HarperCollins, 1993), pp. 24–45.

25. *Calendar of State Papers, Spanish, 1580–86*, 15 May 1582, pp. 366–7.

26. HALE, *Civilization of Europe*, pp. 26–7.

27. GREENBLATT, 'Marlowe and the Will to Absolute Play', pp. 59–60. EMILY BARTELS, *Spectacles of Strangeness: Imperialism, Alienation, and Marlowe* (Philadelphia, University of Pennsylvania Press, 1993), pp. 56–7.

28. BARTELS, *Spectacles of Strangeness*, pp. 60–1, 70–1.

29. BARTELS, ibid., p. 81. THOMAS CARTELLI, *Marlowe, Shakespeare, and the Economy of Theatrical Experience* (Philadelphia, University of Pennsylvania Press, 1991), p. 80.

30. GREENBLATT, 'Marlowe and the Will to Absolute Play', pp. 81–2.

31. PATRICIA FUMERTON, *Cultural Aesthetics: Renaissance Literature and the Practice of Social Ornament* (Chicago, University of Chicago Press, 1991), pp. 180–5.

32. WILLAN, *Early History*, p. 152.

33. R.M. CROSSKEY, 'Hakluyt's Accounts of Sir Jerome Bowes' Embassy to Ivan IV', *Slavonic and East European Review*, 61 (1983), pp. 546–64, esp. 563–4.

34. MARJORIE GARBER, ' "Here's Nothing Writ": Scribe, Script, and Circumscription in Marlowe's Plays', *Theatre Journal*, 36 (1984), pp. 302–3.

35. For a monumental exposition of this thesis, see ROBERT BRENNER, *Merchants and Revolution: Commercial Change, Political Conflict, and London's Overseas Trade, 1550–1653* (Cambridge, Cambridge University Press, 1993). On the Muscovy Company and its influence 'at the core of the eastward thrust during the second half of the sixteenth century', see pp. 13–14, 20–1, 78–9.

36. EDWARD SAID, *Orientalism: Western Conceptions of the Orient* (Harmondsworth, Penguin, 1991), pp. 60–3.

37. JEAN-CHRISTOPHE AGNEW, *Worlds Apart: The Market and the Theater in Anglo-American Thought, 1550–1750* (Cambridge, Cambridge University Press, 1986), pp. 41–3.

38. For the coexistence of trading and raiding, see ANDREWS, *Elizabethan Privateering*, pp. 229–38; and A. PÉROTIN-DUMON, 'The Pirate and the Emperor: Power and the Law on the Seas', in *The Political Economy of Merchant Empires: State Power and World Trade*, ed. JAMES D. TRACY (Cambridge, Cambridge University Press, 1991), pp. 196–227. See also, M.T. BURNETT, 'Tamburlaine: An Elizabethan Vagabond', *Studies in Philology*, 84 (1987), pp. 308–23.

39. MICHEL DE MONTAIGNE, *Essays*, trans. G.B. IVES (New York, Oxford University Press, 1946), book 3, chap. 13, 1464.

40. GEOFFREY PARKER, *The Military Revolution: Military Innovation and the Rise of the West, 1500–1800* (Cambridge, Cambridge University Press, 1988).

41. P. KOCHER, 'Marlowe's Art of War', *Studies in Philology*, 39 (1942), pp. 207–45. In 1567 Elizabeth sent Ivan two dozen architects and craftsmen to 'make

castles, towers, and palaces' for his fortification program; see WRETTS-SMITH, 'English in Russia', p. 99.

42. Marlowe's estimates for Tamburlaine's armies follow the exaggerated reports of Ivan's forces by observers such as HORSEY, *Travels*: 'He having strengthened himself by an invincible power of these Tartars . . . sets forward with an army of an hundred thousand horse and fifty thousand foot, cannon, and all artillery, munition and provisions, towards Livonia' (p. 266).

43. See, for example, UNA ELLIS-FERMOR's introduction to *The Works and Life of Christopher Marlowe: Tamburlaine the Great*, gen. ed. ROBERT HOPE CAVE (London, Methuen, 1930), pp. 23–30. The single exception to the neglect of Marlowe's Muscovy is A.L. Rowse, who thirty years ago wondered 'that people have not thought of the parallel between Tamburlaine's personality and career, the savagery and barbaric splendour, blood-lust and mania, and that of the contemporary ruler of Russia, who was a figure well-known to the Elizabethans' (A.L. ROWSE, *Christopher Marlowe: A Biography* (London, Macmillan, 1964), p. 69).

44. Sigismund quoted in FUHRMANN, *Origins of Capitalism in Russia*, pp. 43–4. See also W. KIRCHNER, 'Entrepreneurial Activity in Russian–Western Relations during the Sixteenth Century', *Explorations in Entrepreneurial History*, 8 (1956), pp. 250–1; and T. ESPER, 'A Sixteenth-Century Anti-Russian Arms Embargo', *Jarhbucher fur Geschichte Osteuropas*, 15 (1967), pp. 180–96; WILLAN, *Early History*, pp. 64–6. HORSEY, *Travels*, pp. 267–8. It was during the Livonian War that Ivan slaughtered prisoners who had surrendered under a 'dejective flag of truce' (p. 266), a crime that may have suggested Tamburlaine's tactics.

45. HORSEY, *Travels*, p. 269; and STEPHEN GRAHAM, *Ivan the Terrible: The Life of Ivan IV of Russia* (1933; rpt., New York, Ernest Benn, 1968), pp. 216–20. Modern estimates of the number of Ivan's victims at Novgorod range from 40,000 to 60,000.

46. HORSEY, *Travels*, pp. 294–8.

47. The link with *Tamburlaine* (and its implications for dating) was suggested in EDMUND KERCHEVEV CHAMBERS, *The Elizabethan Stage*, 5 vols (Oxford, Oxford University Press, 1923), 2:135; and *The Times Literary Supplement*, 28 August 1930, p. 684.

48. WILLAN, *Early History*, p. 64. Full details of the secret treaty (Public Records Office, State Papers, 193/161/fols 9–12) which was signed in 1569 and renewed in 1577 and 1582, were printed for the first time in H.R. HUTTENBACH, 'New Archival Material on the Anglo-Russian Treaty of Queen Elizabeth I and Tsar Ivan IV', *Slavonic and Eastern European Review*, 49 (1971), pp. 535–49. Item 3 states that each ruler will 'aid and assist the other with men, treasure, munition, and all things necessary for war' (p. 546).

49. WILLAN, *Early History*, p. 91. I. GREY, 'Ivan the Terrible and Elizabeth of England', *History Today*, 12 (1962), pp. 648–51; A.F. STUART, 'Early Russian Embassies to Britain', *Twentieth Century Russia*, 2 (1917), pp. 281–7.

50. HORSEY, *Travels*, p. 298. In 1581 Horsey valued a consignment of armaments, carried in 'thirteen tall ships', at £9,000, which suggests that they made up as much as ninety percent of exports to Russia in the period. See also, S. YAKOBSON, 'Early Anglo-Russian Relations, 1553–1613', *Slavonic and Eastern European Review*, 13 (1935), pp. 597–610, esp. p. 602.

51. FRANCIS BACON, *The Works of Francis Bacon*, ed. JAMES SPEDDING, 14 vols (London, Longman, 1857–74), 8:30; quoted in M.S. ANDERSON, 'English Views of Russia in the Seventeenth Century', *Slavonic and Eastern European Review*, 33 (1955), p. 143.

52. PHILIP SIDNEY, 'Astrophil and Stella', sonnet 2, lines 10–11, in *The Poems of Sir Philip Sidney*, ed. WILLIAM RINGLER (Oxford, Clarendon Press, 1962), p. 166. M. PERRIE, 'The Popular Image of Ivan the Terrible', *Slavonic and Eastern European Review*, 56 (1978), p. 275; S.H. BARON, 'Ivan the Terrible, Giles Fletcher and the Muscovite Merchantry', *Slavonic and Eastern European Review*, 56 (1978), pp. 568–9. Significantly, in the only other English Renaissance play set in Russia, *The Loyal Subject* (1618), Giles Fletcher's nephew John drew a coded analogy between his hero, an old general of the reign of Ivan, and Raleigh, as a tribute to a dying breed of privateers.

53. SAMUEL PURCHAS, *Hakluytus Posthumus, or Purchas His Pilgrims*, 20 vols (Glasgow, James MacLehose, 1905–7), 14:113; quoted in K. ANDREWS (note 20), p. 143.

54. J. BARCLAY, *The Mirror of Minds, or Icon Animarum* (London, 1631), pp. 125–8; quoted in K. ANDREWS, p. 145. For the conceptual confusion into which capitalism was thrown by the Muscovite state, with its 'mixture of Tartar and Byzantine elements' and 'extreme barbarity', see A. BESANÇON, 'The Russian Case', in *Europe and the Rise of Capitalism*, ed. JEAN BAECHLER, J.A. HALL, and M. MANN (Oxford: Blackwell, 1988), pp. 160–3.

55. The idea of linking the Mediterranean with the Indian Ocean across the Suez isthmus was, in fact, a project of the Levant merchants from the 1570s; see HALE, *Civilization of Europe*, p. 147.

56. *Calendar of State Papers, Domestic, James I* 9 (1611–18): 29 April 1613, pp. 181–2, and 27 October 1613, p. 208; I. LUBIMENKO, 'A Project for the Acquisition of Russia by James I', *English Historical Review*, 29 (1914), pp. 246–46: C.S.L. DUNNING, 'A Letter to James I Concerning the English Plan for Military Intervention in Russia', *Slavonic and Eastern European Review*, 67 (1989) pp. 94–108, and 'James I, the Russia Company, and the Protectorate Over North Russia', *Albion*, 21 (1989), pp. 206–26. See also, J. CHAMBERLAIN, *The Chamberlain Letters*, ed. ELIZABETH M. THOMSON (London, Murray, 1965), 29 April 1613: 'The King doth so apprehend the matter that he saith he never affected anything more than this, so that he doth not doubt of success, and makes account of sending ten or twelve thousand men' (p. 210). Chamberlain believed that only the death of Prince Henry prevented the project, for otherwise James 'would send them his second son to be their Emperor' (which may explain why Russia reacted so strongly to the execution of Charles I that relations with England were frozen for half a century).

57. WILLAN, *Early History*, pp. 4–5.

58. GREENBLATT, 'Marlowe and the Will to Absolute Play', pp. 66–7.

59. IMMANUEL WALLERSTEIN, *Historical Capitalism* (London, Verso, 1983), pp. 30–1; 56–7. SIMON SHEPHERD, *Marlowe and the Politics of Elizabethan Theatre* (Brighton, Harvester, 1986), pp. 149, 151.

60. SHEPHERD, ibid., p. 151.

61. ALAN SINFIELD, *Faultlines: Cultural Materialism and the Politics of Dissident Reading* (Oxford, Oxford University Press, 1992), p. 241.

62. The earliest formulation of the concept of consideration (which shifted contract law from a gift- to an exchange-economy) was in 1549, and it was in the 1560s that accountability of agreements came to depend on presence of consideration. The principle was affirmed in *Golding's Case* (1586). See A.W.B. SIMPSON, *A History of the Common Law of Contract: The Rise of the Action of Assumpsit* (Oxford, Clarendon Press, 1987), pp. 318–19. Robert Poley, a business agent of the Walsinghams, returned from The Hague on the

morning of Marlowe's murder, to meet with the victim and two other of Walsingham's agents, Ingram Frizer and Nicholas Skeres. See BAKELESS, *Tragicall History*, p. 178.

63. BAKELESS, ibid., pp. 167–8.

64. Ironically, considering Marlowe's identification with Icarus, the outstanding account concerned payment for wax delivered to the royal household since 1587. After cordage, wax was the most important commodity supplied by the Company. See WILLAN, *Early History*, pp. 183–4.

65. WILLAN ibid., pp. 249–61. Horsey began to collate his diplomatic memoirs sometime before the death of Walsingham, their dedicatee, in 1590. They exist in a single manuscript in the British Museum, Harleian MS. 1813, and were first published by EDWARD A. BOND in *Russia at the Close of the Sixteenth Century* (London, Hakluyt Society, 1856). The archives of the Russia Company were destroyed in the Great Fire, but would have contained all letters sent from Moscow to the Company's board of directors. In their absence, HORSEY's *Travels* must stand as an approximation of the information available to Marlowe's Kent patrons about their Asian investments.

66. Ivan was reported by contemporaries to have had a homosexual relationship with his favourite, Theodor Basmanov; see HEINRICH VON STADEN, *The Land and Government of Muscovy*, trans. T. ESPER (Stanford, CA, Stanford University Press, 1967), p. 35; and H.F. GRAHAM (ed.), ' "A Brief Account of the Character and Brutal Rule of Vasil'evich, Tyrant of Muscovy": Albert Schlichting on Ivan Groznyi', *Canadian–American Slavic Studies*, 9 (1975), p. 216. For a psychosexual biography, see ROBERT OWEN CRUMMEY, 'New Wine in Old Bottles?: Ivan IV and Novgorod', in *Ivan the Terrible: A Quatercentenary Celebration of His Death, Russian History*, 14 (1987), pp. 68–9.

67. HORSEY, *Travels*, p. 280.

68. R.K. MASSIE, *Peter the Great: His Life and World* (London, Victor Gollancz 1981), p. 209.

9 Marlowe, Marx, and Anti-Semitism*

Stephen Greenblatt

One influence on New Historicism was the philosopher Nietzsche, fashionable in the 1980s because his image of history as an endless game of the will to power was so contrary to Marx's idealistic belief in progress. Stephen Greenblatt's essay on *The Jew of Malta* was a signal, therefore, of how far Marx had fallen, when he deployed Marlowe to probe the communist's anti-Semitic politics, as opposed to the dramatist's Nietzschean cynicism. Marx and Marlowe both view the Jew as the embodiment of capitalism, on this reading, but whereas the philosopher imagines a world purged of 'Judaic' greed, the playwright heroises Barabas as a personification of eternal human destructiveness. Greenblatt's major book, *Renaissance Self-Fashioning* (1980), would belie its own title by showing how the individual subject was an 'ideological product' of power relations, and in this earlier article Marlowe's self-destructive Jew already reflects such post-political disenchantment with dreams of freedom. As he disappears in his own trap, Barabas seems, in fact, to figure the nihilism of Greenblatt's Berkeley colleague, Michel Foucault, who likewise preached a 'dispossession of the self, an extended vanishing'. There is irony that the play is thereby made the cue for one of Greenblatt's most bitterly personal essays; but unlike gay theorists, who read him as a spur to liberation, this Jewish critic sees no comfort in Marlowe's staging of society as a vast concentration camp. Instead, it is for its universal *contempt* that Marlowe's 'inexcusable' anti-Semitic text speaks to an age without hope of liberation. As much about post-modern America as pre-modern England, Greenblatt's bleak version of *The Jew of Malta* reveals how New Historicism boxed itself into a corner that was neither new nor strictly historicist.

A fantasy: Barabas, the Jew of Malta, had two children. The eldest, Abigail, sickened by the revelation that her father had murdered her

* Reprinted from *Critical Inquiry*, 5 (1978), 40–58.

Christian suitor, converted and entered a nunnery. The other child, a son, likewise apostatized; indeed he wrote a violently anti-Semitic pamphlet denouncing the essence of his father's religion as huckstering, its basis self-interest, its jealous god money. The pamphlet concluded with a call for the emancipation of mankind from Judaism, but, curiously, the son did not convert to Christianity and try to assimilate. On the contrary, he insisted that his father's hated religion was simply the practical essence of Christianity, the thing itself stripped of its spiritual mystifications. The Christians who prided themselves on their superiority to Jews were themselves practicing Judaism in their daily lives, worshipping money, serving egoistic need, buying and selling men as commodities, as so many pounds of flesh. The son's name, of course, was Karl Marx.

The purpose of this chapter is to read Marlowe's *The Jew of Malta* in the light of Marx's 'On the Jewish Question'.[1] Fantasy aside, this is neither an obvious nor a particularly promising enterprise. There was no 'Jewish Question' in Marlowe's England; there were scarcely any Jews.[2] Civil society, the rights of man, the political state, the concept of citizenship – Marx's basic terms – would have been quite incomprehensible to an Elizabethan. Marx's central theme, that political emancipation is not the same as human emancipation, would likewise have been incomprehensible in an age in which there was scarcely a conception of politics, in the modern sense, let alone a dream that man might some day be emancipated from both state and religion. Marx's discourse is informed by the Enlightenment, the American and French Revolutions, Feuerbach's analysis of religion, and the growth of capitalism; its occasion depends upon the particular, historically determined situation of the Ashkenazic Jews of nineteenth-century Germany; its rhetoric is colored both by the virulent modern strain of popular anti-Semitism and by the author's own troubled relationship to the religion of his fathers.[3]

Nevertheless, Marx's essay has a profound bearing upon *The Jew of Malta*; their conjunction enriches our understanding of the authors' relation to ideology and, more generally, raises fruitful questions about a Marxist reading of literature. The fact that both works use the figure of the perfidious Jew provides a powerful interpretative link between Renaissance and modern thought, for despite the great differences to which I have just pointed, this shared reference is not an accident or a mirage. 'On the Jewish Question' represents the nineteenth-century development of a late sixteenth-century idea or, more accurately, a late sixteenth-century trope. Marlowe and Marx seize upon the Jew as a kind of powerful rhetorical device, a way of marshaling deep popular hatred and clarifying its object. The Jew is charged not with racial deviance or religious impiety but with economic and social crime, crime that is committed not only *against* the dominant Christian society but, in less 'pure' form, by that society. Both writers hope to focus attention upon activity that is seen as at once alien and yet central to the life of the community and to direct against the activity the anti-Semitic feeling of the audience. The Jews themselves in their real historical situation are finally incidental in these works, Marx's as well as Marlowe's, except insofar as they excite the fear and loathing of the great mass of Christians. It is this privileged access to mass psychology by means of a semi-mythical figure linked in the popular imagination with usury, sharp dealing, and ruthless cunning that attracts both the sixteenth-century playwright and the nineteenth-century polemicist.[4]

Twentieth-century history has demonstrated with numbing force how tragically misguided this rhetorical strategy was, how utterly it underestimated the irrationality, the fixation upon its object, and the persistence of anti-Semitism. The Christian hatred of the Jew, nurtured by popular superstition, middle-class *ressentiment*, the frequent complicity of Church and state, the place of the Jews in the European economy, and the complex religious and cultural barriers, would not be so easily turned against a particular structure of economic or social relations or a cast of mind that crossed racial and religious boundaries but would light with murderous force upon the whole Jewish community. It is folly to attempt to use a people as a rhetorical device or to exploit popular prejudice as a force for constructive change, let alone moral enlightenment. Even granting that historical hindsight gives us an unearned wisdom, even granting all of the mitigating intentions with which the authors evidently used the figure of the Jew, we are obliged to acknowledge that there is something unsavory, inexcusable, about both works. Their nature is subdued to what it works in, like the dyer's hand; they are, I would insist, defiled by the dark forces they are trying to exploit, used by what they are trying to use. But this acknowledgement, necessary if we are to keep our moral bearings and look unflinchingly at the horrors of our history, is not identical with understanding. The latter will come only by patiently exploring what I have called the shared rhetorical strategy of *The Jew of Malta* and 'On the Jewish Question'.

I will begin by looking briefly at a famous use of the Jewish stereotype that contrasts sharply with Marlowe's and Marx's. *The Merchant of Venice* is built around a series of decisive structural conflicts – Old Law versus New Law, Justice versus Mercy, Revenge versus Love, Calculation versus Recklessness, Thrift versus Prodigality – all of which are focused upon the central dramatic conflict of Jew and Gentile or, more precisely, of Jewish fiscalism and Gentile mercantilism.[5] The great economic utility of Shylock – and of the Jew in this period – is his possession of liquid assets, assets which he is committed, for his very existence, to employ actively.[6] In general, in the northern Italian city-states, when the Christian merchants were weaker, the Jewish moneylenders were stronger; in Venice as Brian Pullan has shown, there was a vigorous attempt by the merchant class to undermine the power of Jewish moneylenders through the establishment of the Monte di Caritá, Christian lending institutions that would disrupt the Jews' 'bargains' by providing interest-free loans.[7] All of this seems to be reflected in the hatred Shylock and Antonio have for each other, hatred Antonio attributes to the fact that he has 'oft deliver'd from his forfeitures / Many that have at times made moan to me' (3.3.22–23).[8]

If Shylock is set against Antonio on grounds of fiscalism versus mercantilism, he is set against Portia on grounds equally based upon the economic position of Jews in early modern Europe. As Jacob Katz observes, the constant application of capital, to which the Jews were committed, precluded investment in immovable property. The law did not permit the Jew to acquire land, and the Jew, for his part, did not attempt to secure such permission:

> Landed property attracted the ordinary burgher who attained
> wealth because of the feeling of stability and economic security
> it gave him and the social prestige involved. But in his peculiar
> situation, the Jew would set no great store by either. He could
> not hope to perpetuate his wealth in that locality, nor did he
> seek a niche in the dominant social and economic hierarchy. The
> economic nexus linking the Jew with his environment was purely
> instrumental.[9]

In Shakespeare's play this economic nexus is suggested above all by Shylock's usury, but it is also symbolized by his nonparticipation in Venetian society, his cold, empty house, and such subtle indicators of value as his hostility to masquing – 'the vile squealing of the wryneck'd fife' (2.5.30). All of this is in sharp contrast to Portia, who has plenty of liquid assets; she can offer at a moment's notice enough gold to pay Antonio's 3000-ducat debt 'twenty times over' (3.2.306). But her special values in the play are bound up with her house at Belmont and all it represents: its starlit garden, enchanting music, hospitality, social prestige. That is, the economic nexus linking Portia with her environment is precisely *not* instrumental; her world is not a field in which she operates for profit, but a living web of noble values and moral orderliness.

Shylock is the antithesis of this world, as he is of the Christian
mercantilism of Venice. He is the 'alien', the 'stranger cur', 'a kind of
devil', in short, the 'faithless Jew'. Even the language he shares with
the Christian Venetians does not provide a bridge between them; he
may use the same words, but he uses them in a wholly different
sense:

> Shylock: Antonio is a good man.
> Bassanio: Have you heard any imputation to the contrary?
> Shylock: Ho no, no, no, no: my meaning in saying he is a good
>   man, is to have you understand that he is sufficient.
>
> (1.3.10–15)

Shylock needs to explain his use of the apparently innocuous 'good
man', as he will later be pressed to explain why he insists, against all
reason and self-interest, upon his bond: linguistically, psychologically,
ethically, as well as religiously, he is different. To be sure, he appeals
at moments to his sameness – 'Hath not a Jew eyes?' – and this
sameness runs like a dark current through the play, intimating secret
bonds that no one, not even the audience, can fully acknowledge.
For if Shakespeare subtly suggests obscure links between Jew and
Gentile, he compels the audience to transform its disturbing
perception of sameness into a reassuring perception of difference.
Indeed the Jew seems to embody the abstract principle of *difference*
itself, the principle to which he appeals when the Duke demands an
explanation for his malice:

> Some men there are love not a gaping pig!
> Some that are mad if they behold a cat!
> And others when the bagpipe sings i'th'nose,
> Cannot contain their urine. . . .
>
> (4.1.46–49)

The examples would be whimsical – evoking a motive no grander
than allegory – were they not spoken by Shylock, knife in hand;
instead, they bespeak impulses utterly inaccessible to reason and
persuasion; they embody what the rational mind, intent upon
establishing an absolute category of difference, terms *madness*.

The Jew of Malta opens with an apparent gesture toward the
same principle of differentiation that governs *The Merchant of Venice*.
Marlowe's Jew is introduced in the prologue by Macheuill as one
'Who smiles to see how full his bags are cramb'd'; he enters, then,
already trailing clouds of ignomiy, already a 'marked case'. But

while never relinquishing the anti-Semitic stereotype, Marlowe quickly suggests that the Jew is not the exception to but rather the true representative of his society. Though he begins with a paean to liquid assets, Barabas is not primarily a usurer, set off by his hated occupation from the rest of the community, but a great merchant, sending his argosies around the world exactly as Shakespeare's much-loved Antonio does. His pursuit of wealth does not mark him out but rather establishes him – if anything, rather respectably – in the midst of all the other forces in the play: the Turks exacting tribute from the Christians; the Christians expropriating money from the Jews; the convent profiting from these expropriations; religious orders competing for wealthy converts; the prostitute plying her trade and the blackmailer his. When the governor of Malta asks the Turkish 'Bashaw', 'What wind drives you thus into *Malta* rhode?' the latter replies with perfect frankness, 'The wind that bloweth all the world besides, / Desire of gold' (3.5.2–4). Barabas's own desire of gold, so eloquently voiced at the start and vividly enacted in the scene in which he hugs his money bags, is the glowing core of that passion which fires all the characters. To be sure, other values are expressed – love, faith, and honor – but as private values, these are revealed to be hopelessly fragile, while as public values, they are revealed to be mere screens for powerful economic forces. Thus, on the one hand, Abigail, Don Mathias, and the nuns are killed off with remarkable ease and, in effect, with the complicity of the laughing audience. (The audience of the Royal Shakespeare Company's brilliant 1964 production roared with delight when the poisoned nuns came tumbling out of the house.)[10] On the other hand, the public invocation of Christian ethics or knightly honor is always linked by Marlowe to baser motives. The knights concern themselves with Barabas's 'inherent sinne' only at the moment when they are about to preach him out of his possessions, while the decision to resist the 'barbarous mis-beleeuing *Turkes*' facilitates all too easily the sale into slavery of a shipload of Turkish captives. The religious and political ideology that seems at first to govern Christian attitudes toward infidels in fact does nothing of the sort; this ideology is clearly subordinated to considerations of profit. In Marx's terms, both religion and the political state are shown to rest upon the foundation of civil society which is entirely governed by the relentless pursuit of money.

Because of the primacy of money, Barabas, for all the contempt heaped upon him, is seen as the dominant spirit of the play, its most energetic and inventive force. A victim at the level of religion and political power, he is, in effect, emancipated at the level of civil society, emancipated in Marx's contemptuous use of the word:

The Jew has emancipated himself in a Jewish manner, not only by acquiring the power of money, but also because *money* had become, through him and also apart from him, a world power, while the practical Jewish spirit has become the practical spirit of the Christian nations. The Jews have emancipated themselves in so far as the Christians have become Jews.

(p. 35)

Barabas's avarice, egotism, duplicity, and murderous cunning do not signal his exclusion from the world of Malta but rather his central place within it. His 'Judaism' is, again in Marx's words, 'a universal *antisocial* element of the *present time*' (p. 34).

For neither Marlowe nor Marx does this recognition signal a turning away from Jew-baiting; if anything, Jew-baiting is intensified even as the hostility it excites is directed as well against Christian society. Thus Marlowe never discredits anti-Semitism, but he does discredit early in the play a 'Christian' social concern that might otherwise have been used to counter a specifically Jewish antisocial element. When the governor of Malta seizes the wealth of the Jews on the grounds that it is 'better one want for a common good, / Then many perish for a private man' (1.2.102–3), an audience at all familiar with the New Testament will hear in these words echoes not of Christ but of Caiaphas and, a few lines further on, of Pilate.[11] There are, to be sure, moments of social solidarity – as when the Jews gather around Barabas to comfort him or when Ferneze and Katherine together mourn the death of their sons – but they are brief and ineffectual. The true emblem of the society of the play is the slave market where 'Every ones price is written on his back' (2.3.4).[12] Here in the marketplace men are literally turned, in Marx's phrase, 'into *alienable*, saleable objects, in thrall to egoistic need and huckstering' (p. 39). And at this level of society, the religious and political barriers fall away: the Jew buys a Turk at the Christian slave market. Such is the triumph of civil society.

For Marlowe as for Marx, the dominant mode of perceiving the world, in a society hagridden by the power of money and given over to the slave market, is *contempt*, contempt aroused in the beholders of such a society and, as important, governing the behavior of those who bring it into being and function within it. This is Barabas's constant attitude, virtually his signature; his withering scorn lights not only on the Christian rulers of Malta ('thus slaves will learn', he sneers, when the defeated governor is forced into submission [5.2.50]), but on his daughter's suitor ('the slave looks like a hogs cheek new sindg'd' [2.3.45]), his daughter ('An *Hebrew* borne, and would become a Christian. / *Cazzo, diabolo*' [4.1.20–1]), his slave Ithamore ('Thus every

146

villain ambles after wealth / Although he ne're be richer then in
hope' [3.4.53–4]), the Turks ('How the slave jeers at him', observes
the governor of Barabas greeting Calymath [5.5.59]), the pimp,
Pilia-Borza ('a shaggy, totter'd staring slave' [4.3.6]), his fellow Jews
('See the simplicity of these base slaves' [1.2.219]), and even, when
he has blundered by making the poison too weak, himself ('What a
damn'd slave was I' [5.1.25]). Barabas's frequent asides assure us that
he is feeling contempt even when he is not openly expressing it, and
the reiteration of the derogatory epithet 'slave' firmly anchors this
contempt in the structure of relations that governs the play. Barabas's
liberality in bestowing this epithet – from the governor to the pimp
– reflects the extraordinary unity of the structure, its intricate series
of mirror images: Pilia-Borza's extortion racket is repeated at the
'national' level in the extortion of the Jewish community's wealth
and at the international level in the Turkish extortion of the Christian
tribute. It is as if the play were depicting Renaissance international
relations as a kind of glorified gangsterism, a vast 'protection' racket.[13]

At all levels of society in Marlowe's play and behind each version
of the racket (and making it possible) is violence or the threat of
violence, and so here too Barabas's murderousness is presented both
as a characteristic of his accursed tribe and as the expression of a
universal phenomenon. This expression, to be sure, is extravagant –
he is responsible, directly or indirectly, for the deaths of Mathias,
Lodowick, Abigail, Pilia-Borza, Bellamira, Ithamore, Friar Jacamo,
Friar Barnadine, and innumerable poisoned nuns and massacred
soldiers – but then everything about Barabas is extravagant: he is
more contemptuous than anyone else, more resourceful, cynical,
egotistical, and avaricious. The difference, however, in each of these
cases is of degree rather than of kind; Barabas expresses in extreme,
unmediated form the motives that have been partially disguised by
the spiritual humbug of Christianity. Barabas cannot *in the last
analysis* be assimilated to his world – Marlowe ultimately veers away
from so entirely sociological a conception – but it is important to
grasp the great extent to which the Jew is *brought into being* by the
Christian society around him. His extraordinary energy does not alter
the fact of his passivity throughout the play; his actions are always
responses to the initiatives of others. Not only is the plot of the whole
play set in motion by the governor's expropriation of Barabas's
wealth, but each of Barabas's particular plots is a reaction to what he
perceives as a provocation or a threat. Only his final stratagem – the
betrayal of the Turks – seems an exception, since the Jew is for once
in power, but even this fatal blunder is a response to his perfectly
sound perception that '*Malta* hates me, and in hating me / My life's
in danger' (5.2.31).

Barabas's passivity sits strangely with his entire domination of the spirit of the play, and, once again, we may turn to Marx for an explication:

> Judaism could not create a new world. It could only bring the new creations and conditions of the world within its own sphere of activity, because practical need, the spirit of which is self-interest, is always passive, cannot expand at will, but *finds* itself extended as a result of the continued development of society.
>
> (p. 38)

Though the Jew is identified here with the spirit of egotism and selfish need, his success is credited to the triumph of Christianity which 'objectifies' and hence alienates all national, natural, moral, and theoretical relationships, dissolving 'the human world into a world of atomistic, antagonistic individuals' (p. 39). The concrete emblem of this alienation in Marlowe's play is the slave market: its ideological expression is the religious chauvinism that sees Jews as inherently sinful, Turks as barbarous misbelievers.

The Jew of Malta ends on a powerfully ironic note of this 'spiritual egoism' (to use Marx's phrase) when the governor celebrates the treacherous destruction of Barabas and the Turks by giving due praise 'Neither to Fate nor Fortune, but to Heaven' (5.5.131). (Once again, the [Stratford] audience guffawed at this bit of hypocritical sententiousness.) But we do not have to wait until the closing moments of the play to witness the Christian practice of alienation. It is, as I have suggested, present throughout and nowhere more powerfully than in the figure of Barabas himself. For not only are Barabas's actions called forth by Christian actions, but his identity itself is to a great extent the product of the Christian conception of a Jew's identity. This is not entirely the case: Marlowe invokes an 'indigenous' Judaism in the wicked parody of the materialism of Job and in Barabas's repeated invocation of Hebraic exclusivism ('These swine-eating Christians', etc.). Nevertheless, Barabas's sense of himself, his characteristic response to the world, and his self-presentation are very largely constructed out of the materials of the dominant, Christian culture. This is nowhere more evident than in his speech which is virtually composed of hard little aphorisms, cynical adages, worldly maxims – all the neatly packaged nastiness of his society. Where Shylock, as we have seen, is differentiated from the Christians even in his use of the common language, Barabas is inscribed at the center of the society of the play, a society whose speech is a tissue of aphorisms. Whole speeches are little more than strings of sayings: maxims are exchanged, inverted, employed as weapons; the characters enact and even deliberately 'stage' proverbs

(with all of the manic energy of Breughel's 'Netherlandish Proverbs').
When Barabas, intent upon poisoning the nuns, calls for the pot of
rice porridge, Ithamore carries it to him along with a ladle, explaining
that since 'the proverb saies, he that eats with the devil had need for
a long spoone, I have brought you a Ladle' (3.4.58–60).[14] And when
Barabas and Ithamore together strangle Friar Barnadine, to whom
Abigail has revealed their crimes in confession, the Jew explains,
'Blame not us but the proverb, Confess & be hang'd' (4.1.149).

Proverbs in *The Jew of Malta* are a kind of currency, the compressed
ideological wealth of the society. Their terseness corresponds to that
concentration of material wealth that Barabas celebrates: 'Infinite
riches in a little roome.' Barabas's own store of these ideological
riches comprises the most cynical and self-serving portion:

Who is honour'd now but for his wealth?

(1.1.115)

Ego mihimet sum semper proximus.

(1.1.192)

A reaching thought will search his deepest wits,
And cast with cunning for the time to come.

(1.2.226)

. . . in extremity
We ought to make bar of no policy.

(1.2.278–9)

. . . Religion
Hides many mischiefs from suspicion.

(1.2.290–1)

Now will I show myself to have more of the Serpent
Then the Dove; that is, more knave than fool.

(2.3.36–7)

Faith is not to be held with Heretics.

(2.3.316)

For he that liveth in Authority,
And neither gets him friends, nor fills his bags,
Lives like the Ass that *Æsope* speaketh of,
That labours with a load of bread and wine,
And leaves it off to snap on Thistle tops.

(5.2.39–43)

For so I live, perish may all the world.

(5.5.12)

149

This is not the exotic language of the Jews but the product of the whole society, indeed its most familiar and ordinary face. And as the essence of proverbs is their anonymity, the effect of their recurrent use by Barabas is to render him more and more typical, to *de-individualize* him. This is, of course, the opposite of the usual process. Most dramatic characters – Shylock is the appropriate example – accumulate identity in the course of their play; Barabas loses it. He is never again as distinct and unique an individual as he is in the first moments:

> Goe tell 'em the Jew of *Malta* sent thee, man:
> Tush, who amongst 'em knowes not *Barabas?*
>
> (1.1.68–9)

Even his account of his past – killing sick people or poisoning wells – tends to make him more vague and unreal, accommodating him to an abstract, anti-Semitic fantasy of a Jew's past. The shift that critics have noted in Barabas's language, from the resonant eloquence of the opening to the terse irony of the close, is part of Marlowe's rhetorical design. It is one of the ways in which he reveals Barabas as the alienated essence of Christian society.

Even the Jew's exclusion from political power does not mark him off decisively from Christian society; rather it enacts, as Marx puts it, 'the contradiction between politics and the power of money'. The relationship between Barabas and the world of the play is almost perfectly expressed by Marx's own aphorisms:

> The Jew, who occupies a distinctive place in civil society, only manifests in a distinctive way the Judaism of civil society.
>
> Judaism has been preserved, not in spite of history, but by history.
>
> It is from its own entrails that civil society ceaselessly engenders the Jew.
>
> (p. 36)

With these aphorisms we are close to the heart of *The Jew of Malta*, as close, in any case, as Marx's 'On the Jewish Question' will take us. But precisely at this point we should, I think, feel a certain uneasiness, for where Marx would collapse the Jew into 'the Judaism of civil society', Marlowe insists upon elements of Barabas's character which do sharply and qualitatively distinguish him even from the world that has engendered him and whose spirit he expresses. For his own part, Barabas insistently excludes himself from all groups, Turks, Christians, *and* Jews:

Nay, let 'em combat, conquer, and kill all,
So they spare me, my daughter, and my wealth.

$$(1.1.155-6)$$

By itself this sentiment is not surprising; it is simply the expression of
that ruthless egotism fostered by the whole society. But Barabas does
seem set apart from everyone in the play, especially in his cold clarity
of vision, his apparent freedom from all ideology. 'A counterfeit
profession is better / Then unseen hypocrisy' (1.2.302–3), he tells his
daughter. In the long run, the play challenges this conviction, at least
from the point of view of survival; the governor, who is the very
embodiment of 'unseen hypocrisy', eventually triumphs over the
Jew's 'counterfeit profession'. But Marlowe uses the distinction to
direct the audience's allegiance toward Barabas; to lie and to know
that one is lying seems more attractive, more moral even, than to lie
and believe that one is telling the truth.

The ethical basis of such a discrimination does not bear scrutiny;
what matters is that the audience becomes Barabas's accomplice. And
the pact is affirmed over and over again in Barabas's frequent,
malevolently comic asides:

Lodowick:	Good *Barabas* glance not at our holy Nuns
Barabas:	No, but I do it through a burning zeal,
	Hoping ere long to set the house a fire. (Aside)

$$(2.3.90-2)$$

Years ago, in Naples, I watched a deft pickpocket lift a camera from
a tourist's shoulder bag and replace it instantaneously with a rock of
equal weight. The thief spotted me watching but did not run away –
instead he winked, and I was frozen in mute complicity. In *The Jew
of Malta*, the audience's conventional silence becomes the silence of
the passive accomplice, winked at by his fellow criminal. Such a
relationship is, of course, itself conventional. The Jew has, for the
audience, something of the attractiveness of the wily, misused slave
in Roman comedy who is always on the brink of disaster, always
revealed to have a trick or two up his sleeve. The mythic core of this
character's endless resourcefulness is comic resurrection, and, though
Barabas is destined for a darker end, he is granted at least one such
moment: thrown over the city walls and left for dead, he springs up
full of scheming energy. At this moment, as elsewhere in the play,
the audience waits expectantly for Barabas's recovery, *wills* his
continued existence, and hence identifies with him.[15]

Along with this identification, the audience grants Barabas certain
traditional rights by allowing him the privileged status of unmasker

or satirist. Where in Marx's 'On the Jewish question' there is an unvoiced but essential boundary between the author, who stands free of the social structure he excoriates, and the Jew, who is the quintessential product of that social structure, in Marlowe's play the boundary is blurred and the Jew linked in subtle ways with the playwright. The result is that even as the audience perceives Barabas as the alienated essence of Christian society, it identifies with Barabas as the scourge of that society.

The most striking indication of a subtle link between Marlowe and his hero, a link that distinguishes the Jew from the world around him and justifies the audience's identification with him, is Barabas's unique capacity for what one must call aesthetic experience. In his opening soliloquy this is manifested as an eloquent appreciation of his wealth:

> Bags of fiery *Opals, Saphires, Amatists,*
> *Jacints,* hard *Topas,* grass-green *Emeralds,*
> Beauteous *Rubies,* sparkling *Diamonds,*
> And seildsene costly stones. . . .
>
> (1.1.25–8)

Though the passion for wealth is widely shared, no one else in the play is capable of such a response. And it becomes clear that it is not only wealth that excites Barabas's energy, eloquence, and delight; money is not finally the jealous god of the Jew of Malta. To be sure, Barabas does speak to the end of turning a profit, but wealth is gradually displaced as the *exclusive* object of his concern; his main object through the latter half of the play seems to be revenge, at any cost, upon the Christians. Then, with his attempt to destroy the Turks and restore the Christians to power, it becomes evident that even revenge is not Barabas's exclusive object. At the end he seems to be pursuing deception virtually for its own sake:

> why, is not this
> A kingly kinde of trade to purchase Townes
> By treachery, and sell 'em by deceit?
> Now tell me, worldlings, vnderneath the sunne
> If greater falsehood euer has bin done.
>
> (5.5.49–53)

As Barabas, hammer in hand, constructs the machinery for this climactic falsehood, it is difficult not to equate him with the playwright himself, constructing the plot, and Marlowe appears consciously to encourage this perception: 'Leave nothing loose, all

leveld to my mind', Barabas instructs his carpenters, 'Why now I
see that you have Art indeed' (5.5.5–6). Deception here takes on
something of the status of literary art, and we might recall that
Plato's rival Gorgias held that deception – *apate* – is the very essence
of the creative imagination: the tragic artist's special power is the
power to deceive. Such a conception of art does not preclude its
claim to strip away fraud since tragedy 'with its myths and emotions
has created a deception such that its successful practitioner is nearer
to reality than the unsuccessful, and the man who lets himself be
deceived is wiser than he who does not'. This paradox in Gorgias
depends upon an epistemology and ontology summed up in his
proposition that 'Nothing whatever exists'. And, as I have argued
elsewhere, it is precisely this dark vision, this denial of Being, that
haunts all of Marlowe's plays.[16]

. Barabas devises falsehoods so eagerly because he is himself a
falsehood, a fiction composed of the sleaziest materials in his culture.
At times he seems almost aware of himself as such: 'we are villaines
both' (2.3.219), he announces to Ithamore after they have run through
a catalog of outrageous, blatantly fictional misdeeds. In celebrating
deception, he is celebrating himself – not simply his cunning, his
power to impose himself on others, his inventiveness, but his very
distance from ontological fullness. Barabas is the Jewish Knight of
Non-Being. From this perspective, the language shift, to which I
alluded earlier, is a deliberate assault upon that immediacy, that
sense of presence, evoked at the beginning in Barabas's rich poetry
with its confident sense of realized identity. 'Infinite riches in a little
roome' is speech dreaming its plenitude, its *possession* of being.[17]
Without that opening soliloquy, so unlike anything Barabas speaks
thereafter, we would have no norm by which to measure his
effacement; he exists subsequently in the failure of the opening
rhetoric to return, in the spaces between his words, in his lack of
substance. He is a thing of nothing.

This is why the particular objects Barabas sets for himself and
passionately pursues seem nonetheless curiously unreal: nothing can
desire nothing. But if there is no substance, within or without, there
remains in Barabas an intense, playful energy. Marlowe's hero is not
defined finally by the particular object he pursues but by the eerie
playfulness with which he pursues it. This playfulness manifests
itself as cruel humor, murderous practical jokes, a penchant for the
outlandish and the absurd, delight in role-playing, entire absorption
in the game at hand and consequent indifference to what lies outside
the boundaries of the game, radical insensitivity to human
complexity and suffering, extreme but disciplined aggression,
hostility to transcendence and indeed to the whole metaphysics of

presence. There is some evidence for a similar dark playfulness in Marlowe's own career, with the comic (and extremely dangerous) blasphemies, the nearly overt (and equally dangerous) homosexuality, the mysterious stint as double agent, and, of course the cruel, aggressive plays themselves. The will to play flaunts society's cherished orthodoxies, embraces what the culture finds loathsome or frightening, transforms the serious into the joke and then unsettles the category of the joke by taking it seriously. For Barabas, as for Marlowe himself, this is play on the brink of an abyss, *absolute* play.

Nothing could be further from Marx. To be sure, Marx dreamed of play as the very center of social existence but only in a society transformed by communism. The essential quality of this revolutionary playfulness is the return of man's powers to himself through the abolition of the division of labor and hence a liberated polymorphousness. [. . .] But precisely by locating this experience in an historical or, if you will, posthistorical moment, Marx cuts literature off from absolute play, from its essence as Marlowe conceives it. Before its concrete, material realization in a truly communist society, play can never be in and for itself; it is rather a way station, a form of planning, a mode at once of criticism and of prophecy. The vision of the revolutionary society for Marx, like the apocalyptic vision in Christianity, undermines the autonomy of play and renders it a critical reflection upon everything that exists or a model of nonalienated labor.[18] As the former, play may keep man from being locked in the reified structures of his particular society; as the latter, it may keep alive in a dark time certain vital human possibilities. But it is not emancipation itself which must always be pursued beyond the particular moments of liberated artistic play.[19]

It is this passionate, relentless pursuit of emancipation that governs Marx's rhetorical strategy in 'On the Jewish Question', and it is this rhetorical strategy – the quest for a world without 'Jews' or 'Judaism' – that is ultimately blocked in *The Jew of Malta* by Marlowe's absolute play, that is, by his buried identification with Barabas. This identification should not be overstated: Barabas is not, after all, an artist; the trap door and cauldron are not a playwright's plot but a Machiavelli's. The connection between the artist and the Jew is only strong enough to complicate the conclusion, based on our use of Marx's essay, that Barabas is the alienated essence of Christian society. To shore up this conclusion, we could argue that Barabas's passion for deceptive play does not exist for its own sake but rather to serve his instinct for survival: 'For so I live, perish may all the world' (5.5.12). Such an argument would serve to reintegrate Barabas into the now familiar world of rapacious egotism. Yet beneath this

egotism, so zestfully proclaimed in his asides, lies a dark, indeed
scarcely visible, but potent self-destructiveness.

This self-destructiveness certainly does not exist at the level of
conscious motivation, and with a character who manifests as little
interiority as Barabas, it is difficult and quite possibly pointless to
talk of unconscious motivation. The self-destructiveness rather is built
into the very structure of Barabas's identity. He is determined, he
says, to survive, determined not to be 'a senseless lump of clay /
That will with every water wash to dirt' (1.2.221–2), determined not
to 'vanish ore the earth in ayre, / And leave no memory that e're
I was' (1.2.270–1). Yet the play as a whole depicts Barabas's own
commitment to just such erosion of himself as a complex, integrated
subject. Having cut himself off from everyone and everything, neither
persecuted outsider nor accepted insider, he is a far more shadowy
figure at the close than he was at the start. That he dies in his own
trap is no accident, nor is it solely the result of the governor's
superior cunning: his career is in its very essence suicidal. He
proclaims that he always wants to serve his own self-interest: '*Ego
mihimet sum semper proximus*' (1.1.192); but where exactly is the self
whose interests he serves? Even the Latin tag betrays an ominous
self-distance: 'I am always my own neighbor', or even, 'I am always
next to myself'. Beneath the noisy protestations of self-interest, his
career is a steady, stealthy dispossession of himself, an extended
vanishing, an assault upon the subject.

Once again we might attempt to reintegrate Barabas into his
world and find in his self-destructiveness the supreme expression
of that 'human self-estrangement' Marx saw embodied in the Jew.
But we are prevented from doing so by the uncanny sense that we
have an unmistakable complicity in Barbaras's whole career, that
Marlowe would have us admire Barabas's progress toward the
boiling cauldron as he would have us admire the Jew's cynical
clarity of vision and his playfulness. Where Marx depicts human
self-estrangement in order to turn his readers toward pursuit of
human emancipation, Marlowe depicts something very similar
in order to disabuse his audience of certain illusions. And the
greatest of these illusions is that human emancipation can be
achieved.

Marx can finally envisage the liberation of mankind from what
he inexcusably calls 'Judaism'. Marlowe cannot. In fact, Marlowe
celebrates his Jew for being clearer, smarter, and more self-
destructive than the Christians whose underlying values Barabas
travesties and transcends. Self-destructiveness in the play, as
elsewhere in Marlowe's work, is a much-admired virtue, for it is
the sign that the hero has divested himself of hope and committed

himself instead to the anarchic, playful discharge of his energy. Nothing stands in the way of this discharge, not even survival, and certainly not that imaginary construction, that collection of social scraps and offal, that is Barabas's identity. This identity – everything that marks him as at once his society's most-hated enemy and its most characteristic product – is in the last analysis subordinate to his radical will to play, the will that is inseparable from the process that destroys him.

The Jew of Malta diverges most crucially from Marx at the point at which the latter invokes, in effect, what Ernst Bloch calls the principle of hope. In Marx there is the principle of hope without the will to play; in Marlowe, the will to play without the principle of hope.

Notes

1. All citations to Marlowe's *The Jew of Malta* (*Complete Works*, ed. C.F. TUCKER BROOKE [Oxford: Clarendon Press, 1910]) and Marx's 'On the Jewish question' (*Early Writings*, trans. and ed. T.B. BOTTOMORE [New York: Watts, 1963]) will appear in the text.

2. On Jews in Renaissance England, see CECIL ROTH, *A History of the Jews in England* (Oxford: Clarendon Press, 1964); SALO W. BARON, *A Social and Religious History of the Jews*, 2 edn, vol. 2, *Citizen or Alien Conjurer* (New York: Columbia University Press, 1967); and C.J. SISSON, 'A Colony of Jews in Shakespeare's London', *Essays and Studies*, 22 (1937), pp. 38–51.

3. On Marx's essay, see SHLOMO AVINIERI, *The Social and Political Thought of Karl Marx* (Cambridge: Cambridge University Press, 1968), pp. 43–6; ISAIAH BERLIN, *Karl Marx: His Life and Environment*, 3rd edn (London, 1963), pp. 27, 99–100; JEAN-YVES CALVEZ, *La Pensée de Karl Marx*, 6th edn (Paris, 1956), pp. 64–78; FRANZ MEHRING, *Karl Marx: The Story of His Life*, trans. EDWARD FITZGERALD (Ann Arbor, MI: Ann Arbor University Press, 1962), pp. 68–73; ROBERT C. TUCKER, *Philosophy and Myth in Karl Marx* (Cambridge: Cambridge University Press, 1961), pp. 111–13; and ISTVAN MESZAROS, *Marx's Theory of Alienation* (London: Merlin Press, 1970), pp. 28–31, 71–4.

4. Anti-Semitism, it should be emphasized, is never merely a trope to be adopted or discarded by an author as he might choose to employ zeugma or eschew personification. It is charged from the start with irrationality and bad faith and only partly rationalized as a rhetorical strategy. Marlowe depicts his Jew with the compulsive cruelty that characterizes virtually all of his work, while Marx's essay obviously has elements of a sharp, even hysterical, denial of his religious background. It is particularly tempting to reduce the latter work to a dark chapter in its author's personal history. The links I am attempting to establish with Marlowe or the more direct link with Feuerbach, however, locate the essay in a far wider context. Still, the extreme violence of the latter half of Marx's work and his utter separation of himself from the people he excoriates undoubtedly owe much to his personal situation. It is interesting that the tone of the attack on the Jews rises to an almost ecstatic disgust at the moment when Marx seems to be locating the Jews most clearly as a product of bourgeois culture; it is as if Marx were eager to prove that he is in no way excusing or forgiving the Jews.

5. All citations to *The Merchant of Venice*, ed. JOHN RUSSELL BROWN (Cambridge, MA: Harvard University Press, 1955), will appear in the text. There is a useful summary of the voluminous criticism of the play by NORMAN RABKIN, 'Meaning and Shakespeare', in *Shakespeare 1971*, ed. CLIFFORD LEECH and J.M.R. MARGESON, Proceedings of the World Shakespeare Congress, Vancouver, 1971 (Toronto: Toronto University Press, 1972), pp. 89–106. Of particular importance are C.L. BARBER's chapter on the play in *Shakespeare's Festive Comedy* (Princeton, NJ, 1959) and BARBARA LEWALSKI's 'Biblical allusion and allegory in *The Merchant of Venice*', *Shakespeare Quarterly* 13 (1962), pp. 327–43. On usury and Shakespeare's play, see JOHN W. DRAPER, 'Usury in *The Merchant of Venice*', *Modern Philology* 33 (1935), pp. 37–47; E.C. PETTER, '*The Merchant of Venice* and the problem of usury', *Essays and Studies* 31 (1946), pp. 19–33; and BENJAMIN NELSON, *The Idea of Usury: From Tribal Brotherhood to Universal Otherhood* (Princeton, NJ: Princeton University Press, 1949). On fiscalism and mercantilism, see IMMANUEL WALLERSTEIN, *The Modern World-System: Capitalist Agriculture and the Origins of the European World-Economy in the Sixteenth Century* (New York: Columbia University Press, 1974), pp. 147–51.

6. See JACOB KATZ, *Tradition and Crisis: Jewish Society at the End of the Middle Ages* (1st edn, 1958; New York: Free Press of Glencoe, 1971), pp. 46–7; see also ANTHONY MOLHO, 'A note on Jewish moneylenders in Tuscany in the late trecento and early quattrocento', in *Renaissance Studies in Honor of Hans Baron*, ed. ANTHONY MOLHO and JOHN A. TEDESCHI (Florence, 1971), pp. 101–17.

7. See BRIAN PULLAN, *Rich and Poor in Renaissance Venice: The Social Institutions of a Catholic State, to 1620* (Oxford: Oxford University Press, 1971).

8. Shylock seems, in part at least, to confirm this notion at 3.1.46ff.

9. Katz, *Tradition and Crisis*, pp. 47–8.

10. This was the invention of the director, Clifford Williams; in Marlowe's text only the dying Abigail appears. There is a discussion of this and other productions of Marlowe's play in JAMES L. SMITH's '*The Jew of Malta* in the theatre', in *Christopher Marlowe*, ed. BRIAN MORRIS, Mermaid Critical Commentaries (London: Ernest Benn, 1968), pp. 1–23.

11. See G.K. HUNTER, 'The Theology of Marlowe's *The Jew of Malta*', *Journal of the Warburg and Courtauld Institutes* 27 (1964), p. 236.

12. Shylock attempts to make this a similarly central issue in the trial scene, but, as we might expect, the attempt fails (4.1.90–100).

13. FREDERIC C. LANE, *Venice and History* (Baltimore, MD: Johns Hopkins University Press, 1966).

14. For the Jew as devil, see JOSHUA TRACHTENBERG, *The Devil and the Jews: The Medieval Conception of the Jew and its Relation to Modern Antisemitism* (New Haven, CT: Yale University Press, 1943).

15. See my 'The false ending in *Volpone*', *Journal of English and Germanic Philology*, 75 (1976), 93.

16. For Gorgias, see MARIO UNTERSTEINER, *The Sophists*, trans. KATHLEEN FREEMAN (Oxford: Oxford University Press, 1954), p. 113; THOMAS G. ROSENMEYER, 'Gorgias, Aeschylus, and *Apate*', *American Journal of Philology* 76 (1955), pp. 255–60. For Marlowe's 'Gorgian' aesthetic, see my 'Marlowe and Renaissance Self-Fashioning', in *Two Renaissance Mythmakers*, ed. ALVIN B. KERNAN, Selected Papers from the English Institute 1975–76 (Baltimore, MD: Johns Hopkins University Press, 1977).

17. For an illuminating discussion of this concept of presence in Western ontotheology, see JACQUES DERRIDA, *Of Grammatology*, trans. GAYATRI CHAKRAVORTY SPIVAK (Baltimore, MD: Johns Hopkins University Press, 1974), pp. 27–73

18. On the problematical status of play in Marx's thought, see FRANCIS HEARN, 'Toward a critical theory of play', *Telos* 30 (1976–77), pp. 145–60; on art as a model of nonalienated labor, see HANS ROBERT JAUSS, 'The idealist embarrassment: observations on Marxist aesthetics', *New Literary History* 7 (1975), pp. 191–208.

19. The most searching exploration in Marxist thought of these 'moments' of emancipation is by JÜRGEN HABERMAS; see esp. 'Toward a theory of communicative competence', *Recent Sociology*, no. 2, ed. HANS PETER DREITZEL (New York: Macmillan, 1970), pp. 115–48; and *Knowledge and Human Interests*, trans. JEREMY J. SHAPIRO (Boston, MA: Beacon Press, 1971). For an ambitious exploration of the opposition of play and seriousness in Renaissance culture, see RICHARD A. LANHAM, *The Motives of Eloquence: Literary Rhetoric in the Renaissance* (New Haven, CT: Yale University Press, 1976).

10 Malta: *The Jew of Malta*, and the Fictions of Difference*

EMILY BARTELS

In reading *The Jew of Malta* as a crude incitement to anti-Semitism, New Historicists were reacting to the sour suspicion of the Western canon in multi-ethnic America. By contrast, Emily Bartels's essay demonstrated how a stricter historicism might release the radical potential of such a classic text. Whereas Stephen Greenblatt had seen Marlowe's cynical Jew as an incarnation of all that Christianity despises and dreads, Bartels disrupts this anachronistic binarism by restoring the play to the multi-racial Mediterranean where it is actually set. What was so crucial about Malta, she explains, was its location in the no-man's land between Christendom and Islam, where the European presence was Spain: England's Catholic foe. It is upon this historical irony that Marlowe pivots his plot, with Del Bosco, the Spanish admiral, and Calymath, the Turkish commander, each misrepresenting the island as their own in a dichotomy between the Other and the Same. By introducing third parties, like the slave Ithamore, however, the dramatist undermines the polarities on which such empires depend, and in Barabas creates an interloper so protean as to expose the fictions on which identity itself is built. Dating from the end of the Cold War, when the United States was suddenly bereft of an 'Evil Empire' to oppose, Bartels's analysis breaks the dualism between subversion and containment that had gridlocked New Historicism, reconfiguring Marlowe as an unacknowledged precursor of the (Algerian Jewish) philosopher Jacques Derrida in his refusal to privilege either East or West, Turk or Christian, or Alien or Self. Here and in her 1993 book, *Spectacles of Strangeness*, Bartels repositions Marlowe as a post-modern before the fact, deconstructing the stereotypes of difference that enable racism, mysogyny, or homophobia to thrive.

* Reprinted from *English Literary Renaissance*, 20 (1990), 1–16.

As Europe's fervor for geographic exploration in the sixteenth and seventeenth centuries led to continued confrontations with other worlds and peoples, the 'fascination with the idea of the stranger in a strange land' – a phrase which Stephen Greenblatt uses, appropriately, to characterize Christopher Marlowe's plays – became increasingly characteristic of European society.[1] The popularity and necessity of such texts as Hakluyt's *Voyages* or John White's 'true pictures and fashions' of the newly discovered people of North America attest to this fascination. And so too does the short-lived but significant preoccupation (extending only from the mid-sixteenth to mid-seventeenth centuries) with the 'Wunderkammer' – a collection of such curiosities as an Indian axe, an African charm made of teeth, a mummified child, and the 'bauble and bells of Henry VIII's fool'.[2] The wonder-cabinet itself suggests Europe's desire to bring the 'infinite riches' of the world outside into its own 'little room', to enclose and somehow to contain, if not to categorize, these fragments of other worlds and peoples.[3] This act of enclosure provides a fitting image for the form which encounters with strange new worlds inevitably took, as confrontation was translated into domination, and exploration into colonization.

These continued encounters with the 'other', however, necessitated a concomitant confrontation with self, provoking a re-evaluation of the known in relation to the newly discovered unknown. Significantly, and ironically, England's preoccupation with strangers and strange lands intensified the culture's re-examination of its own estranged others (such as the poor and insane), and led to the institution of 'poor laws' (however ineffectual) and to the institutionalization of the mad.[4] The inclusion of King Henry's fool's 'bauble and bells' amid the collection of marvels suggests the blurring between cultures, as England recognized the other within itself. This recognition could only be a threat to a society whose self-definition depended upon continued assertions of a ruling and stabilizing orthodoxy, assertions so prevalent and persuasive that critics even in our era have upheld the myth of a singular and stable 'Elizabethan world picture'. Consequently, with the emergence of colonialist exploits came also the insistence upon the otherness of the other, upon the absolute difference between the dominating and the dominated culture.

Edward Said's study of 'orientalism' has established assertions of absolute difference as essential to Europe's domination of the Orient and has uncovered crucial discursive strategies marking and enabling European domination more generally.[5] Europe, Said argues, creates an artificial boundary between itself as a civilized and orderly establishment (the 'ours') and the savage and mysterious other world (the 'theirs'), displacing everything it considers, or wishes to consider, other to itself (barbarity or excessive sensuality, for example) onto the Orient. Through this binary opposition Europe secures its own supremacy and suppresses the threatening unknowableness of the Orient by defining this other in its own European terms. The 'truth' of such categorization is subverted, however, by Africa. For, as Christopher Miller has argued, with Europe as the self and the Orient as the Other, Africa can only be a third term outside the binarism, and it figures as 'the Orient's orient' or 'the Other's other' – a term which here (as in Lacan) has no fixed meaning.[6] Consequently, the attempts within Africanist discourse to impose such meaning result in ambiguities and contradictions, as Europe projects onto this 'empty slate' both what it embraces as self and what it displaces as other. In both cases, representation of the other within Europe's colonizing discourses emerges as representation of the self, and assertions of absolute difference as 'matters of strategy rather than truth'.[7]

As new historicists have suggested, such strategies of power were also being enacted on the Renaissance stage, not merely to reproduce but rather to enforce or subvert (or, paradoxically, both) the *modus operandi* of the state. Yet, as the emergence of the 'Wunderkammer' demonstrates, colonialist interest had already become important in the mid-sixteenth century. Christopher Marlowe's plays, produced in the 1580s and 1590s, record that interest, with their characteristic exotic presentations of foreign worlds and peoples. Significantly, instead of bringing to the stage a collection of exotic 'others' as a curious display, these texts expose and undermine the discourses of power which attempt to colonize and contain those others by ultimately revealing the fictionality of myths of domination and difference. *The Jew of Malta*, particularly, centers on and subverts colonialist constructs. By offering Barabas 'the Jew' as its main character, the play provokes readings which center on the Semitism or anti-Semitism of his characterization, of the text, and of the playwright; yet significantly, it contextualizes its representation of the Jew amid imperialist conflicts and reveals the stereotype as a product not of religious but of colonialist competitions.

What is perhaps most problematic about *The Jew of Malta* – and what therefore receives prominent critical attention – is its seemingly anti-Semitic stereotype of the Jew. Greenblatt, for example, suggests that Marlowe's 'figure of the Jew' is, for its Christian audience, 'an embodiment . . . of all they loathe and fear, all that appears stubbornly, irreducibly different', a 'marked case' who 'enters already trailing clouds of ignominy'.[8] That ignominy was asserted and enforced in the mystery plays (still being played throughout the sixteenth century) which presented the Jew, ostentatiously marked by a large nose and red wig and beard, as histrionically greedy, deceitful,

villainous, and faithless.[9] Marlowe's play clearly evokes that
stereotype as it costumes Barabas in a long nose and possibly red hair
as well and introduces him counting and fondling his 'infinite riches'
(1.1.37). Its title – in contrast to all of his others (*Dido, Tamburlaine,
Doctor Faustus*, and *Edward II*) which name the main character –
privileges type, as it presents 'the Jew' rather than Barabas. Machevill
seconds this emphasis in his prologue by announcing the play as 'the
tragedy of a Jew', and further abnegates the title character's
individuality by using 'a' rather than 'the' here (Pro. 30).

Yet the title links Barabas's identity as 'the Jew' to his position
as a figure 'of Malta', and that link, often overlooked by critics
preoccupied and persuaded by the apparently anti-Semitic
stereotype, is crucial to an understanding of the figure and of the
play. For the text is structured around two separate but parallel
events: the external domination of outside authorities over Malta,
and the internal domination of the inside authority (Ferneze) over
the Jews, and over Barabas in particular as their representative.
The representation of Malta establishes a context of colonialism,
and its link to the representation of Barabas insists that we view the
stereotype of the Jew in relation to that context – that we consider
what it means to be 'of Malta' before or while deciding what it
means to be 'the Jew', and that we recognize colonialism as a central
concern of the text, as of its extra-theatrical context.

Renaissance plays situated the Jew in foreign worlds, not only to
reproduce the historical alienation of Jews from England but also
to enhance the otherness of the figure. Italy became the favored
setting for Shakespeare and those who followed as a place whose
contamination both enforced and was enforced by the preconceptions
of the Jew as villain.[10] Although this predilection post-dates Marlowe,
it highlights the uniqueness of his use of setting, for he associates
his Jew with a place defined not by corruption, but by imperialist
conflicts of significant consequence to England's national security.

Because of its location in the Mediterranean Sea, Malta remained a
strategic post for both trading and war, and consequently an object of
continued imperialist domination. Europe's interest in the island was
heightened by the unsuccessful Turkish siege of 1565 which, had it
succeeded, would have given the Turks a threatening control over
Mediterranean commerce and defense.[11] In response to this event,
England launched an 'ideological campaign' against the Turks as
'aggressor', taking on Malta's cause with an eye to her own national
security.[12] In setting his tragedy in Malta, Marlowe exploits
contemporary interest in imperialist activity (which did not end with
the siege), and takes advantage of its extra-theatrical importance to
enforce its significance within the play.

The play, in fact, builds on the historical base and places Malta in a position of subjugation by rewriting history and presenting the Turks as victorious in their siege. When the Governor first appears, the autonomy of his rule is being overridden by the dictates of the Turkish Calymath, who demands (and receives) acquiescence to his father's long-standing tributary league. Ferneze first exercises and defines his authority in relation to the Turkish cause, as he extorts payment from the Jews (an action which provides the internal parallel to the external domination, and to which I will return). Although he subsequently turns against the Turks, his rebellion is dictated by the Spanish Del Bosco, who arrives in Act Two to announce that his king 'hath title to this isle' and to impose yet another external claim over Malta (2.2.37). Although silent through most of the play, Del Bosco appears continually with Ferneze, and even as the Governor ultimately triumphs over Turk and Jew, the Spaniard stands beside him, reminding us of Spain's imperialist intentions, of Del Bosco's warning that the Spanish king 'means quickly to expel' Ferneze and his knights from Malta (2.2.37–38).[13]

In giving Spain the defining voice over Malta, Marlowe's play exposes and undermines the strategies enabling imperialistic power – strategies which depend upon discursive assertions of absolute difference between an 'ours' and a 'theirs', an Establishment and an Outsider. Del Bosco enforces his claim by rewriting Malta's allegiance to Turkey as a pre-established opposition. He directs Ferneze to:

Remember that, to Europe's shame,
The Christian isle of Rhodes, from whence you came,
Was lately lost, and you were stated here
To be at deadly enmity with Turks.

(2.2.30–33)

Del Bosco defines Malta as a Christian, European 'ours', 'stated' as an Establishment to act against an alien, Turkish 'theirs'. His directive calls up the historical prototype for Ferneze and his knights, the Knights of St John, who were organized to defend the Christian world against the Turkish 'infidel', and who were driven in their campaign from Rhodes and (in 1530) to Malta, their last and most permanent outpost.[14] His subsequent demonization of the Turks as 'barbarous' and 'misbelieving' (2.2.46) echoes the European prejudice against the Turks evident in *Othello*, for example, where the general wonders if his unruly soldiers have all 'turned Turks' (2.3.169).

Perhaps because Del Bosco's terms seem to fit so well with historical prejudices, critics have endorsed the binary opposition which he proposes. J.B. Steane, for example, reads Ferneze's overthrow of

163

Barabas and Calymath as the triumph of Establishment over Outsider, and suggests a simple referentiality between Malta and Establishment, and between Turk (as well as Jew, which I'll leave aside for the moment) and Outsider.[15] Yet the 'facts' of the play resist such organization, for the Turks are neither the quintessential nor the only Outsiders here, and Malta is not an autonomous Establishment. Calymath, far from seeming a savage, 'misbelieving' barbarian, acts on law (whose origination under his father's rule suggests an established patriarchal order) and with moderation; in contrast to his basso Callapine, he is willing to extend the deadline for Ferneze's payment.[16] Although Del Bosco labels the Turks the only threatening Outsider, the country which he represents is equally 'outside' Malta – and Elizabethan England.

Del Bosco's attempts to define Malta as the Establishment are actually attempts to enforce the authority of Spain. The simple dichotomy which he imposes strategically overlooks the fact that Malta is the object and not the subject of imperialist conflict, a conflict in which Spain's own interests (like England's) are very much at stake. For the Turks are in competition with Spain, not Malta, and for, not against, Malta. Instead of being easily distinguished as Establishment and Outsider, the two main contenders (both Outsiders to the Elizabethan world) are positioned within the text as competing Establishments, both 'outside' the only domain we see. The play, then, subverts the simple binarism which Del Bosco imposes both by exposing three terms where he acknowledges only two and by undermining the difference between 'ours' and 'theirs' upon which his imperializing discourse depends. Moreover, the play represents Malta itself as a place of difference – not in relation to some other, but within itself, and precisely because of its undefinable position outside, rather than within, a binary opposition. As the object of the imperialist conflict, the island emerges in Marlowe's play as a third term whose meaning (as Miller suggests of Africa) is dictated from without rather than derived from within. What Malta 'means' within the text depends upon the discourses imposed upon it (predominantly here, by Spain), discourses which enable the self-assertion and self-empowerment of that dominating subject.

Yet the relation between the subject and object of domination is problematized by Ferneze's complicity in his own subjugation: he misreads domination as alliance and alternately adopts the dictates of both imperializing powers. The play leaves ambiguous how conscious this misreading is on his part, how much a product of blindness or insight, naïveté or cunning. Yet whether or not Ferneze chooses subjugation with an eye to possible self-empowerment, it is clear that he uses his subjection to both Turkey and Spain for his own exercise of authority (in the first case over the Jews and, in the second, over the Turks and Jews). The Governor, in effect, exchanges a place as the colonized for a place as the colonizer, displacing his powerlessness onto an other (which he must create as other) as a strategic defense against his own disempowerment. The text, then, implicates the object of domination as it undermines the discourses of the dominating subject, subverting the distinction (which it provokes) between dominator and dominated, as between 'ours' and 'theirs', Establishment and Outsider, and suggesting imperialism as a self-perpetuating chain reaction. The colonized have access to power only by becoming colonizers themselves and, ironically, by reinscribing the kind of discrimination which has enabled their own disempowerment.

The play exposes the production of imperialist fictions as self-perpetuating by linking Ferneze's dominance under the Turks to his domination over the Jews, and representing the stereotype of the Jew as a product of an internal domination which not merely mirrors but also derives from the external one. Clearly, Ferneze's exploitation of the Jews emerges in response to the Turkish demand for money, as he shifts the responsibility for payment from himself to them. In associating the Governor with the Knights of St John, the play enforces his role as a colonizer, for the historical Knights colonized a series of islands (Malta the most prominent and most permanent among them) in their attempts to secure a base for their campaigns. Although officially they were committed to preserving native rights and customs, their domination often devolved into dictatorships, and their enterprises involved economic as well as Christian gains.[17] The Knights stood as a threat to Elizabethan England because of their militant Catholicism and their control over Mediterranean commerce, and the play encourages its audiences' prejudices against them as it erases the one historical event (their success in freeing Europe from the Turks) which secured what was already very limited English support after the Reformation.[18]

Apart from this historical context, Ferneze's position as a colonialist becomes increasingly clear as what it means to be 'of Malta' becomes increasingly unclear. The text leaves ambiguous who, if anyone, is originally and authentically Maltese by peopling the island with multifarious groups and nationalities (Italians, 'Grecians, Turks, and Afric Moors', the Knights, and the Jews), suggesting that to be of Malta means, in effect, not to be, originally, of Malta (2.2.9).[19] The Governor, however, exploits that ambiguity and circumscribes the citizenry of Malta in his own terms and for his own profit. When he needs money to meet Calymath's demands, he scapegoats the Jews as 'the inhabitants of Malta' and makes Barabas, as a representative citizen, responsible for the 'common good' (1.2.21, 102). Although Barabas is well established within the community of merchants (and, as he himself emphasizes, as 'the Jew of Malta'), he protests that he and his fellow Jews are 'strangers' here (1.2.61). In presenting these two equally unsubstantiated claims, the text undermines both. This undecidability exposes Ferneze's attempts to designate a clearly defined citizenry as a product of discourse, a colonizing discourse which imposes its own terms on the object (or subjects) it would control and contain.

Ferneze's representation of Barabas as Jew emerges as a part of that same discourse, and of that same conversation.[20] Although Barabas places himself in a position of difference (as a 'stranger') to escape taxation, Ferneze (who is as much a stranger here) translates that difference as religious rather than national, in terms which allow him (as the national distinction does not) to distinguish the Jews as subversively other, as the heathen 'theirs' to his Christian 'ours'. The Jews are 'infidels', 'accursed in the sight of heaven', and his tolerance of their 'hateful lives' has led, he argues, to the 'taxes and afflictions' of Malta (1.2.66–67). In establishing this Christian/Jew dichotomy, Ferneze assigns a fixed meaning to the Jew, defining him as everything he, as Christian, is not (in the same way that Europe, according to Said, defines the Orient as everything Europe is not, or wishes it were not). Europe's domination of other worlds is marked by attempts to circumscribe each in fixed terms, for mastery over the dominated other is enabled and signified by knowledge of it. Ferneze's circumscription of the Jew as the Christian other emerges as just such a production and enforcement of knowledge, especially as it reinscribes the stereotype already established on the stage by the faithless, greedy, and deceitful Jews of the mystery plays, endorsed by the audiences offstage, and quickly embraced by the audiences onstage.

The play, however, undermines the knowledge, the rigid Christian/Jew dichotomy and its allied stereotype, that Ferneze promotes and exposes discrepancies within his colonizing discourse which unfix his terms. The Governor's insistence on religious difference is immediately subverted by his laws, which rewrite the distinction in economic terms. According to the written edicts, if a Jew refuses to pay the tax, he 'shall straight become a Christian': no longer a source of money, he can no longer be a Jew (1.2.75–76). This slippage between religious signifiers and their secular signifieds is further exacerbated as he identifies his 'profession' as his belief, but defines Barabas's 'profession' as money-making, imposing a double standard and assigning the Jew only a secular identity.[21] While Ferneze asserts of the Christians that 'to stain our hands with blood / Is far from us and our profession' (1.2.148–49), he protests Barabas's claims to righteousness, retorting, 'Sham'st thou not to justify thyself / As if we knew not thy profession?' (1.2.123–24).

The Governor's attempts to establish the Jew as other (and a stereotypical other) are undermined not only by the gaps between his religious terms and their secular signifieds, but also by the discrepancies between the distinctions which he asserts and the similarities which we see. As critics have often noted, the play offers a cast of characters all too like Barabas in those aspects – 'avarice, egotism, duplicity, and murderous cunning' – which his onstage (and offstage) audiences use to set him off as Other, to enforce the stereotype of the Jew.[22] Ferneze demonizes Barabas for his interest in money while clearly seconding that interest and desiring that the Jew 'live still' in Malta and 'get more' (1.2.105–6). Although Greenblatt argues that such similarities undermine the Christianity of the Christians, he suggests nonetheless that the text upholds the anti-Semitic stereotype and represents its Jew as a 'stock type of demonic villainy'.[23] Yet because the stereotype signifies and therefore depends upon recognizable difference, the play's refusal to validate that difference has the effect of invalidating the stereotype and the discourses from which it derives.

Ferneze's representation of the internal situation is as much at odds with the facts as is Del Bosco's reading of the external affairs, for both impose a rigid binarism on a contention which involves three terms rather than two. The opponent who necessitates and determines the Governor's policy is not the Jew but the Turk: the 'taxes and afflictions' imposed upon Malta have absolutely nothing to do with the Jews and everything to do with the Turks. Just as Del Bosco rewrites Spain's opposition to Turkey as a conflict between Malta and Turkey, so too does Ferneze rewrite his relation to the Turks as a conflict between Christians and Jews. As I have suggested, the play is structured around this parallel between the two figures and their respective impositions of power, emphasizing the Governor's role as a colonizer by linking him to figures whose colonialist aims are explicit rather than implicit, and highlighting the strategic fictions of both. This parallel is also reinforced as Marlowe strategically delays, in both the external and internal situations, the introduction of the figure whose presence subverts colonialist dichotomies – in the first case, Del Bosco (who reminds us of Spain's role in what he misrepresents as a conflict between Malta and Turkey) and, in the second, Ithamore (who reminds us of the Turk's role in what Ferneze misrepresents as a conflict between Christians and Jews).

It is not only Ithamore's presence which calls Ferneze's discourse into question, but also his own description of Barabas, as he – speaking,

like the Governor, from a position of subjugation – attempts to place
himself in a position of domination by demonizing the Jew as a
'strange thing' (4.4.82). In Ithamore's case as in Ferneze's, the play
exposes similarities where he marks difference. Despite Ithamore's
exaggerated appetites for rice and murder, his scurrilous appearance,
and the fact of his circumcision (which Barabas notes earlier as a trait
shared by 'both'), the slave demonizes his master as one who 'lives
upon pickled grasshoppers and sauced mushrooms', who 'never
put on a clean shirt since he was circumcised', whose hat 'Judas
left under the elder when he hanged himself' (4.4.82–90). Barabas
himself underscores the fictional nature of this representation, as he,
present here and disguised as a Frenchman, objects in asides to each
of Ithamore's claims. His comic and transparent portrayal of a
Frenchman – who also figured in the Elizabethan imagination as
an alien usually despised – displays all the more obviously the
representation (or misrepresentation) of an other as a self-
empowering fiction.[24]

Despite Ferneze's attempts to define Barabas through an absolute
binarism and as a stereotypical other, the Jew emerges here, like
Malta, as a third term outside the dominant opposition (Christian
versus Turk). In his case, as in Malta's and Africa's, the term
represents absence rather than presence, an 'empty slate' whose
definition is dictated from without and not derived from within.[25]
In a useful discussion of colonialist discourse, Homi Bhabha argues
that the 'anxious repetition' of stereotypes reveals the colonizer's
desire to contain the colonized within known and knowable terms
but, at the same time, betrays an awareness (however sublimated)
that such containment and the knowing it professes are not possible.[26]
It is precisely this recognition which Marlowe's play brings to the
foreground as it rehearses the stereotype of the Jew. For instead of
validating the stereotype, the play creates a tension between the
discourses which attempt to script Barabas a fixed and knowable role
as 'the Jew' and Barabas's persistence as the unknowable object of
those discourses – a tension acted out offstage between critics who
attempt to 'explain' Barabas and his motivations, and the text which
defies such explanation.

The wide divergence in these critical opinions attests to the
impossibility of knowing who this subject really is. To some, Barabas
is a sympathetic and even praiseworthy hero, a figure 'conscious
of being hated and want[ing] to be loved'; to others, he is the
'quintessential alien', or worse, 'a mere monster brought in with
a large painted nose to please the rabble'.[27] The differences
between readings of the character suggest a difference within the
characterization, and critics, unable to locate the 'true' Barabas, have

located a significant gap in his characterization between Acts Two and Three, and have used unintentional authorial unevenness as an excuse for and an answer to that difference.[28] Yet the discrepancy within his characterization extends throughout the text and emerges not as a textual problem but as a strategy of representation – a strategy which exposes the impossibility of defining Barabas absolutely and, therefore, of stereotyping the Jew.

The fictions which Barabas constructs to hide himself and his 'many mischiefs' from the onstage audiences also occlude the view of Marlowe's audiences (1.2.291); for the play refuses its spectators a privileged position of knowledge. Like the characters, we are continually surprised as what seems a sincere speech or action is suddenly betrayed as pretense – as Barabas bemoans his initial loss of wealth only to discover a substantial hidden store, for example, or as he embraces Ithamore as his heir and partner in crime only to vow vengeance against him immediately thereafter, or as he dies and rises again.[29] And what motivates Barabas is as undefinable as his schemes are unpredictable, inasmuch as he offers a series of conflicting goals – his ducats, his daughter, revenge – to justify his deeds. The play, then, defines its protagonist by difference, not between himself and a Christian other (as does Ferneze), but between his various self-representations: by a difference within the characterization rather than between the characters, making him unknowable rather than known.

Marlowe represents and exposes this strategy of characterization in Barabas's own self-representation, as he undermines his identity as the Jew by presenting himself in answer to different aspects of the stereotype, ultimately unfixing the stereotypical terms. As he laments to Ferneze over his lost fortune, for example, Barabas plays a figure of greed, destroyed because the Governor has 'my wealth, the labour of my life, The comfort of mine age, my children's hope' (1.2.153–54). As he meets Katherine in the marketplace he becomes a learned Jew pondering the Maccabees, and pretends to be offering her son Jewish law and not his Jewish daughter. To gain the aid of the villainous Ithamore, Barabas reduces himself to a circumcised, anti-Christian villain and directs his new slave to 'make account of me / As of thy fellow. We are villains both, / Both circumcised. We hate Christians both' (2.3.218–20). The discrepancies within Barabas's representations of the Jew, like those within the text's, expose this identity as a fictional construct, exploited as strategy and not offered as 'truth'.

Barabas's profession of 'fellow-ship' with Ithamore suggests the strategy he exploits throughout as he represents himself in terms familiar to, because shared by, his respective audiences: to Ferneze, whose desire for money necessitates and dominates their first interchange, he plays a greedy Jew; to Ithamore, who promotes villainy as his most valuable asset, he plays the deceitful villain.[30] As Barabas fashions his role of difference from the 'materials' of his spectators, he masks his threatening unknowableness and plays to their need for a knowable 'other'.[31] He allows himself, in effect, to be invented by the figures (Ferneze and Ithamore particularly) whose own assertions of authority depend upon the presence and the subjugation of a containable other.[32] Consequently, he is embraced within and not alienated from his society – so much so, in fact, that Ferneze directs him to 'live still' in Malta, that Lodowick and Mathias contend for his daughter, and Friars Barnardine and Jacomo for his wealth (1.2.106).

Yet instead of endorsing this reinscription of the stereotype, the play makes a tragedy of such 'self-colonization', rendering identity dependent upon external terms, whether dictated by the self or by another. Barabas's continual role-playing puts him in a position of absence behind the discourses which he and others impose. Although his control over the action is clearly increased by his literal absence (and, interestingly though not surprisingly, decreased as his direct involvement in his plots increases), his control over his own identity is made problematic by his symbolic absence, which not only allows him to manipulate others but also allows others to manipulate him. At the end of the play, just as the cauldron and trap which he constructs are all too easily appropriated by Ferneze for ends completely and fatally at odds with Barabas's own designs, so also is the identity which he constructs. Shouting from the pit, Barabas claims credit for all his schemes, identifies himself by name (and not as the Jew), and enforces his own authority by asserting his superior knowledge and reiterating a self-authorizing 'I':

> Know, Governor, 'twas I that slew thy son,
> I fram'd the challenge that did make them meet.
> Know, Calymath, I aim'd thy overthrow:
> And, had I but escap'd this stratagem,
> I would have brought confusion on you all.
>
> (5.5.86–90)

Catherine Belsey has recently emphasized the irony of assertions of self which are coupled to and dependent upon a character's ultimate loss of identity, and has suggested that, instead of exalting the unified humanist subject, such declarations attest to its absence.[33] Barabas's self-assertion here is no exception. For despite his claims to autonomy as he orders Calymath and Ferneze to 'know you cannot help me now' and his attempts to end his life 'with resolution', the

Malta: The Jew of Malta, *and the Fictions of Difference*

Governor deprives Barabas of his name, his singularity, and his voice, and proffers Barabas's final plot as an example of 'the unhallow'd deeds of Jews', which he himself has effectively circumvented (5.5.97). In this final scene, as Barabas falls into a 'deep pit past recovery', with Ferneze standing above, his literal position mirrors the symbolic position through which he has defined himself and has been defined, a position of absence beneath the discourses of a dominating authority (5.5.38). Ferneze all too easily appropriates 'a Jew's courtesy' for his own self-empowerment, for his subjugation of the Jew allows him to escape the domination of the Turks (5.5.115). The play, however, creates a telling link between his position and Barabas's, for Del Bosco stands beside Ferneze – the colonizing voice behind the colonizing voice – reminding us that Malta too is an object of colonialist discourse, and demanding that we recognize how much that discourse has to do with the Jew of Malta, the figure and the play.

Notes

1. STEPHEN GREENBLATT, *Renaissance Self-Fashioning: From More to Shakespeare* (Chicago: Chicago University Press, 1980), p. 194. Portions of this essay were first presented at the Modern Language Association convention held in San Francisco in December, 1987. My deepest thanks go to Ann Coiro, Mary Crane, Naomi Miller, and Susan Wolfson for their invaluable suggestions and encouragement.

2. STEVEN MULLANEY, *The Place of the Stage: License, Play, and Power in Renaissance England* (Chicago: Chicago University Press, 1988), p. 60. MARGARET T. HODGEN's *Early Anthropology in the Sixteenth and Seventeenth Centuries* discusses these cabinets also, amid a survey of various kinds of Renaissance collections (Philadelphia: University of Pennsylvania Press, 1964).

3. Mullaney argues that what keeps the 'wunderkammer' distinct from museums is the fact that the collectors made no attempt to categorize the objects within their collections.

4. MULLANEY, *The Place of the Stage*, p. 71. Cross-cultural expansion was only one of many factors prompting social revaluation and change. For a fuller view of these conditions, see, for example, KEITH WRIGHTSON, *English Society, 1580–1680* (New Brunswick, 1982), and J.A. SHARPE, *Early Modern England: A Social History, 1550–1760* (London: Edward Arnold, 1987).

5. EDWARD SAID, *Orientalism* (London: Routledge, 1978).

6. CHRISTOPHER MILLER, *Blank Darkness: Africanist Discourse in French* (Chicago: Chicago University Press, 1985), pp. 15–16.

7. BARBARA JOHNSON, 'Thresholds of difference: structures of address in Zora Neale Hurston', *Critical Inquiry*, 12 (1985), p. 285.

8. GREENBLATT, *Renaissance Self-Fashioning*, p. 203. See also, JEAN-MARIE MAGUIN, 'The Jew of Malta: Marlowe's ideological stance and the play-world's ethos', *Cahiers Elisabéthains*, 27 (1985), pp. 17–26; ALFRED HARBAGE, 'Innocent

171

Christopher Marlowe

Barabas', *Tulane Drama Review*, 8 (4) (1964), pp. 47–58; and G.K. HUNTER, 'The theology of Marlowe's *The Jew of Malta*', *Journal of the Warburg and Courtauld Institutes*, 27 (1964), pp. 211–40.

9. In *The School of Abuse* (1579), Stephen Gosson mentions a lost play, *The Jew*, which also reinforces the stereotype as it exposes 'the greedinesse of worldly chusers and bloody minds of usurers' (cited in M.J. LANDA, *The Jew in Drama* [Port Washington, NY: King & Son, 1926], p. 47). For further discussion of medieval and Renaissance preconceptions of the Jew, see also EDGAR ROSENBERG, 'The Jew in Western drama', in *The Jew in English Drama: An Annotated Bibliography*, comp. EDWARD D. COLEMAN (New York: New York Public Library, 1968); ESTHER L. PANITZ, *The Alien in Their Midst: Images of Jews in English Literature* (London: Faileigh Dickinson University Press, 1981); and JOSHUA TRACHTENBERG, *The Devil and the Jews: The Medieval Conception of the Jew and Its Relation to Modern Antisemitism* (New Haven: Yale University Press, 1961).

10. ROSENBERG, 'The Jew in Western drama', pp. 7–9.

11. JOHN BAKELESS, *The Tragicall History of Christopher Marlowe* (Cambridge, MA: Harvard University Press, 1942), p. 59.

12. SIMON SHEPHERD, *Marlowe and the Politics of Elizabethan Theatre* (Brighton: Harvester, 1986), p. 170. The self-interestedness of England's support betrays itself clearly two centuries later, as England annexes Malta as a colony.

13. Barker and Hulme note that *The Tempest* is 'symbolically silent about Prospero's own act of usurpation' and suggest that this 'occlusion of the play's initial colonial moment' is itself an act of 'colonialist legitimation', as the colonizer enforces his illegitimate claim first by denial, then by 'retrospective justification' (pp. 200–1). Del Bosco's silence, although not coupled to belated justification, suggests a similar occlusion which allows both Ferneze and critics to overlook a crucial colonial moment which (as I suggest below) hangs over the fate of Malta even as the play closes.

14. My discussion of the history of Malta and the Knights has been informed by MATURIN M. BALLOU, *The Story of Malta* (Boston, MA: Houghton Mifflin & Co. 1893), and ERIC BROCKMAN, *Last Bastion: Sketches of the Maltese Islands* (London: Darton, Longman & Todd, 1961).

15. J.B. STEANE, *Marlowe: A Critical Study* (Cambridge: Cambridge University Press, 1964), p. 169.

16. While Callapine – whose name recalls the rash son of Bajazeth in *Tamburlaine* – objects to allowing 'more than is in our commission' (1.2.22), Calymath exercises 'a little courtesy' and justifies a lenient treatment on the grounds that "Tis more kingly to obtain by peace / Than to enforce conditions by constraint' (1.2.25–26). This positive representation picks up on England's somewhat contradictory view of the Turks. For while they were abhorred as infidels, they were also – though less prominently – admired for their martial prowess, discipline, and unity. For further treatment of this issue, see SHEPHERD, *Marlowe*, pp. 143–4, and SAMUEL CHEW, *The Crescent and the Rose: Islam and England during the Renaissance* (New York: Octagon Books, 1937), pp. 108–21.

17. BALLOU, *The Story of Malta*, p. 276; BROCKMAN, *Last Bastion*, p. 127.

18. England's official lack of support for the Knights is evident both in Queen Elizabeth's letter to the Grand Master of Malta which commends them for their efforts against the Turks but refuses them royal favor because of their Catholicism, and in her reassertion of Henry VIII's decree which dissolved

172

the English faction of the order. (ANDREW P. VELLA, *An Elizabethan–Ottoman Conspiracy* [Malta: Royal University of Malta Press, 1972], pp. 12–13.)

19. Even when Barabas is disguised as a Frenchman and speaks in a foreign tongue (a comic mix of French and English), he is treated as no more of an outsider than any of the other foreign nationals on the island.

20. Cartelli notes that 'it is, of course, in the nature of colonial encounters that stereotypes are privileged at the expense of distinctions' (THOMAS CARTELLI, *Marlowe, Shakespeare and the Economy of Theatrical Experience* [Philadelphia: University of Pennsylvania Press, 1997], p. 109).

21. Because the secular connotation of 'profession' (i.e., occupation) was new to the language in 1541, its use here might have been particularly notable to the Elizabethan viewers.

22. GREENBLATT, *Renaissance Self-fashioning*, p. 203.

23. Ibid., p. 203.

24. Because 'the great immigration' in England between 1567 and 1580 'was of *French*, not Jews', the Frenchman was a more present, and perhaps more threatening, alien than the Jew (SHEPHERD, *Marlowe*, p. 176).

25. MILLER, *Blank Darkness*, p. 16.

26. HOMI BHABHA, 'The other question: the stereotype and colonial discourse', *Screen*, 24 (1983), p. 18.

27. HARRY LEVIN, *The Overreacher: A Study of Christopher Marlowe* (Cambridge, MA: Harvard University Press, 1952), p. 62; GREENBLATT, *Renaissance Self-fashioning*, p. 196; CHARLES LAMB, *Specimens of English Dramatic Poets* (1808), p. 31, quoted in N.W. Bawcutt's introduction to the Revels edition of the play. In an introduction to *Christopher Marlowe: Modern Critical Views*, HAROLD BLOOM offers an appropriate summation of what 'modern critical views' of the play suggest: 'Barabas defies reduction' (New York: Chelsea House, 1986), p. 4.

28. Critics have even explained the discrepancy within Barabas's characterization by attributing the first two acts to Marlowe and the last three to some other, unknown author. See BAKELESS, *Marlowe*, e.g., p. 328.

29. Lawrence Danson notes, 'With Barabas we must be on guard both because he takes us into his confidence . . . and also because he reserves the right to trick us, his accomplices'; 'Christopher Marlowe: the questioner', *English Literary Renaissance*, 12 (1) (1982), p. 8.

30. Katharine is the exception here, for although Barabas's choice to play the learned Jew in her presence seems appropriate to her civility, the text does not explicitly characterize her by a love of learning (perhaps because her role is minor and her characterization brief).

31. Greenblatt argues that 'Barabas's sense of himself, his characteristic response to the world, and his self-presentation are very largely constructed out of the materials of the dominant Christian culture', but he reads this self-fashioning merely as a product of acculturation and not as the calculated strategy which I suggest here (p. 207).

32. Greenblatt offers a useful discussion of the construction, by an authority, of a convenient and necessary other. See 'Invisible bullets: Renaissance authority and its subversion, *Henry IV* and *Henry V*', in *Political Shakespeare*, pp. 18–47.

33. CATHERINE BELSEY, *The Subject of Tragedy: Identity and Difference in Renaissance Drama* (London: Methuen, 1985), p. 36.

11 King Edward's Body*

THOMAS CARTELLI

Marlowe's iconoclastic contrast to other Elizabethan dramatists begs a vital question about his attitude to his audience, a problem critics have habitually elided by normalising his texts. In a rare Renaissance application of 'Reader Response' theory, Thomas Cartelli seeks instead to reconstruct the collective mentality of the Londoners who applauded Marlowe's diabolic plots. Here he is less concerned with the economic or social status of the Bankside spectators than their reactions to extreme sensations, such as the on-stage sodomy of Edward with a 'red-hot spit'. From the instant when Edward's lover Gaveston seduces the (male) viewers with his 'decadent' vision of 'a lovely boy in Dian's shape', Marlowe succeeds in 'restructuring their moral and sexual priorities', according to Cartelli, and thereby induces complicity in the final outrage perpetrated upon the body of the king. It is the regicide Lightborn who emerges as the hero of *Edward II* in this account, his pornographic performance being a literalisation of Gaveston's sado-masochistic 'snuff' fantasy and a metonym for the play-wright's own profession as purveyor of 'perverse pleasures' of erotic degradation. Though Cartelli relates this theatre of cruelty to Machiavelli, Marlowe resembles Jean Genet on this view, and the excitement he provokes by such spectacles seems to prompt similar qualms in American eyes as the homoerotic photographs of Robert Mapplethorpe or violence in contemporary films like *Crash*. Cartelli's implied distinction between 'decadence' and 'normality' may be anachronistic and even homophobic, but his essay is a sharp reminder of Marlowe's continuing capacity to shock.

---

* Reprinted from *Marlowe, Shakespeare, and the Economy of Theatrical Experience* (Philadelphia, University of Pennsylvania Press, 1991), 121–35.

The Machiavellian Playwright

Machiavellism, as it was popularly understood and as Marlowe chose to understand it in his plays and offstage pronouncements, seems to have functioned as a particularly enabling source of theatrical energy for Marlowe. In the plays that followed *1 and 2 Tamburlaine*, it provided a sustained focus for him in his position as a master fabricator and purveyor of fantasies for the Elizabethan public theater. Marlowe was responsive not only to the theatrical possibilities of the Machiavellian character-type – with which he works overtly in *Edward II, The Jew of Malta*, and *The Massacre at Paris* – but also to the seductive potential of a Machiavellian approach to his audience, which he realized by making the manipulation of audience response a virtual policy of playmaking. Marlowe was also acutely responsive to the destabilizing appeal of Machiavelli's ideas.[1] His indebtedness to Machiavelli can be detected both in the style and content of his plays, each of which presents political and religious contention in terms of the self-interested pursuit of power, and treats the exercise of power as the most desirable of activities for the 'aspiring mind'. It is discernible as well in the notorious Baines deposition where we gain privileged insight into Marlowe's habit of entertaining the kinds of thoughts his contemporaries chose to attribute to marginal figures in their midst.[2]

A revealing pattern emerges from Marlowe's appropriation of Machiavelli's penchant for demystification in the Baines deposition. In one item, for example, Marlowe remarks Moses's ability as a subtle, educated man to manipulate 'a rude and gross people', while in another he identifies religion as a means of social control by contending, 'That the first beginning of Religion was only to keep men in awe'. He thus expresses an ambivalent attitude towards the lawgiver, successively identifying himself as an unawed analyst of the mysteries of power, as an admirer of the cultivater of mysteries, and as a skeptical degrader of Moses himself. In affirming, in Baines's words, 'that Moses was but a Juggler & that one Hariot's being Sir W Raleighs man Can do more than he', Marlowe attempts to deny Moses's claim to authority while expressing his own pleasure in the prospect of the gifted scholar's ability to master and manipulate a culture's belief system. If Baines's words be credited, Marlowe represents here his capacity at once to anatomize and celebrate the workings of power.

In *Doctor Faustus*, his most celebrated achievement, we again find Marlowe casting about in seemingly opposed directions at one and the same time. At one moment, he has Mephistophilis offer a metaphysical portrayal of hell which is at odds with the anachronistic infernal machines he elsewhere introduces into the play. His protagonist, Faustus, mouths opinions that resemble those attributed to Marlowe in the Baines deposition, but is nonetheless presented as a misguided soul whose mistakes would be worthy of ridicule were they not so fatally consequential. Faustus is himself a mystified demystifier, and his damnation recuperates the very world-view Marlowe is alleged to have repeatedly mocked in his offstage conversations. (cf. Greenblatt, 1977: 53) Yet, to further complicate matters, this recuperation of what Wilbur Sanders calls 'the old scholastic cosmos' (1968: 229) may spring from the same fascination with power and the powerful, and lack of sympathy for the powerless, that we witness in the Baines deposition and throughout the Tamburlaine plays, and not, as others have argued, from some obscurely orthodox religious motivation.

From this brief inventory we can isolate some frequently perceived characteristics of Marlowe's writing, namely, his lack of human(e) sympathy; his preoccupation with power and the powerful; his chronic or, more precisely, compulsive heterodoxy; and the apparent contradictions between his intellectual radicalism and the orthodox endings of several of his plays. The former characteristics are apparent in his fascination with the manipulation of belief systems and in his lack of interest in the effects of their manipulation on those he revealingly calls a 'rude and gross people'. The contradictions are discernible in his tendency to demystify one embodiment of authority only to identify with another.

The Power of Pleasure

The intricacy of Marlowe's approach to received ideas and the structures of power is especially evident in the opening and closing movements of *Edward II* where his compulsion to demystify runs squarely against the expectations aroused by his cultivation of what appear to be morally exemplary set pieces. In the first scene of the play Marlowe pits the insidious attractions of Gaveston against the more modest ambitions for employment of three poor men. The lines of sympathy appear clearly drawn here, especially given the scene's formal consistency with those sequences in *Doctor Faustus* and earlier moralities in which characters discredit themselves in the eyes of the audience by pursuing selfish or deceptive designs at the expense either of their souls or of the common good. However, in this instance, as elsewhere in his work, Marlowe subordinates moral expectation to the pragmatics of self-interest, and valorizes his transvaluation by giving Gaveston privileged access to an audience that might otherwise be repulsed by his behavior.

Dramatically positioned in the role of the play's Presenter,
Gaveston begins by establishing a tone of amorous negligence that
privileges the exclusive pleasures of a personal relationship with
royalty:

> The sight of London to my exiled eyes
> Is as Elysium to a new-come soul;
> Not that I love the city or the men,
> But that it harbors him I hold so dear,
> The king, upon whose bosom let me die,
> And with the world be still at enmity.
>
> (I. i. 10–15)

The extended egotism of Gaveston's romantic conceit is licensed by
the freedom from subservience to others Gaveston imagines his
alliance with the king will allow him to enjoy:

> Farewell base stooping to the lordly peers.
> My knee shall bow to none but to the king.
> As for the multitude that are but sparks,
> Raked up in embers of their poverty –
> *Tanti*; I'll fawn first on the wind
> That glanceth at my lips and flieth away.
>
> (I. i. 18–23)

The confidently derisive manner in which Gaveston expresses his
contempt for rich and poor alike seems designed less to alienate his
audience than to solicit its responsive investment in his fantasy of
self-enrichment. As if to test the appeal of this suspect but aspiring
gentleman to an audience otherwise apt to censure so mercenary a
sensibility, Marlowe again draws on the contemporary phenomenon
of masterless men in the entrance of three supplicants for Gaveston's
favor:

Gaveston.	But how now, what are these?
	Enter three Poor Men.
Poor Men.	Such as desire your worship's service.
Gaveston.	What canst thou do?
First Poor Man.	I can ride.
Gaveston.	But I have no horses. What art thou?
Second Poor Man.	A traveler.
Gaveston.	Let me see – thou wouldst do well
	To wait at my trencher and tell me lies at
	dinner time,

Christopher Marlowe

	And as I like your discoursing, I'll have you.
	And what art thou?
Third Poor Man.	A soldier, that hath served against the Scot.
Gaveston.	Why, there are hospitals for such as you.
	I have no war, and therefore, sir, be gone.
Third Poor Man.	Farewell, and perish by a soldier's hand,
	That wouldst reward them with an hospital.
Gaveston.	Ay, ay, these words of his move me as much
	As if a goose should play the porpentine
	And dart her plumes, thinking to pierce my breast.

(I. i. 24–41)

Gaveston playfully adopts attitudes towards the lower orders that
were characteristic of a ruling class with little patience either for
the indolent poor or for the indolence enforced upon those whose
capacity for service had been exhausted ('there are hospitals for such
as you'). Setting himself up as a parodic version of a contemporary
gentleman who enlists servants 'to tell [him] lies at dinner time',
Gaveston both focuses and deflects the rampant hostility of the
Elizabethan poor toward the gentry. He simultaneously reveals
and revels in the haughtiness of the high born, eliding the fact that
to 'the lordly peers' he is, himself, nothing more than a more
sophisticated species of masterless man. In so doing, he carves out
an ambiguous but appealing position for himself as someone who
aspires to more than any poor man could appreciate or any aristocrat
could countenance.[3]

While Gaveston ultimately chooses to disguise his contempt for the
common man by 'flattering' his servitors and 'mak[ing] them live in
hope', as he reveals in a subsequent aside, he is far more candid with
the audience to whom he confides his true designs in the speech that
succeeds the poor men's exit:

| *Poor Men.* | We will wait here about the court. |

Exeunt

Gaveston.	Do. These are not men for me,
	I must have wanton poets, pleasant wits,
	Musicians, that with touching of a string
	May draw the pliant king which way I please.
	Music and poetry is his delight,
	Therefore I'll have Italian masks by night,
	Sweet speeches, comedies, and pleasing shows,
	And in the day, when he shall walk abroad,
	Like sylvan nymphs my pages shall be clad,
	My men, like satyrs grazing on the lawns,

Shall with their goat-feet dance an antic hay.
Sometime a lovely boy in Dian's shape,
With hair that gilds the water as it glides,
Crownets of pearle about his naked arms,
And in his sportful hands an olive tree,
To hide those parts which men delight to see,
Shall bathe him in a spring; and there hard by,
One like Actaeon peeping through the grove,
Shall by the angry goddess be transformed,
And running in the likeness of an hart,
By yelping hounds pulled down, and seem to die –
Such things as these best please his majesty.

(I. i. 49–71)

What Marlowe aims at here is less a subversion of the conventional preference for the normative than a normalizing of the attractions of the deviant or unusual. He proceeds by making Gaveston the eloquent champion of desires and pleasures that are decidedly more 'curious' than the mundane needs of three poor men. In offering a splendidly imagined representation of what life may resemble when the marginal becomes mainstream, Gaveston effectively depicts the normative as the product of a limited and limiting consciousness of life's possibilities: as something that may surely satisfy the desires of those who identify with his would-be servants, but that cannot satisfy men like him.

There are, of course, any number of ways for an audience to respond to this speech, but only one that Marlowe would probably endorse. On the one hand, the playgoer may feel that Gaveston's attitudes toward his suitors and Edward alike are both morally and politically reprehensible. From this perspective, Gaveston appears poised to plunder both the body-politic of England and the king's body that should otherwise preside over the commonwealth and commonweal. On the other hand, the playgoer may find Gaveston's flawlessly designed plans so seductive that consideration of their practical consequences becomes submerged in the anticipation of their realization. There is, I would submit, something alluringly decadent in Gaveston's conceit which (like many decadent things) plays upon the deepest springs of our responses, co-habiting, as it were, with our most studied and settled repressions. And what is more, Gaveston (or, more correctly, Marlowe) seems to know this. Gaveston audaciously registers the implicit consent of the audience in his depiction of the artful striptease performed by 'a lovely boy in Dian's shape' who holds 'in his sportful hands an olive tree, / To hide those parts which men delight to see'. It is, of course, the homoeroticism of this imagined masque that constitutes its primary challenge to the audience since (sexual prejudices being what they were – and are) if a lovely girl were substituted for the lovely boy, the scenario would not be considered decadent at all but merely lascivious, conforming as it would to the less intricate delights of 'The Passionate Shepherd'. One cannot respond fully to Gaveston's images and the lyrical swing with which they are described without implicitly associating oneself with the men (not just *some* men, but, as Gaveston has it, simply 'men') who 'delight to see' the boy-Dian's private parts. For a playgoer can hardly register satisfaction with Gaveston's proposed masque without also sanctioning what its realization involves: namely, an inversion of the normative heterosexual order. If Gaveston succeeds in making accomplices of playgoers who are psychologically responsive to his suggestions, then he succeeds as well in at least temporarily restructuring their moral and sexual priorities, which restructuring can only occur in concert with the demystification of their starting positions.[4]

Like Shakespeare's Edmund or Iago, Gaveston is, of course, the reigning demon of his dramatic world who, in attempting to seduce the audience into identifying with his designs, is presumably meant to stimulate its resistance as well. But Marlowe's work in this kind may be distinguished from Shakespeare's on the ground that where Shakespeare generally attempts to recuperate the subversions of the moral and political order he dramatizes, Marlowe generally seeks to enforce them. In *Edward II*, for instance, when the play-proper begins and Gaveston withdraws to the margins of the stage, his seemingly marginal fantasy of an eroticized court life maintains its theatrical appeal in the face of the fierce but decidedly stiff aggression of the peers. In rendering the lords their aesthetic due in brief, pointed asides, Gaveston deflates their moral self-righteousness and makes the patriotic positions they assume seem what Marlowe shows them to be in the course of the play, namely, defenses of their own prerogatives and preoccupations:

> *Mort. jun.*   Mine uncle here, this earl, and I myself
> Were sworn to your father at his death,
> That he should ne'er return into the realm.
> And know, my lord, ere I will break my oath,
> This sword of mine, that should offend your foes,
> Shall sleep within the scabbard at thy need,
> And underneath thy banners march who will,
> For Mortimer will hang his armor up.
>
> *Gavest.*   *Mort Dieu!* [Aside.]

(I. i. 82–90)

Gaveston's dramatic status, in respect to such moments, has often been critically misconstrued because the values he ridicules are superficially akin to those Marlowe celebrates in the *Tamburlaine* plays – masculine pride, martial fervor, etc. In fact, the peers' values are only poor and petty shadows of Tamburlaine's ethic of omnipotence, and the peers themselves actually more closely resemble the vaunting Bajazeth and his confederates who brag and bluster themselves into prominence, than they do Tamburlaine himself. It takes also only an elementary comparison of Mortimers senior and junior with their more noble likenesses in *Richard II* – Bolingbroke and John of Gaunt, for example – to conclude that Marlowe did not, like Shakespeare, intend to censure his weak king's party by immediate reference to representatives of superior values.[5] This early exchange between Edward and his nobles provides, then, a second instance of Marlowe's inversion of the dramatic import of the exemplary set-piece, in this case one that has its analogues in the meetings between an unwise king and his virtuous ministers. And it too appears to be indebted to a Machiavellian habit of mind that schematizes such contentions not in terms of moral polarities but in terms of the struggle of two parties competing for power.

I am careful to add this last observation because I believe that the critical application of moral distinctions to Marlowe's plays is frequently misplaced, especially given the extent to which Marlowe's thinking appears to be influenced by the materialist bias of Machiavellian political analysis. A morally oriented criticism is also disabled by its incapacity to offer authoritative evaluations of contentions that Marlowe characteristically resolves in terms of their competing theatrical appeal. The scene under scrutiny, for example, resolves itself in a manner that most commentators find disturbing, with Gaveston running into Edward's embrace; summarily being 'created' Lord High Chamberlain, secretary of state, Earl of Cornwall, and King and Lord of Man; and mightily abusing the Bishop of Coventry. But in theatrical terms, the long-postponed (and recently forbidden) reunion of Edward and Gaveston energetically opposes itself to the pompous puritanism of the lords; the creation of the base-born Gaveston as a veritable lord of misrule subverts the lords' emphasis on the exclusivity of their power and position; and Gaveston's abuse of the bishop is licensed both by its sheer audacity and by an anticlerical pronouncement that would surely have found a responsive auditory in the anti-papist environment of the 1590s: 'What should a priest do with so fair a house? / A prison may beseem his holiness' (1.2.206–7).

In short, Marlowe carnivalizes Edward's and Gaveston's deviations from orthodox social and political behavior. By making the king himself and his base-born favorite the agents of anti-authoritarian misrule, he establishes a provocative alliance between royalty and presumption, united in an erotically charged assault on the constraints imposed on both by an aggressive peerage and an entrenched church. Mortimer and his confederates are cast as counter-fantasists in this theatrical transaction, as the puritanical enemies of pleasure who aim to suppress violently any deviation from their colorless and self-interested rule. The prospect of a carnivalized court presided over by a sexually 'ambiguous' lord of misrule whose intentions and interests are, moreover, anti-populist in the extreme may not, admittedly, have warmed the heart of an Elizabethan playgoer who saw any possibility of the same being realized in fact. But 'fact' is neither the province of the drama itself, nor the point of reference for audience reception or receptivity. And although the playgoer's capacity for engagement is at least partly rooted in the facts of his or her life and preoccupations, it is how the dramatist reconstructs those facts to fit the forms of the playgoer's fantasy that will largely dictate the nature of audience response.

The common critical view that the audience of *Edward II* will, for example, identify with the three poor men whom Gaveston rejects and ridicules assumes that the 'average' Elizabethan playgoer will operate imaginatively in accord with a normative Christian or humanist imperative grounded in compassion, while the comparatively unprivileged playgoer will respond in a class-interested manner to Gaveston's provocation. Such an assumption not only assigns specific moral and political profiles to playgoers who may have made their judgments on more self-interested or psychological grounds; it assigns the same profile to Marlowe as well whose capacity to treat such schematic material in unorthodox ways and to construct unorthodox positions for the audience to inhabit is retrospectively inhibited and repressed. Marlowe may actually have intended the three poor men to arouse the revulsion of an audience distanced by their own privileges or their desire for psychic relief from scenes of social misery in which they might otherwise find themselves implicated: a possibility that 'facts' about Elizabethan playwrights and playgoers drawn from the domain of professed or prescribed cultural practices and beliefs cannot provide for. Such facts exclude the fantasy life of Marlowe's audience to which the unachieved ambitions and unrealized dreams of Gaveston appear to be addressed. If, however, fantasies are accorded the same phenomenal status as facts, then we may contend that it is the audience's presumed eagerness to raise its own station in life and desire to have its difference from such poor specimens of humanity confirmed that Gaveston and Marlowe play upon here. As Gaveston turns from his supplicants and says, 'These are not men for me,' he may well be suggesting that braver spirits are likelier to be found in the audience, among those who aspire to conditions where what they are in fact may give place to what they are or would be in fantasy.[6]

Of course, both here and in the scenes that focus on Edward and Gaveston's conflict with the peerage, Marlowe cultivates the possibility of an opposing point of view, one grounded either in the audience's conceivable resistance to the homoerotic union of king and minion or in a more consciously political preference for the position of the nobles. Nevertheless, Marlowe's disposition of dramatic energy clearly favors the theatrically appealing interchange of love and power focused on Edward and Gaveston, and later extended to include Spencer and Baldock, a pair of masterless men in whom a decidedly Machiavellian opportunism takes precedence over the fawning servility of the three poor man. And it is, finally, Marlowe's privileging of the erotic and political conjunction of king and aspiring commoner in each instance that similarly takes precedence in helping to situate the possibly resistant playgoer in a corresponding position.

The Pleasures of Power

Marlowe's decision to privilege Edward's and Gaveston's iconoclastic contestation of the nobility's claim to superiority is generically consistent with his treatment of Tamburlaine's and Faustus's respective approaches to the structures of secular and religious power. But it has, perhaps, an even stronger autobiographical component. Whereas Tamburlaine and Faustus embody fantasies Marlowe presumably shared with a great many of his contemporaries, Gaveston and his successors, Spencer and Baldock, are marginal figures with whom we may identify the marginalized preoccupations of Marlowe's abbreviated life. In addition to an alleged taste for young boys, Gaveston shares with Marlowe the desire to make a place for himself in the world through his creative resources. Cynical and clever, unawed by the mystifications that restrict the imaginative range of their contemporaries, both Gaveston and Marlowe conceive and invent 'pleasing shows' of the erotically charged Ovidian variety. They share an anti-populist contempt for the common man, and aspire to an anti-humanist position of power unmediated either by conscience or concern for the commonweal.[7] Marlowe's other apparent preference for a behind-the-scenes role in the exercise of power is possibly expressed in his introduction of Spencer Junior and Baldock in Act II, scene i, where Spencer defines the qualifications required of the self-made courtier in stage-Machiavellian terms: 'You must be proud, bold, pleasant, resolute, / And now and then stab, as occasion serves' (II. i. 42–43). For his part, Baldock plays an even more proximate role in relation to Marlowe's offstage career as scholar and spy when he speaks of the 'formal toys' that disguise the pedant's preference for intrigue and the licentious life of the court. In this instance, we may well be witnessing the former Cambridge scholar's inscription of his own aspirations into the only play in the language that makes the life and loves of a conspicuously homosexual king the object of sustained dramatic scrutiny.[8]

For Marlowe, Edward's weakness as a king does not derive simply from an extreme self-indulgence. It is exacerbated by a jealous and homophobic peerage that repeatedly oversteps the bounds of accepted feudal behavior, motivated more by class animosity and personal insecurity than by a concern for good government. Marlowe makes this peerage unsympathetic both in terms of its rhetorical self-display and its actions. Edward's love for Gaveston is, for example, flatteringly contrasted with Mortimer's equally exploitative but romantically lackluster liaison with Isabella; Gaveston's mistreatment of the bishop of Coventry is greatly overmatched by his vicious murder at the hands of the treacherous Warwick; and Edward's various transgressions are obscured by the relentlessly sadistic ministrations of Mortimer's henchmen.

Whereas Marlowe discredits the peers at every turn – making Mortimer one of the stiffest, least theatrical Elizabethan stage-villains on record – his compulsion to demystify self-justifying behavior is often withheld with respect to Edward, whose claim to power is seldom dramatically disputed so long as he is capable of sustaining it. I add this qualification because Marlowe shifts his dramatic point of view when Edward no longer provides him with the pleasure and security the playwright appears to have enjoyed in allying himself with the agents and executors of secular power. Once Edward surrenders the prerogatives of power to Mortimer, the king's body becomes a site both for the power of the usurper to play itself out upon and for Marlowe to anatomize and demystify.

The body of the king – 'upon whose bosom' Gaveston is content to die and upon whose senses Gaveston desires to play – is subjected, in the closing movement of *Edward II*, to indignities that rival and, ultimately, exceed those visited upon Tamburlaine's opponents. And while Edward elicits considerably more sympathy than does the Governor of Babylon, the completeness of his subjection to Mortimer and his henchmen also elicits from Marlowe yet another shift in perspective in the direction of those who now 'mak[e] Fortune's wheel turn as [they] please' (V. ii. 53). Most prominent among the temptations that Marlowe indulges in the scenes of Edward's suffering is his refusal to mystify the harsh facts he found in his sources and, hence, make the physical reduction of a king any more momentous than that of other victims of state-sponsored violence.

Licensed by Mortimer to 'amplify' Edward's grief by whatever means they can devise, Matrevis, Gurney, and, later, Lightborn operate on Edward's presumably sovereign body with the same freedom from constraint that Gaveston enjoys as he 'frolics' with Edward's private body and preys on the body-politic of England. The subjection of King Edward's body to what could either be construed as competing or complementary forms of violation thus serves to demystify the sovereign's claim to exemption from a common humanity and *to make common* otherwise extraordinary acts of transgression. This effort at demystification helps to explain Marlowe's selective divergences from his source in Stow where Edward's sufferings are in some sense dignified by his Christ-like endurance of a crown of hay and his poignant provision of tears in place of warm water for his shaving.[9] In Marlowe's play, Edward's abasement is presented with a gruff, mocking economy of word and gesture:

King Edward.	O, water, gentle friends, to cool my thirst
	And clear my body from foul excrements.
Matrevis.	Here's channel water, as our charge is given.
	Sit down, for we'll be barbers to your grace.
King Edward.	Traitors, away! What, will you murder me,
	Or choke your sovereign with puddle water?
Gurney.	No, but wash your face and shave away your beard,
	Lest you be known and so rescued.
Matrevis.	Why strive you thus? Your labor is in vain.
King Edward.	The wren may strive against the lion's strength,
	But all in vain; so vainly do I strive
	To seek for mercy at a tyrant's hand.

> *They wash him with puddle water,*
> *and shave his beard away.*
> (V. iii. 25–36)

While the forced shaving of Edward 'with puddle water' surely must arouse the sympathy of most playgoers, the sympathy that a playgoer feels must be extended to a king whose majesty is now sufficiently sullied to make him indistinguishable from his own most abject subjects. Subjecting Edward to the meanest, most debasing ministrations, Matrevis and Gurney dramatically enact the kind of 'deconsecration of sovereignty' that Franco Moretti positions historically as the enabling medium of a 'real' king's eventual decapitation. But what Moretti sees as a long-term historical process that has its roots in the development of English tragic form and its culmination in the execution of Charles I in 1649, Marlowe presents in the concentrated span of five acts and in a manner even more threatening to the residual claims of absolute sovereignty.[10]

In preparing and performing Edward's execution, Mortimer's henchman, Lightborn, orchestrates a violently literal version of Gaveston's erotic fantasy. As an informed manipulator of men and situations in the typical stage-Machiavellian mode, Lightborn not only knows how 'to draw the pliant king which way' he chooses, but knows also what it is men most fear and desire. His refinement of brutality (under the sponsorship of the state) is, in its way, the consummation of Gaveston's pornographic refinement of eroticism, and, indeed, contains a marked erotic element with the king, as Actaeon, being seduced into a death that is not simply apparent. Lightborn's craft also insidiously recalls the craft of the playwright himself, as does his goal, which involves not only the violation of the king's body but the demystification of the royal prerogatives that made that body appear kingly. When, for example, Edward enjoins Lightborn, 'Tell Isabel the Queen, I looked not thus, / When for her sake I ran at tilt in France, / And there unhorsed the duke of Clermont' (V. v. 67–69) and then attempts to bribe Lightborn with the present of his last jewel, the audience is compelled to register the utter irrelevance of royal presumption when royalty is rendered powerless. And, as playgoers watch Edward acquiesce to Lightborn's ministrations like a child trying to overcome his fear of the dark, they are compelled to register also the utter arbitrariness of social distinctions in the face of the only prerogatives that matter in the end, namely, the prerogatives of power. They are also encouraged to participate to some extent in Lightborn's own interest in the proceedings, which involves manipulating Edward, in an ostensibly sympathetic manner, into assuming a position most conducive to the planned mode of execution: 'O speak no more, my lord; this breaks my heart. / Lie on this bed, and rest yourself awhile' (V. v. 70–71).[11]

Apart from Edward's passivity and the insidiousness of the proceedings, the most striking aspects of the murder scene are the speed, specificity, and professional detachment of Lightborn as he goes about his business. The brutal economy with which he finally identifies his mission; his indifference to anything other than Edward's body as he executes his designs; and the pride with which he practices his craft conspicuously call attention to themselves, and further mediate our sympathetic involvement with Edward's sufferings. Indeed, Marlowe seems to want us to admire the precision of the execution almost more than he wants to shock us with the terrible logic of its composition. When Lightborn turns to his onstage auditors, Matrevis and Gurney (who will soon murder *him* with the same professional detachment, though without his theatrical flair), and says, 'Tell me sirs, was it not bravely done?' (V. vi. 115), he does not simply express his perverse pleasure in the deed he has done, but challenges the offstage audience to acknowledge its complicity in his performance.[12]

Compared to the closing movement of *Edward II*, the murder of Clarence in *Richard III* and of the king in *Richard II* are humanist fantasies. The stripped-down image Marlowe draws of the weak, enfeebled king, lying prone and submissive on his bed, while his murderers move purposefully about the room to execute a murder that is also a rape, even exceeds in horror – and daring – Shakespeare's depiction of Gloucester's blinding in *King Lear*. And as is the case in the latter scene, the playwright situates the spectating subject in a position of affiliated agency with the transgressive actor and action. As Lightborn efficiently lulls Edward into submission, has a table placed over his body to contain his cries and movements, and drives a hot poker into Edward's anus to leave no noticeable mark of violence upon his body, the conventional separation between audience and stage is temporarily suspended: theater assumes the immediacy and materiality of an actual event. The audience's presumptive sympathy for Edward and censure of Lightborn become bound up with the respective success each has in commanding his theatrical properties. Voluntary witnesses at the scene of royalty's abjection and sovereignty's deconsecration, Marlowe's audience may well have experienced feelings of transgressive release and excitation at Lightborn's professional command of these proceedings: feelings that would be inconsistent with a normatively prescribed sympathy for the royal victim of violence sponsored by a precipitately constructed state. Indeed, I would submit that in his studied failure to provide (as Shakespeare is careful to provide in *Richard III* and *Richard II*) any mention of repentance or mark of indecision on the part of his assassins, much less any act of intervention as Shakespeare supplies in *Lear*, Marlowe encourages his audience to *will* Edward's murder, to participate vicariously in the climactic act of demystification it observes.[13]

Notes

1. Like many of his contemporaries, Marlowe was also responsive to ideas that were merely attributed to Machiavelli. See, for example, Ribner (1954: 349–56). For detailed examinations of popular conceptions and misconceptions of Machiavellism, see Praz (1958) and Raab (1964).

2. In the course of his provocative commentary on the Baines deposition, Jonathan Goldberg observes: 'The theater was permitted to rehearse the dark side of Elizabethan culture; it was a recreative spot where sedition could wear the face of play, where authors could make assertions as potent as monarchs'. In the theater, kings were the puppets of writers, greatness was mimed, atheists, rebels, magicians, and sodomites could be publicly displayed. And nowhere, of course, more strikingly than in Marlowe's heroes, . . . Marlowe's identity in his culture comes from his rehearsal of these counterpositions, and the words of Richard Baines, government spy, report how Marlowe, a fellow spy, acquired a counteridentity at once countenanced and denounced by his society' (1984: 376–7; also, Chapter 3 in this volume).

3. Marlowe's decision to depart from Holinshed's description of Gaveston as 'an esquire of Gascoine' (*Chronicles* II: 539), hence, to downgrade his social standing to that of a well-placed commoner or minor gentleman, is itself ambiguous, though it probably has its basis in the repeated placement of his protagonists – e.g., Tamburlaine and Faustus – in the ranks of those who aspire to higher stations than those to which they were born. Cf. Summers (1974: 161–2) and Cohen (1985: 232–7).

4. This kind of 'restructuring' may, of course, have been even more difficult for female playgoers to negotiate. Such moments in Marlowe provide perhaps overly suitable examples of Barbara Hodgdon's conclusion regarding female spectatorship, namely, that 'there is pleasure, no end of pleasure, only not for a female spectator' (1990: 258).

5. The 'elementary' nature of the comparison is, I should add, more obvious to myself than to most other commentators on the play. Cohen (1985), for example, reproduces a critical commonplace in contending that 'greater sympathy' is evoked 'for the aristocracy than for the monarchy in the first half of the play'. Cohen also asserts that Gaveston and his successors Spencer and Baldock are 'treated with far less sympathy' than are characters like Tamburlaine, Barabas, and Faustus who similarly 'stand outside the traditional ruling class, with which their aspirations bring them into conflict' (1985: 237).

6. It hardly seems coincidental that in order to effect the last stage of Christopher Sly's 'transformation' into a lord in *The Taming of the Shrew*, Shakespeare has his 'real' lord and that lord's servants liberally borrow from Gaveston's sylvan fantasy:

> *Second Servant.* Dost thou love pictures? We will fetch thee straight
> Adonis painted by a running brook,
> And Cytherea all in sedges hid,
> Which seem to move and wanton with her breath,
> Even as the waving sedges play with wind.
> *Lord.* We'll show thee Io as she was a maid,
> And how she was beguiled and surpris'd,
> As lively painted as the deed was done.
>
> (Ind. ii. 49–56)

It is, however, more difficult to determine whether Shakespeare is burlesquing the device he deploys here, criticizing the susceptibility of the low-born and illiterate to such elaborate seductions, or simply confirming the theatrical appeal of such conceits.

7. The most astute discussion of the possible relationship between Marlowe's apparent homosexuality and the social positions maintained in plays like *Edward II* is offered by Huebert who notes, for example, that an Elizabethan 'homosexual could come to think of himself as an outlaw, living always in

defiance of the sacred and secular code, and requiring at all times the support of influential protectors against even the bare possibility of a legal reckoning. Desire, for such a man, would be by its very nature an act of defiance' (1984: 212).

8. The negligible attention traditionally accorded the homosexual orientation of *Edward II* is in the process of being redressed by a new generation of Renaissance scholars. Summers is one of the few, comparatively traditional scholars to acknowledge Marlowe's favorable treatment of homosexuality in *Edward II* (1974: 155–86). Kuriyama (1980) breaks some new ground in making Marlowe's sexuality a sustained focus in her psychoanalytically oriented book. More recent and more adventurous appraisals of Marlowe's homosexuality are offered by Huebert (1984), Shepherd (1986), Goldberg (1984), and Porter (1989).

9. While I am indebted to Sanders (1968) for bringing these divergences to light, I find them operating to decidedly different effects from those he describes, which 'tempt' him 'to mutter piously, "What a scene Shakespeare would have made of it!"' (1968: 130). To support his conclusions, Sanders quotes the following excerpt from Stow, *Annales* (1615: 226): 'These champions bring Edward towards Barkley, being guarded with a rabble of hellhounds, along by the Grange belonging to the Castle of Bristowe, where that wicked man Gorney, making a crown of hay, put it on his head, and the soldiers that were present, scoffed and mocked him beyond all measure, . . . Moreover, devising to disfigure him that he might not be known, they determined for to shave as well the hair of his head, as also of his beard: wherefore, as in their journey, they travelled by a little water which ran in a ditch, they commanded him to light from his horse to be shaven, to whom, being set on a moale hill, a Barber came unto him with a basin of cold water taken out of the ditch, to shave him withall, saying unto the king, that that water should serve for that time. To whom Edward answered, that would they, noulde they, he would have warm water for his beard; and, to the end that he might keep his promise, he began to weep, and to shed tears plentifully.'

10. Moretti (1981) begins his essay with a discussion of the contention between royalty and aristocracy in *Gorboduc*, the terms of which may easily (and profitably) be transposed to *Edward II*. Moretti argues, for example, that when 'tragedy performs the degradation of the cultural image of the sovereign, it deprives the monarchy of its central bastion, its ultimate weapon' (1981: 9) a feat that *Edward II* 'performs' repeatedly, just as it similarly reduces the prescribed 'collaboration between different organs [of the body politic] for the benefit of the whole' to a 'contest' of individual wills and self-interest (ibid.: 12).

11. In sexual terms, Edward represents for Lightborn the perfect object of perverse erotic satisfaction, blending the vulnerability of the child with the desperation of a man deprived of all other significant human contact. Toby Robertson (1964), in a discussion of his 1958 Marlowe Society production of the play, calls this episode 'almost the last "love scene" in the play', and describes its enactment in the following manner: 'We played this with Edward almost lying in Lightborn's lap and sort of crooning to him. He's very gently stroking him and it became like a child asking for love, wanting love, affection' (1964: 179).

12. Cf. Greenblatt (1977: 52) who writes that 'in *Edward II*, Marlowe uses the emblematic method of admonitory drama, but uses it to such devastating effect that the audience recoils from it in disgust. Edward's grisly execution is, as orthodox interpreters of the play have correctly insisted, iconographically "appropriate," but this very appropriateness can only be established *at the*

expense of every complex, sympathetic human feeling evoked by the play. The audience is forced to confront its insistence upon coherence, and the result is a profound questioning of the way audiences constitute meaning in plays and in life.' I attempt to provide one kind of answer to this 'profound questioning of the way audiences constitute meaning in *plays*.' I would add (and hope) that audiences do not 'constitute meaning' in the same way in life.

13. Cohen (1985) concludes his discussion of the play by stating that '*Edward II* constitutes a typical act of demystification, powerful in its destructiveness, but incapable of producing a constructive alternative'. He adds: 'This is to say, however, that Marlowe does what Shakespeare does not and vice versa, . . . (1985: 239). It should be clear from each of my discussions of Marlowe that I do not believe Marlowe was at all interested in 'producing a constructive alternative'.

References

COHEN, WALTER, *Drama of a Nation: Public Theater in Renaissance England and Spain* (Ithaca, NY: Cornell University Press, 1985).

GOLDBERG, JONATHAN, 'Sodomy and society: the case of Christopher Marlowe', *Southwest Review*, 69 (1984), pp. 371–8.

GREENBLATT, STEPHEN J., 'Marlowe and Renaissance self-fashioning', in ALVIN KERNAN (ed.), *Two Renaissance Mythmakers: Christopher Marlowe and Ben Jonson* (Baltimore, MD: Johns Hopkins University Press, 1977, pp. 41–69).

HODGDON, BARBARA, 'He do Cressida in different voices', *English Literary Renaissance*, 20 (2) (1990), pp. 254–86.

HUEBERT, RONALD, 'Tobacco and boys and Marlowe', *Sewanee Review*, XCII (2) (1984), pp. 206–24.

KURIYAMA, CONSTANCE BROWN, *Hammer or Anvil: Psychological Patterns in Christopher Marlowe's Plays* (New Brunswick, NJ: Rutgers University Press, 1980).

MORETTI, FRANCO, ' "A huge eclipse": tragic form and the deconsecration of sovereignty', *Genre*, 15 (1981), pp. 7–40.

PORTER, JOSEPH, 'Marlowe, Shakespeare, and the canonization of heterosexuality', *South Atlantic Quarterly*, 88 (1) (1989), pp. 127–47.

PRAZ, MARIO, ' "The politic brain": Machiavelli and the Elizabethans', in *The Flaming Heart* (New York: W.W. Norton, 1958, pp. 90–145).

RAAB, FELIX, *The English Face of Machiavelli* (London: Routledge & Kegan Paul, 1964).

RIBNER, IRVING, 'Marlowe and Machiavelli', *Comparative Literature*, 6 (1954), pp. 349–56.

ROBERTSON, TOBY, 'Directing *Edward II*'. *TDR*, 8 (4) (1964), pp. 174–83.

SANDERS, WILBUR, *The Dramatist and the Received Idea* (Cambridge: Cambridge University Press, 1968).

SHEPHERD, SIMON, *Marlowe and the Politics of Elizabethan Theatre* (New York: St Martin's Press, 1986).

SUMMERS, CLAUDE J., *Christopher Marlowe and the Politics of Power* (Salzburg: Salzburg Studies in English Literature, 22, 1974).

12 Marlowe and the Observation of Men*

JOHN ARCHER

Foucault's impact on Renaissance studies is due to the importance he assigns the era in a shift in *ways of seeing* from spectacle to observation (or from sovereignty to surveillance). Theatre was a prime instrument of this monopolisation of vision by the state, but, as John Archer shows in his study of Elizabethan spying, Marlowe also staged the anxiety of the victims of this new system of scopic control. *Edward II* is crucial to this story, which hinges on Freud's theory of a link between homosexuality and the fear of being the object of the gaze which he termed *paranoia*. The play is literally *paranoid*, therefore, in presenting a world of eroticised boys reorganised into compulsory heterosexuality under the eyes of an all-seeing authority, a process that mirrors the erotics of Queen Elizabeth's court. Thus, the royal favourites, Gaveston and Spencer, figure Marlowe's own position as spy and dramatist in a culture moving from display to discipline – and from pederasty to patriarchy – through the games of patrons with their pawns. Like Foucault, Archer recalls that love of boys had been the cement that held society together before the invention of the nuclear family, here represented by Mortimer and the Queen. Written while Marlowe was an agent for the pederastic King James, *Edward II* therefore records a point when same-sex relations were an 'unspoken affirmation' of the law: an affirmation made explicit in *Massacre at Paris*, where the boys' zone is a cordon about the King and his Protestant cause. The murder of Henri III in that play, however, is relayed by an 'English agent' who may stand for the author: an omen of his own fate in the new age of surveillance. Archer's essay highlight's Marlowe's relevance to both theory and practice: in this case, the philosophy of the gaze and the history of gays themselves.

* Reprinted from *Sovereignty and Intelligence: Spying and Court Culture in the English Renaissance* (Stanford, CA, Stanford University Press, 1993), 69–94.

The commonest spy, Nashe's Jack Wilton observed, 'must be familiar with all and trust none, drink, carouse, and lecher with him out of whom he hopes to wring any matter, swear and forswear, rather than be suspected, and, in a word, have the Art of dissembling at his fingers ends as perfect as any Courtier'.[1] Though at opposite ends of the social scale, the spy and the courtier employ the same strategy of simulation and dissimulation, as Bacon would call it. Sexuality forms part of the intelligencer's tactics as well as the courtier's; later, Jonson would link the two figures in Captain Hungry and the 'young Statesmen' who lie with him to get information.[2] The relation between knowledge and the body is more immediate for the common spy than for the chivalric performer, however, as Jack's ambiguous injunction that one must 'lecher with' one's victims suggests.

Nashe's friend Christopher Marlowe can be viewed as a writer situated at the margins of court society and its sexual anxieties rather than its center. Francis Meres claimed that '*Marlow* was stabbed to death by a bawdy Servingman, a rivall of his in his lewde love'.[3] An inaccurate account of Marlowe's murder, Meres's statement is nevertheless a vestige of the contemporary gossip that associated an excessive sexuality with Marlowe and his way of life. [. . .] A spy himself, Marlowe was allowed to enter an alternative realm of subversion otherwise inaccessible to those in authority. A Machiavellian attitude toward religion and royal authority coincided with the homosexuality imputed to Marlowe. Furthermore, as we shall see, Marlowe himself attempted to realize this self-construction through the characters he created within the licensed transgression of the stage. Yet Marlowe was also negotiating his identity with Elizabethan society through the dispersed mechanism of the patronage system, the collective medium of the theater, and the often violent world of London's urban subculture. In a sense, all accounts of Marlowe's life, including the one that I have assembled below, are traces of his failed attempt to fashion himself as the intimate servant of the great. The ruins of this self-construction can be seen in plays like *Doctor Faustus*, *Edward II*, and *The Massacre at Paris*, where Marlowe described the combination of politics and sexuality at court as an outside observer, a servant of the servants of the prince.

Marlowe's career as a spy resembled in some ways that of Maliverny Catlyn, one of Walsingham's principal agents, though Marlowe did not share Catlyn's Protestant aversion to the theater. Religious fervor may have joined with the need for ready cash to impel Catlyn, a soldier and something of a scholar, to become a spy, but he must have been a good actor himself. He had fought in the Netherlands, where he may already have been employed in spying of some sort. After a dispute with his commander, Catlyn fled to Rouen, and in 1586 he wrote to Walsingham offering his services as someone who had infiltrated English Catholic circles in France. Next he was placed in jail, first at Portsmouth and then, by his own request, in the Marshalsea, to spy on imprisoned priests and find out about future invasion plans. After Catlyn's release, Walsingham sent him among the Catholics of the northern counties at least twice; back in London, Catlyn claimed to have gained the confidence of a suspect nobleman before disappearing for good.

Like Catlyn, Marlowe was an educated man who seems to have been employed in France and the Low Countries, after which he returned to England, more than likely as a prisoner. He had already spent two weeks in Newgate in 1587 after a street brawl in which the poet Thomas Watson stepped in to kill his opponent. Marlowe 'had thus an excellent opportunity of becoming acquainted with the prisoners', as Mark Eccles puts it, and it may have been at this time that he met 'one Poley prisoner in Newgate' who taught him how to counterfeit.[4] Marlowe probably had other prison experiences as well. In May 1593 the Privy Council had him arrested; he was released, but was killed in a fight a few weeks later. Catlyn had gone on to become one of Walsingham's better agents in England, but Marlowe somehow fell prey to the intelligence apparatus he had served on the Continent.

A clearer pattern emerges when the case histories of Catlyn and Marlowe are compared with those of other spies that Conyers Read and Lawrence Stone have documented. According to Stone, the typical intelligencer began as a stool pigeon. Thrown into prison, 'the unfortunate would insensibly drift into offering himself as a spy. Cleared of his debts and given money for his journey, he would set out boldly on his travels to the enemy country.' Where a journey to the Continent was involved, the agent would often be imprisoned by a Catholic power, 'turned', and dispatched to England as the agent of a new master.[5] Walsingham avoided sending Catlyn back to Europe altogether; Marlowe seems never to have lost the taint, whether fact or rumor, of the early association of his name with Rheims, the site of a notorious Catholic seminary.[6]

This association cropped up in March 1587, when the Privy Council itself demanded that Cambridge grant him his MA degree despite the report that 'Christopher Morley was determined to have gone beyond the seas to Rheims and there to remaine'. Although he had often been absent from Cambridge, the Council assured the university that Marlowe 'had behaved him self orderly and discreetly whereby he had done her majesty good service, and deserved to be awarded for his faithful dealing'. Hearsay about his papist leanings should be put to rest 'because it was not her majesty's pleasure that any one employed as he had been in matters touching the benefit of his Country should be defamed by those that are ignorant in th'affaires he went about'.[7] Marlowe was awarded his MA by the following September.

There is evidence that Marlowe continued in government service abroad after the controversy over his degree. In October 1587 a 'Mr. Morley' is mentioned as one of Burghley's messengers in Utrecht, and 'Mr. Marlin' evidently served the English envoy to Henri of Navarre in a similar capacity during part of 1591–92. In March 1592 one 'Marlin' was employed as a courier between besieged Rouen and Dieppe, and then sent on to Robert Cecil in London.[8] If Marlowe was employed in some or all of these European missions, it is easy to see why he continued to be suspected of crypto-Catholicism by those who were ignorant of the affairs he went about, and perhaps by some who weren't. The most interesting, and most certain, escapade involved his only recorded encounter with Richard Baines, the spy who after Marlowe's murder submitted the report on his supposed beliefs. January 1592 found Baines and 'Christofer Marly' in the custody of Sir Robert Sidney, who had succeeded his brother Philip as the commander of Flushing. We have Sidney's letter to Burghley describing the case: Marlowe and a goldsmith had been picked up for trying to counterfeit Dutch shillings after Baines, who shared lodgings with them, reported the plan to Sir Robert. Baines and Marlowe promptly accused each other of intending 'to go to the Enemy or to Rome'.[9] The Baines libel states that Marlowe claimed to have as good a right to coin as the queen, and that he knew a prisoner in Newgate who had taught him how to exercise this right.[10] The counterfeiting charge seems to have been scored from the original document, but it was not out of place: according to Mark Eccles, Elizabethan authorities 'as a matter of course examined prisoners at the same time on coining and religion'.[11] Marlowe was sent back to London by Sidney. But during the following March he may have been employed on the Continent again and then sent home with a message for Cecil. In May 1592 'Christofer Marle' was bound over by a pair of Shoreditch constables.[12]

If Marlowe was the Morley and Marlin mentioned above, he evidently did much of his work for Burghley and his son Robert Cecil rather than for Walsingham, even though he was also patronized by Thomas Walsingham, Sir Francis's relative and sometime agent.[13] Robert Sidney had written to Burghley, and Burghley may have interceded for his prisoner, just as the Council had intervened to get Marlowe his MA. Unfortunately, Marlowe remained unlucky in his choice of roommates. When Thomas Kyd was arrested early in May 1593 on suspicion of circulating libels against the state, he probably offered to turn queen's evidence against the man with whom he had lived for a while a few years earlier.[14] Kyd was found in possession of a manuscript copy of a book called *The Fall of the Late Arian* that was deemed to contain heretical material. After Marlowe's death, Kyd wrote two letters to the lord keeper. In the first he claimed that the book was Marlowe's, and that their papers had become mixed together when they shared chambers; the second letter accuses his former acquaintance in some detail of mocking the Scriptures.[15] It is possible that Kyd had already denounced him under interrogation, leading to Marlowe's own arrest on 20 May at Thomas Walsingham's house near Greenwich by order of the Privy Council.

Despite the gravity of such charges, Marlowe must once more have been granted an early release, for at the end of May we find him in Deptford, a short distance away. The circumstances of his murder there by Ingram Friser have inspired several attempts to explain the killing as a political assassination.[16] Nicholas Skeres and the notorious Robert Poley were present at the death; although both spied on the Babington conspirators, Poley had been an agent of Francis Walsingham and remained associated with the Cecils, and Skeres was connected with Robert Devereux, earl of Essex.[17] In the early 1590s Essex was trying to establish secret contacts with James VI of Scotland as the most likely successor to the English throne; in his second letter to the lord keeper, Kyd later claimed that Marlowe had also been planning to go over to James, as his friend Matthew Roydon had done.[18] Essex and Robert Cecil were building rival espionage networks during these years; in some obscure way Marlowe may have been a minor casualty in the struggle for Elizabeth's intelligence patronage in the wake of Francis Walsingham's death in 1590.[19]

[...]

Marlowe was also supposed to have maintained 'That all they that love not Tobacco and Boys were fools'. He said that St John was Christ's bedfellow, and 'that he used him as the sinners of Sodoma'.[20] Kyd corroborated this allegation: 'He would report St John to be our saviour Christ's Alexis I cover it with reverence and trembling that is that Christ did love him with an extraordinary love.'[21] Taken together, the accusations of Kyd and Baines suggest that the company of poets, scientists, and spies kept by the Marlowe of the London years constituted an urban subculture in which religious skepticism, a natural history that veered toward the occult, and homosexuality were all involved.

Yet Alan Bray has usefully questioned the applicability of the term 'homosexuality', a clinical category from the late nineteenth century, to the early modern period. According to Bray, what we would now call homosexual practices may have been, in fact probably were, quite common, but they usually passed unrecognized as such by society at large, and even by the men who participated in them. Intimate sleeping arrangements were common at all levels in the Renaissance household. The laborer Meredith Davy's sexual relations with the boy he was sleeping with were eventually caught out by a third chambermate and reported to a magistrate, but Davy swore that he had no idea he was a sodomite and was allowed by the court and his employer to continue sharing the boy's bed.[22] 'Sodomy' was the name for a terrible force outside the order of creation that could nevertheless erupt in everyone, a threat associated with Satan, witchcraft, and the Roman Catholic church.[23]

Most recent studies agree that a male homosexual subculture, with its own codes of behavior and mutual recognition, did not exist in England toward the end of the sixteenth century.[24] Yet if homosexual practice did not form the basis of a subculture in Renaissance England, it was nevertheless part of the 'surculture' of aristocratic patronage that also produced the developing mechanisms of espionage and surveillance. I am coining this term to designate those overarching social practices that are at once 'above' the threshold of visibility, and yet too large to be seen in full by their participants, too taken for granted. Patronage among aristocrats, and between aristocrats and their less well-born clients, was the crown of such a surculture in sixteenth-century England. In a discussion of 'paederastice' in Edmund Spenser's *Shepheardes Calander* and his 'familiar letters' to Gabriel Harvey, Jonathan Goldberg has demonstrated that male homosexual practice was fleetingly exposed when it was understood as a sign of subordination within the patronage relationship, and then only upon the moment when this relationship came to an end.[25] As 'sodomy', it threatened society from without, or from deep within, but as 'pederasty' it paradoxically served as the barely visible mortar that held the social framework together at its surface.[26]

Baines's implication that Marlowe was a lover of boys made him doubly subversive, then – not only was Baines's Marlowe a sodomite, but as a sodomite he assumed the dominant position within his relationships, thus usurping and parodying the role of patron. Yet Marlowe had already trumped such an imposed 'counter-identity' by uniting patronage and sodomy in the person of the sovereign. In *Edward II* he explores the pattern of all patronage relationships in early modern England – that between the sovereign and the sovereign's favorite. Marlowe's own patron Ralegh was either Elizabeth's current favorite while the play was being written, or had just fallen out of her good graces because of his secret marriage to Elizabeth Throckmorton.[27] *Edward II* both underwrites the political erotics of Elizabeth's court examined above and criticizes its compulsory heterosociality by imagining a male monarch, courted by male suitors, and threatened by over-mighty male subjects. In doing so, it once again both conceals and reveals the paradoxical link between patronage and homoeroticism as subversive practice and social bond.

The parallel between Edward and Elizabeth is established in the soliloquy by Piers Gaveston that opens the play, where he proclaims: 'The sight of *London* to my exiled eyes, / Is as *Elizium* to a new come soule.'[28] Edward, like Elizabeth, is fond of courtly entertainments (I. 1. 54–56), and he tries to contain aristocratic resistance to his rule through a chivalric tournament. But the barons plan to bear emblems to the joust that attack Gaveston as an ambitious flatterer, comparing him to a flying fish or, in the younger Mortimer's device, a canker that creeps up a lofty cedar tree (II. 2. 16–18).[29] Edward's tenuous court society soon dissolves into concealed conspiracy, then open rebellion because of the barons' jealousy of his favorite, Gaveston. The new regime of Mortimer and Isabella, Edward's rejected queen, fails to control the unstable relationship between sexuality and power.

The shift from stability to antagonism, and from courtly display to secret observation, is foreshadowed in the first 100 lines or so of the text. First we witness the undermining of feudal bonds by patronage and the unstable relationships it fosters. Gaveston enters reading the letter from the newly crowned Edward that has summoned him back from exile in France. Subsequent events, like Gaveston's banishment, his recall, and Edward's murder, will be accompanied by less intimate documents and messages; sovereignty and its abuse are construed in terms of writing throughout this play.[30] The king's personal letter is a sign of Gaveston's new power. He will base his prestige solely upon physical proximity to Edward, rather than on the existing system of competition and compromise with the monarch's more aristocratic followers. 'Farewell base stooping to the lordly peers', he resolves, 'My knee shall bow to none but to the king' (I. 1. 18–19). Three 'poor men' then enter and pay suit to the reinstated favorite, who mocks them but determines to 'flatter these, and make them live in hope' (I. 1. 43). This piece of business again shows the audience Gaveston's position in the chain of royal patronage. He will serve as a self-interested intermediary between commoners and king, circumventing the feudal power of the magnates.

And yet, he concludes, 'these are not men for me'. Edward delights in display, in comedies and Italian masques, so Gaveston wants poets, musicians, and dancers for followers, men who 'with touching of a string / May draw the pliant king which way I please' (I. 1. 49–53). The court itself is transformed into such a 'pleasing show' in Gaveston's plans, for he next imagines Edward walking abroad and happening upon a scene suddenly populated by his favorite's men. Gaveston's pages will dress like nymphs, while his satyrs 'graze' upon the lawn and dance an antic hay. Courtly display becomes identical with the display of the male body, as indeed it often was at Elizabeth's court. But here the sovereign's gaze is a homoerotic one, although it is constructed through a cross-dressing masquerade that simultaneously cancels and affirms heterosexual desire:

> Sometime a lovely boy in *Dian's* shape,
> With hair that gilds the water as it glides,
> Crownets of pearle about his naked arms,
> And in his sportful hands an Olive tree,
> To hide those parts which men delight to see,
> Shall bathe him in a spring, and there hard by,
> One like *Actaeon* peeping through the grove,
> Shall by the angry goddess be transformed,
> And running in the likeness of an Hart,
> By yelping hounds pulled down, and seem to die.
>
> (I. 1. 61–70)

Gaveston's fantasy about the observation of men resolves itself into a well-known emblem of the dangers that access to the sovereign's person and its secrets can bring, and immediately after the Actaeon set piece, we see how precarious Gaveston's position actually is.[31] Edward enters, pursued by the angry barons, the hounds who will eventually pull both the king and his darling down. Gaveston withdraws from his contemplation of erotic display to spy upon the argument, making comments upon the scene like a spectator in the theater. The movement from display to surveillance in the opening scene of *Edward II* informs the ensuing action. No sooner is Gaveston apprehended and killed than Edward adopts his more devious client, Hugh Spenser, in his stead (III. 1. 144).

When the feudal hierarchy is replaced by the exercise of royal patronage it formerly tolerated and contained, the duplicity that underlies all social bonds in court society is given free rein, and espionage becomes the prime way of dealing with these new political relations. To some extent, Edward's relationship with his new favorite Spenser parodies his old love with Gaveston, yet there is little question of there having been any originary honesty in the earlier bond – Spenser's machinations retrospectively reveal the

policy that lay behind Gaveston's rhetoric. Still, policy and affection
were more closely entwined for Gaveston than his successor, and
only after Gaveston's fall does it become possible to speak of honesty
and dishonesty in royal clientage. When we first see Spenser, he
is a hanger-on in the household of the recently deceased duke of
Gloucester, whose title he will one day be granted. Spenser, who is
depicted as something of a university wit (see IV. 7. 16–19), is asked
by Baldock, his scholarly sidekick, which noble patron he will now
follow. 'Not *Mortimer*, nor any of his side', he replies, 'Because the
king and he are enemies' (II. 1. 4–5). Gaveston, newly created 'the
liberall earle of *Cornewall*', is his man, Spenser discloses, and he
means to become not his 'follower' but his 'companion', 'for he loves
me well, / And would have once preferred me to the king' (II. 1. 13–
14). There is little of the spurned lover in Spenser, however. Gaveston
has been newly exiled, but

> A friend of mine told me in secrecy,
> That he's repealed, and sent for back again,
> And even now, a post came from the court,
> With letters to our lady from the King,
> And as she read, she smiled, which makes me think,
> It is about her lover *Gaveston*.
>
> (II. 1. 17–22)

The lady here is the daughter of the dead duke of Gloucester, whom
Edward intends that Gaveston should marry.

Spenser already has at least one informant at court, and he is
clearly an adept at the courtly art of human observation, able to read
in his mistress's looks the news of her betrothed's return. He also is
an adept at 'turning' others' spies. After Gaveston's death, Spenser
seeks to please Edward by employing Levune, Queen Isabella's spy
in the French court, against the queen herself (III. 1. 60–65). Isabella
escapes to the Continent with plans to invade England and place the
young prince on the throne, but Levune successfully bribes the
French not to aid her, and reports back her resort to Flanders in a
message that Spenser reads aloud to Edward (III. 1. 262–71; IV. 1.
28–36). Marlowe may have served as a messenger between France
and England during or shortly after the composition of *Edward II*
sometime in 1591–92. The relics of his self-construction in the
play are found in the scholar Baldock, in the agent Levune, and in
Gaveston, the would-be homoerotic masquer of the first scene, but
they may be seen in the ambitious Spenser as well.

With Spenser, a heightened sense of deceit and dissimulation enters
the drama. '*Baldock*, you must cast the scholer off', he tells his friend,

> And learn to court it like a Gentleman,
> Tis not a black coat and a little band,
>
> . . . .
>
> Can get you any favour with great men.
> You must be proud, bold, pleasant, resolute,
> And now and then, stab as occasion serves.
>
> (II. 1. 31–33, 41–43)

Baldock assures Spenser that he is ready to follow this code of pretense and self-concealment; despite his 'curate-like' attire, he is 'inwardly licentious enough, / And apt for any kinde of villanie' (II. 1. 50–51). As the new favorite, Spenser appropriates the courtly conventions that Edward and Gaveston followed, taking up one of the mythological allusions that characterized their discourse. He tells Levune to bribe the French, so that 'all enchanted like the guard, / That suffered *Jove* to pass in showers of gold / To *Danae*', they will refuse to help Queen Isabella (III. 1. 266–68). Edward had once greeted Gaveston by comparing himself to the lovers of Danaë who 'Desired her more, and waxt outragous' when she was confined in the brazen tower (II. 2. 52–56). Edward's figure of desire has become Spenser's Machiavellian conceit. The discourse of transgressive sexuality is re-absorbed opportunistically into quotidian politics as soon as its deeper function in court society is glimpsed.

Throughout *Edward II*, the homoerotic desire that cements social bonds between men is at once revealed and concealed, and the neoclassical parallels that pepper courtly language in the play aid this paradoxical effect. When Gaveston imagines himself as Leander and Edward, implicitly, as Hero, in the soliloquy that begins the action, there is no lascivious Neptune to intercept his channel crossing as there is in Marlowe's contemporary poem. Even Edward's comparison of himself to Hercules and Gaveston to Hilas, it could be argued, functions as a reference to an earlier and alien realm of sexual possibility remote from present realities.[32] Old Mortimer apologizes for Edward's relationship with Gaveston through classical examples that justify the homoerotics of power and knowledge. 'The mightiest kings have had their minions', he says, 'Great *Alexander* loved *Ephestion* . . . And for *Patroclus* stern *Achilis* droopt' (I. 4. 391–94). More examples follow, yet all this is seemingly beside the point. 'Uncle, his wanton humor grieves not me', the younger Mortimer replies, 'But this I scorn, that one so basely born, / Should by his sovereigns favour grow so pert' (I. 4. 402–4). Young Mortimer's complaint is repeated several times elsewhere in the play. The barons read Edward's relationship with his minion principally as an extension of the patronage system beyond the feudal hierarchy of mutual obligation that has heretofore contained it.

Yet young Mortimer himself sees more of a sexual threat in Gaveston than his initial response to his uncle lets on. As his choler builds, he dwells on the minion's appearance:

> I have not seen a dapper jack so brisk,
> He wears a short Italian hooded cloak,
> Larded with pearle, and in his tuskan cap
> A jewel of more value then the crown.

> (I. 4. 412–15)

This virtual blazon is followed by the complaint that Gaveston and the king 'From out a window, laugh at such as we . . . and jest at our attire. / Uncle, 'tis this that makes me impatient' (I. 4. 17–19). Mortimer's paranoia under such observation, and his own close observation of Gaveston, reveals a confused perception of the dangers that homosexuality poses to the homosocial world of the feudal court, where king and nobles should 'love' one another according to their rank. (See I. 1. 80, 100.)

One character who does seem to understand the erotics of power is the spurned queen. She calls Gaveston 'a bawd to his affections' before Edward (I. 4. 151), and tells the clueless peers of her husband's displays of devotion to him: 'He claps his cheeks, and hangs about his neck, / Smiles in his face, and whispers in his ears' (I. 2. 51–52). Old Mortimer, seemingly uncomprehending, can only reply 'Is it not strange, that he is thus bewitched?' (I. 2. 55). When Isabella addresses the troops before the final battle (a rare example of overreaching rhetoric from a woman in Marlowe), she apostrophizes her husband as a king

> Whose loosness hath betrayed thy land to spoil,
> And made the channels overflow with blood,
> Of thine own people patron shouldst thou be
> But thou –

> (IV. 4. 11–14)

She is cut off, typically, by a condescending remark from young Mortimer, who has become her lover. Mortimer may well feel that any reference to kings' patronizing their people, rather than sustaining their nobles, will merely perpetuate the threat that Gaveston and Spenser have posed. His subsequent speech to the soldiers emphasizes 'All homage, fealty, and forwardness' to the prince, a return to feudal categories that also allows him to speak for Isabella, 'That *England's* queen in peace may repossess / Her dignities and honors' (IV. 4. 20, 24–25). Yet Mortimer himself eventually turns to the practice of patronage, if not its public display, to consolidate the power he derives from his erotic link to the queen he claims to represent.

It is Isabella who comes up with the governing mythological symbol for the mutual involvement of patronage and physical love between men:

> Like frantic *Juno* will I fill the earth,
> With gastly murmur of my sighs and cries,
> For never doted *Jove* on *Ganymede*,
> So much as he on cursed *Gaveston*.

> (I. 4. 178–81)

Her allusion to Jupiter's cupbearer recalls the opening scene of Marlowe's *Dido, Queen of Carthage*, a play that can be related to *Edward II* through the figure of Ganymede in other ways.[33] [. . .] At first, the queen's urging of her son's claim to the throne seems to position the boy as a rival to Edward's latest Ganymede. The prince goes along with this strategy, saying 'I warrant you, I'll win his highness quickly, / A loves me better than a thousand *Spencers*' (IV. 2. 6–7). After Edward is captured and Spenser disposed of, the little family that Mortimer creates as a vehicle for his own power is an obviously artificial construction (V. 2. 1–20). He makes his affair with Isabella the means of reining in the prince's right as lord protector. 'Let not that *Mortimer* protect my son', Edward rages, 'More safety is there in a Tiger's jaws, / Then his imbrasements' (V. 1. 115–17). Mortimer's attempt to control the prince is a failed imitation of Edward's position as father, patron, and lover of boys or young men. The displaced eroticism in his alternate embracement and coercion of the prince is signaled by Mortimer's own fantasy of schoolmasterly violence: 'I view the prince with *Aristarchus* eyes, / Whose looks were as a breeching to a boy' (V. 4. 54–55). But the nuclear family that Mortimer, self-appointed tutor and foster father, sets up is a fragile and inadequate alternative to older institutions like patronage, pederasty, and the dynastic household, all of which do a better job of managing the erotics of court power.[34]

Before his construction collapses, however, Mortimer consolidates his power by arranging the murder of the king. He does so through the well-known device of the 'unpointed' Latin message *Edwardum occidere nolite timere bonum est*, which can be read by his agents the jailers to mean either 'Kill not the king 'tis good to fear the worst', or 'Fear not to kill the king 'tis good he die' (V. 4. 8–12). We have already seen sovereign power abused through language, particularly written language, and here the instability of writing would seemingly permit power to erase its abuse. If sodomy is a crime 'without a name among Christians', it seems that regicide is not to be named either. Both actions mark the ethical limits of the early modern moral field. Sovereign and sodomite are opposites; when brought together, one of them must die, the sodomite if power justly travels downward, the king if its course is reversed, *contra naturam*.

But what if sodomite and sovereign are the same? 'In the darkest region of the political field', Foucault writes, 'the condemned man represents the symmetrical, inverted figure of the king. We should analyse what might be called, in homage to Kantorowicz, "the lesser body of the condemned man".'[35] But placing king and *condamné* – each with his own legal body, ceremony, and theoretical discourse – at opposite poles from one another obscures the ritual similarities between these figures, similarities that persisted despite the late medieval attempt to separate the monarch from the risk of death. As Kantorowicz himself remarks of *Richard II*, 'Kingship itself comes to mean Death, and nothing but Death. . . . The king that "never dies" here has been replaced by the king that always dies and suffers death more cruelly than other mortals.'[36] These words apply equally to *Edward II*, the impossible memory of which Shakespeare was in some sense trying to obliterate in his play.

Edward's death is more cruel than other mortals', certainly more cruel than Richard's. The assassin Lightborn calls for a red-hot spit as well as a table and feather bed – its presence betokens the chronicle tradition in which Edward was impaled in a tacit, but grossly parodic, specification of sodomy, as well as pressed to death. Both forms of execution were employed so as not to leave a mark on the corpse, and thus Edward's end embodies the unspeakability of regicide and of sodomy as well. However, Marlowe elides the tradition about the apparently woundless death in his version of the king's murder, and the brand-like spit can be seen as an attempt to 'write' onto him the homoeroticism constantly ascribed to him.[37] Such writing remains unstable, perhaps partly illegible, yet Lightborn's initial approach and Edward's response, in which he gives his executioner a jewel, darkly rehearse the dynamics of his generous courtship of Gaveston and Spenser. But finally it is regicide and not sodomy that is fully recognized and punished.

For the conceit of the unpointed message fails – the prince, now Edward III, has Mortimer beheaded after identifying his hand-writing. One of the jailers has escaped, rumor is afoot, and the barons back up the young king: popular voice, consensus, and sovereign hegemony outstrip mere writing and through his son's decision produce the truth of Edward II's murder, for 'in me my loving father

speaks' (V. 6. 41). The king's second body lives on in Edward III,
confirming social hierarchies against excessive adulteration by
patronage and the manipulative regime of writing that is linked to it
in this play. Despite his use of feudal language in public, Mortimer's
regime operated through patronage after all. He extended the
principle of Gaveston's and Spenser's ascendancy, although without
violating existing hierarchies of sexuality and gender, similarly
basing his power upon his relationship with royal bodies – his sexual
conquest of the queen and his paternal, but erotically tinged,
relationship with her son. Mortimer unites the nuclear family,
patronage, and rule by the pen when he vaunts:

> The prince I rule, the queen do I command,
> And with a lowly conge to the ground,
> The proudest lords salute me as I pass,
> I seal, I cancel, I do what I will.

'Mine enemies will I plague, my friends advance', he concludes,
'And what I list command, who dare controle?' (V. 4. 48–51, 67–68).
'Control' here carries a range of meanings similar to its French
cognate *contreroller* in Montaigne; it can signify both domination and
scrutiny.[38] When Edward's brother Kent asks the queen how the
imprisoned king will be treated, Mortimer cuts in with ''Tis not in
her control, nor in ours, / But as the realm and parlement shall
please' (IV. 6. 35–36). But the king's fate is controlled by Mortimer, as
is Kent's – ''tis good to look to him betimes', he warns Isabella in an
aside (IV. 6. 39). The king exercises his authority by bestowing favor
on whom he pleases; thus 'Triumpheth *England's Edward* with his
friends', as Edward himself rejoices before the fight, 'And triumph
Edward with his friends uncontrolled' (IV. 3. 2–3). Yet Edward
recognizes the limits of royal power in the deposition scene through
a metaphor of opacity and light:

> But what are kings, when regiment is gone,
> But perfect shadows in a sun-shine day?
> My nobles rule, I bear the name of king,
> I wear the crown, but am controlled by them.

> (V. 1. 26–29)

The sovereign is watched over and to some extent controlled by his
court after all, and he is eventually removed by that court from the
presence chamber to the dungeon. Mortimer suffers a similar fate
when the prince turns on him and regains control of the barons.

Bad as Edward's rule may have been, Marlowe depicts Mortimer's usurpation as worse. Edward resolves at one point to 'Make *England's* civil towns huge heaps of stones' in defiance of the nobles – 'A desperate and unnatural resolution', as Warwick exclaims (III. 1. 215, 217). His own brother, Kent, calls him an 'Unnatural king, to slaughter noble men / And cherish flatterers' (IV. 1. 8–9). It is Edward's violence and his trust in hangers-on, and not his desires, that Kent regards as unnatural or monstrous. But Edward is after all England's anointed monarch, and Kent resolves covertly to support his brother once he is defeated and captured. 'Rain showers of vengeance on my cursed head / Thou God', he prays, 'to whom in justice it belongs / To punish this unnatural revolt' (IV. 6. 7–9). The unnatural is now associated with bearing arms against 'Thy lawful king thy sovereign' (IV. 6. 4–5). Marlowe's play renders any easy distinction between the natural and the unnatural impossible, opening a space for homoerotic desire that is seemingly tangential to transgressions of hierarchy.[39]

In Elizabeth's England, Edward's cause must finally appear to be the better one because he embodies legitimate sovereign power. But Marlowe's plays also contain an implicit challenge to Elizabeth's politics of heterosexual courtship. In *Dido*, Aeneas's sojourn on 'this courteous Coast' (I. 1. 232) is clearly portrayed as a voluntary submission to the 'female drudgery' of court life, where 'wanton motions of alluring eyes, / Effeminate our minds inur'd to war' (IV. 3. 55, 35–36). Here, effeminacy is associated with heterosexuality, not with love between men.[40] There is an unmistakable reference to Elizabeth herself in *Dido*, which may have been performed before her by the Children of Her Majesty's Chapel. 'O hear *Iarbus* plaining prayers', Dido's rejected suitor complains, 'Whose hideous echoes make the welkin howle, / And all the woods *Eliza* to resound' (IV. 2. 8–10). 'Elissa' is an alternative name for the Carthaginian queen in the *Aeneid*. That the echo of the name is 'hideous' here may signal the play's subtle critique of Elizabeth's courtly reign. A sexuality 'uncontrolled' by external powers became the hallmark of English sovereignty with Henry VIII's first divorce and the Reformation, and it remained so under his daughter Elizabeth. An uncontrolled homosexuality is the unspoken affirmation of sovereignty in *Edward II*, as it was to be when James I came to the throne a decade later.

In *The Massacre at Paris*, the monarch's sexuality once more becomes the hidden spring of the action. In a curious scene, the logician Ramus and his 'bedfellow', Taleus, are killed during the St Bartholomew's Day massacre by Anjou, the future King Henry III, while the diabolical Guise looks on. The pair then plan 'To get those pedants from the King *Navarre*, / That are tutors to him and the

prince of *Condy*' (I. 7. 65–6). Navarre's tutors, who recall Baldock and
Spenser, are a dim anticipation of Henry III's own minions later in
the drama, a group about the throne for whom physical intimacy and
knowledge of a political kind are closely allied. Guise is determined
to kill the clients of the enemy king, just as he manipulates first
Charles IX and then Henry himself through their bodily pleasures.

Unlike Edward II's barons, the Guise has learned to manage the
'pleasures uncontrolled' of his monarch, allowing him to weaken his
body and his realm by treating him like a child (I. 2. 70). So far the
Guise has succeeded with the infantilized king where Mortimer failed
to manipulate either Edward or his young son. But when Charles
begins to regret the massacre, his mother Catherine de Médicis
poisons him and places his brother on the throne. Henry III seems
even more tractable than Charles, as Catherine assures the Cardinal
of Lorraine:

> His mind you see runs on his minions,
> And all his heaven is to delight himself:
> And whilst he sleeps securely thus in ease,
> Thy brother *Guise* and we may now provide.
>
> (III. 2. 45–8)

Henry, unlike Edward II, is a monarch who can be controlled
because of his favorites, not in spite of them.

Yet the Guise runs afoul of Henry because the sexual energy
that surrounds the king breaks its bounds and invades his own
household. One of Henry's principal minions is carrying on an affair
with the duchess of Guise. 'Sweet *Mugeroune*, 'tis he that hath my
heart', she says, making the political parallel clear, 'And *Guise* usurps
it, cause I am his wife' (IV. 1. 4–5). Her husband pries into the letter
she is writing to her lover and arranges his assassination. When
Henry makes horns at the Guise and teases him about 'the letter
gentle sir, / Which your wife writ to my dear Minion' (IV. 3. 12–13),
the jealous husband scorns the king's love for his favorites and
openly threatens Mugeroun.

The violence that follows is set loose by the unstable combination
of disruptive sexual desire and royal patronage. The Guise murders
Mugeroun in a scene that is juxtaposed with Navarre's fair and open
defeat of the minion Joyeux in battle. Henry's relationship with
Epernoun, another minion, leads to his unexpected conversion to the
side of Navarre and the queen of England. Epernoun informs upon
the Guise, telling the king that he has raised an army to depose Henry
for affronting the pope, and that he is funded by Rome and Spain.
'I, those are they that feed him with their gold', Henry agrees, 'To

countermand our will and check our friends' (IV. 5. 41–2). Henry's similarity to Marlowe's other minion-minded king is emphasized by his violent threat against the pope as he lies dying at the end of the play: 'I'll fire his crased buildings and enforce / The papal towers to kiss the lowly earth' (V. 5. 63–4). These lines are almost identical with the words Edward speaks when he rails at Rome after the clergy side with the barons against Gaveston (*Edward II*, I. 4. 100–101). Henry is assassinated because he lured the Guise himself to his death at the hands of hired killers after entering into an alliance with Navarre.

Catherine de Médicis pines away and dies when she hears the news of the Guise's murder. Marlowe's handling of the queen mother exhibits the same anxieties over the mixing of political power with female sexuality that animate Sidney in the *New Arcadia*. Catherine dominates the stage in the early throne scenes, muttering in the first one that she will dissolve the celebration of Navarre's marriage 'with blood and cruelty' and calling openly for Guise's massacre plans in the second (I. 1. 26; I. 4. 28). She is given to repeating resolutions like 'I'll rule *France*' and 'while she lives, *Katherine* will be Queen'; she murders one son and determines to kill another should he not follow her behests. Yet it is the Guise who emerges as the active villain in the events Marlowe dramatizes, more strongly in the *Massacre* than the pamphlet literature that influenced it.[41]

After the Guise is done away with, an almost anonymous Jacobin friar volunteers to assassinate Henry III; the dying king interprets his own murder as a warning to Elizabeth. This chain of antagonists – Catherine, the Guise, the friar – indicates the changes that had taken place in English anxieties about Catholic conspiracy during the period covered by the play. In 1572, the year of Navarre's marriage and the massacre, the dangers of a French marriage for Elizabeth were uppermost in people's minds. Fears of a dynastic Catholic plot embodied in Catherine de Médicis were carried over well into the mid-1580s as Alençon's negotiations with Elizabeth dragged on. In the meantime, however, priests began to infiltrate Scotland and England, and with the Throckmorton Plot it finally became clear that Spain was allied with the Guisan faction in France rather than with the French crown. This realization was marked by Henri III's assassination of Guise and Catherine's subsequent death in 1588, the year of the Armada. The murder of Henri by a clergyman in 1589, on the heels of the Babington Plot to kill Elizabeth and put Mary Stuart on the throne, confirmed English anxieties about a large-scale invasion of devious and regicidal Catholic agents. The connection between the Guise and Spain is stressed in *The Massacre at Paris* as if to revise the faults in Walsingham's actual intelligence of affairs in France before the mid-1580s.[42]

The historical Guise had in fact established the college for priestly agents at Rheims, as Henry later discloses. Marlowe's character boasts that

Paris hath full five hundred Colleges,
As Monastries, Priories, Abbies and halls,
Wherein are thirty thousand able men,
Besides a thousand sturdy student Catholics,
And more: of my knowledge in one cloister keeps,
Five hundred fat Franciscan Friars and priests.

(I. 2. 80–5)

Marlowe, as we have seen, may have attended Guise's seminary at Rheims sometime before 1587. The phrase 'of my knowledge' sounds like something out of a spy's report rather than the Guise talking to himself; the public theater has become the forum for the display of secret intelligence, and for an admonition to the queen and her ministers. At the end of the drama, a taciturn 'English Agent' is suddenly summoned by the dying king, who resolves: 'I'll send my sister *England* news of this, / And give her warning of her trecherous foes' (V. 5. 51–2).

H.J. Oliver tentatively identifies the Agent with Walsingham; this may be correct in a symbolic way, but Walsingham was ambassador to France during the St Bartholomew's Day massacre in 1572, not in 1589.[43] Sir Edward Stafford filled the post the year Henri was killed, yet he was visiting England at the time. His servant, one William Lyly, acted in his place. Lyly was a tireless dispatcher of intelligence reports, and his account to Elizabeth of the murder and the role he played afterwards is remarkably similar to Marlowe's dramatization. The friar, 'in making him a monastical reverence, with a knife which he held in his sleeve struck the King under the short ribs, to have pierced his bowels; which the King with his own hand, seeing the motion . . . with great courage and force got the knife from him and therewith gave the Jacobin two blows', killing him. Henri spoke to Lyly a short while later, telling him: 'I am sure the Queen your mistress will be sorry for this, but I hope it shall be quickly healed and so I pray you write her from me'.[44] Having killed the assassin with his own weapon, Marlowe's Henry proclaims:

Agent for *England*, send thy mistress word,
What this detested Jacobin hath done.
Tell her for all this that I hope to live.

(V. 5. 56–8)

It is possible that Marlowe knew someone who was acquainted with Lyly or his report.[45] Is Lyly the mysterious English Agent? In a sense he is, but the Agent is also a figure for Marlowe, or rather for the playwright-spy who must warn Elizabeth and her subjects of regicidal Catholic plotters, making public what he claims covertly to have witnessed.

As Oliver notes, it is likely that, in addition to the information gathering among pamphlets and chronicles that eventually went into *The Massacre at Paris*, 'Marlowe may well have spoken with men who saw, or even took part in, the actions he portrays in his play'.[46] He may have served, after all, as the messenger of the English representative to Henri of Navarre in the early 1590s. When he was arrested in Flushing for coining in January 1592, Marlowe claimed to be well known to the earl of Northumberland and Lord Strange – a little unwisely, since both noblemen possessed Catholic associations and occult interests.[47] It was Strange's company, however, who performed *The Massacre* in 1593. The play was most probably composed in 1592, and Marlowe must have written it under the shadow of Baines's first round of accusations.[48] If he was the 'Marlin' of Rouen, he was in France on government service again in March. Marlin was sent back to London, and we know that Marlowe ran into trouble with the law there once more in May. He got into yet another fight in Canterbury during September of the same year – could the *Massacre* have been written in the intervening months, between brawls?[49] It is possible that Marlowe composed it in prison, although we have evidence that he was free later in the year.

If Marlowe intended to exorcise or excoriate an atheistic Catholicism through the Guise, he may have succeeded only in bringing more suspicion upon himself. When the Guise vaunts 'My policy hath fram'd religion' (I. 2. 65), he sounds a little like the Marlowe of the Baines report, who maintained 'that the first beginning of Religion was only to keep men in awe'.[50] In any case, Marlowe had a reputation to live down and, perhaps, a job to perform, and in *The Massacre at Paris* he decries the Guisan atheism and papistry with which Baines was already linking his name.

The play is unique among Marlowe's works for the propagandistic stance it assumes toward the events it portrays. This is partly because it depicts current events, Henry's 'news'. It has come down to us in a 'corrupt' form, but the contribution of voices other than Marlowe's, the voices perhaps of actors reconstructing from memory a text that must also have elicited a vigorous audience response, adds to the element of popular mythology that was already present in the original. And if Marlowe's public affected his plays, the plays reacted in turn upon their audience. According to Stephen Greenblatt, sixteenth-century drama 'depended upon and fostered in its audience *observation*, the close reading of gesture and speech as manifestations of character and intention'.[51] The representation of mutual observation at court in the theater of the period rendered it imitable, extending it outside the circle of court culture to the common spectator, a shift in emphasis from the erotics of courtly display and scrutiny to an uneasy awareness of overarching surveillance. The works signed by Marlowe that I have discussed here register this movement from the viewpoint of a playwright and spy. Display becomes public spectacle and observation the grounds for a generalized paranoia. Yet in constructing both his self and his sovereigns through his sexuality, Marlowe's theater stages history from below in another way, engaging the paranoia of the heterosocial court and affective family through dramatic representations of the social bonds that preceded them.

Notes

1. THOMAS NASHE, *The Unfortunate Traveller* (1594), p. 220. Subsequent references will be included in the text.

2. BEN JONSON, 'To Captayne Hungry', lines 19–21, *Ben Jonson [Works]*, ed. C.H. HERFORD et al. (Oxford: Clarendon, 1947), 8: 69.

3. FRANCIS MERES, *Palladis Tamia* (London, 1598; reprint, New York: Scholars' Facsimiles, 1938), pp. 286v–287r.

4. MARK ECCLES, *Christopher Marlowe in London* (Cambridge, MA: Harvard University Press, 1934), p. 36.

5. LAWRENCE STONE, *Sir Horatio Palavicino: An Elizabethan* (Oxford: Clarendon Press, 1956), pp. 234–5; CONYERS READ, *Mr Secretary Walsingham and the Policy of Queen Elizabeth* (3 vols, Cambridge, MA: Harvard University Press, 1925), 2: 322–35. Spies in the service of Burghley and his son Robert Cecil after Walsingham's death followed more or less the same pattern: see P.M. HANDOVER, *The Second Cecil* (London: Eyre & Spottiswoode, 1959), p. 103.

6. READ, *Walsingham*, 2: 329.

7. JOHN BAKELESS, *The Tragicall History of Christopher Marlowe*, 2 vols (Cambridge, MA: Harvard University Press, 1942), 1: 77; italics removed.

8. BAKELESS, 1: 84; PHILIP HENDERSON, 'Marlowe as a messenger', letter to the editor in *The Times Literary Supplement*, 12 June 1953, p. 381. Both these names are variant spellings of 'Marlowe' – the dramatist seems to have preferred 'Marley' himself: BAKELESS, 1: 96, x.

9. R.B. WERNHAM, 'Christopher Marlowe at Flushing in 1592', *English Historical Review*, 91 (1976), pp. 344–5. For a summary of, and some useful additions to, scholarship on Baines, see CONSTANCE BROWN KURIYAMA, 'Marlowe's nemesis: the identity of Richard Baines', in KENNETH FRIEDENREICH, ROMA GILL and CONSTANCE BROWN KURIYAMA (eds), *'A Poet and a filthy Play-maker': New Essays on Christopher Marlowe* (New York: AMS Press, 1988), pp. 343–60.

10. Quoted in Clifford Leech, *Christopher Marlowe: Poet for the Stage*, ed. Anne Lancashire (New York: AMS Press, 1986), p. 9. Leech gives the original text of the Baines report in full. I have also found his concise summary of events in Marlowe's life on pp. 2–11 very helpful.

11. Eccles, p. 37.

12. Bakeless, 1: 104–5; William Urry, *Christopher Marlowe and Canterbury* (London: Faber and Faber, 1988), pp. 64–5. This meant that Marlowe would be fined a sum of money should he fail to keep the peace.

13. Kuriyama, 'Marlowe's nemesis' (p. 357) comes to a similar conclusion.

14. Kyd may have been the unlucky one. Verses threatening aliens in London were found tacked on the wall of the Dutch Church yard in May 1593; this 'Dutch Church Libel' was glossed with the words '*per* Tamburlaine', an apparent attribution that may have led the authorities to stumble across Kyd in the course of tracking down Marlowe. See Arthur Freeman, 'Marlowe, Kyd, and the Dutch Church Libel', *English Literary Renaissance*, 3 (1973), pp. 44–52.

15. The letters are reproduced in A.D. Wraight, *In Search of Christopher Marlowe* (New York: Vanguard Press, 1965), pp. 314–16.

16. See Bakeless, 1: 142–84; and J. Leslie Hotson, *The Death of Christopher Marlowe* (Cambridge, MA: Harvard University Press, 1925). It is to Hotson that we owe the discovery of most of the documents relating to Marlowe's death and his Cambridge days. Urry, in *Christopher Marlowe* (pp. 97–8), discusses and disposes of most of the conspiracy theories: it used to be thought that Thomas Walsingham's wife, Audrey Shelton, was involved, for Frizer went on to become her business agent, but there is no evidence that the couple were married as early as 1593. Yet Urry also intimates that Marlowe's contacts with both espionage and court circles may have played some role in his murder; he shows, for instance, that Marlowe was killed in the house of a respectable widow who was mentioned in the will of one of the queen's gentlewomen (pp. 84–6).

17. On Frizer and Skeres, see Bakeless, *Tragicall History*, 1: 163–71, 180–2. The best account of Poley is in Frederick Boas, *Christopher Marlowe: A Biographical and Critical Study* (Oxford: Clarendon Press, 1940), pp. 263–8. Boas reveals that Poley was a double-agent who spied for Mary Stuart as a servant in Sidney's household at Walsingham's estate, Barn Elms. According to Urry, in May 1593 Poley had just returned from a mission to the Hague (p. 86). Urry (*Christopher Marlowe*, p. 68) has also turned up evidence that Poley must have passed through Canterbury twice bearing messages from the court to Dover and back again in September 1592, when Marlowe was also in Canterbury facing yet another assault charge.

18. Wraight, *Marlowe*, p. 316.

19. A letter survives from the spy Thomas Drury to Anthony Bacon, brother of Francis Bacon and chief intelligencer for Essex. Drury complains that he has not been awarded 100 crowns by the City of London for obtaining information about a mutinous libel; the City had offered such a reward in May 1593, during the investigation that led to Kyd's arrest. The libel he brought to light was also connected with a book and some articles of atheism, and his contact had been 'one Mr. Bayns'. If the book was *The Fall of the Late Arian*, and the libel the Dutch Church Libel or Baine's 'libel' against Marlowe, then Marlowe's old enemy may have been involved in Kyd's, and thus his own, arrest. Furthermore, the possibility of a connection to the Essex faction through Anthony Bacon cannot be discounted. See S.E. Sprot, 'Drury and

Marlowe', *Times Literary Supplement*, 2 August 1974, p. 840, and URRY, *Christopher Marlowe*, pp. 78–9.

20. LEECH, *Marlowe*, p. 9.

21. WRAIGHT, *Marlowe*, p. 316; contractions removed. Corydon's love for the young Alexis forms the subject of Virgil's second Eclogue.

22. ALAN BRAY, *Homosexuality in Renaissance England* (London: Gay Men's Press, 1982), pp. 48, 67, 77.

23. Ibid., pp. 70–6, 15–20.

24. In addition to Bray, see ARTHUR N. GILBERT, 'Conceptions of homosexuality and sodomy in western history', *Journal of Homosexuality*, 6 (1–2) (1980–81), pp. 57–68; DAVID F. GREENBERG, *The Construction of Homosexuality* (Chicago: University of Chicago Press, 1988), and ED COHEN, 'Legislating the norm: from sodomy to gross indecency', in RONALD R. BUTTERS, JOHN H. CLUM, and MICHAEL MOON (eds), *Displacing Homophobia* (Durham, NC: Duke University Press, 1989), pp. 169–205. See as well the articles by Stephen Orgell and Jonathan Goldberg in the same volume. On 'constructivist' as opposed to 'essentialist' approaches to homosexuality, see MARTIN DUBERMAN, MARTHA VICINUS, and GEORGE CHAUNCEY, JR (eds), 'Introduction', *Hidden from History: Reclaiming the Gay and Lesbian Past* (New York: New American Library, 1989), pp. 1–13. Valerie Traub cautions us that the stress on urbanization and its subcultures may reflect a male perspective on early modern sexualities. I owe much to her broader reading of homoerotic desire in the period: VALERIE TRAUB, 'Desire and the difference it makes', in VALERIE WAYNE (ed.), *The Matter of Difference: Materialist Feminist Criticism of Shakespeare* (Ithaca, NY: Cornell University Press, 1991), pp. 81–114 (on urbanization, see p. 110, n. 24). I am also indebted to GREGORY BREDBECK's important book *Sodomy and Interpretation: Marlowe to Milton* (Ithaca, NY: Cornell University Press, 1991), which provides a nuanced reading of antiessentialist arguments about the construction of male homosexual identity in the period; see particularly his first and fourth chapters. Jonathan Dollimore likewise advocates a strategic use of essentialist presuppositions when considering homosexuality in early modern Europe. See JONATHAN DOLLIMORE, *Sexual Dissidence: Augustine to Wilde, Freud to Foucault* (Oxford: Clarendon Press, 1991). On the notion of subculture in general, see DICK HEBDIGE, *Subculture: The Meaning of Style* (London: Methuen, 1979).

25. JONATHAN GOLDBERG, 'Colin to Hobbinol: Spenser's familiar letters', in *Displacing Homophobia*, pp. 121–2. Spenser left Harvey's university patronage for service as the Bishop of Rochester's secretary; his duties as secretary are uncertain, but it is interesting to note that he was probably employed by his next patron, Leicester, as a confidential messenger – that is, a spy. See J. SMITH and E. DE SELINCOURT, 'Introduction', *The Poetical Works of Edmund Spenser* (Oxford: Oxford University Press, 1912), p. xii.

26. Alan Bray's recent work has also concerned patronage among men, male homosexual practice, and ideas of 'manliness'. See ALAN BRAY, 'Homosexuality and the signs of male friendship in Elizabethan England', *History Workshop Journal*, 26 (1990), pp. 1–15.

27. *Edward II* was written either in the winter months of 1592–93, or sometime in 1591. See CHRISTOPHER MARLOWE, *The Complete Works of Christopher Marlowe*, 2nd edn, 2 vols (Cambridge: Cambridge University Press, 1981), 2: 12. Ralegh and his wife were imprisoned by Elizabeth in August 1592 after he tried to depart for the West Indies without her permission; the queen had discovered that Elizabeth Throckmorton was pregnant as early as February. The secret

marriage may date from 1588. See JOHN W. SHIRLEY (ed.), *Thomas Harriot: Renaissance Scientist* (Oxford: Clarendon Press, 1974), pp. 177–8.

28. Christopher Marlowe, *Edward II*, I. 1. 10–11, in *Complete Works*, 2nd edn, vol. 2. Further references to Marlowe's works will be from this edition and will be placed in parentheses. The probable pun was a familiar one: for instance, 'Elizium' is the name of Eliza's, or Queen Elizabeth's, realm in George Peele's entertainment *The Araygnement of Paris* (ca. 1582).

29. Richard C. McCoy briefly compares Edward's tournament in Marlowe's play with Elizabeth's more successful containment of her nobles' aggression in the Fortress of Perfect Beauty tilt. See RICHARD C. McCOY, *The Rites of Knighthood: The Literature and Politics of Elizabethan Chivalry* (Berkeley: University of California Press, 1989), p. 62. On the failure of Elizabeth's 'chivalric compromise' later in her reign, see his chapter on the Earl of Essex.

30. See SIMON SHEPHERD, *Marlowe and the Politics of Elizabethan Theater* (Brighton: Harvester, 1986), p. 115. I would like to acknowledge a general debt to Shepherd's reading of Marlowe, and particularly of *Edward II*, throughout what follows.

31. See LEONARD BARKAN, 'Diana and Actaeon: the myth as synthesis', *English Literary Renaissance*, 10 (1980), pp. 317–59.

32. Compare BRAY, *Homosexuality in Renaissance England*, pp. 62–7.

33. On Ganymede and male homosexuality during the Middle Ages and Renaissance, see JOHN BOSWELL, *Christianity, Social Tolerance, and Homosexuality* (Chicago: University of Chicago Press, 1980), chapter 9; JAMES M. SASLOW, *Ganymede in the Renaissance: Homosexuality in Art and Society* (New Haven, CT: Yale University Press, 1986), and LEONARD BARKAN, *Transuming Passion: Ganymede and the Erotics of Humanism* (Stanford, CA: Stanford University Press, 1991). In discussing two poems in which Ganymede debates Helen and Hebe on the merits of same-sex love, Boswell links this figure to the short-lived emergence of a homosexual identity in twelfth-century Europe, and Saslow (p. 117) relates the medieval context to Marlowe's *Dido, Queen of Carthage*. Barkan's book is a general meditation on Ganymede in humanist thought and the visual arts.

34. My reading of the Ganymede pattern in *Dido* and *Edward II* is corroborated by two rather different discussions. Saslow, *Ganymede* (chapter 5), demonstrates that in northern European art of the seventeenth century, Ganymede was appropriated for the celebration of the dynastic link between father and son and thus ceased to be a cipher for sexual love between men; he traces this development back to Vasari's designs for Cosimo de' Medici's rooms in the Palazzo Vecchio in Florence during the 1550s (pp. 168–70). Eve Kosofsky Sedgwick shows how the dynastic order itself finally breaks down in the 'paranoid' Gothic novel of early nineteenth-century England, where 'the hero intrusively and in effect violently carves a *small*, *male*, *intimate* family for himself out of what had in each case originally been an untidy, non-nuclear group of cohabitants', EVE KOSOFSKY SEDGWICK, *Between Men: English Literature and Male Homosocial Desire* (New York: Columbia University Press, 1985), pp. 116–17 (original emphasis). *Dido* registers the first of these transitions, while the proto-Gothic *Edward II* projects the second through the hero-villain Mortimer.

35. MICHEL FOUCAULT, *Discipline and Punish: The Birth of the Prison*, trans. ALAN SHERIDAN (New York: Vintage Books, 1979), p. 29. I have tacitly corrected a spelling error, and modified the translation with reference to *Surveiller et punir*, p. 34.

36. ERNST KANTOROWICZ, *The King's Two Bodies: A Study in Medieval Political Theology* (Princeton: Princeton University Press, 1957), p. 30.

37. BREDBECK, *Sodomy and Interpretation*, p. 76. On Edward's murder and Holinshed's *Chronicle*, see also BRUCE R. SMITH, *Homosexual Desire in Shakespeare's England: A Cultural Poetics* (Chicago: University of Chicago Press, 1991), pp. 220–1.

38. Compare, for instance, Shakespeare's *Twelfth Night*, II. 5. 67.

39. See SMITH, *Homosexual Desire*, pp. 219–20.

40. Philip Sidney, *The Countess of Pembroke's Arcadia (The New Arcadia)*, ed. VICTOR SKRETKOWICZ (Oxford: Clarendon Press, 1987), p. 78.

41. P.H. KOCHER, 'Contemporary pamphlet backgrounds for Marlowe's *The Massacre at Paris*', *Modern Language Quarterly*, 8 (1947), pp. 151–73, and see his 'Francois Hotman and Marlowe's *The Massacre at Paris*', *PMLA*, 56 (1941), pp. 349–68.

42. See READ, *Walsingham*, 2: 380–6, 389, 3: 1–48.

43. H.J. OLIVER, 'Introduction', in CHRISTOPHER MARLOWE, *The Massacre at Paris* (London: Methuen, 1968), p. 94.

44. Quoted in R.B. WERNHAM, *After the Armada: Elizabethan England and the Struggle for Western Europe, 1588–95* (Oxford: Clarendon Press, 1984), p. 146. See also JULIA BRIGGS, 'Marlowe's *Massacre at Paris*: a reconsideration', *Review of English Studies*, 34 (1983), p. 271, n. 38.

45. Marlowe attended the King's School in Cambridge with a William Lyly, who was the younger brother of John Lyly, author of *Euphues*; the elder Lyly appears to have had another brother named William as well. I have not been able to determine if either of these Williams was the diplomatic Lyly, but it is possible that Marlowe had an intimate source of intelligence for his assassination scene. See URRY, *Christopher Marlowe*, p. 102.

46. OLIVER, 'Introduction', p. lxiii. URRY, in *Christopher Marlowe* (pp. 2–3), points out that the Canterbury of Marlowe's childhood harbored many Huguenot refugees after 1572, some of whom may have circulated first-hand accounts of the massacre itself.

47. WERNHAM, 'Christopher Marlowe', p. 345. Kuriyama ('Marlowe's nemesis', p. 357) suggests that Marlowe may have been spying on both noblemen for the Cecils – his statement that he was 'very well known' to them may hint at this rather than simply laying claim to their patronage.

48. On the date of the play, see OLIVER, 'Introduction', p. lii.

49. ECCLES, pp. 102–13; HENDERSON, 'Messenger', p. 381; WILLIAM URRY, *Marlowe and Canterbury* (London: Faber and Faber, 1988), 136.

50. LEECH, *Christopher Marlowe*, p. 8.

51. STEPHEN GREENBLATT, 'The cultivation of anxiety: King Lear and his heirs', *Raritan*, 2 (1982), p. 103; Greenblatt's emphasis.

13 The Rites of Violence: Marlowe's *Massacre at Paris**

Julia Briggs

The historical turn in Renaissance studies was accelerated by the French *Annales* school of historians, who view local archives within long-term structures, and especially by Emmanuel Le Roy Ladurie's pathbreaking book on a massacre which erupted during Mardi Gras in 1580: *Carnival at Romans*. Commentators had always seen popular violence as spontaneous anarchy, but Ladurie excavated its symbolic meanings. So, when the citizens of Romans paraded *en fête* to butcher their neighbours, they knew that (contrary to Marxists like Mikhail Bakhtin) carnival is not a liberation, but a licence to kill the scapegoats. This grim insight has been extended to the whole of the French Wars of Religion by Natalie Zemon Davis, and it is her study of 'the rites of violence' that underpins Julia Briggs's microhistory of Marlowe's *Massacre at Paris*. Like a real riot, the play had been misread by critics as a chaotic mêlée, but Briggs contends that it simply repeats the ritual programme of its subject, the horrific Saint Bartholomew's Day Massacre. As a secret agent, Marlowe had penetrated the terrorist Catholic League, and it was his undercover operations which supplied him with a justification for slaughtering Protestants: as a purification ritual. The result, according to this reading, is a text that accurately records the atrocities of 1572, though with savage festive humour. An example of the fascination in the 1980s with folk customs, Briggs's essay is true to the *Annales* rule of 'history from below' in revealing how high art depends on low culture. But it is most typical of the New Historicism in its dark interpretation of Renaissance carnival as a brutal purging. Marlowe becomes less a renegade in this context, and more a reporter on the contemporary slaughter of the innocents, like the painter Brueghel.

---

* Reprinted from *Review of English Studies*, 34 (1983), 257–78.

Among the small corpus of Marlowe's plays, *The Massacre at Paris* has done nothing or worse than nothing to enhance its author's reputation. Critics have been exceptionally consistent in disparaging it. John Payne Collier, writing in 1820, anticipated many later comments when he declared it to be 'obviously a work of great haste, and got up for the purpose of gratifying the vulgar feeling at that date against popery: indeed, it has hardly anything to recommend it'.[1] His opinion has been widely endorsed by modern critics. One in particular, Wilbur Sanders in *The Dramatist and the Received Idea*, has taken the general condemnation a stage further, entitling his chapter on *The Massacre* 'Dramatist as Jingoist'. For him, Marlowe is 'a brutal, chauvinistic propagandist', the play 'a prostitution of art'.[2] Here even its initial popularity becomes a point of criticism, since it is seen as pandering to the most vulgar religious intolerance.

After a first performance in January 1593 (marked with Henslowe's cryptic 'ne'), *The Massacre at Paris* was played ten times during the summer of 1594, when the theatres reopened, the takings being high at the outset.[3] Henry IV's recent conversion, his coronation and entry into Paris would have enhanced its interest, while casting an ironic light on the final scene which depicts his declaration for the Protestant cause. The play was one of the earliest to present recent historical and contemporary political events on the English stage, though it is amusing to note that Marlowe's subject-matter had been anticipated by a French playwright, Pierre Matthieu, whose *La Guisiade*, published at Lyons in 1589, apparently went into three editions within the year.[4] The latter's success is only to be explained in terms of topicality and pro-League sympathies. The play itself is a plodding neo-classical tragedy in which the climax, the murder of the Guise, inevitably takes place off-stage, to be reported by a messenger and commented on by a chorus. It is most unlikely to have reached Marlowe's notice. Nearer home, Peele's *Battle of Alcazar* (1589) was concerned with similarly recent events, but these were altogether more remote from English concerns than the French civil wars being fought out across the Channel. Government censorship was subsequently to discourage the presentation of such potentially inflammatory topics on the stage.

Given the great interest of its subject-matter, it is particularly frustrating that the text we have is not that of the play written by Marlowe and first performed by Lord Strange's men, but a garbled and confused memory of that play which must, when complete, have been half as long again. [. . .] The plea that this is a poor text cannot, of course, be used to redeem a play which, in the form that it has reached us, is clearly very far from being a masterpiece. Two widespread assumptions about the play, however, do seem worth challenging: that it is 'obviously' a piece of crude Protestant propaganda, and that it is historically misleading. The very obviousness of the first supposition ought to arouse suspicion, for in Marlowe's dramaturgy things are so seldom exactly what they seem. The second assumption implies that Marlowe substantially misrepresented the main characters, and perhaps their actions too, in accord with a popular political bias. Yet although Marlowe did not have access to the wide variety of sources available to modern historians, his account comes much closer to historical fact than has been previously acknowledged; it is at least arguable that he represents the events much as they would have struck an impartial observer of the time.[5] In his presentation of the massacre itself he appears to have reproduced with remarkable accuracy forms of ritualized violence peculiar to the French religious wars.

It would be naïve to suppose that the problem of the French Huguenots was ever a simple or clear-cut issue as far as the English were concerned. They were not merely persecuted co-religionists whose wrongs at the hands of the Catholics, the international conspiracies of Spain, the Jesuits, and the Pope, required rectification. They were also rebels against their lawful king, and were gradually evolving a theory of justified political resistance which had developed among the refugees from Mary Tudor, and would be remembered by the opponents of Charles I. In the years in which the play takes place, far from prosecuting a religious war against the French in support of the Huguenot cause, Elizabeth was engaged in lengthy negotiations for a marriage with the king's brother; her support for the French monarchy was motivated almost as much by a desire for good order as by her fear of Spain. An ultra-Protestant standpoint ran the risk of undermining the sacred institution of kingship if it presented the Huguenot cause too sympathetically. John Stubbs had expressed such a view of the events of the massacre in his pamphlet attacking the proposed French match, *The Discovery of a Gaping Gulf* (1579): 'The last act was very lamentable. A King falsified his sworn word, the marriage of a King's sister imbrued with blood; a King murdered his subjects.'[6] Stubbs had his right hand cut off for his impudence. The direct expression of the kind of ultra-Protestant views that Marlowe has often been credited with in this play, far from guaranteeing financial reward, as some critics have supposed, might well risk official correction.

What makes the policy of religious intolerance advocated in the play's final scenes look suspiciously ironic, however, is that the effects of such policies had themselves already been vividly dramatized in the earlier scenes showing the massacre. Marlowe, faced with the apparently endless cycle of retaliation that characterized the French

217

civil wars, like many of his contemporaries, must have come to doubt whether 'one more act of violence could cure a world whose malady was aimless violence'.[7] Elsewhere his plays reveal his fascination with morally complex situations it is hard to understand why this play has traditionally been regarded as the exception. In her book on Marlowe, Judith Weil argues persuasively for a more equivocal reading, asserting that 'irony pervades *The Massacre at Paris*, an irony dependent less upon "hard" allusions, more upon dramatic structure and implicit ideas'.[8] Effectively ignoring its political context, Judith Weil concludes that it is more complex and characteristic of its author than had previously been acknowledged.

One of Wilbur Sanders's most important contentions, and one that recurs in other criticisms of the play, is that it 'is notable for a crippling dependence on source material which was, in itself, vacuous'. This view is derived from evidence provided by Paul Kocher in three articles which set out to identify Marlowe's sources from contemporary pamphlets.[9] Professor Kocher's knowledge of these is impressive and scholarly, but when his methodology is examined it turns out to be suspect. His articles are based on the unadmitted assumption that Marlowe derived all his information from written source-material, all of which is assumed to have survived. But this is patently unlikely, granted that the events of the second half of the play, from the Huguenot victory at Coutras in 1587 (IV. 4.) to the end, had occurred within five years of the play's composition. In these years Marlowe travelled abroad and was associated with government agents working for Mr Secretary Walsingham, on whose desk the foreign dispatches arrived (and who had himself been in Paris in 1572).[10]

The full inadequacy of Professor Kocher's method is exposed when he criticizes as yet another piece of Protestant propaganda Marlowe's presentation of Henry III dismissing his council: the King declares

> Make a discharge of all my council straight,
> And I'll subscribe my name and seal it straight.—
> My head shall be my council, they are false;
> And, Epernoun, I will be rul'd by thee.

> (IV. 5. 78–81)

Professor Kocher comments 'I know of no published statement that Henry made any formal dismissal of these corrupt advisers after the Barricades. Marlowe seems to use the idea merely to symbolize the definite crystallization of the king's enmity for the Guise.'[11] That he did not know of any such published statement does not, however, mean that the incident did not occur, carrying exactly the significance that Marlowe gives it in his text – it was part of the run-up to Henry's assassination of the Guise. There is an account of Henry's dismissal of his council in the *Calendar of State Papers Foreign* and a list by Burghley of the ministers involved, while in France l'Estoile recorded it in his *Journal*.[12] Wilbur Sanders, however, further compounds Professor Kocher's error when he writes 'In order to smooth over this transition [Marlowe] is obliged to invent another incident – Henry's dismissal of his council and his adherence to the anti-League hero, Epernoun.'[13] In fact, neither of these two plot elements was invented by Marlowe.

After the death of Joyeuse at Coutras, Henry III became markedly more dependent on the Duke of Epernon. As we shall see, that dependence was the subject of endless indecent speculations in League pamphlets and was sometimes even attributed to witchcraft. When Dr Sanders asserts that he has found 'no evidence to modify the clear-cut conclusions [Kocher] advances',[14] we may be justified in wondering whether he ever looked for any. On the other hand, likely though it is, it is not possible to prove positively that Marlowe made use of oral information, rather than written sources. The mistake of Orleans for Lyons as the town where Dumaine (otherwise Duke of Mayenne) was staying when he received news of his brother's assassination (xxi. 128; xxiii. 11)[15] suggests a mishearing, rather than a misreading, but it may represent a failure of our text rather than a significant authorial mistake.

If we look again, with an open mind, at the play's relation to its sources, we shall find that Marlowe has done exactly what he might have been expected to do. The play deals with two main sequences of events, the first centred upon the massacre itself in 1572 (Acts I–III), the second presenting selected events from 1587 up to Henry III's murder and the accession of Henry IV in 1589 (Acts IV–V). Since the first sequence occurred when he was a small child, Marlowe is naturally forced to rely extensively on a source-book for this. He used François Hotman's *De Furoribus Gallicis* or *A true and plaine report of the Furious outrages of Fraunce* . . . , published in 1573 and subsequently as the tenth book of Jean de Serres's *Three Partes of Commentaries . . . of the Civill warres of Fraunce* (1574). Evidently a work with a strong Protestant bias, this was also the obvious source-book for an English writer to use. When we come to the more recent sequence of events, however, of which Marlowe is more likely to have known from hearsay, there is no such single source. A variety of pamphlets, some pro-Huguenot, some pro-Catholic League, contributed details, but one significant event at least, Henry's dismissal of his council (referred to earlier), is not traced to any source at all, and two details concerning the murder of the Guise brothers seem only to be traceable to pro-League pamphlets. What does not accord with the received view of the play as a piece of blatant Protestant propaganda, is that the whole section of the play centring on the murder of the Guise is actually treated, not from the Huguenot viewpoint at all, but from the League viewpoint. That Marlowe should have been familiar with the League view of these events is less surprising if we recall that he may have visited Rheims in 1587; a note from the Privy Council to the Cambridge authorities insists that he had no intention of doing so, but this official denial may reasonably arouse suspicion. If he was, as seems probable, a member of Walsingham's counter-espionage system, he would have mingled with Catholics and have learnt to recognize their attitudes.

The League pamphlets, printed in Paris, indulged in the most extravagant character assassinations of Henry III (whom they consistently demoted to 'Henry of Valois') for his failure to adopt their own hard line on the Huguenot issue.[16] Marlowe's play presents Henry's dependence on the advice and energy of the Duke of Epernon in a manner slightly reminiscent of Mycetes and his favourite Meander in *Tamburlaine* or, more closely and significantly, Edward II and Gaveston. He may even have been prompted to write his history of *Edward II* by the striking parallels it offered to the story of Henry III which he had so recently dramatized, parallels developed in the notorious League pamphlet of Jean Boucher, *Histoire tragique et mémorable de Pierre de Gaverston*, published in July 1588. Its preface makes explicit the analogies between the Gascons, Gaveston and Epernon, both uniquely favoured by the King, both lining their pockets at the expense of church and commonwealth, both protectors of heretics who threatened the well-being of the realm. Boucher then turns to Edward, whose depravities are requited both by his own shameful death, impaled upon 'a red-hot spit', and that of his subsequent favourite Spenser, slain 'in detestation of his sodomy'. Two aspects of Marlowe's Edward II are perhaps more appropriate to Henry III: his delight in extravagant, even transvestite entertainments, as outlined by Gaveston in the opening scene (I. i. 54–70), and the row with the Bishop of Canterbury that develops into a full-scale denunciation of Rome (I. iv. 96–103), closely parallel to Henry's in *The Massacre* (V. 5. 58–63), but (predictably) better preserved. Boucher's pamphlet made a strong impression. Edward II was also cited, on occasion, as a warning to Henry III that kings might be deposed.[17] Explicit accusations of homosexuality were frequently made against the King, in particular with Epernon.[18]

Wilbur Sanders describes Marlowe as 'condoning the assassination of the Guise',[19] but the text suggests rather the reverse. Indeed Marlowe appears to have introduced four special features into his account of the Guise's death with the specific intention of swinging our sympathies away from Henry and towards the Guise and the murdered Cardinal, his brother. Such a shift of attitude might be seen to parallel those scenes in *Edward II* where Isabel's plight is treated more sympathetically than Edward's. The first of these four features is Marlowe's alteration of the established series of occurrences leading up to the Guise's murder. Instead of having the Guise murdered as he approaches Henry's cabinet but before he reaches it, Marlowe shows him being assassinated as he leaves Henry's chamber, after having been lulled into a state of false confidence by Henry's treacherous reassurances:

> So; now sues the King for favour to the Guise,
> And all his minions stoop when I command.
> Why, this 'tis to have an army in the field.
>
> (V. 2. 50–2)

crows the Guise as the murderers are about to set on him. It is a moment of pure hubris, close in tone to Mortimer's soliloquy near the end of *Edward II*:

> The prince I rule, the queen do I command:
> And with a lowly congé to the ground
> The proudest lords salute me as I pass.
>
> (V. iv. 48–50)

Like the Guise, Mortimer is about to touch that point of Fortune's wheel

> to which when men aspire,
> They tumble headlong down.
>
> (V. vi. 60–1)

Henry is traditionally supposed to have reassured the Guise of his goodwill towards him at Blois, during the period prior to the murder. This act of honeyed hypocrisy on Henry's part is a favourite theme of contemporary League pamphlets, but Marlowe altered all the known sources in juxtaposing this reassurance to the murder itself, so that the one occurs minutes after the other. The change emphasizes both the Guise's fatal pride and Henry's bad faith, hot versus cold Machiavellism. Eagerly anticipating the Guise's death, Henry intends to repay his cousin's treasons with treachery:

> Breathe out that life wherein my death was hid,
> And end thy endless treasons with thy death.
>
> (V. 2. 26–7)

To redress the balance, the Guise must die cursing the Huguenots and invoking the revenge of the Pope, Parma, and Philip of Spain (V. 2. 82–6). Henry then denounces his plotting and malevolence against Elizabeth (V. 2. 101–5), but after such a cowardly and self-interested action, his words sound hollow and uneasily self-justifying.

The second feature, much emphasized by League pamphlets and vividly brought out in Marlowe's treatment, is the personal courage shown by the Guise in the face of death. The line 'Yet Caesar shall go forth' (V. 2. 67), spoken by the Guise after the third murderer's warning, also occurs in Shakespeare's *Julius Caesar*, written six or seven years later, and may have been remembered from there in the existing text, but it is unlikely that something to this effect does not belong here, since twenty lines later the Guise declares 'Thus Caesar did go forth, and thus he died' (V. 2. 87) – that is to say, 'thus he went forth, bravely, despite warnings' and 'thus he died, treacherously murdered by a trusted friend'. The first comparison of the Guise to Caesar is made in his long opening soliloquy (I. 2. 95); it is possible that originally the play included others, now lost. Caesar, with his much-debated aspirations to kingship, his personal courage, his desire for power was an equivocal figure not unlike the Guise. League pamphleteers seem to have been fond of drawing analogies between them.[20]

The third feature is the introduction of the Guise's son to view his father's body; this is clearly gratuitous unless Marlowe intends to incriminate Henry III thoroughly. As a detail it is likely to be apocryphal, only to be found in a pro-League pamphlet. According to one source, the son on seeing his father 'began to spew out threatening words against the father's assassins'.[21] In Marlowe, the son's gesture of offering to throw his dagger is childishly ineffectual (unlike the boy Edward III's condemnation of Mortimer), but his words are less easily dismissed:

Art thou king, and hast done this bloody deed?

(V. 2. 121)

The final feature, also traceable to a League pamphlet, is the mockery of the Cardinal of Lorraine before his strangulation;[22] again, the sympathy aroused here is for the victim and against the King.

Marlowe's intention in presenting the murders of the Guise brothers from the League point of view was not, however, to blacken Henry III or to give the League a fair hearing, even though that may be part of the effect. The alterations he makes are all designed to remind the audience of something they have seen before. In altering the sequence of the Guise's fatal visit to Henry's cabinet, he does not merely emphasize Henry's treachery, he also reminds us of his brother's. Charles IX had visited the wounded Admiral to reassure him of his friendship and good faith (I. 4. 52–67), having agreed to the massacre earlier in the same scene (I. 4. 25). Both Charles IX and Henry III gave promises they knew they were about to break, and sanctioned murders. The incredulous words of the Guise's son confronting his father's corpse, recall John Stubbs's indictment of Charles IX for his part in the massacre: 'A King falsified his sworn word . . . a King murdered his subjects.' The parallel was noted by contemporaries.

The Admiral Coligny's fate is itself significantly echoed in the Guise's murder. Both die bravely, while the Guise's triumph over Coligny is ironically echoed in Henry's triumph over the Guise; Henry, in his turn, will fall victim to the Friar a few scenes later. It is tempting to speculate that a stage direction is missing at Henry's gloating

Monsieur of Lorraine, sink away to hell!

(V. 2. 94)

on which he treads or stamps on the Guise's body, recalling the latter's treatment of the Admiral:

The Duke of Guise stamps on thy lifeless bulk!

(I. 5. 41)

Henry is certainly reported by League pamphleteers to have kicked the corpse. The moderate Catholic l'Estoile recognized the irony of that gesture, recording in his *Journal* that the King 'Kicked the poor corpse in the face as the Duke had kicked the Admiral'.[23] The play exhibits many such dramatic ironies characteristic of revenge tragedy. The presentation of the Cardinal's murder presses home, with macabre humour, the sacrilege of killing God's ministers:

Card.	Murder me not, I am a cardinal.
First Murd.	Wert thou the Pope, thou mightst not 'scape from us.
Card.	What, will you file your hands with churchmen's blood?
Sec. Murd.	Shed your blood? O Lord, no: for we intend to strangle you.

(V. 3. 1–5)

The shedding of churchmen's blood had figured significantly in the massacre, where a similarly gruesome jocularity had accompanied the murders of the ministers Leranne (who does not figure as a preacher in Marlowe's source) and Seroune. Leranne, like the Cardinal, appeals in vain for clerical exemption (I. 7. 3–4).

The play's structure thus turns on the ironic relation between the massacre of the Huguenots and the murder of the Guise brothers, an event that was frequently referred to as a massacre by League pamphleteers. If Marlowe's original title was, as Henslowe recorded it in the majority of his entries, simply 'the masacer', the word may have been intended to refer to both events, or at least to gain a further resonance from the later murders. It is striking that the word 'massacre', originally meaning a shambles or butchery, appears to have arrived in England in the wake of St Bartholomew's Day. Its earliest use, according to the *Oxford English Dictionary*, was in 1581; there are several other occurrences listed from the 1580s, but most examples are contemporary with or occur after Marlowe's play. The word's novelty and its strong connection with these particular events of French history is likely to have given it a special impact.[24]

While it is not suggested that Marlowe saw the massacre and the murders as strictly comparable, as some of his contemporaries did, his dramatic treatment of them aimed to bring out their resemblances, above all in their combination of royal treachery and sacrilegious violence against men of the church, each instance serving to invite the next retaliation. In structure this play may be compared to that of *Doctor Faustus*, where again two focal episodes are at once paralleled and ironically reversed: the scene of Faustus's fatal pact, with the clock striking midnight and the words

> Faustus, thou art safe:
> Cast no more doubts! Mephostophilis, come,
> And bring glad tidings from great Lucifer.
>
> (V. 26–8)[25]

corresponds closely and contrasts dramatically with the final soliloquy as midnight strikes:

> Ugly hell, gape not! Come not, Lucifer;
> I'll burn my books! Ah, Mephostophilis!
>
> (XIX. 189–90)

In *Faustus* the central episodes constituting the twenty-four years of the pact degenerate towards comic padding, and a similar tendency is apparent in *The Massacre*, where the play's centre, the fifteen years from 1572 to 1587, is chiefly represented by the joke-book episode of the cutpurse at Henry's coronation (III. 2. 29–33) and the cuckolding of the Guise (IV. 3. 1–16), which, like the Benvolio episode in *Faustus*, is mainly the occasion for a series of indecent puns.

In choosing to concentrate almost exclusively on two episodes, Marlowe deliberately omitted from the action Henry III's younger brother the Duke d'Alençon, familiar from his lengthy and abortive negotiations for a marriage to Elizabeth. Marlowe also fused (or confused) two individuals when the elder Cardinal of Lorraine, who was associated with the massacre and died in 1574, is identified with his nephew, the Cardinal of Guise, murdered by Henry's assassins on the day after his brother the Duke. Such omissions underline the dramatist's intention of focusing on these two episodes above all; by paralleling the murder of the Guise brothers with St Bartholomew's Day, Marlowe can bring out the extent to which personal spite motivated both actions, even as their protagonists exploited the more impersonal forces of the two opposed religious faiths. Though not specifically referred to in the play as we have it, the Guise had used the massacre partly to indulge a personal vendetta against the Admiral, as well as to activate anti-Huguenot elements in Paris. Later Marlowe makes Henry taunt the Guise with his wife's unfaithfulness. The Guise retaliates by having the King's *mignon* Mugeron murdered[26] and collects an army for himself. Henry responds to the Guise's open challenge to his power by murdering him and his brother the Cardinal. Beneath reasons of state lurk personal animosities.

The Guise's open challenge to the King (IV. 5. 44–54) is the nearest Marlowe came to depicting the important events that occurred at Paris in May 1588, known as the Day of the Barricades. By passing over it, Marlowe gave up an obvious opportunity to blacken the Guise's character, if that was really his intention, since the Guise, by returning to Paris against Henry's express command, had committed an act of open rebellion, comparable to the Essex rebellion of 1601, except that it succeeded. He might well have had misgivings about presenting an act of Catholic rebellion against a reigning monarch on the English stage, where such a thing was still feared, even though the Armada experience had proved it a most unlikely eventuality. It might have been taken in the wrong way, and the subject was certainly a delicate one. Our assumption that this play voices only obvious Protestant propaganda may be no sounder than the traditional assumption that Shakespeare unhesitatingly endorsed the rights of the anointed king in *Richard II*.

If Henry III's murder of the Guise brothers reveals his treachery and hypocrisy, his subsequent turning to Navarre for aid in capturing the infuriated and League-dominated Paris might be interpreted as cynical rather than idealistic, another politic about-turn. It is the Guise who announces in his opening soliloquy his intention of using religion for his own ends, but neither this nor his admitted allegiance to the teachings of Machiavelli are confined exclusively to him. Like Barabas, the Jew of Malta, he merely voices openly the values that his enemies adhere to secretly. Henry's shift from enjoying an active part in the massacre to accepting Huguenot aid against the unforgiving forces of the League looks opportunist, to say the least. Obviously his assassination by a League fanatic provides a motive for anti-Catholic sentiments, but there is nothing to show that his earlier change of allegiance sprang from a genuine change of heart, rather than political necessity. If Protestant pamphlets viewed the Guise as a Machiavel, the League pamphlets, among them some Marlowe may have used to provide particular details of the Guise murders, saw Henry in the same light: an atheist and Machiavel, he wears alternately the mask of the fox and the lion.[27]

Henry's partiality for England, so enthusiastically attested in the play's final scenes, was another favourite theme of League pamphleteers, for whom his acceptance of the Order of the Garter represented a feeble, if not a positively dangerous dependence on 'the English Jezebel'.[28] Although from one point of view the final scenes invite an uncomplicated Protestant reaction, from another they are quite congruent with the League attitudes so frequently reflected in the second half of the play. Henry's siege of Paris, his support for Navarre and Elizabeth, and the commitment that these implied were seen as threats to the Catholic religion, so serious – to some ways of thinking – as to justify assassination. Marlowe may also have intended Henry's death to provide a special irony for those in the know. The dying King certainly announced Navarre his heir, but far from begging him to espouse the Protestant cause, he in fact urged him to convert to Catholicism, as the dispatches to Walsingham make clear. Henry IV's first public commitment was not to the Huguenots – it was an undertaking to defend the French Catholic Church. Whatever Marlowe was to present, it certainly could not be the unpalatable truth about Henry III's last hours, or Henry IV's first ones.[29] A neat reversal of facts may have been intended to amuse the informed; it may even be intended as rabble-rousing Protestantism, yet the religious intolerance of proposals to 'fire Paris where these treacherous rebels lurk', to 'fire accursed Rome', to 'whet your sword on Sixtus' blood' is nevertheless uneasily reminiscent of the mindless savagery and the hatred of the clergy that inspired the massacre itself. The apparently unqualified enthusiasm of the ending of *Tamburlaine Part II*, where the victor's sons are directed to carry on conquering, induces a similar unease.

At the simplest level, Henry's final and mythical conversion to the Protestant faith may be intended to increase our sympathy for his murder, just as at the end of *Edward II* the King's cruel death provokes our pity; but Henry's murder is firmly conceived as a direct consequence of his own treachery to the Guise brothers, and it is not so much Henry as the Guise who dies a memorable death, despite his avowals of loyalty to Spain and the Pope. The Guise is presented as a typical Machiavel, ambitious, ruthless, consciously dissimulating, yet possessed of the demonic virtues of courage and restless energy.[30] His alliance with Catherine de Medici, apparently Marlowe's invention, seems natural enough since, according to the English view of her, Catherine was Machiavellism incarnate, having been born and bred in Florence and coming from a family indissolubly linked with that philosopher. She was, in any case, unpopular with both sides. Jean de Serres, writing for the Protestants, and Jean Boucher, writing for the League, both found a sinister significance in her reported words to Henry as he left for Poland: 'Goe, thou shalt not remayne long in Polonia'. Both juxtaposed them with Charles IX's death, supposedly from poison.[31]

Henry of Navarre remains the most problematical figure in the play, especially since what little he has to say is so unconvincingly sanctimonious that it is tempting to interpret him as yet another political operator, exploiting religious fervour to bring him one step nearer the crown, in the manner of the Guise. Marlowe may have felt inhibited by Navarre's enormous popularity in this country where he was regarded as a hero from the outset; his nickname – 'the Great' – certainly survived his conversion to Catholicism in the year after Marlowe's death.[32] Yet his position during the wars of religion was an awkward one. Marlowe makes Henry III refer to him as 'the rebellious king Navarre', and though the point is not laboured, the wonderful victory at Coutras, won against all the odds, was by the same token an act of rebellion and a defeat for the forces of the King.

Whatever reservations may remain with regard to Navarre's fine sentiments or the Guise's gross cynicism, the play's obvious tendency is to invite our approval of the former and our condemnation of the latter. At the same time, granted his early dependence on a Protestant source and his alteration of certain minor elements, Marlowe does not seriously distort the main historical facts in his representation of them. The Guise was undoubtedly in the pay of Philip of Spain and committed, as he explained in a letter to the Spanish ambassador Mendoza, to a policy of total extermination of the Huguenots. The Pope may not unreasonably be thought to have encouraged acts of violence against Protestants – both he and Philip II were eager for the Admiral's murder in 1572, and the St Bartholomew massacre was celebrated by a *Te Deum* at Rome and a special medallion struck to commemorate the holy event.[33] The excommunication of Henry III in

227

retaliation for the Cardinal's murder made him an obvious target
for ultra-Catholic fanatics such as had murdered William of Orange
in 1584, and would later murder Henry IV. In the interests of
impartiality it should be added that Protestants frequently acted with
comparable brutality and cunning. It was the contemporary essayist
Michel de Montaigne who pointed out that some of the barbarous
acts committed in his lifetime in the name of piety and religion made
cannibalism look humane by comparison.[34] Marlowe may have
intended his gruesome chronicle to yield a comparable moral.

Finally, Marlowe's dramatization of the events of the massacre
itself is worth closer analysis than it has yet received. Obviously he
employs dramatic licence in making the Guise and Henry of Anjou
enact a significant number of murders themselves, though it is widely
reported that the Guise wiped the blood from the Admiral's face
after his corpse had been thrown from the window to ensure that it
really was that of his old enemy, and it is not inconceivable that he
also kicked him. Marlowe endows the Guise with a sinister sense
of humour, partly though not wholly responsible for the particular
vein of comic-macabre that accompanies the murders, and usually
regarded as a hallmark of Marlowe's dramaturgy. A comparable vein
of grim comedy and ritualized violence is also to be found in some of
Shakespeare's early work. It belongs to a continuous dramatic tradition
that can be traced back to the treatment of Christ's scourging and
crucifixion in the mystery plays. There nevertheless remain some
striking parallels between the scenes Marlowe here presents and
contemporary accounts of the behaviour of rioting crowds during the
French religious wars. Judith Weil has observed of the play that 'the
regular connection of ceremonial with violent behaviour can scarcely
be accidental'. The nature of this connection is illuminated by the
work of the social historian of France, Natalie Zemon Davis, whose
article 'The Rites of Violence' examines in careful detail a number
of incidents that occurred during the wars of religion, several of
which bear a notable resemblance in tone to scenes from Marlowe's
play. Professor Davis shows that ceremonies provided the most
frequent occasion for religious riots, and particularly those where the
participants held opposing views as to how these should be conducted.
Marlowe's recognition that this was indeed the case is evident from
the way he begins his play with the royal marriage, described by
Davis as a characteristic scenario for what followed: 'a marriage –
one of the great rites of passage, but here, . . . conflict over whether
its form should be Catholic or Protestant.'[35]

In religious riots the elements of violence are anything but random
or chaotic, as they are, for example, when the angry mob tears Cinna
the poet in Shakespeare's *Julius Caesar* merely because he has the

same name as Cinna the conspirator, and they are anyway looking for someone to tear. Instead, as Davis persuasively argues, such riots are commonly ritualized into challenges, mock trials, mock services, mock exorcisms, behaviour that parodies or echoes existing formulae. Objects, primarily those with religious significance, are commonly involved, being mocked, broken, or ritually defiled, one underlying cause for this being the extent to which religious differences themselves centred on the significance and meaning of particular objects. Davis lists numerous examples of the mocking demands of crowds, often insisting on the value or worthlessness of particular objects or emblems, according to their beliefs.[36] In such a context, the exchange before the murder of the Admiral no longer sounds merely Marlovian; it assumes the ring of authenticity:

> *Adm.*   O let me pray before I die!
> *Gon.*   Then pray unto our Lady; kiss this cross.
>
>   (I. 5. 27–8)

The cross is that formed by the hilt of the dagger with which Gonzago proceeds to stab his victim. The mockery that so frequently accompanied acts of violence might also involve parodies of religious ritual – so Protestants murdered at Mâcon in 1562 had a distorted version of the blessing from Numbers recited over them: 'The Lord God of Huguenots keep you, the great Devil bless you, the Lord make his face to shine upon you who play the dead.'[37] This may be compared with the treatment of the minister Leranne whose assertion that he is a preacher of the word of God is answered by the Guise's mockery of the opening of a Protestant sermon:

> 'Dearly beloved brother' – thus 'tis written.
> *He stabs him.*
>
>   (I. 7. 5)

while Henry of Anjou adds, for good measure,

> Stay, my Lord, let me begin the psalm.

Psalm singing had, of course, replaced the traditional words of the mass in Protestant services, while Huguenot pastors, as Marlowe shows, were obvious targets in religious riots. Davis has commented on these grim travesties: 'With such actions, the crowds seem to be moving back and forth between the rites of violence and the realms of comedy. Are we at a Mardi Gras game, with its parodies and topsy-turvy mockery?'[38]

Underneath the murderous cruelty of many incidents of this kind lay a conviction of pollution, the Protestants believing that the priests and clergy had filled God's house and his services with corruption, against which they reacted by committing acts of desecration and sacrilege, while Catholics were, in their turn, eager to purge their country of the spreading uncleanness represented by the heretics. In this light, murder became a rite of purification, and the destruction by fire or water of the corpses of the profane assumed a special significance. Protestant victims were often drowned or thrown into rivers (in Marlowe's account of the massacre, those who have taken refuge in the Seine are to be shot at) since water was envisaged as washing away their evil, as if in baptism or exorcism. But the body of the Admiral, leader of the Huguenots, is symbolically a source of pollution too powerful and pervasive to be dealt with by any single method, neither fire nor water being, by themselves, adequate.[39] The point is sharply made in a scene that is otherwise difficult to explain, since Anjou had already given orders (I. 5. 41–7) that the Admiral's head and hands should be cut off and his body dragged to the gallows:

(II. 2.) *Enter two with the* ADMIRAL's *body.*
1. Now, sirrah, what shall we do with the Admiral?
2. Why, let us burn him for an heretic.
1. O no, his body will infect the fire, and the fire the air, and so we shall be poisoned with him.
2. What shall we do, then?
1. Let's throw him into the river.
2. O, 'twill corrupt the water, and the water the fish, and by the fish, ourselves when we eat them.
1. Then throw him into the ditch.
2. No, no, to decide all doubts, be ruled by me: let's hang him here upon this tree.

Henry III after the murder of the Guise brothers, faced with what might be thought to be a comparable problem in reverse, took the precaution of burning their bodies and scattering their ashes so that they should not acquire the power of relics, a measure that further enraged his League opponents.

The assumption that murder constitutes a ritual purification was one of the strategies used by the rioters to create the psychological conditions necessary for guilt-free violence. Their victims must be seen as vermin, filth, no longer human beings resembling themselves, who might thus challenge pity. Similarly, laughter and mockery, as Davis brings out, hid from the rioters 'a full knowledge of what they were doing'.[40] This gruesome aspect of the psychology of violence was fully grasped by Marlowe, as can be seen from his other plays, but nowhere was it put to such sustained or historically authentic use as in *The Massacre of Paris*, a play that, as the theatre critic Robert Cushman wrote, 'tells you more about the springs of atrocity than any more tasteful piece'.[41] It remains to decide what effect this presentation of the rites of violence was intended to have on an audience, and here there are clearly two different possibilities. If the alienating character of the stage is emphasized, the audience's reaction to the relished comic violence they witness will be one of disapproval, even of intense disgust – the thud of the Admiral's body as it falls from the upper stage, the gratuitous taunting and mocking of helpless victims, the preacher Seroune murdered before his wife's eyes – surely invite the pity of the victims' co-religionists, and the laughter and games thus appear as the sick-making self-deceptions they really are.

Alternatively, the Elizabethan audience may have reacted to the violence with excitement, as if they were watching real events, witnessing an execution or participating in a lynching, so that they laughed with the murderers, thus freeing themselves of responsibility and compassion, as the religious rioters themselves seem to have done. Even so, such a reaction would have forced a Protestant audience to see the massacre from a standpoint identical with that of the Catholic murderers, an insight which no other dramatist was to give them and which, in itself, is surely a refutation of the claim that the play is merely jingoist, a crude piece of Protestant propaganda. The scenes of the massacre may be viewed either as a subtle, perhaps even a humane, analysis of contemporary crowd violence and religious hatred, or as black comedy that paradoxically invites its audience to laugh at helpless Protestant victims. Either way, it must be conceded that *The Massacre* is something more than a tract on their behalf. What is needed now is a wider view of the play that poses such dilemmas, that asks us to weigh the murder of the Huguenot victims of St Bartholomew against the murder of the Guise brothers, and to see the outcome of that as a further murder, this time of the King himself. In such a context the rabid attack on Catholics, Rome, and the Pope with which the play ends rather resembles a compulsive reopening of unhealed wounds than a pious manifesto for the future.

Notes

1. *Marlowe: The Critical Heritage*, ed. MILLAR MACLURE (London: Routledge, 1979), p. 83. See also pp. 94, 104, 163, 180.

2. WILBUR SANDERS, *The Dramatist and the Received Idea* (Cambridge: Cambridge University Press, 1968), pp. 20, 36.

3. *Henslowe's Diary*, ed. R.A. FOAKES and R.T. RICKERT (Cambridge, 1968), pp. 20, 22–4.

4. For this reference and for many others to French sources, I am indebted to my husband, Robin Briggs, whose ideas and suggestions have contributed substantially to what follows.

5. A comparable claim has been made recently for the authenticity of *Edward II*. NATALIE FRYDE asserts in *The Tyranny and Fall of Edward II, 1321–1326* (Cambridge: Cambridge University Press, 1979), p. 7, that 'Marlowe's play . . . has captured the essential atmosphere of the regime perhaps better than any historian has since been able to do'.

6. JOHN STUBBS, *The Discovery of a Gaping Gulf*, ed. LLOYD E. BERRY (Charlottesville: University of Virginia Press, 1968), p. 25.

7. GARRETT MATTINGLY, *The Defeat of the Spanish Armada* (London: Jonathan Cape, 1983), p. 50.

8. JUDITH WEIL, *Christopher Marlowe – Merlin's Prophet* (Cambridge, 1977), p. 82.

9. SANDERS, *The Dramatist*, p. 23. P.H. KOCHER, 'François Hotman and Marlowe's *The Massacre at Paris'*, *Proceedings of the Modern Language Association of America*, lvi (1941), pp. 349–68; 'Contemporary pamphlet background for Marlowe's *The Massacre at Paris'*, *Modern Language Quarterly* (*MLQ*), viii (1947), pp. 151–73, 309–18.

10. R.B. WERNHAM, 'Christopher Marlowe at Flushing in 1592', *English Historical Review*, xci (April 1976), pp. 344–5. On his connection with government agents, see PIERRE LEFRANC, *Sir Walter Raleigh Ecrivain* (Paris, 1968), pp. 363–79, 657.

11. *MLQ*, viii (1947), p. 172.

12. ERNEST LAVISSE, *Histoire de France*, vol. 6 (I): (*1559–1598*), by Jean H. Mariéjol (Paris, 1904), p. 279. *Calendar of State Papers Foreign*, Elizabeth XXII, 178 (1 Sept. 1588: Stafford to Walsingham), 208 (20 Sept. 1588: notes by Burghley). PIERRE DE L'ESTOILE, *Journal du règne de Henri III*, ed. L.-R. LEFÈVRE (Paris, 1943), p. 572. See also Mattingly, op. cit., p. 316.

13. SANDERS, *The Dramatist*, p. 27, who further makes the untenable assertion that 'the intimacy between the King and Epernoun, however gratifying to the opponents of the League, has no foundation in contemporary reports'. See MATTINGLY, op. cit., p. 198, and nn. 17, 18, below.

14. SANDERS, *The Dramatist*, p. 23.

15. Discussed by KOCHER, *MLQ*, viii (1947), p. 159.

16. DENIS PALLIER has listed these in *Recherches sur l'imprimerie à Paris pendant la Ligue (1585–1594)* (Paris, 1976).

17. JEAN BOUCHER, *Histoire . . . de Pierre de Gaverston* (Paris, 1588), p. 14. References to Marlowe's *Edward II* are to Roma Gill's edition (Oxford, 1967). L'Estoile refers to Henry's tastes for transvestism (*Journal*, p. 142) and comments on Boucher's pamphlet (p. 569). Later pamphlets also refer to Epernon as Gaveston, e.g., *L'Atheisme de Henry de Valoys* (Paris, 1589), p. 30. Edward II's deposition is referred to in *De l'Excommunication et censures Ecclesiastiques* (Paris, 1589), p. 72.

18. Henry's supposed homosexuality is referred to widely, e.g., *Le Martyre des Deux Freres* ([Paris], 1598), p. 23; with Epernon, p. 7; with Longnac (Captain

of the Guard and murderer of the Guise), p. 36; *Le Faux-Visage Descouvert du fin Renard de la France* (Paris, 1589), p. 22; strongly implied in Boucher's *La Vie et Faits Notables de Henry de Valois* ([Paris], 1589), p. 35. Epernon was frequently described as a sorcerer who entertained familiar spirits and had cast a spell over the King e.g., *La Grande Diablerie de Jean Vallette* ([Paris], 1589), *passim*; *L'Atheisme de Henry*, pp. 13, 19, 23; *Responce faicte à la declaratiō de Henry* ([Paris], 1589), p. 7; and many other examples.

19. SANDERS, *The Dramatist*, p. 26.

20. KOCHER, *MLQ*, viii (1947), p. 155. See *Le Faux-Visage Descouvert*, p. 9, for example.

21. Cited by KOCHER, *MLQ*, viii (1947), p. 156.

22. *Le Martyre des Deux Freres*, p. 48; cited by KOCHER, *MLQ*, viii (1947), p. 156.

23. For example BOUCHER, in *La Vie et Faits Notables*, p. 136; L'ESTOILE, *Journal*, p. 581.

24. A list of League pamphlets that refer to the murder of the Guise brothers as a massacre in their titles or subtitles includes those numbered by PALLIER (*Recherches*) as follows: 286, 289, 290, 295, 298, 306, 342, 374, 382, 398, 436. See also *Le Martyre des Deux Freres*, pp. 38, 39, 43, 49, 55, 63; *De l' Excommunication*, pp. 17, 28, 45, 53, 66, 68, 70. HENSLOWE (ed. cit., pp. 20, 22–4) lists two performances of 'the gvyes'; thereafter the play is referred to as 'the masacer' (with spelling variations) on nine further occasions. Later records (pp. 76, 82, 182–5, 187) refer to transactions concerning 'the Guise', but once (3 Nov. 1601, p. 183) it is called 'the masaker of france'. It is highly probable that both titles refer to Marlowe's play.

25. References are to the Revels edition, ed. JOHN D. JUMP (London: Edward Arnold, 1962).

26. Here too, Marlowe has confused, or more probably conflated, two individuals, both *mignons* of the King, both of whom died violently within a few months of one another: Maugiron was killed in a duel in April 1578, while Saint-Mégrin, notoriously the Duchess of Guise's lover, was assassinated in July, apparently at the Duke's instigation. See L'ESTOILE, *Journal*, pp. 190–1, 205. KOCHER exceptionally concedes Marlowe an unknown contemporary source for the incident, *MLQ*, viii (1947), pp. 169–70.

27. Machiavelli's recommendation to the prince to imitate both the fox and the lion was followed by Henry, according to *Le Martyre des Deux Freres*, p. 9, and the influence of his atheistical teachings on the King figures in *L'Atheisme de Henry*, pp. 15, 16, 28; his maxim that the prince is not obliged to keep his word is adopted by Henry in *De l'Excommunication*, p. 55, and *Le Faux-Visage Descouvert*, p. 17.

28. Henry's alliance with Elizabeth is frequently seen as evidence of his secret intention to overthrow the Catholic faith, e.g., *De l'Excommunication*, pp. 11, 75; *La Vie et Faits Notables*, p. 106 (where it prompts the Guise to establish the Catholic League in retaliation). In *Le Martyre des Deux Freres*, p. 9, Henry names the Queen 'sa bonne soeur' (cf. Marlowe's 'my sister England', xxiv. 50). Henry's murder of the Guise and his siege of Paris effectively forced him to seek help from Navarre and support from England.

29. Marlowe has made Henry's death-bed scene a curious mixture of fact and fiction. His message to Elizabeth, 'Tell her for all this, that I hope to live' (xxiv. 57) is close to the message sent back from Henry by William Lyly: 'I am sure the Queen, your mistress, will be sorry for this, but I hope it shall quickly be healed, and so I pray write unto her for me', *Calendar of State*

Papers Foreign, Elizabeth XXIII, 394 (22 July/1 Aug. 1589: William Lyly to the Queen). John Welles, however, reported to Walsingham, 'The King did pray the King of Navarre to live and die a Catholic, and so he hath promised all the nobility and doth go to Mass', ibid. 405 (29 July/8 Aug. 1589). For Henry IV's Declaration of St Cloud, see DE LAMAR JENSEN, *Diplomacy and Dogmatism: Bernardino de Mendoza and the French Catholic League* (Cambridge, MA: Harvard University Press, 1964), p. 192.

30. But see KOCHER, *MLQ*, viii (1947), p. 314.

31. A.G. DICKENS, 'The Elizabethans and St Bartholomew', p. 61; DONALD R. KELLEY, 'Martyrs, myths and the massacre: the background of St Bartholomew', p. 194; both articles in *The Massacre of St. Bartholomew – Reappraisals and Documents*, ed. ALFRED SOMAN (The Hague: Martinus Nijheff, 1974). Jean de Serres is cited by KOCHER, *MLQ*, viii (1947), p. 166; BOUCHER, *La Vie et Faits Notables*, p. 17.

32. JUDITH WEIL, *Marlowe*, pp. 89–90; KOCHER, *PMLA*, lvi (1941), p. 368; A.G. DICKENS, 'The Elizabethans', p. 57.

33. DE LAMAR JENSEN, *Diplomacy and Dogmatism*, pp. 53, 54; JEAN DE CROZE, *Les Guises, les Valois et Phillipe II* (Paris, 1866), ii. 361 (Guise to Mendoza, 13 Oct. 1588) and see also i. 349 (Guise to Mendoza, 25 Aug. 1585), ii. 283 (Guise to Mendoza, 2 Apr. 1587); N.M. SUTHERLAND, *The Massacre of St Bartholomew and the European Conflict 1559–1572* (London, 1973), pp. 331, 344; ROBERT M. KINGDON, 'Reactions to the St Bartholomew Massacres in Geneva and Rome', in ALFRED SOMAN, *The Massacre of St Bartholomew*, p. 43.

34. 'Je pense qu'il y a plus de barbarie à manger un homme vivant qu'à le manger mort, à deschirer par tourmens et par geénes, un corps encore plein de sentiment, le faire rostir par le menu, le faire mordre et meurtrir aux chiens et aux porceaux (comme nous l'avons, non seulement leu, mais veu de fresche memoire, non entre des ennemis anciens, mais entre des voisins et concitoyens, et, qui pis est, sous pretexte de pieté et de religion), que de le rostir et manger apres qu'il est trespassé.' ('Des cannibales', in *Essais de Michel de Montaigne*, ed. A. THIBAUDET (Paris, 1946), p. 217.)

35. JUDITH WEIL, *Marlowe*, p. 85. NATALIE ZEMON DAVIS, 'The rites of violence', reprinted in *Society and Culture in Early Modern France* (London: Polity Press, 1975), p. 173.

36. DAVIS, 'The rites of violence', p. 157. See also LE ROY LADURIE, *Paysans de Languedoc* (Paris, 1966), vol. i, p. 398 n. 5.

37. DAVIS, 'The rites of violence', p. 181.

38. Ibid., pp. 175, 180.

39. Ibid., pp. 159, 162. See also JANINE ESTÉBE, *Tocsin pour un massacre – la saison des Saint-Barthélemy* (Pairs, 1968), pp. 197–8.

40. DAVIS, 'The rites of violence', p. 181; MONTAIGNE, 'Des cannibales', cited above.

41. ROBERT CUSHMAN, reviewing a recent production of *The Massacre at Paris* by the Glasgow Citizens' company for *The Observer*, 8 Feb. 1981.

14 *Doctor Faustus*: Subversion through Transgression*

Jonathan Dollimore

Jonathan Dollimore's impact on Renaissance studies in the 1980s was due to his philosophical training at a time when critics were avid for – but inept in – French theory, and his work was characterised by a rigid repetition of existentialist formulae, such as that (since *existence* precedes *essence*) all 'nature' is culture. Most Sartrian is Dollimore's obsession with freedom and transgression, which finds a similar focus in Marlowe as Sartre discovered in Genet. His reading of *Doctor Faustus* is as a parable of the intellectual in a divided universe, the overall subject of his much-hyped book, *Radical Tragedy*. Traditional criticism had idealised Faustus as the prototypical Renaissance Man, insurgent against medieval authority, but Dollimore perceives that it is the very limits imposed by orthodoxy which constitute his dissidence, since there can be no subversion without containment. So, the Wittenberg scholar is a product of the Protestant religion which ultimately destroys him, but it is the puerility of his pact with the Devil which exposes the tyranny of the God he denies. The spin on this version of the free will problem comes from Foucault, who likewise held that power and transgression are locked in an endless dialectic, such that there can be no judge without criminal, or God without sin. And just as Foucault supported prisoners' and gay protest groups, so Dollimore draws hope from the dissident ability to subvert a dominant discourse from within. Like an academic on the contemporary university campus, 'Defiant, masochistic, yet wilful', Faustus seems to figure not only Marlowe here, but the critic himself in the pose of existential rebel, doomed to repeat his ever more futile provocations.

One problem in particular has exercised critics of *Dr Faustus*: its structure, inherited from the morality form, apparently negates what

* Extracted from *Radical Tragedy: Religion, Ideology and Power in the Drama of Shakespeare and his Contemporaries* (Hemel Hempstead, Harvester Wheatsheaf, 1984), 109–19.

the play experientially affirms – the heroic aspiration of 'Renaissance man'. Behind this discrepancy some have discerned a tension between, on the one hand, the moral and theological imperatives of a severe Christian orthodoxy and, on the other, an affirmation of Faustus as 'the epitome of Renaissance aspiration . . . all the divine discontent, the unwearied and unsatisfied striving after knowledge that marked the age in which Marlowe wrote' (Roma Gill, ed. *Dr Faustus*, p. xix).

Critical opinion has tended to see the tension resolved one way or another – that is, to read the play as ultimately vindicating either Faustus or the morality structure. But such resolution is what *Dr Faustus* as interrogative text resists.[1] It seems always to represent paradox – religious and tragic – as insecurely and provocatively ambiguous or, worse, as openly contradictory. Not surprisingly Max Bluestone, after surveying some eighty recent studies of *Dr Faustus*, as well as the play itself, remains unconvinced of their more or less equally divided attempts to find in it an orthodox or heterodox principle of resolution. On the contrary: 'conflict and contradiction inhere everywhere in the world of this play' ('*Libido Speculandi*: Doctrine and Dramaturgy in Contemporary Interpretations of Marlowe's *Dr Faustus*', p. 55). If this is correct then we might see it as an integral aspect of what *Dr Faustus* is best understood as: not an affirmation of Divine Law, or conversely of Renaissance Man, but an exploration of subversion through transgression.

Limit and Transgression

What Erasmus had said many years before against Luther indicates the parameters of *Dr Faustus*'s limiting structure:

> Suppose for a moment that it were true in a certain sense, as Augustine says somewhere, that 'God works in us good and evil, and rewards his own good works in us, and punishes his evil works in us'. . . . Who will be able to bring himself to love God with all his heart when He created hell seething with eternal torments in order to punish His own misdeeds in His victims as though He took delight in human torments?
>
> (*Renaissance Views of Man*, ed. S. Davies, p. 92)

But Faustus is not *identified* independently of this limiting structure and any attempt to interpret the play as Renaissance man breaking out of medieval chains always founders on this point: Faustus is constituted by the very limiting structure which he transgresses and his transgression is both despite and because of that fact.

Faustus is situated at the centre of a violently divided universe. To the extent that conflict and contradiction are represented as actually of its essence, it appears to be Manichean; thus Faustus asks 'where is the place that men call hell?', and Mephostophilis replies 'Within the bowels of these elements', adding:

> when all the world dissolves
> And every creature shall be purify'd,
> All places shall be hell that is not heaven.

> (I. 5. 127–9)

If 'purified' means 'no longer mixed, but of one essence, either wholly good or wholly evil' (*Marlowe's Dr Faustus*, Parallel Texts, p. 330), then the division suggested is indeed Manichean.[2] But more important than the question of precise origins is the fact that not only heaven and hell but God and Lucifer, the Good Angel and the Bad Angel, are polar opposites whose axes pass through and constitute human consciousness. Somewhat similarly, for Mephostophilis hell is not a place but a state of consciousness:

> Hell hath no limits, nor is circumscrib'd
> In one self place, but where we are is hell,
> And where hell is, there must we ever be.

> (I. 5. 122–4)

From Faustus's point of view – one never free-ranging but always coterminous with his position – God and Lucifer seem equally responsible in his final destruction, two supreme agents of power deeply antagonistic to each other yet temporarily co-operating in his demise.[3] Faustus is indeed their subject, the site of their power struggle. For his part God is possessed of tyrannical power – 'heavy wrath', while at the beginning of Act I scene 5 Lucifer, Beelzebub and Mephostophilis enter syndicate-like 'To view the *subjects* of our monarchy'. Earlier Faustus had asked why Lucifer wanted his soul; it will, replies Mephostophilis, 'Enlarge his kingdom' (I. 5. 40). In Faustus's final soliloquy both God and Lucifer are spatially located as the opposites which, *between them*, destroy him:

> O, I'll leap up to my God! Who pulls me down?

> see where God
> Stretcheth out his arm and bends his ireful brows

> My God, my God! Look not so fierce on me!

> Ugly hell, gape not! Come not, Lucifer.

> (V. 2. 145, 150–1, 187, 189)

Before this the representatives of God and Lucifer have bombarded
Faustus with conflicting accounts of his identity, position and destiny.
Again, the question of whether in principle Faustus can repent, what
is the point of no return, is less important than the fact that he is
located on the axes of contradictions which cripple and finally
destroy him.

By contrast, when, in Marlowe's earlier play, Tamburlaine speaks
of the 'four elements/Warring within our breasts for regiment' he is
speaking of a dynamic conflict conducive to the will to power – one
which 'Doth teach us all to have aspiring minds' (1. II. vii. 18–20) –
not the stultifying contradiction which constitutes Faustus and his
universe. On this point alone *Tamburlaine* presents a fascinating
contrast with *Dr Faustus*. With his indomitable will to power and
warrior prowess, Tamburlaine really does approximate to the self-
determining hero bent on transcendent autonomy – a kind of fantasy
on the Renaissance theme of aspiring man. With *Dr Faustus* almost
the reverse is true: transgression is born not of a liberating sense
of freedom to deny or retrieve origin, nor from an excess of life
breaking repressive bounds. It is rather a transgression rooted in
an *impasse* of despair.

Even before he abjures God, Faustus expresses a sense of being
isolated and trapped; an insecurity verging on despair pre-exists a
damnation which, by a perverse act of free will, he 'chooses'. Arrogant
he certainly is, but it is wrong to see Faustus at the outset as secure
in the knowledge that existing forms of knowledge are inadequate.
Rather, his search for a more complete knowledge is itself a search
for security. For Faustus, 'born, of parents base of stock', and now
both socially and geographically displaced (Prologue, ll. 11, 13–19),
no teleological integration of identity, self-consciousness and purpose
obtains. In the opening scene he attempts to convince himself of
the worth of several professions – divinity, medicine, law, and then
divinity again – only to reject each in turn; in this he is almost schizoid:

> Having commenc'd, be a divine in show,
> Yet level at the end of every art,
> And live and die in Aristotle's works.
> Sweet Analytics, 'tis thou hast ravish'd me!
>
> When all is done, divinity is best.
>
> Philosophy is odious and obscure,
> Both law and physic are for petty wits,
> Divinity is basest of the three,
> Unpleasant, harsh, contemptible, and vile.
>
> (I. 1. 3–6, 37, 105–8)

As he shakes free of spurious orthodoxy and the role of the
conventional scholar, Faustus's insecurity intensifies. A determination
to be 'resolved' of all ambiguities, to be 'resolute' and show fortitude
is only a recurring struggle to escape agonised irresolution.

This initial desperation and insecurity, just as much as a
subsequent fear of impending damnation, suggests why his search
for knowledge so easily lapses into hedonistic recklessness and
fatuous, self-forgetful 'delight'. Wagner cannot comprehend this
psychology of despair:

> I think my master means to die shortly:
> He has made his will and given me his wealth.
>
> I wonder what he means. If death were nigh,
> He would not banquet and carouse and swill
> Amongst the students.
>
> (V. 1. 1–2, 5–7)

Faustus knew from the outset what he would eventually incur.
He willingly 'surrenders up . . . his soul' for twenty-four years of
'voluptuousness' in the knowledge that 'eternal death' will be the
result (I. 3. 90–4). At the end of the first scene he exits declaring
'This night I'll conjure though I die therefor'. Later he reflects: 'long
ere this I should have done the deed [i.e. suicide] / Had not sweet
pleasure conquer'd deep despair' (II. 1. 24–5). This is a despairing
hedonism rooted in the fatalism of his opening soliloquy: 'If we say
that we have no sin, we deceive ourselves, and there's no truth in us.
Why, then, belike we must sin, and so consequently die' (I. 1. 41–4).
Half-serious, half-facetious, Faustus registers a sense of human-kind
as miscreated.

Tamburlaine's will to power leads to liberation through
transgression. Faustus's pact with the devil, because an act of
transgression without hope of liberation, is at once rebellious,
masochistic and despairing. The protestant God – 'an arbitrary and
wilful, omnipotent and universal tyrant' (Walzer, p. 151) – demanded
of each subject that s/he submit personally and without mediation.
The modes of power formerly incorporated in mediating institutions
and practices now devolve on Him and, to some extent and
unintentionally, on His subject: abject before God, the subject takes
on a new importance in virtue of just this direct relation.[4] Further,
although God is remote and inscrutable he is also intimately
conceived: 'The principal worship of God hath two parts. One is to
yield subjection to him, the other to draw near to him and to cleave
unto him' (Perkins, *An Instruction Touching Religious or Divine*

Worship, p. 313). Such perhaps are the conditions for masochistic transgression: intimacy becomes the means of a defiance of power, the new-found importance of the subject the impetus of that defiance, the abjectness of the subject its self-sacrificial nature. (We may even see here the origins of sub-cultural transgression: the identity conferred upon the deviant by the dominant culture enables resistance as well as oppression.)

Foucault has written: 'limit and transgression depend on each other for whatever density of being they possess: a limit could not exist if it were absolutely uncrossable and, reciprocally, transgression would be pointless if it merely crossed a limit composed of illusions and shadows' (*Language, Counter-Memory, Practice*, p. 34). It is a phenomenon of which the anti-essentialist writers of the Renaissance [such as Montaigne] were aware: 'Superiority and inferiority, mastery and subjection, are jointly tied unto a natural kind of envy and contestation; they must perpetually enter-spoil one another' (Montaigne, *Essays*, III. 153).

In the morality plays sin tended to involve blindness to the rightness of God's law, while repentance and redemption involved a renewed apprehension of it. In *Dr Faustus* however sin is not the error of fallen judgement but a conscious and deliberate transgression of limit. It is a limit which, among other things, renders God remote and inscrutable yet subjects the individual to constant surveillance and correction; which holds the individual subject terrifyingly responsible for the fallen human condition while disallowing him or her any subjective power of redemption. Out of such conditions is born a mode of transgression identifiably protestant in origin: despairing yet defiant, masochistic yet wilful. Faustus is abject yet his is an abjectness which is strangely inseparable from arrogance, which reproaches the authority which demands it, which is not so much subdued as incited by that same authority:

Faustus: I gave . . . my soul for my cunning.
All: God forbid!
Faustus: God forbade it indeed; but Faustus hath done it.

(V. 2. 65–7)

Mephostophilis well understands transgressive desire; it is why he does not deceive Faustus about the reality of hell. It suggests too why he conceives of hell in the way he does; although his sense of it as a state of being and consciousness can be seen as a powerful recuperation of hell at a time when its material existence as a *place* of future punishment was being questioned, it is also an arrogant appropriation of hell, an incorporating of it into the consciousness of the subject.

240

A ritual pact advances a desire which cancels fear long enough to pass the point of no return:

Lo, Mephostophilis, for love of thee
Faustus hath cut his arm, and with his proper blood
Assures his soul to be great Lucifer's,
Chief lord and regent of perpetual night.
View here this blood that trickles from mine arm,
And let it be propitious for my wish.

(I. 5. 54–8)

But his blood congeals, preventing him from signing the pact. Mephostophilis exits to fetch 'fire to dissolve it'. It is a simple yet brilliant moment of dramatic suspense, one which invites us to dwell on the full extent of the violation about to be enacted. Faustus finally signs but only after the most daring blasphemy of all: 'Now will I make an end immediately / ... *Consummatum est*: this bill is ended' (I. 5. 71–3). In transgressing utterly and desperately God's law, he appropriates Christianity's supreme image of masochistic sacrifice:[5] Christ dying on the cross – and his dying words (John xix:30). Faustus is not liberating himself, he is ending himself: 'it is finished'. Stephen Greenblatt is surely right to find in Marlowe's work 'a subversive identification with the alien', one which 'flaunts society's cherished orthodoxies, embraces what the culture finds loathsome or frightening' (*Renaissance Self-Fashioning*, pp. 203, 220). But what is also worth remarking about this particular moment is the way that a subversive identification with the alien is achieved and heightened through travesty of one such cherished orthodoxy.

Power and the Unitary Soul

For Augustine the conflict which man experiences is not (as the Manichean heresy insisted) between two contrary souls or two contrary substances – rather, one soul fluctuates between contrary wills. On some occasions *Dr Faustus* clearly assumes the Augustinian conception of the soul; on others – those expressive of or consonant with the Manichean implications of universal conflict – it presents Faustus as divided and, indeed, constituted by that division. The distinction which Augustine makes between the will as opposed to the soul as the site of conflict and division may now seem to be semantic merely; in fact it was and remains of the utmost importance. For one thing, as *Dr Faustus* makes clear, the unitary soul – unitary in the sense of being essentially indivisible and eternal – is the absolute precondition for the exercise of divine power:

O, no end is limited to damned souls.
Why wert thou not a creature wanting soul?
Or why is this immortal that thou hast?
Ah, Pythagoras' *metempsychosis*, were that true,
This soul should fly from me and I be chang'd
Unto some brutish beast: all beasts are happy,
For when they die
Their souls are soon dissolv'd in elements;
But mine must live still to be plagu'd in hell.

(V. 2. 181–9)

Further, the unitary soul – unitary now in the sense of being
essentially incorruptible – figures even in those manifestations
of Christianity which depict the human condition in the most
pessimistic of terms and human freedom as thereby intensely
problematic. The English Calvinist William Perkins indicates why,
even for a theology as severe as his, this had to be so. If sin were
a corruption of man's 'substance' then not only could he not be
immortal (and thereby subjected to the eternal torment which
Faustus incurs), but Christ could not have taken on his nature:

Sin is not a corruption of man's substance, but only of his faculties.
Otherwise neither could men's soul be immortal, nor Christ take
upon him man's nature.

(Perkins, 1970, p. 168)

Once sin or evil is allowed to penetrate to the core of God's subject
(as opposed to being, say, an inextricable part of that subject's fallen
condition) the most fundamental contradiction in Christian theology is
reactivated: evil is of the essence of God's creation. This is of course
only a more extreme instance of another familiar problem: how is
evil possible in a world created by an omnipotent God? To put the
blame on Adam only begs the further question: Why did God make
Adam potentially evil? (Compare Nashe's impudent gloss: 'Adam
never fell till God made fools' [*The Unfortunate Traveller*, p. 269]).

Calvin, however, comes close to allowing what Perkins and
Augustine felt it necessary to deny: evil and conflict do penetrate to
the core of God's subject. For Calvin the soul is an essence, immortal
and created by God. But to suggest that it partakes of *God's* essence is
a 'monstrous' blasphemy: 'if the soul of man is a portion transmitted
from the essence of God, the divine nature must not only be liable to
passion and change, but also to ignorance, evil desires, infirmity, and
all kinds of vice' (*Institutes*, I. xv. 5). Given the implication that these
imperfections actually constitute the soul, it is not surprising that

'everyone feels that the soul itself is a receptacle for all kinds of pollution'. Elsewhere we are told that the soul, 'teeming with . . . seeds of vice . . . is altogether devoid of good' (I. xv; ii, iii). Here is yet another stress point in protestantism and one which plays like Dr Faustus exploit: if human beings perpetuate disorder it is because they have been created disordered.

The final chorus of the play tells us that Dr Faustus involved himself with 'unlawful things' and thereby practised 'more than heavenly power permits' (ll. 6, 8). It is a transgression which has revealed the limiting structure of Faustus's universe for what it is, namely, 'heavenly *power*'. Faustus has to be destroyed since in a very real sense the credibility of that heavenly power depends upon it. And yet the punitive intervention which validates divine power also compromises it: far from justice, law and authority being what legitimates power, it appears, by the end of the play, to be the other way around: power establishes the limits of all those things.

It might be objected that the distinction between justice and power is a modern one and, in Elizabethan England, even if entertained, would be easily absorbed in one or another of the paradoxes which constituted the Christian faith. And yet: if there is one thing that can be said with certainty about this period it is that God in the form of 'mere arbitrary will omnipotent' could not 'keep men in awe'. We can infer as much from many texts, one of which was Lawne's *Abridgement* of Calvin's *Institutes*, translated in 1587 – around the time of the writing of *Dr Faustus*. The book presents and tries to answer, in dialogue form, objections to Calvin's theology. On the question of predestination the 'Objector' contends that 'to adjudge to destruction whom he will, is more agreeable to the lust of a tyrant, than to the lawful sentence of a judge'. The 'Reply' to this is as arbitrary and tyrannical as the God which the Objector envisages as unsatisfactory: 'it is a point of bold wickedness even so much as to inquire the causes of God's will' (p. 222; quoted from Sinfield, p. 171). It is an exchange which addresses directly the question of whether a tyrannical God is or is not grounds for discontent. Even more important perhaps is its unintentional foregrounding of the fact that, as embodiment of naked power alone, God could so easily be collapsed into those tyrants who, we are repeatedly told by writers in this period, exploited Him as ideological mystification of their own power. Not surprisingly, the concept of 'heavenly power' interrogated in *Dr Faustus* was soon to lose credibility, and it did so in part precisely because of such interrogation.

Dr Faustus is important for subsequent tragedy for these reasons and at least one other: in transgressing and demystifying the limiting structure of his world without there ever existing the possibility of his escaping it, Faustus can be seen as an important precursor of the malcontented protagonist of Jacobean tragedy. Only for the latter, the limiting structure comes to be primarily a socio-political one.

Lastly, if it is correct that censorship resulted in *Dr Faustus* being one of the last plays of its kind – it being forbidden thereafter to interrogate religious issues so directly – we might expect the transgressive impulse in the later plays to take on different forms. This is in fact exactly what we do find; and one such form involves a strategy already referred to – the inscribing of a subversive discourse within an orthodox one, a vindication of the letter of an orthodoxy while subverting its spirit.

Notes

1. This concept, originating in a classification of Benveniste's, is developed by CATHERINE BELSEY in *Critical Practice*, chapter 4.

2. The Manichean implications of protestantism are apparent from this assertion of Luther's: 'Christians know there are two kingdoms in the world, which are bitterly opposed to each other. In one of them Satan reigns. . . . He holds captive to his will all who are not snatched away from him by the Spirit of Christ. . . . In the other Kingdom, Christ reigns, and his kingdom ceaselessly resists and makes war on the kingdom of Satan' (*Luther and Erasmus*, ed. RUPP, pp. 327–8; see also PETER LAKE, *Moderate Puritans and the Elizabethan Church*, pp. 144–5). J.P. BROCKBANK, in a discussion of the Manichean background of *Dr Faustus*, notes similarities between Faustus and the Manichean bishop of the same name mentioned by Augustine in the *Confessions* – himself an adherent of the Manichean faith for nine years; on Manicheanism generally, see also JOHN HICK, *Evil and the God of Love*, chapter 3.

3. Cf. WALZER: 'The imagery of warfare was constant in Calvin's writing'; specifically of course, warfare between God and Satan (*The Revolution of the Saints*, p. 65).

4. Cf. C. BURGES, *The First Sermon* (1641): 'A man once married to the Lord by covenant may without arrogancy say: this righteousness is my righteousness . . . this loving kindness, these mercies, this faithfulness, which I see in thee . . . is mine, for my comfort . . . direction, salvation, and what not' (p. 61; quoted from CONRAD RUSSELL, *Crisis of Parliaments*, p. 204).

5. MARGARET WALTERS reminds us how Christian iconography came to glorify masochism, especially in its treatment of crucifixion. Adoration is transferred from aggressor to victim, the latter suffering in order to propitiate a vengeful, patriarchal God (*The Nude Male*, p. 10; see also pp. 72–5). Faustus's transgression becomes subversive in being submissive yet the reverse of propitiatory.

References

BELSEY, CATHERINE, *Critical Practice* (London: Methuen, 1980).

BLUESTONE, MAX, '*Libido speculandi*: doctrine and dramaturgy in contemporary interpretations of Marlowe's *Doctor Faustus*', in N. RABKIN (ed.), *Reinterpretations of Elizabethan Drama* (New York: Columbia University Press, 1969).

Doctor Faustus: *Subversion through Transgression*

BROCKBANK, J.P., *Marlowe: Dr Faustus* (London: Arnold, 1962).

CALVIN, JOHN, *Institutes*, trans. HENRY BEVERIDGE, 2 vols (London: Clarke, 1949).

DAVIES, STEVIE, *Renaissance Views of Man* (Manchester: Manchester University Press, 1978).

FOUCAULT, MICHEL, *Language, Counter-Memory, Practice* (Ithaca, NY: Cornell University Press, 1977).

GREENBLATT, STEPHEN, *Renaissance Self-Fashioning* (Chicago: University of Chicago Press, 1980).

HICK, JOHN, *Evil and the God of Love* (Glasgow: Collins, The Fontana Library, 1968).

LAKE, PETER, *Moderate Puritans and the Elizabethan Church* (Cambridge: Cambridge University Press, 1982).

LAWNE, WILLIAM, *An Abridgement of the Institution of Christian Religion*, trans. CHRISTOPHER FETHERSTONE (Edinburgh, 1587).

MARLOWE, CHRISTOPHER, *Dr Faustus 1604–16, Parallel Texts*, ed. W.W. GREG (Oxford: Clarendon Press, 1950).

MARLOWE, CHRISTOPHER, *Dr Faustus*, ed. ROMA GILL (London: Benn, 1965).

MONTAIGNE, MICHEL, *Essays*, trans. JOHN FLORIO, 3 vols (London: Dent, 1965).

NASHE, THOMAS, *The Unfortunate Traveller and other Works*, ed. J.B. STEANE (Harmondsworth: Penguin, 1972).

PERKINS, WILLIAM, *Works*, ed. I. BREWARD (Abingdon: Sutton Courtenay Press, 1970).

RUPP, E. GORDON (ed.), *Luther and Erasmus: Free Will and Salvation* (London: SCM, 1969).

RUSSELL, CONRAD, *The Crisis of Parliaments* (London: Oxford University Press, 1971).

SINFIELD, ALAN, *Literature in Protestant England 1560–1660* (London: Croom Helm, 1982).

WALTERS, MARGARET, *The Nude Male: A New Perspective* (New York and London: Paddington Press, 1978).

WALZER, MICHAEL, *The Revolution of the Saints: A Study in the Origins of Radical Politics* (London: Weidenfeld & Nicolson, 1966).

15   Bruno and Marlowe: *Doctor Faustus**

Hilary Gatti

In *The Massacre at Paris* Marlowe had staged the murder of Ramus by Guise, and *Doctor Faustus* opens with his assassination in Faustus's mind. As Hilary Gatti explains, the Sorbonne professor who, in Guise's contemptuous words, 'Did never sound anything to the depth', represents an academic tradition which Faustus uses only to discard. His own project, by contrast, is to solve 'the central problem of his time': the contradiction between Christian dogma and intellectual freedom. Read in this light, Faustus's true adversary is not the Protestant orthodoxy invoked by the Chorus, but Hell itself, represented by the Grand Inquisitor, Mephistophilis. His tragedy is that of a whole generation of intellectuals, Gatti argues, torn between the Good Reformation Angel and the Bad Angel of the Catholic Counter-Reformation: like Giordano Bruno, who trounced the Oxford dons only to be burned by the Venetian Inquisition. The pessimism of the play is therefore that Faustus's rebellion against Protestant Wittenberg is ultimately controlled by Rome, and that even in death he is confined to the medieval dogma of his confessor Mephistophilis. This is an interpretation of a piece with the New Historicist dictum that the human subject is constructed by and in texts, but with an attention to the exact details of those texts which belongs to a *newer* and more stringent historicism. Once again, it is the spirit of Foucault that hovers here, with his insistence that as knowledge is power, it is those who write (or burn) the books who determine truth.

'Divinity, Adieu'

Faustus's opening monologue, as he sits alone in his room in Wittemberg trying to 'settle' his studies, is a brilliantly synthetic,

---

* Reprinted from *The Renaissance Drama of Knowledge: Giordano Bruno in England* (London, Routledge, 1989), 89–113.

radical review of the orthodox culture of the late sixteenth century: a Christian culture whose intellectual structure was still predominantly Aristotelian and which presents itself to Marlowe with its Protestant face. The first crux of the monologue is Marlowe's choice of the order in which to develop his review of this cultural situation. He begins not with the question of faith, nor with a primarily theological argument, but with the question of logic. Faustus thus approaches his problem in philosophical terms, choosing to reject initially the authority of Aristotelian analytics.

Aristotle, the master of 'sweet Analytikes', is presented at first in an impetus of unreserved acceptance, almost a poetic embrace ('tis thou hast ravished me'). The verse is immediately qualified with a Latin definition of the aims of logic: *'Bene disserere est finis logices'* (To dispute well is the end of logic). This complicates the question under review, for although his name is not explicitly linked to Aristotle's, the verse, as Marlowe critics have long recognized, is the opening sentence of the *First Book of Dialectic* of Peter Ramus. The influence of Ramist logic throughout the Protestant countries of Europe was rapidly growing in this period, and was strong in both the English universities, but particularly Cambridge where Marlowe himself had studied. Faustus's rejection of the traditional logic is thus a double act of deliberate cultural provocation: not only Aristotle is swept aside but with him the modern logician acclaimed by the Protestant cultures as the great reformer, the inventor of a new and simplified method of reasoning in the search for truth.

Yet the terms in which this rejection is developed suggest an extremely complex, even ambiguous, relationship between Faustus and Ramist logic. For his rejection of Ramus's definition has no psychological build-up or descriptive preparation, but is itself stated as a logical proposition. As such, it is a logical proposition of a peculiarly Ramist flavour, reflecting two special tenets of Ramist thinking: the necessity for brief, clear-cut discourse, and the particular emphasis placed upon the 'figure of difference' or the 'definition of dissimilitude', which was to make Ramist discourse a sharp instrument in controversial argument. In Chapter XI of his *Logike*, Ramus insists on the importance of developing with particular clarity differing arguments of dissent from a stated proposition: 'The agreeable argument being expounded, now followeth the disagreeable, which dissenteth from the matter. The arguments disagreeable are equally known among themselves, and disproveth equally one another: yet by their dissention, they do more clearly appear'. The movement of Marlowe's poetry in Faustus's opening lines suggests that he was using Ramist logical concepts (generally interpreted today as differing in emphasis rather than kind from the basic tenets of Aristotelian analytics) in a radical rejection of traditional logic itself as the highway towards the new knowledge he dreams of:[1]

> live and die in *Aristotles* works.
> Sweet *Analytikes*, tis thou hast ravished me,
> *Bene disserere est finis logices.*
> Is to dispute well Logikes chiefest end?
> Affords this Art no greater miracle?
> Then read no more, thou hast attain'd that end;
> A greater subject fitteth *Faustus* wit.[2]

It is in terms of this same logical movement from 'agreeable argument' to 'disagreeable', or clear-cut dissent, that Faustus's monologue develops in its second section: a rapid invocation and rejection of the disciplines at the basis of the academic life of the period. First of all medicine is reviewed and then law, in the figures of Galen and Justinian: names closely linked to Aristotelian methods and doctrines. Marlowe offers no explicitly named alternative authorities, but his rejection of Galen clearly invokes Paracelsian concepts of magical healing, thus linking Faustus to an already developed, if semi-underground, English school of 'alternative' medicine and alchemical enquiry.[3] It is in this part of the monologue that a closely related Hermetic image of man as magus begins to emerge in terms of a provocatively stated concept of a human intellect capable of achieving, through its enquiry into natural truths, almost divine vision and powers. Marlowe at once states this concept as an act of intellectual liberation, exposing the dreary drudge of routine academic enquiry, the fastidious professor who Faustus himself had been until only a few minutes back, in all his obsequious respect of the cultural status quo: 'This study fits a Mercenary drudge / Who aims at nothing but external trash / Too servile and illiberal for me.'[4]

It is only when this sense of man as free to achieve for himself, through his own intellectual impetus, an almost divine status has already been hinted at that Faustus reaches, in the central verses of his monologue, the hard kernel of his problem: his studies of divinity. In eleven terse and concise verses he offers to his audience his answer to the problem at the centre of his culture. And he does it, as his culture was doing in academic places throughout Europe, by linking the problems of divinity to the methods of traditional logic. Here, in fact, Faustus reaches back beyond Ramus and picks up the traditional, accepted method of Aristotelian reasoning. For he ironically and provocatively rejects the Christian godhead by developing from biblical sources a regular and, in logical terms, perfectly acceptable syllogism: 'The reward of sin is death? that's hard. . . . If we say that we have no sin we deceive our selves. . . . Why then belike we must sin, and so consequently die.' It has often been pointed out by Marlowe's commentators that the syllogism is a traditional one, to which Christianity offered its answer by the Christian act of salvation itself: faith in Christ's mercy breaks up the apparently acceptable logic of the syllogism. In fact Faustus fails to quote his biblical sources in full, giving only the opening part of Romans 6:23 and failing to add the following and opposing proposition, 'but the gift of God is eternal life through Jesus Christ our Lord'.[5] The fact that Faustus does not qualify the syllogism with this central tenet of the Christian doctrine has seemed to some an act of intellectual irresponsibility, or even of almost infantile, wilful forgetfulness.[6] But Marlowe makes it quite clear that it is to be seen as a deliberate intellectual choice, and he leaves his audience in no doubt as to the considerations which lead Faustus to that choice. The Christian solution to the drastic conclusion to the syllogism is rejected on two grounds: first of all because its concept of death in terms of rewards and punishments leaves open the possibility of everlasting torment; and secondly because it develops a doctrine which leaves man dependent for his salvation on an act of mercy on the part of God: 'What doctrine call you this? *Che sera sera:* / What will be, shall be; *Divinity*, adieu.'[7]

Once again the deliberate and daring provocation offered by Faustus's reasoning (it must be remembered that Marlowe connects him constantly with Wittemberg, the intellectual centre of Protestant Christianity) can only be fully understood in terms of the historical situation which Marlowe was expressing. He was writing at the end of a century in which opposing Christian factions had been making ever more drastic use of visions of hell and eternal punishment to ensure the obedience of their adherents. Writers such as Thomas Beard on the Protestant side or the notorious English Jesuit Robert Parsons were equally unscrupulous in conjuring up visions of the tortures awaiting those who died with the wrong beliefs; and men like the playwright Robert Greene, who cursed Marlowe's influence on him with the last strokes of his pen, were dying filled with horror at the fate which might await them. It is against this vision of death as, for some at least, an 'everlasting punishment', that Faustus reacts already at the opening of his drama; and it is in a much expanded, anguished meditation on the same subject that Marlowe will depict his death. In part, Marlowe's play can be seen as an early text making a plea for a 'decline of hell': certainly Faustus refuses an idea of death which involves the possibility of such a fate.[8] But his refusal appears to be also a protest against some of the special tenets of

Protestant Christianity, and particularly against Luther's vision of a humanity saved from eternal punishment entirely by an act of faith in God's mercy, and not at all by its own works.[9]

Marlowe is expressing here, in the dialectic between his Chorus and Faustus, one of the fundamental issues of his times: man's new faith in his own intellectual resources against a deeply rooted Christian concept of the vanity of human endeavour alone. The issue was acutely felt by the newly emerging magus of the sixteenth century, as well as by his more scientific counterpart in the century to come. Cornelius Agrippa, whose *De occulta philosophia* (1533) had become established as one of the central texts on magic of the century, and whom Faustus will acknowledge explicitly as his master, hoping to become 'as cunning as Agrippa was, / Whose shadows made all Europe honour him', had also written his widely read attack on the vanity and uncertainty of arts and sciences, *De vanitate scientiarum* (1530). Here the natural magic of the philosophers is depicted, in terms which the Chorus would certainly have approved, as 'oftentimes . . . entangled in the crafts and errors of the devills of hell'.[10] Agrippa seems to have oscillated rather ambiguously between two opposing positions, but later more scientific enquirers would feel the need to resolve the dilemma. On the Protestant side, efforts to do so would be especially concerned with the question of vindicating an active concept of enquiring man against the dominating theories of predestination. Bacon will elaborate with care, at the beginning of the seventeenth century, his theory of first and second causes, limiting the activity of the modern scientist to the latter but claiming for him, in his proper sphere, unreserved freedom of enquiry. Once again Marlowe expresses in Faustus's opening monologue a particular moment of exasperation and a particularly dramatic solution to the dilemma. Opposing himself without compromise to the warning and admonitions of the Chorus, Faustus not only omits to qualify his syllogism with the central statement of Christian belief, but cuts short all niceties of theological debate by bidding *'Divinity*, adieu'.

At this point in his monologue, Faustus also abandons the rigorous logical structure which has so far informed the pattern of his reasoning, and Marlowe's poetry opens out into freer and more impetuous rhythms invoking an alternative 'metaphysic', which is at the same time a different concept of man and a different way of reaching the heavens. The conventional magical symbols which Faustus invokes – 'Lines, Circles, Signes, Letters and Characters' – appear here in the impetus of Marlowe's poetry as the means of satisfying Faustus's desire to achieve new forms of knowledge unknown so far to man. Although he appeals to the traditional 'Negromantic books', Faustus's image of the knowledge he yearns for is represented in terms of new, unlimited spaces for the human mind to move in, and looks forward to new forms of power and dominion over the forces of nature which will make of the 'Studious Artisan' a triumphant demi-god.

The points at which this monologue connects with and echoes the thought as well as the poetry of Giordano Bruno are so many that it is difficult to select precise passages for comparison. All the arguments Faustus touches on find their counterpart in similar terms in Bruno's works: the initial love, followed by the violent repudiation of Aristotle; the dismissal of Galenic medicine in favour of Paracelsus; the particularly strong attack on the Protestant refusal of works and on concepts of predestination; the refusal of the Christian incarnation in favour of a metaphysic which sees the whole universe as the sign or seal of the divine intelligence; the reference to traditional magic as a means of achieving new knowledge of and powers over the natural world; and finally the inebriating vision of a human mind capable of reaching unbounded vistas of knowledge and truth, becoming assimilated, in its moment of understanding and power, into the divine whole. The very concept of an intellectual-poetical biography of the mind in its action of repudiating accepted cultural methods and doctrines to reach out into vastly expanded spaces of new learning and understanding of the universe recalls the *Heroici furori,* a text which would later be used by Northumberland as his primary source for his own intellectual biography. But the Bruno text which offers the closest parallels to Faustus's opening soliloquy is the *De la causa,* the second of his Italian dialogues written in London. This work opens with a strong attack against the academic culture of the period, particularly in its pedantic dependence on Aristotelian doctrine. Bruno is burning with indignation against an English academic tradition which he sees as exhausting itself in ever more subtle disputes while ignoring the true substance of metaphysical enquiry. The statutes of Oxford university, we are reminded, which the student is obliged to obey on his oath, include the principle that none be promoted to the rank of doctor or allowed to teach Philosophy and Theology if he has not drunk from the fountain of Aristotle.[11]

It is in the third dialogue of the *De la causa* that Bruno also launches his heaviest attack on Peter Ramus. Ramus's attack on Aristotelian logic, which one might have expected Bruno to appreciate, is heavily criticized as misdirected, and insufficient to save the French logician himself from the accusation of being still, in the end, a pedantic grammarian. The whole story of the dispute has been told by Frances Yates in her *Art of Memory,* where it is judged as 'one of the most basic of all Elizabethan controversies';[12] and one which surely Marlowe is recalling in Faustus's repudiation of Ramist logic

which leads him, in the final lines of his monologue, to an alternative
metaphysic of 'things': 'All things that move between the quiet poles'.
In the context of this anti-Ramist dispute, Faustus's monologue can be
seen as a rejection of his academic-Ramist self to assume the part of a
'sound Magician' intent on penetrating the secrets of the universe:

> Emperors and Kings,
> Are but obey'd in their several Provinces:
> Nor can they raise the wind, or rend the clouds:
> But his dominion that exceeds in this,
> Stretcheth as far as doth the mind of man:
> A sound Magician is a Demi-god,
> Here tire my brains to get a Deity.

> (I. 1. 56–62)

Mephostophilis: Words as Deceit

No sooner has Faustus decided to dedicate himself to the
'metaphysics of Magicians' than he is visited by a Good and a
Bad Angel:

> GOOD ANGEL.   O *Faustus*, lay that damned book aside,
>   And gaze not on it least it tempt thy soul,
>   And heap God's heavy wrath upon thy head.
>   Read, read the Scriptures: that is blasphemy.
> BAD ANGEL.   Go forward *Faustus* in that famous Art
>   Wherein all natures treasury is contain'd:
>   Be thou on earth as *Jove* is in the skye,
>   Lord and Commander of these elements.

> (I. 2. 69–76)

The two angels are traditional figures taken straight out of the
medieval drama, and the theme of the two books which they
introduce is also traditional and of medieval origin. The damned
book is obviously a necromantic book such as the *Picatrix*, one of the
most popular of the medieval magical works, originally written in
Arabic, probably in the twelfth century, but widely available to the
Renaissance reader in Latin translation. It is certainly a necromantic
book of spells in which Faustus finds his instructions for his first
attempts at conjuring. But the terms in which the Bad Angel refers
to the 'damned book' indicate that Marlowe is deliberately treating
these traditional themes in the light of new emphases and experiences
which had been slowly developing in his century. For the Bad Angel

sees 'Negromantic Art' as one 'wherein all natures treasury is contain'd'. He is thus placing the book of God or the Scriptures against the symbol of a 'book of nature', creating a contraposition through which the consciousness of a new more scientific enquiry into the truths of nature would gradually develop. Thus, Marlowe's Faustus experiences the typical ambiguities of his period. He is unhesitant in accepting the Bad Angel's invitation to study the art 'Wherein all natures treasury is contain'd', but the ends he is pursuing through that art are uncertainly defined. At times he expresses his desired end in terms of the penetrating of Orphic or Pythagorean mystical secrets beyond the veil of an obscure, phenomenal natural world. Faustus will thus instruct his spirits to 'read me strange Philosophy', while he approves the promise of Cornelius: 'Then doubt not *Faustus* but to be renown'd, / And more frequented for this mystery, / Than heretofore the *Delphian* Oracle'. Yet such occult and mystical definitions of his purpose are rare. Rather than a purifying ascent beyond an obscure, phenomenal natural world, Faustus's dominating passion appears the bending and controlling of that world to his will and desire. In Faustus the will to knowledge is also a will to power; and Marlowe's poetry accepts and accentuates the identification by expressing Faustus's aims as magician in terms of an almost physical appetite for new forms of control and power over the natural world:

> How am I glutted with conceit of this?
> Shall I make spirits fetch me what I please?
> Resolve me of all ambiguities?
> Perform what desperate enterprise I will?
>
> (I. 1. 77–80)

When Marlowe introduces Mephostophilis, Faustus's deceiving demon, he presents him in strictly traditional terms as the servant of Lucifer and the powers of hell, developing his theme with subtle differences of emphasis which will make of Faustus's tragedy a primarily human rather than supernatural or demonic experience. Most particularly is this evident where Mephostophilis, like the Good and Bad Angels, becomes associated with the theme of books, which are language or words. For Mephostophilis, it soon becomes clear, is not only the guardian but also the censor of the books on which Faustus depends for his speculative adventure in search of new forms of truth.[13] In a central moment of Faustus's eager dialogue with his newly conjured demon, Mephostophilis presents him with a book of powerful spells, presumably more powerful than those in the book which Faustus has already used to conjure Mephostophilis himself.

Inexplicably, Faustus not only at once accepts the new necromantic book, but repeats his request to Mephostophilis, who yet again offers him the book he asks for. The really important aspect of this scene, however, is the fact that Faustus is not satisfied with these multiple necromantic books:

FAUSTUS. Now would I have a book where I might see all characters of planets of the heavens, that I might know their motions and dispositions.
MEPHOS. Here they are too. *Turne to them*
FAUSTUS. Nay let me have one book more, and then I have done, wherein I might see all plants, herbs and trees that grow upon the earth.
MEPHOS. Here they be.
FAUSTUS. O thou art deceived.
MEPHOS. Tut I warrant thee. *Turne to them*
(I. 5. 172–82)

The inexplicable repetition concerning the gift of the necromantic books, and the abrupt ending of this scene after Faustus's crucial 'O thou art deceived', clearly suggest that the text is imperfect and has been interfered with and cut. We are at once reminded of another (historically true) scene similarly interfered with and cut: Bruno's Oxford débâcle. Here too the drama centred on a book, and just such a one as Faustus demands of Mephostophilis: 'where I might see all characters of planets of the heavens, that I might know their motions and dispositions'. The book in question was Copernicus's *De revolutionibus orbium caelestium*, and Bruno's reference to it as the book which revealed a new message of natural truth had caused the Oxford dons to accuse him of madness and interrupt his lectures. In the words of an indignant contemporary witness of this seminal Elizabethan scene:

when he had more boldly than wisely, got up into the highest place of our best & most renowned school, stripping up his sleeves like some Juggler, he undertook among very many other matters to set on foot the opinion of Copernicus, that the earth did go round, and the heavens did stand still; whereas in truth it was his own head which rather did run round, & his brains did not stand still.

Less than a year later Bruno published his *Cena de le ceneri*, where he not only returned the Oxford dons' insults with as good as he got, but continued with undiminished vigour to propose the book of Copernicus as the new message of truth about the cosmos. But he knew by then how strong the resistance to the new message was, and in his text he represents it in the figures of the supercilious Torquato and the pedantic Nundinio, who express here the 'discourteous incivility and the imprudent ignorance' of the doctors, refusing to listen to the new message but hurrying away still convinced of the fitness and unchangeable justness of the traditional Aristotelian cosmology. The dramatic clash within the text was punctually reflected in the outside London world by a reaction so harsh and scandalized to the publication of Bruno's book that he was forced to stay closed indoors and seek protection against bodily harm.[14]

There could be no question, only a few years later, and with Bruno himself by then in prison and on trial, of the public theatres of London accepting an open debate into the Copernican question. The fact that in *Dr Faustus* Marlowe makes no mention of Copernicanism does not necessarily mean that he was unaware of this revolutionary theory. It is true that in none of his writings – as they have reached us – does Marlowe ever mention a heliocentric universe, while his poetic imagery often contemplates a 'centric' earth and the revolving spheres; none the less, many of his critics have found it surprising and even contradictory that he did not include Copernicanism among his unorthodox and unlicensed opinions.[15] His documented intimacy with Thomas Harriot and Walter Warner, who were confirmed Copernicans, suggests it as a probability; and his evident relationship to Bruno in other contexts makes it unlikely that he could have ignored this central element of Bruno's cosmic vision. Such considerations give a precise meaning to the crucial point in the drama when Faustus looks through the book offered him by Mephostophilis presenting the truth about the universe, and cries in disappointment: 'O thou art deceived'. It is a cry which echoes through the immediately succeeding scene, the famous astronomical debate (or 'dispute' of 'divine Astrology' as Faustus calls it) which Faustus and Mephostophilis undertake in his study. The scene is a key one, for in it the demonic role of Mephostophilis becomes comprehensible in a new light.[16] No longer a traditional devil or fearful fiend, he suddenly appears in recognizably human and historical terms as an Aristotelian academician. Nor is he any less fearful for that. Seen in Brunian terms, he is the most deadly of enemies: the doctor who interrupted his Oxford lectures, the Torquato of the *Cena*, perhaps even the Inquisitor already officiating at Bruno's trial in Venice: the voice of a rigorously exposed, centuries-old cosmology integrated into a traditional, theological vision of the universe.

[. . .]

In Bruno's text, Bruno intervenes and disputes with Torquato in heated terms, defending the Copernican cosmology. Torquato leaves the supper indignantly after Bruno has 'revealed his ignorance'. Faustus, on the other hand, is obliged by Mephostophilis to remain within the Ptolemaic universe; but then the 'book' revealing the new cosmic truth he had asked for has been denied him. Marlowe makes it clear enough that Faustus is as dissatisfied with Mephostophilis's reasoning as Bruno was with Torquato's. For when his final question, 'Why are not Conjunctions, Oppositions, Aspects, Eclipses, all at one time, but in some years we have more, in some less?' has received the smooth, expected answer: *'Per inequalem motum respectu totius'* (because of the spheres' unequal motion with regard to the whole), Faustus replies with a drily ironic: 'Well, I am answer'd: now tell me who made the world?' (II. 1. 63–9).

If the scene of the astronomical debate is considered in the context of Faustus's overall interrogation of Mephostophilis in the first part of the drama, it can be seen how the tension on the stage is derived precisely from Mephostophilis's expertise in frustrating Faustus's eager desire to break new boundaries of knowledge. Nowhere does Mephostophilis allow him so much as to crack the compact shell of conventional dogma and explanation: to Faustus's questioning of the nature of demons and hell, he replies with the accepted biblical explanation of the war in heaven and the defeat of the over-proud Lucifer; to the questions on the nature of the cosmos he replies with an already accepted if debated version of the Ptolemaic-Aristotelian hypothesis; to Faustus's ultimate question about the creator and the creation, he returns a scandalized refusal to offer to man knowledge beyond his station. Systematically and inexorably Faustus is drawn back into the traditional dichotomy between good and evil, salvation and sin; and it is a 'distressed' Faustus, as he describes himself, who finishes his first attempt to 'raise the winds' and 'rend the clouds' by watching that most dreary of tired spectacles conjured up for him by Lucifer himself: the procession of the seven deadly sins.[17]

Words, Bruno had written, must be the servants of meanings, not meanings the servants of words as the grammarians make them.

We will have made a real beginning when we have uprooted from the depths of the shadows the most famous assertions of antiquity together with the ancient words: we shall be inventors, if necessary, of new words, whatever their origin might be, in harmony with the novelty of the doctrine.[18]

It is here that Faustus, to use another Brunian expression, loses the race, unable to pit against the smooth expertise of Mephostophilis's oratory new doctrines and new words. He can only ask question upon question, and cry disappointedly at the familiar, expected answers: 'O thou art deceived'. It is surely with dramatic irony that when Marlowe's Faustus finally travels through the heavens, as the *Faust-book* required, to investigate the true nature of the cosmos, the dramatist does not allow the journey to be described by Faustus himself (who might have told a very different story), but presents it through the entirely orthodox words of the Chorus:[19]

> Learned *Faustus*
> To find the secrets of Astronomy,
> Graven in the booke of *Joves* high firmament,
> Did mount him up to scale *Olimpus* top.
> Where sitting in a Chariot burning bright,
> Drawne by the strength of yoked Dragons neckes;
> He viewes the cloudes, the Planets, and the Starres,
> The Tropicks, Zones, and quarters of the skye,
> From the bright circle of the horned Moone,
> Even to the height of *Primum Mobile*:
> And whirling round with this circumference,
> Within the concave compasse of the Pole,
> From East to West his Dragons swiftly glide,
> And in eight daies did bring him home againe.

(III. 1. 1–14)

Faustus's Death: 'I'll Burn My Books'

'Let him kiss me with the kisses of his mouth . . . Stay me with flagons, comfort me with apples: for I am sick of love.' Quoting these verses from the Song of Solomon, Bruno in Dialogue Four of the First Part of the *Heroici Furori* expresses his sense of the search for knowledge in its culminating moment when the mind dissolves itself in the object. The language he is using, as Bruno himself underlines, is that of the mystical death of the soul, called by the cabbalists the kiss of death. In the Psalms, the kiss becomes a sleep: 'I will not give sleep to mine eyes, or slumber to mine eyelids, until I find out a place for the Lord'.[20] Mystical and Neoplatonic imagery appears to dominate the concept of knowledge Bruno is expressing here, although the passage culminates in an image which gives the traditional theme new and different emphases. The heroic searcher seems, it is true, to be tending towards a pure reality of forms or ideas, beyond the phenomenal, natural world, but in the end Bruno's philosophy in this passage, as in previous dialogues, denies the Platonic dichotomy, and

257

the final image of the object desired by the intellect modulates from the Platonic 'fountain' of ideas into an Epicurean 'ocean' of truth and goodness, identifiable with the natural universe itself.[21]

[...]

We know that prominent figures such as Ralegh and members of the Northumberland circle shared similar views on the soul and on death which were frowned on by the authorities. Nashe's attack against the so-called 'atheists' in *Pierce Penilesse his supplication to the devill*, which corresponds so exactly to the probable date of composition of *Dr Faustus* in 1592, was primarily directed against Harriot, who was known to be closely connected with Marlowe: 'I hear say there be Mathematicians abroad, that will prove men before Adam, and they are harboured in high places, who will maintain it to the death, that there are no devils'.[22] One of the 'high places' frequented by both Harriot and Marlowe was the household of Ralegh, whom the Jesuit Parsons had accused of forming a 'School of Atheism' and whose religious views would be the subject of an official investigation shortly after Marlowe's death.[23] It is in this enquiry that we hear news of the famous dinner party where Ralegh's brother had scoffed at the views on the soul proposed by an Anglican clergyman, Ralph Ironside, who recorded:

> Towards the end of supper ... Master Raleigh demands of me, what danger he might incur by such speeches? whereunto I answered, the wages of sin ... is death eternal, both of the body, and of the soul also. Soul quoth Master Carew Raleigh, what is that?[24]

Similarly conflicting concepts of the soul and death lie behind the whole dramatic development of the final scene of Faustus's tragedy. And the lucidity with which Marlowe poses the problem as essentially a metaphysical rather than a religious one clearly links him to Bruno's philosophy. It is a point which Marlowe's critics have not sufficiently clarified, for they have always approached Faustus's death scene in moral terms, pointing out how even in the extreme moment of his history Faustus fails to repent and save himself from eternal torment. But Faustus himself clearly defines his situation as an intellectual rather than a moral dilemma, and he does this by underlining his link with Wittemberg. For it is here in the country of Paracelsus and Agrippa, and the historical Faustus (and indeed where Bruno himself had taught), that books 'wherein all natures treasury is contain'd' had convinced Marlowe's Faustus to make an irrevocable intellectual choice: to embrace an alternative metaphysic which implied alternative concepts of knowledge but also of the

258

soul and of death. But it was here too that Luther had powerfully
reinforced a vision of the universe balanced between heaven and hell,
the joy of eternal salvation and the despair of eternal punishment,
with the individual soul as the prize to be won in this cosmic struggle.
Faustus carries both visions within him, together with the lucid
knowledge that having embraced an alternative metaphysic he can
no longer be saved in Christian terms, while nevertheless living as he
does in the very centre of Protestant Christianity he has no means of
escape from a death he must experience in the terms of his world:

> the serpent that tempted *Eve* may be saved, but not Faustus. Ah
> gentlemen, hear me with patience, and tremble not at my speeches.
> Though my heart pant and quiver to remember that I have been
> a student here these thirty years, O would I had never seen
> *Wittemberg*, never read book: and what wonders I have done, all
> *Germany* can witness, yea all the world: for which *Faustus* hath lost
> both *Germany* and the world, yea heaven itself: heaven the seat of
> God, the Throne of the Blessed, the Kingdom of Joy, and must
> remain in hell for ever. Sweet friends, what shall become of *Faustus*
> being in hell for ever?
>
> (V. 2. 44–54)

It is in the poetic development of the tensions between two
conflicting images of the universe, and two concepts of knowledge
and of death in that universe, that Marlowe writes his greatest and
final dramatic monologue. A universe in which time brings man
inexorably to death, and in which death means God or the devil,
eternal joy or eternal despair.

> Stand still you ever moving Spheres of heaven,
> That time may cease, and midnight never come. . . .
> The Stars move still, Time runs, the Clock will strike.
>
> (V. 2. 146–53)

Throughout the first part of his speech Faustus experiences his
death in a Christian universe, in despair at the impossibility of being
able to save himself in terms which he has chosen to renounce, and
in fear of the consequences which necessarily follow:

> The devil will come, and *Faustus* must be damn'd.
> O I'll leap up to my God: who pulls me down?
> See see where Christ's blood streams in the firmament,
> One drop would save my soul, half a drop, ah my
> Christ.
>
> (V. 2. 54–7)

Yet for Faustus it is only a momentary vision ('Where is it now? 'tis gone') which is quickly replaced by that of another God, more wrathful and less merciful, of the Old rather than the New Testament. In front of this vision Faustus, developing a complex set of biblical references, can only wish to hide himself in the earth, or to have his soul separated from his body by the force of the storm clouds 'So that my soul may but ascend to heaven'. Then this vision too fades away to leave only the certainty of damnation. And it is here that Faustus's mind turns at last to the ideas of death implied in the metaphysics he himself has embraced:

> Why wert thou not a creature wanting soul?
> Or why is this immortal that thou hast?
> Ah *Pythagoras' Metemsycosis*; were that true,
> This soul should flie from me, and I be chang'd
> Unto some brutish beast.
> All beasts are happy, for when they die,
> Their souls are soon dissolv'd in elements,
> But mine must live still to be plagu'd in hell.[25]

The search therefore is no longer for forms of salvation of his soul within a Christian or Hebraic universe, impossible for Faustus for whom such images are visions briefly conjured up but soon gone again. Here instead we have a metaphysical hypothesis which, if true, as Faustus lucidly realizes, would allow him to die, even if he has failed in his heroic attempts to gain new forms of knowledge, in quite different terms. Above all to die without fear, as Bruno had claimed:

> Every production, of whatever sort it is, is an alteration, in which the substance remains the same; for it is only one, there is only one divine and immortal being. This is what Pythagoras meant, who does not fear death but expects a process of change.[26]

It is in such a vision of death that Faustus's mind longs to come to rest in the last poignant verses of his monologue, which bring him finally to a concept both Epicurean and Brunian of the soul as a drop of water (an image clearly related both to Epicurean and Brunian atomism) which resolves at the death-moment into the universal ocean:

> O Soul be chang'd into little water drops,
> And fall into the Ocean, ne're be found.
> *Thunder, and enter the devils.*[27]

The attempt to escape from the metaphysic which dominates his culture has failed, and the last, tragic moments of Dr Faustus on

earth are an expression of his despairing recognition of that failure:
he has no choice but to die in terms of the inevitable scenario.

My God, my God, look not so fierce on me;
Adders and serpents, let me breathe a while:
Ugly hell gape not; come not *Lucifer*,
I'll burn my books; ah *Mephostophilis*.

Exeunt with him.

Marlowe creates in these final verses of Faustus's monologue a
subtle contrast between two forms of purification on death. On one
side we have the painless purification of water imagery in the vision
of the ocean silently absorbing, as one of its cosmic rights, its
component 'little water drops'; on the other the roaring, hissing,
punishing purification by thunder, serpents, damnation, and hell-fire.
Faustus's mind clearly tends with ardent desire towards the first of
these visions, although he realizes by now that he can only express
such a vision in hypothetical grammatical forms ('Why wert thou
not', 'Or why is this', O soul be chang'd'). The alternative form of
purification, which is warded off for as long as possible by Faustus's
ever weaker negative verbs ('Ugly hell gape not; come not *Lucifer*')
is only irrevocably accepted in the final line, and in a spirit of
despairing, exhausted recognition of a fact and its consequences.[28]
Rather than repenting, Faustus recognizes in his final words the force
of a reigning metaphysic too strong and entrenched to resist. As in
his opening monologue, although with a far deeper anguish which
Marlowe's poetry evokes powerfully in the broken irregularity of his
pentameters, Faustus's mind is working according to a logical pattern
of thought centred on the theme of a choice of alternative books.
With his alternative metaphysic, or art 'wherein all naturs treasury
is contain'd', relegated to the status of a dangerous heresy by the
realities of the situation in that particular Wittemberg (which can
stand as well, in this context, for Bruno's Oxford or Venice or
Rome) Faustus brings his speech and his life to a close with lucid
if exhausted logical precision on the inevitable consequences
of his intellectual adventure: 'I'll burn my books; ah
Mephostophilis'.

The pessimism of Marlowe's final tragic vision is only partially
qualified by the brief comments of the two scholars who discover
Faustus's dead body. For them Faustus's story is not to be concluded
on a purely negative note. Although they recognize that in religious
terms his experience must be accepted as a negative lesson, they
express an understanding of the intellectual dilemma which the
Faustian story represents:

> tho *Faustus* end be such
> As every Christian heart laments to think on:
> Yet for he was a Scholar, once admired
> For wondrous knowledge in our Germane schools,
> We'll give his mangled limbs due burial:
> And all the Students clothed in mourning black,
> Shall wait upon his heavy funeral.

(V. 3. 13–19)

Such ambivalence is at once suffocated by the Chorus, who close the tragedy, as it had begun, on a note of unequivocal orthodoxy, bringing the intellectual experience represented by Faustus under a moral and theological sign of rigorous negativity. As in the opening of the tragedy, the Chorus uses a pagan symbol to express the Faustian intelligence, recognized as having made an attempt to re-establish the values of *'Apollo's* laurel bough'. But the bough has been duly burnt, and the lesson must be learned by the audience who are recalled by the Chorus to the values (which are also linguistic and dramatic forms and formulas) of the medieval morality play:

> regard his hellish fall,
> Whose fiendful fortune may exhort the wise
> Only to wonder at unlawful things,
> Whose deepness doth intice such forward wits,
> To practise more than heavenly power permits.

(V. 3. 24–8)

The question here is not whether Marlowe's schematically conceived, theologically dominated Middle Ages fully represent the complex characteristics of that period. He is writing in a recognizable Renaissance convention which underlined its own achievements as a reawakening of lost forms of thought and knowledge, and marked out the centuries intervening between the illuminated cultures of classical antiquity and the modern rebirth as a period of shadows and darkness. But Marlowe was also writing in the agitated, blood-filled final years of the sixteenth century, in a Europe torn by the struggle between Reformation and Counter-Reformation, with even the comparatively peaceful Elizabethan England overshadowed by increasing religious tensions and oppressive legislation, aggravated by growing political uncertainty due to the ageing of the Virgin Queen. In such a situation, Marlowe brings his final tragedy to a close on a note of fierce intellectual pessimism which consciously projects his audience backward into a past age. The intellectual impulses forward seem to be irrevocably blocked by the Chorus's assumption of its own intellectual authority and dominion. It has taken possession in its own terms of the classical images which define the Faustian attempts to break new intellectual territory. Icarus has fallen as the Chorus predicted, and Apollo's laurel bough has burnt. Both a new science and a new poetry or drama appear irrevocably compromised; and Marlowe's final moment of tragic vision seems to lead with both a logical and biographical inevitability towards his shadowy and premature death.

I have suggested that Bruno's thought, and above all his uncompromising search for new forms of knowledge of the natural world, informs Marlowe's conception of the Faustian figure. Had Marlowe lived to the end of the century, he would have seen Bruno die in terms which he himself already foresaw as inevitable, burned at the stake by the Inquisition. But had he followed Bruno's final days in all their dramatic complexity, he would also have heard him making his celebrated and extreme claim that he did not want or have to retract, that he had nothing which needed retraction and that he did not know of anything he should retract: a stand which a few days later Bruno qualified by his penetrating statement to his judges that perhaps they pronounced against him with more fear than he received his sentence.[29] It is tempting to speculate whether a more mature Marlowe, if he had followed the Brunian experience through to the end, might not have found there that movement forward against all odds towards new forms of liberty and knowledge which his tragedy, in its last moments, seems to deny.

Notes

1. See ROSAMUND TUVE, *Elizabethan and Metaphysical Imagery* (Chicago: Chicago University Press, 1947), in particular Chapter XII, 'Ramist Logic: Certain General Conceptions affecting Imagery'. On Ramus's method in its historical context, see W.J. ONG, SJ, *Ramus: Method and the Decay of Dialogue* (Cambridge, MA, Harvard University Press, 1958), and the relevant sections in C. VASOLI, *La dialettica e la retorica dell'Umanesimo* (Milan, 1968). On Ramus's influence in England, see W.S. HOWELL, *Logic and Rhetoric in England, 1500–1700* (Princeton, NJ, Princeton University Press, 1956), pp. 146–282, and, more recently, G. OLDRINI, 'Le particolarità del ramismo inglese', *Rinascento*, 1985, pp. 19–80.

2. *Dr Faustus*, I, i, pp. 162–3.

3. See A.G. DEBUS, *The English Paracelsians*, London, 1965.

4. *Dr Faustus*, I, i, pp. 162–3.

5. The religious aspects of Marlowe's thought and learning are given particularly thorough treatment in P.H. KOCHER, *Christopher Marlowe: A Study of his Thought, Learning and Character* (Chapel Hill, NC, North Carolina University Press, 1946).

6. For an analysis of Faustus's use of Aristotelian and Ramist logical doctrine, see A.N. OKERLUND, 'The Intellectual Folly of Dr Faustus', *Studies in Philology*, 74 (1977), pp. 258–78. I do not, however, agree with the conclusion that Marlowe is necessarily censuring Faustus for his misuse of Ramist concepts.

7. *Dr Faustus*, I, i, pp. 162–3.

8. D.P. WALKER, *The Decline of Hell. Seventeenth Century Discussions of Eternal Torment* (London: Routledge, 1964), outlines the historical terms of the discussion in which I think Marlowe is participating here.

9. Marlowe's knowledge of Luther's and Calvin's works is discussed in KOCHER, *Christopher Marlowe*. The Hermetic conception of the Renaissance magus has been outlined by F.A. YATES in Chapters I–X of *Bruno and the Hermetic Tradition* (London–Chicago: Routledge, 1964), although in *The Occult Philosophy*, she argues that Marlowe was condemning the magus. The clash between the Hermetic conception of the magus and orthodox Protestant views of man is well illustrated in G.F. WALLER, '"This Matching of Contraries": Bruno, Calvin and the Sidney Circle', *Neophilologus*, 56 (1972), pp. 331–43.

10. See Chapter 44, 'Of witching magicke', in the English translation, ed. C.M. DUNN (California: California University Press, 1974), p. 129. The introduction to this edition has some interesting remarks on the relationship between this work of Agrippa's and 'the legend of Faustus, which in many ways symbolizes the intellectual crisis of the sixteenth century' (p. xxii).

11. See *Dialogico italica*, I, pp. 211–12.

12. For Bruno's attack on Ramus, see *Dial. ital.*, I, pp. 260–1. For the conflict between Brunian and Ramist doctrines of memory in Elizabethan England, see F.A. YATES, *The Art of Memory* (London: Routledge, 1966), pp. 260–78.

13. See C. DEFAYE, 'Mephistophilis est-il un démon authentique?', *Etudes anglaises*, janvier–mars (1979), pp. 1–10, for some interesting comments on the peculiar nature of Marlowe's demon.

14. The Oxford don in question was George Abbot whose sneering description of Bruno at Oxford was published in his book *The Reasons which Doctour Hill Hath Brought for the Upholding of Papistry*, 1604 (See Chapter 1, n. 38). The hasty departure of Nundinio and Torquato from the Ash Wednesday supper is described at the end of Dialogue IV of the *Cena* (*Dial. ital.*, I, p. 141). The page contains Bruno's famous misreading of Copernicus's description of the movements of the earth and moon, which repeats a similar error made by Pontus de Tyard in his French translation of 1552: see Aquilecchia's text of the *Cena* (Turin, 1955), p. 201, nn. 19–20. The persecution suffered by Bruno after the publication of the *Cena* is hinted at in the *Proemiale epistola* and Dialogue I of the *De la causa*.

15. I agree with Kocher (see n. 5) who refuses to consider as truly Copernican the verses in *Tamburlaine* sometimes considered as expressing a heliocentric universe. The critics who remain perplexed by Marlowe's apparent ignorance of Copernicanism are those who consider him an advanced Renaissance thinker, and include Kocher himself and HARRY LEVIN in *The Overreacher* (London, 1954).

16. *Dr Faustus*, II, i, pp. 179–82.

17. I have made no attempt here to relate the Mephostophilist–Faustus relationship to Bruno's theory of 'linking' as a magical–erotic technique which allows one mind to control and dominate another. This theory was fully developed only in Bruno's late works on magic, unpublished in his life time.

18. See *Op. lat.*, I, iii, p. 135.

19. There is, of course, no Chorus in the *Faust-book*. Marlowe is using a dramatic convention to express the sermonizing, disapproving tones of the anonymous, Lutheran *Faust-book* author. In the *Faust-book* it is Faust himself who describes his journey through the heavens in a letter to 'a friend in Liptzig' (see *The Historie*, Chapter XXI). Unfortunately, as Johnson pointed out, his description is based on an 'ignorant jumble of wholly unscientific astronomical lore'.

20. Song of Solomon 1:2 and 2:5. My quotations are from the English Authorized Version of 1611. Bruno, like Marlowe's Faustus, was probably quoting from the Latin of Jerome's Bible, where the sense is slightly different: 'Osculetur me osculo oris sui. . . . Fulcite me floribus, stipate me malis; quia amore langueo'; Psalm 132: 4–5: 'Si dedero somnum oculis meis dormitationem, Et requiem temporibus meis'.

21. See *Dial. ital.*, II, pp. 1011–12.

22. T. NASHE, *Pierce Penilesse his supplication to the devill* (London, 1592). See T. NASHE, *Works*, ed. R.B. McKERROW (Oxford: Clarendon Press, 1966), I, p. 172.

23. Modern scholars underline the context of fierce religious polemic which stimulated Parsons's tract and point out that no historical evidence of the existence of such a 'school' supports his assertion. See E.A. STRATHMANN, *Sir Walter Ralegh: A Study in Elizabethan Skepticism* (New York: Columbia University Press, 1951), pp. 25ff., and J.W. SHIRLEY, *Thomas Harriot: A Biography* (Oxford: Oxford University Press, 1983), pp. 179–80.

24. The documents relating to the Ralegh enquiry were published in full by G.B. HARRISON, *Willobie His Avisa* (London: A & C Black, 1926), Appendix III, pp. 255–71. Ironside's report to the Commission is republished in SHIRLEY, *A Biography*, pp. 194–6.

25. *Dr Faustus*, V, ii, p. 222.

26. See *Dial. ital.*, I, p. 324.

27. *Dr Faustus*, V, ii, pp. 225–7.

28. William Empson's brief discussion of Faustus's final verses as an example of his seventh and most conflictual type of ambiguity points out how the weight of Marlowe's verses here falls on the verbs 'gape' and 'come' rather than on the negatives, in which Faustus himself hardly seems any longer to believe. I agree with Empson's reading of the verses, although his conclusions from his reading seem to me arbitrary and unconvincing. See WILLIAM EMPSON, *Seven Types of Ambiguity* (London: Chatto and Windus, 1930).

29. See *Il processo*, p. 105.

Notes on Authors

JOHN ARCHER is Associate Professor of English at the University of New Hampshire. He is the author of *Sovereignty and Intelligence: Spying and Court Culture in the English Renaissance* (1993); and co-editor, with Richard Burt, of *Enclosure Acts: Sexuality, Property and Culture in Early Modern England* (1994).

EMILY BARTELS is Associate Professor of English at Rutgers University. She is the author of *Spectacles of Strangeness: Imperialism, Alienation, and Marlowe* (1993); and editor of *Critical Essays on Christopher Marlowe* (1997).

JULIA BRIGGS is Professor of English Literature at Simon de Montfort University. She is the author of *This Stage-Play World: English Literature and its Background, 1580–1625* (1983; new edition 1997).

THOMAS CARTELLI is Professor of English and Chair of the Department of Humanities at Muhlenberg College. He is the author of *Marlowe, Shakespeare, and the Economy of Theatrical Experience* (1991).

JONATHAN CREWE is Professor of English at Dartmouth College. He is the author of *Trials of Authorship: Anterior Forms and Poetic Reconstruction from Wyatt to Shakespeare* (1990); *Hidden Designs: The Critical Profession and Renaissance Literature* (1986); and *Unredeemed Rhetoric: Thomas Nashe and the Scandal of Authorship* (1982).

JONATHAN DOLLIMORE is Professor of English and Related Literature at the University of York. He is the author of *Death and Desire in Western Culture* (1998); *Sexual Dissidence: Augustine to Wilde, Freud to Foucault* (1991); and *Radical Tragedy: Religion, Ideology and Power in the Drama of Shakespeare and his Contemporaries* (1984).

MARJORIE GARBER is Professor of English and Director of the Centre for Literary and Cultural Studies at Harvard University. Her books include *Vice-Versa: Bisexuality and the Eroticism of Everyday Life* (1995); *Vested Interests: Cross-Dressing and Cultural Anxiety* (1992); and *Shakespeare's Ghost Writers: Literature as Uncanny Causality* (1987).

HILARY GATTI teaches at the Universita degli studi di Roma. She is the author of *Giordano Bruno and Renaissance Science* (1998); and *The Renaissance Drama of Knowledge: Giordano Bruno in England* (1989).

JONATHAN GOLDBERG is Professor of English at Duke University. His books include *Sodometries: Renaissance Texts, Modern Sexualities* (1992); and he has edited *Reclaiming Sodom* (1994); and *Queering the Renaissance* (1994).

STEPHEN GREENBLATT is Professor of English at Harvard University and General Editor of the Norton Shakespeare. His books include *Marvelous Possessions: the Wonder of the New World* (1991); *Learning to Curse: Essays in Early Modern Culture* (1990); and *Shakespearean Negotiations: the Circulation of Social Energy in Renaissance England* (1988).

SIMON SHEPHERD is Professor of Drama at Goldsmiths College, University of London. He is the author, with Peter Womack, of *English Drama: A Cultural History* (1996); and of *Because We're Queers: The Life and Times of Kenneth Halliwell and Joe Orton* (1989); and the editor of *Coming on Strong: Gay Politics and Culture* (1989).

ALAN SINFIELD is Professor of English in the School of Cultural and Community Studies at the University of Sussex. His books include *Cultural Politics, Queer Reading* (1994); *The Wilde Century: Effeminacy, Oscar Wilde and the Queer Moment* (1994); and *Faultlines: Cultural Materialism and the Politics of Dissident Reading* (1992).

RICHARD WILSON is Professor of Renaissance Studies at the University of Lancaster and Director of the Shakespeare Programme at Hoghton Tower. He is the author of *Will Power: Essays on Shakespearean Authority* (1993); and *'Julius Caesar': A Critical Study* (1992); and co-editor, with Richard Dutton, of *New Historicism and Renaissance Drama* (1992).

Further Reading

The history of Marlowe criticism has been surveyed in WILLIAM TYDEMAN and VIVIEN THOMAS, *State of the Art: Christopher Marlowe: A Guide through the Critical Maze* (Bedminster: Bristol Press, 1989). Though serviceable, this primer gives little sense of the elective affinity with post-structuralist ideas which makes this Elizabethan iconoclast such a challenging subject of contemporary debate. Modern theory erupted into Marlowe studies, however, with STEPHEN GREENBLATT's overview, *Renaissance Self-Fashioning: From More to Shakespeare* (Chicago: Chicago University Press, 1980), which placed the dramatist in the context of an emerging sense of self in sixteenth-century England. What made this book so timely was Greenblatt's dawning realisation – traceable page by page – that his conventional image of the Renaissance as (in a famous formulation) 'the discovery of the world and of the self' had to be entirely reversed in the shadow of Foucault's demolition of the 'repressive hypothesis' – the belief in human emancipation – and of the philosopher's analysis of the early modern period as the threshold not of rights and liberties but of subjection and surveillance. Greenblatt's recantation of his American faith in freedom, as a result of combining Marlowe with Foucault, set the scene, therefore, for New Historicism, with its grim confirmation that 'fashioning oneself and being fashioned by institutions – family, religion, state – were inseparably intertwined'.

Greenblatt's description of Marlowe's doomed but defiant 'will to endless play' established the parameters in which post-modern critics would interpret this pre-modern writer. Thus, for THOMAS CARTELLI, in his *Marlowe, Shakespeare, and the Economy of Theatrical Experience* (Philadelphia: University of Pennsylvania Press, 1991), the Elizabethan playwright was a true *homo ludens*: a grand master of power games, whose heroes expressed the libido of his London spectators. Cartelli's curious extension of Reception Theory to Renaissance texts risked anachronism by proposing to reconstruct the mind-set of the Bankside audience; but his emphasis on the sheer popularity of Marlowe's monsters was a welcome relief from moralising. By contrast, EMILY BARTELS applied a more rigorous historicism to the dramatist in *Spectacles of Strangeness: Imperialism, Alienation, and Marlowe* (Philadelphia: University of Pennsylvania Press, 1993), yet still revealed him to be a Renaissance Joseph Conrad, cynical and nihilistic at the expense of both the coloniser and colonised. This was a refinement of EDWARD SAID's *Orientalism* (London: Routledge, 1978), and one of a wave of New Historicist books that offloaded twentieth-century American colonialist guilt on to the sixteenth-century English empire.

SIMON SHEPHERD's polemic, *Marlowe and the Politics of Elizabethan Theatre* (Hemel Hempstead: Harvester Wheatsheaf, 1986) remains the only full-scale work of British Cultural Materialism devoted to the dramatist, though its sloganising now seems very much of the Thatcher era. It has been valuably supplemented, however, by THOMAS HEALY's study of Marlowe in the 'Writers and their Work' series (Plymouth: Northcote House, 1994), which cements the plays firmly within the Protestant culture they interrogated; and in a more sociological idiom, by ROGER SALES, *Christopher Marlowe* (Basingstoke: Macmillan, 1991). Equally materialist, though from an earlier generation of scholarship, was WILLIAM EMPSON's swansong, *Faustus and the Censor: The English Faust-Book and Marlowe's 'Doctor Faustus'* (Oxford: Oxford University Press, 1987), a perverse attempt to prise an 'original' playtext from the coils of the Elizabethan censors. Finally, in NEIL RHODES's *The Power of Eloquence and English Renaissance Literature* (Hemel Hempstead: Harvester Wheatsheaf, 1992) there is an interpretation which roots Marlowe's totalising will to power in the most material place of all: the language he inflated and deployed.

Future researchers will be indebted to WILLIAM URRY's *Christopher Marlowe and Canterbury* (London: Faber & Faber, 1988), a painstaking compilation by a local Kent historian of evidence, much of it previously unknown, which suggests why cult theories of 'the death of the author' and the inaccessibility of history stand to be chastened by what Foucault admiringly called 'the grey dust of the archives'. Urry's discoveries – such as, that Marlowe died not in a tavern, but in a customs office – have been slow to penetrate the academic industry; but they confirm the claim made by Andrew Butcher in his introduction, that 'decentralising' this author means situating him within the sexual, economic and political relations of his 'highly documented society'. Such is the thrust of the collection of essays edited by DARRYLL GRANTLEY and PETER ROBERTS, proceedings of a conference at the University of Kent at Canterbury, *Christopher Marlowe and English Renaissance Culture* (Aldershot: Scolar Press, 1996); and the implication, too, of the collection edited by ALAN DOWNIE, *Christopher Marlowe: Critical Readings* (Cambridge: Cambridge University Press, 1999). In these historicist books, a material Marlowe at last begins to supplant the figure for so long minimised by formalist literary critics as simply Shakespeare's shadow.

It is Gay Studies and, most recently, Queer Theory which have propelled Marlowe to the centre of current critical thinking. Here, Jonathan Goldberg's work has been decisive in wresting the writer from the prejudices of Feminism, which has consistently imposed heterosexist norms on the all-male Elizabethan theatre. Thus, in JONATHAN GOLDBERG's *Sodometries: Renaissance Tests, Modern Sexualities* (Stanford, CA: Stanford University Press, 1992) he finds Feminists collusive with genocide of natives (slaughtered to rid America of sodomites) in obliterating same-sex relations from Marlowe's stage. In Queer Theory, homosexuality – for so long the demonised darkness of Marlowe studies – is valorised as the dramatist's vital interpretative difference from the regimes he represented. So, GREGORY BREDBECK's *Sodomy and Interpretation: Marlowe to Milton* (Ithaca, NY: Cornell University Press, 1991), JONATHAN DOLLIMORE's *Sexual Dissidence: Augustine to Wilde, Freud to Foucault* (Oxford: Oxford University Press, 1991), and JOHN ARCHER's *Sovereignty and Intelligence: Spying and Court Culture in the English Renaissance* (Stanford, CA: Stanford University Press, 1993), all advocate a strategic emphasis on homosexuality as the key to Marlovian resistance. They build in this way upon the finding of books such as ALAN BRAY's *Homosexuality in Renaissance England* (London: Gay Men's Press, 1982), and BRUCE SMITH's *Homosexual Desire in Shakespeare's England* (Chicago: Chicago University Press, 1991), that though the modern category of the 'homosexual' only dates from the Freudian era, a homosexual community did begin to crystallise around Marlowe's playhouse, and that it was this sub- or 'sur-culture' which equipped the playwright with such a subversive perspective on power and oppression.

Index

Numbers in **bold** type denote main entries

Index